A History of Popular Culture in Japan

A History of Popular Culture in Japan

From the Seventeenth Century to the Present

E. TAYLOR ATKINS

Bloomsbury Academic
An imprint of Bloomsbury Publishing Plc

B L O O M S B U R Y

LONDON · OXFORD · NEW YORK · NEW DELHI · SYDNEY

Bloomsbury Academic
An imprint of Bloomsbury Publishing Plc

50 Bedford Square	1385 Broadway
London	New York
WC1B 3DP	NY 10018
UK	USA

www.bloomsbury.com

BLOOMSBURY and the Diana logo are trademarks of Bloomsbury Publishing Plc

First published 2017
Reprinted 2018

British Library Cataloguing-in-Publication Data

A catalogue record for this book is available from the British Library.

ISBN: HB: 978-1-4742-5853-1
PB: 978-1-4742-5854-8
ePDF: 978-1-4742-5856-2
eBook: 978-1-4742-5855-5

Library of Congress Cataloging-in-Publication Data
A catalog record for this book is available from the Library of Congress.

Cover design: Adriana Brioso

Cover image: Ukiyo-e panel depicting accessories used in Kabuki Theatre, woodcut, Japan,
19th century © De Agostini Picture Library / G. Dagli Orti / Bridgeman Images

Typeset by Newgen Knowledge Works (P) Ltd., Chennai, India
Printed and bound in Great Britain

To find out more about our authors and books visit www.bloomsbury.com. Here you will
find extracts, author interviews, details of forthcoming events and the option to sign up for
our newsletters.

For my dawtas,
Ella Rose and Annabelle
"Your daddy loves you."

CONTENTS

ILLUSTRATIONS

ACKNOWLEDGMENTS

A *History of Popular Culture in Japan* is the product of an upper-level undergraduate course on the subject I developed in 1999 and have taught many times since at Northern Illinois University (NIU), and once at the Japan Center for Michigan Universities. To my knowledge, its historical perspective makes it unique among similarly titled courses. I have been thinking about and rethinking this material for almost two decades. Somehow, Emma Goode of Bloomsbury Press discovered this and approached me with the idea of writing a book based on that course. She insisted there was a market for it and that I should write it. I am grateful for her confidence. It has indeed been a pleasure to get these thoughts out of my head and onto screen and page. I do hope I have not taken the fun out of the subject by thinking so deeply about it, but having written so much scholarship on jazz music, I know from personal experience that analyzing the object of one's ardor need not diminish the pleasure it gives.

There are a number of people to thank for their assistance and contributions to this book. First and foremost, I thank my predecessors and colleagues in Japan studies, most of whom I've never met, for their dedication to careful work using difficult source materials, and their provocative and illuminating ideas. The reader will see how much I relied on their work. Conversations with students in my popular culture class over the years have been fruitful and thought provoking. I am most thankful to those in the spring 2016 section who read drafts of Chapters 3 and 6 and offered meaningful feedback.

My doctoral student Heeyoung Choi has made important contributions to this book. I hired her to find and translate Korean-language sources about Chosŏn embassies to Japan in the early modern period, and from the era of Japanese colonial rule (1910–45). Her work enabled me to include some information that has rarely if ever been addressed in Anglophone scholarship. Sources she found and translated are marked "HYC" in the endnotes. I owe a huge debt of gratitude to former students and colleagues who nominated me for NIU's Presidential Teaching Professorship. The award provided funds to pay Ms. Choi, and a semester's leave from teaching to write the book.

My colleagues in the Midwest Japan Seminar offered terrific advice and encouragement after reading two draft chapters. The feedback of nonspecialists—friends, former students and family members—was just as important as that of Japan scholars, if for different reasons. I am much obliged to members of my family, T. J. Abell, Lindsey Bier, Carolyn Braucher, Sean Farrell, Anne Hanley, Beatrix Hoffman, Christopher Jaffe, Laurel Kirk, Susanne Reece, Jim Schmidt, Andrea Smalley, and Jui-ching Wang. Faults, defects, and shortcomings are my own responsibility.

Transliteration of East Asian words and names adhere to the following systems, except in cases where individuals use idiosyncratic spellings:

1 Japanese (J): Hepburn
2 Korean (K): McCune-Reischauer
3 Taiwanese Hokkien (T): Wade-Giles and Pe̍h-ōe-jī (POJ)
4 Mandarin Chinese (Ch): Hanyu Pinyin

East Asian personal names are in standard order—surnames first—except in cases where authors reverse the order for publishing in Western languages.

Introduction

"Japan is reinventing superpower—again," Douglas McGray wrote in *Foreign Policy* in 2002. "What made Japan a superpower [in the 1980s], more than just a wealthy country, was the way its great firms staked claim to a collective intellectual high ground that left competitors, even in the United States, scrambling to reverse-engineer Japanese successes." At the turn of the millennium, though, Japan's "national swagger is gone, a casualty of a decade-long recession." However, the decline of the gross national product (GNP) has coincided with the ascent of a different kind of global influence, which McGray dubs "gross national cool" (GNC). This new influence was based on the impact of Japanese popular culture—particularly manga, anime, and video games, but also consumer electronics, toys, architecture, fashion, J-Pop music, and cuisine—on leisure activities and popular tastes around the world. McGray contends that its cultural prominence could have broader implications for Japan's international stature: "National cool is an idea, a reminder that commercial trends and products, and a country's knack for spawning them, can serve political and economic ends."[1]

Japanese popular culture (or "J-Cult") has indeed become a major force in the globalization of entertainment media.[2] The animated films of Miyazaki Hayao, video games like *Super Mario Brothers*, foods such as sushi and seaweed salad, and television programs like *Iron Chef* have millions of fans around the world. Thousands of high school and college students enroll in challenging Japanese language classes or study abroad because of their enthusiasm. Some aspire to careers in the Japanese entertainment industry, which hires foreign consultants to hone their products and overseas marketing. The Japanese government has set up a Cool Japan Fund, hoping to make friends abroad and revive the country's sagging economy. Japanese popular culture has become the object of serious academic inquiry, and colleges around the world have added courses on the subject to their curricula.

Usually these classes focus on popular culture of the last two or three decades. But popular culture has a four-century history in Japan; the cities that arose there in the seventeenth century gave birth to one of the earliest markets for commercial entertainment in human history. The following chapters demonstrate that all of the fundamental characteristics of popular culture as we now define it were there. A core mission of this book is to provide a critical introductory history of the foundation on which Pikachū, Sailor Moon, Goku, and Godzilla stand. By "critical," I mean an interpretive framework rather than a narrative one, based on the insights of over a century of theoretical analyses of popular culture and its operation in society.

Many history textbooks unwittingly adhere to radio personality Rush Limbaugh's simplistic definition of the discipline: "History is real simple. You know what history is? It's what happened. It's no more."[3] That's *not* what history is. History is an ongoing, endless process of discovery, interpretation, discussion, and debate. Historians expect their own findings and arguments to be challenged or eclipsed by later generations of scholars who discover new sources or revisit and reinterpret older sources. Good historians know that nothing is immune to change over time, even their own work. Here I avoid an omniscient *narrative* voice, by crediting individual scholars for their discoveries, contributions, and arguments, and highlighting changes in understanding and points of ongoing dispute. I have not, however, shied away from using my own *interpretive* voice. Unlike most textbooks, this one has an argument, or at least a theoretical framework for understanding four centuries of popular culture in Japan. This book is unapologetically not just an assemblage of facts and information. Another scholar writing on the same topic would produce an entirely different work. The discipline conditions me to accept that.

Japan 101

Summarizing nearly two millennia of recorded history in a few pages is a fool's errand, but it would not be the first one I have ever run. There are some basic things about the history of Japan that are necessary to learn before our focus narrows to the history of popular culture. First, here is the conventional chronological periodization:

Period	Dates	Events/Characteristics
Jōmon	ca. 14,000–300 BCE	Japan's Mesolithic age; archipelago inhabited by hunter-gatherers, who may be ancestors of northern Emishi/Ezo/Ainu people
Yayoi	ca. 300 BCE–300 CE	Iron and Bronze age; waves of immigrants from continental Asia—possibly fleeing chaos after collapse of China's Zhōu Dynasty (1046–256 BCE)—introduce wet rice agriculture and metallurgy; Chinese records of visit to Wa (Japan) and shaman-queen Himiko
Kofun	ca. 250–538 CE	Appearance of tomb mounds similar to those found on Korean peninsula, indicating social stratification and regular interaction with continent; consolidation of power by Yamato imperium over regional clans (uji) in western Japan
Asuka	538–710	Further consolidation of Yamato power; introduction of Chinese writing, Confucian thought, and Buddhism, and conflict over imperial patronage of the religion; armed assistance to Paekche in Korean peninsular wars against Silla and Tang China
Nara	710–784	Imperial capital city (modeled on Tang Chinese capital Cháng'ān) built in Nara; implementation of Chinese-style bureaucratic state; growth of institutionalized Buddhism
Heian	794–1185	Capital relocated to Kyōto (after ten years in Nagaoka); gradual retraction of centralized bureaucratic state and increasing local autonomy; era of classical literature (e.g., Tale of Genji) written by female courtiers
Kamakura	1192–1333	First government administered by military shōgun appointed by imperial court and located in Kamakura; administration of provinces by vassal warlords; attempted Mongol invasions of archipelago in 1274 and 1281

Period	Dates	Events/Characteristics
Muromachi	1336–1572	Rule by Ashikaga *shōgun*, based in Kyōto; schism in imperial family, divided into Northern and Southern courts (1334–92); gradual devolution of power to provincial warlords (*daimyō*)
Warring States (*sengoku*)	ca. 1467–1590	Near-constant civil war among autonomous *daimyō*, monastic institutions, other parties; arrival of European missionaries and firearms, and integration of Japan into Indian Ocean commerce; gradual unification by succession of three *daimyō*; invasions of Chosŏn (Korea) in 1592 and 1598
Edo	1600–1868	Tokugawa clan appointed as *shōgun*, based in Edo (now Tokyo), bringing an end to warfare; formalized caste distinctions; explosion of domestic commerce and popular culture; expulsion of Christianity, and diplomacy and trade only with Korea, Ezo, Ryūkyū kingdom, and Netherlands
Meiji	1868–1912	Restoration of imperial rule by Emperor Meiji; promotion of "civilization and enlightenment"; modernization of economy, judiciary, education, arts, military, transportation, and communication along Euro-American lines; acquisition of colonies; creation of constitutional monarchy
Taishō	1912–26	Reign of sickly emperor Yoshihito; Japanese participation in World War I and anti-Bolshevik expedition; growth of popular press, labor movement, feminism, socialism, and anarchism; passage of national security law to suppress leftist extremism; expansion of voting rights to all men without property restrictions
Shōwa	1926–89	Reign of Hirohito; imperialist aggression against China and Southeast Asia; World War II and atomic attacks on Hiroshima and Nagasaki; military occupation by United States and postwar "high-speed growth" via export-oriented economy; "Japan as Number One"
Heisei	1989–present	Reign of Akihito; economic decline and "lost decades" of stagnant growth; international tensions with South Korea and China over history education; demonstrations against US military occupation of Okinawa; earthquakes in Kōbe (1995) and northeast Japan (2011)

Next are the three pillars of traditional Japanese culture: Shintō, Confucianism, and Buddhism. Shintō ("the Way of the gods") refers to hundreds of animistic cults throughout the Japanese archipelago, centered on the belief in ancestral and tutelary spirits (*kami*) inhabiting natural features—local forests, rivers, mountains, and the like—with whom people interact through festivals (*matsuri*), music, dance, and prayers of supplication. Like most polytheistic, animistic religions, Shintō has neither canonical scriptures, codes of ethics, nor a concept of virtuous, omniscient deities (one myth involves a *kami* evacuating his bowels in his sister's palace). Renowned mythologist Joseph Campbell once recounted that when a sociologist asked a Shintō priest about the intricacies of his belief systems, the priest replied, "We do not have ideology. We do not have theology. We dance."

However, Shintō has *political* significance, since the imperial lineage claims descent from the sun goddess Amaterasu-Ōmikami. Historically speaking, "Shintō" is sort of a misleading, anachronistic umbrella term covering all the localized cults: it was originally invented in the sixth century CE to distinguish indigenous faiths from the imported Buddhist religion, and in the nineteenth century the imperial state attempted to create a unified "State Shintō" (*kokka Shintō*) with the imperial family as its primary object of veneration. When Japan ruled Taiwan and Korea in the first half of the twentieth century, imperial shrines were erected in those colonies, and natives urged to pray there. When Korean Christians objected to participating in these rites, Japanese officials responded that the ceremonies were patriotic, not religious, rituals.[4]

Confucianism is the philosophy of Confucius (Kǒng Fūzǐ, 551–497 BCE), an intellectual and teacher who lived amid the chaotic aftermath of the collapse of China's Zhōu Dynasty and the emergence of several "warring states" (476–221 BCE). In these turbulent times, Confucius articulated an ethics of social relations and good governance that he believed the sage-kings (Ch: *xiánwáng*; J: *ken'ō*; K: *hyŏnwang*) of old had upheld, to the benefit of their entire realms. Accepting the naturalness of hierarchy in social relations, he argued that one's nobility and status came not from pedigree but from self-discipline, education, benevolence, and proper observance of ritual and decorum. If the cardinal virtue of filial piety (Ch: *xiào*; J: *kō*; K: *hyo*), reverence for one's parents and ancestors, was practiced by a ruler and his officials, setting a moral example for his subjects, all would be well: harvests would be bountiful, natural disasters held at bay, and order maintained throughout the realm (*tiānxià*, "all under heaven"). Boring as this may sound, it was the ideal of East Asian political culture.

From the sovereign's palace to the humble peasant's home, it is certainly true that for generations people in authority have used *xiào* to justify capricious tyranny toward their inferiors. But at the heart of Confucian ethics was the conveniently forgotten principle of *reciprocity*—loyalty in exchange for benevolence. Long before Spider-Man's epic epiphany, authority figures in East Asia understood that "with great power comes great responsibility."

In Confucius's mind, their thrones were hot seats, conditional on their moral conduct. If they lost their divine right to rule—their "mandate of heaven" (Ch: *tiānmìng*; J: *tenmei*; K: *ch'ŏnun*)—they would be blamed for everything from earthquakes and floods to famine and rural unrest. Ultimately, their dynasties would fall to a (theoretically) more upstanding citizen.

In the seventeenth century, an elaborate, extended version of Confucian thought became the philosophical basis for political and social relations in Japan, China, and Korea. Neo-Confucianism (Ch: *Sòng-Ming lixue*; J: *Shūshigaku*; K: *Sŏngrihak* or *Chujahak*) consists of the teachings of Zhū Xī (1130–1200), who lived during China's Sòng Dynasty (960–1279). Partially a response to Buddhism and Daoism, it expands upon the implied yet unexplored cosmological assumptions of orthodox Confucianism, detecting moral virtues, ideals, and social relations in metaphysics and nature. Through the "investigation of things" (*géwù*) one could discover moral principles (*lǐ*) not just in canonical books but in nature and the mind/heart (Ch: *xīn*; J: *shin*; K: *sim*). Zhū advocated deep, meditative introspection to set the mind aright; since thought and action are inseparable, such moral reflection manifests in righteous conduct. Zhū's commentaries on the classic *Four Books* of the Confucian canon became the basis for the civil service examinations in China under the Ming (1368–1644) and Qing (1644–1911) dynasties, and in Korea under the Chosŏn dynasty (1392–1910). Japanese interest and study of neo-Confucianism was partially sparked by books looted from the Chosŏn royal library when Japanese forces invaded and decimated the Korean peninsula in the 1590s.

Although filial piety became a cornerstone of ethical behavior in Japanese society, there was a twist on Chinese *political* cosmology. From the seventh century Japanese monarchs had adopted Confucian ideals of benevolent kingship, but were exempt from the rise-and-fall "dynastic cycle" because, according to official mythology, the imperial dynasty was founded by Jinmu, a direct descendant of the sun goddess Amaterasu. By definition, the logic went, the Japanese sovereign could not *not* be moral. Chinese political cosmology posited the emperor as the "Son of Heaven" (*tiānzǐ*), with a divine mandate to rule, and to whom lesser kings in surrounding states were to pay tribute. The Japanese imperial court's consistent refusal (after the turn of the sixth and seventh centuries CE) to concede Chinese suzerainty made Japan an outlier in East Asian diplomacy. The dynastic cycle itself was proof enough to Japanese that their emperor (*tennō*, literally "heavenly sovereign") surpassed Chinese and Korean rulers in virtue. Although the actual succession process was frequently turbulent and even violent, Japanese boasted of an "unbroken line" of emperors (*bansei ikkei*) that constituted what is now the oldest surviving hereditary monarchy in the world.

Though its concerns were usually otherworldly, Buddhism served to augment imperial authority, as well. A religion of North Indian origin, Buddhism consisted of the teachings (dharma) of Prince Siddhārtha Gautama (563 or 483?–411 or 400? BCE), intended to alleviate the ceaseless, intrinsic suffering of life in physical form through serene detachment and moral conduct. Buddhists sought release from the endless cycle of physical rebirth (*saṃsāra*) that only perpetuated suffering. Along with meditation, Siddhārtha taught that improvement of one's spiritual development would occur with the accumulation of merit (karma) through goodly thoughts and deeds. With the institutionalization of the faith, innumerable other beliefs and practices accrued to these basic principles.

Buddhism had prospered in China for several centuries by the time Japanese learned of it. Oddly enough, a religion that taught detachment from and spiritual transcendence of the ephemeral material world was presented to the imperial court by an envoy from the Korean kingdom Paekche in 552 as "among all doctrines the most excellent" for the sovereign's prosperity. "Imagine a man in possession of treasures to his heart's content, so that he may satisfy all his wishes in proportion as he used them." Despite controversy and explosive violence later in the sixth century between those who championed the new faith and those who feared the wrath of the indigenous gods, several monarchs patronized Buddhism "for the protection of the state" (*gokoku bukkyō*).⁵ Thus, compared to the Chinese emperor's measly mandate of heaven, Japan's could claim legitimacy based on divine descent from the Sun Goddess, the moral example he set as a Confucian sovereign, and his patronage of the Buddhist dharma.

In addition to these three cornerstones of traditional Japanese culture, I want to highlight four conceptual or thematic frameworks for grasping some important aspects of Japan's recorded history: (1) its geographic location, which paradoxically both protected it from and facilitated relations with its East Asian neighbors and modern imperial powers; (2) tensions between political centralization and local autonomy; (3) a profound shift from egalitarian to patriarchal gender relations over the *longue durée*; and 4) the ill-fitting Chinese and Euro-American ideals of meritocracy within a society in which birth status and lineage remained an important credential. Let us examine these ideas in more detail.

Location

Although frequently described as a "small island country" (*semai shima-guni*) mercifully detached from the sometimes turbulent Asian continent, premodern Japan historically had intermittent yet intense periods of significant contact with neighboring polities in East Asia, particularly those of the Korean peninsula, and less frequently and directly with imperial China. The strait between the Korean peninsula and the Japanese archipelago's southernmost island, Kyūshū, is 200 km, not far enough to impede travel between them, but daunting enough that only twice did foreign military aggression from the continent (in 1274 and 1281, by the Mongol Empire) threaten Japan. The impact of Sinic (Chinese) civilization on Japan extended from political administration to writing, and from Confucian philosophy to Buddhist religion. What we now know as "Japanese culture" is a mélange of East Asian ideas, institutions, arts, and religious beliefs, and indigenous Shintō. Yet because of the political pretensions of its sovereign mentioned above, Japan was *of*, not *in*, the Sinosphere.

In the sixteenth century, during the period of civil unrest known as the Warring States (*sengoku*) period, Japanese had their first contacts with European Christians and enslaved Africans, which eventually linked them to the extensive trade networks of Southeast Asia and the Indian Ocean. Retroactively called "Japan's Christian Century," this period saw the arrival of Portuguese Jesuit and Spanish Dominican and Franciscan missionaries. Regional warlords (*daimyō*) cultivated trade relations with Europeans to obtain luxury items and firearms, which they used against each other in near-constant battle. Japanese adopted everything from bread (*pan*, from the Portuguese *pão*) and battered, deep-fried *tenpura*, to European pantaloons, Marian iconography, and crucifixes. Perhaps as many as 300,000 Japanese converted to Catholicism before all foreign missionaries were evicted and a series of edicts prohibited the religion on pain of death. We will see in Chapter 2 that influential contact with foreigners continued in the following centuries, though on a much smaller and more controlled scale.

In the mid-1800s, insistent demands from the United States, Russia, and several European countries forced Japanese to open their borders to trade and diplomacy. The last *shōgun* was deposed and imperial sovereignty restored (more on this arrangement below). As China and Siam suffered similar bullying, and the rest of Southeast Asia subjected to European colonial rule, Japanese determined not to let cultural pride prevent them from learning what ideas, institutions, and technologies made their tormentors so powerful. From the nineteenth into the early twentieth century, the imperial state created new governmental, educational, judicial, military, financial, and economic institutions based on Western models. Coming full circle, Japanese remade their country from the ground up as they had some twelve hundred years earlier, but along Euro-American lines rather than Chinese.

Governance

From around the sixth century CE, Japan was theoretically ruled by a hereditary monarchy that presided over a centralized administrative bureaucracy. This remained the ideal of governance throughout most of Japan's recorded history, yet there were extended periods during which real power was exercised by provincial strongmen whose loyalty to the imperial court was tenuous and conditional, at best. Frequently, this was because it was difficult to determine who was really in charge.

Over the course of the fifth, sixth, and seventh centuries political authority was consolidated in the hands of a particular lineage group, located in the Yamato plain of west-central Honshū (Japan's largest island). Whereas before, power was shared among several regional chieftains (*uji*) scattered throughout the archipelago, the Yamato royals were eager to solidify their authority through processes of state building they observed in China and the Korean kingdoms Paekche, Silla, and Koguryŏ. By the sixth century the foreign polities recognized the Yamato as the official representatives of what they called the Land of Wa (Ch: Wōguó; K: Waeguk). *Wa* means "dwarf," by the way. Make of that what you will.

In the late seventh and early eighth centuries, the imperial court implemented administrative and penal (*ritsuryō*) reforms to standardize the political, economic, and social structures throughout the realm. All land belonged to the sovereign; provincial governors answered to the court; the emperor dispensed ranks and rewards based on merit rather than heredity; an imperial conscript army was to maintain internal order and guard against foreign threats; a national currency was minted; a (semi-) permanent capital was established in Nara and seventy-four years later in Kyōto. A duckier kingdom could not be found.

But not really. Over the next two centuries the court—sometimes deliberately, sometimes carelessly—delegated increasingly more responsibilities to its provincial representatives. Royals and courtiers were at cross-purposes in that they clung to the idea of a central authority, while also advancing their personal *financial* interests in provincial arrangements that retarded the flow of tax revenues to the capital, and evaded court oversight. That is, as public officials with private economic stakes (*shiki*) throughout the realm they were theoretically governing, they had multiple conflicts of interest. They outsourced internal security and licenses to kill to private warrior bands, having abandoned the conscript army in the late 700s. These armies comprised the first samurai warriors (*bushi*).

In the late twelfth century the emperor Go-Toba (1180–1239) appointed the powerful warrior Minamoto no Yoritomo (1147–99) as "barbarian-subduing generalissimo" (*sei-i tai shōgun*) to pacify and administer his realm through military bonds with provincial warlords. Yet Yoritomo and his successors often acted independently of the imperial court, as did the local warlords who were theoretically his vassals. They were typically inclined to pursue their own interests rather than defer to a central authority. When they did submit, it came at a price. For instance: part (or most) of their remuneration for military service to the court or *shōgun* included booty or spoils from the vanquished foe; when called upon to repel the aforementioned Mongol invasions of 1274 and 1281, there was none to be had. *Bushi* resentment about not being adequately compensated in those campaigns weakened the military government in Kamakura.

This raises a question: why did no *shōgun* attempt to overthrow the monarchy? Were they in such reverent awe of His Majesty's divine lineage that they would rather swallow their swords than harm him? Hardly. In reality, the court was rarely a threat to the interests of whichever tough guy felt the call to govern the realm. If anything, the emperor was so thoroughly *irrelevant* politically that toppling the dynasty would simply invite more trouble than it was worth. Its longevity and the traditions associated with it meant that no one seriously considered setting that particular precedent. There was simply *no need* to do so, when the most powerful man in the realm could simply manipulate the emperor, deploy his symbolic authority and power, and keep him preoccupied performing rites, writing poetry, and producing offspring in his harem. The three families that bore the title *shōgun*—the Minamoto, Ashikaga, and Tokugawa—simply received (or extracted) their positions from the sitting sovereign, basing their legitimacy on his blessing and their military might. Even military strongmen who never earned that title presented themselves as the court's patrons, financing repairs to the royal palace, hosting enthronement ceremonies, and the like. To keep cooperative monarchs on the throne, warlords often expressed preferences about imperial succession. The relationship between court and military, then, was mutually beneficial, requiring none of the messy, unpleasant dynastic overthrows that periodically afflicted China and Korea.

The nadir for centralized authority was the Warring States period (ca. 1467–1590), during which *daimyō*, monastic institutions, and a few autonomous city-states made war on one another and openly defied the hapless court and Ashikaga *shōgun* in Kyōto. Impoverished emperors could not even afford to enthrone themselves with appropriate pomp and dignity. Yet the ideal of a central authority remained compelling, even if everyone involved was in fact thwarting that ideal with their conduct. There was general alarm and discontent with "a realm torn asunder," but no one seemed prepared to sacrifice self-interest in service to its repair. From the 1570s to 1590, however, three men—Oda Nobunaga (1534–82), Toyotomi Hideyoshi (1536 or 1537–1598), and Tokugawa Ieyasu (1534–1616)—successively carried out the work of restoring order and unity, through a combination of diplomacy and alliances, vision and tactical skill, and treachery and warfare. Ieyasu was named *shōgun* in 1603 and began constructing a federal system that balanced Tokugawa supremacy with local autonomy for regional *daimyō*. Japan was at peace for the next two and a half centuries.

After the dissolution of the Tokugawa government in 1868, the new Meiji regime set about strengthening centralized authority in Tokyo, following the examples of constitutional monarchies in Europe. Modern communication and transportation technologies, and administrative and legal structures abetted this process so well that people in the rural provinces, or even in large cities such as Nagoya, Ōsaka, Fukuoka, and Kyōto, could be forgiven for thinking that officials in Tokyo paid them little mind. That sentiment has hardly faded today. The capital region is home to one-tenth of Japan's population, the headquarters of most corporations, the entertainment industry, and political power. In the wake of the triple disaster of March 11, 2011, many in the affected Tōhoku region attributed the lackluster relief effort to the Tokyo-centric bias of the government. Many of the grassroots movements for environmental, anti-nuclear, and social justice emerge in local communities that feel they must take matters into their own hands to survive.

Gender politics

One of the earliest documentary mentions of Japan was written by visitors from China's short-lived Wèi Dynasty (220–65), who found many strange things in the Land of Dwarves, not least of which was a female head of state, the shaman queen Himiko. According to the *Chronicles of Wei* (*Wèizhì*, ca. 297 CE), the strange, tattooed *Wajin* ("people of Wa"; Ch: *Wōrén*) had selected fourteen-year-old Himiko as their ruler after the disastrous reign of a male that had led to some eight decades of "disturbances and warfare." Her court consisted of "one thousand women as attendants, but only one man. He served her food and drink and acted as a medium of communication." Himiko's authority was confirmed through her tributary relationship with the Wèi emperor Cáo Rùi (203–39), who endorsed her rule with a gold seal and graciously christened her "Queen of Wa Friendly to Wèi." Upon her death and interment in a massive tomb mound, a man succeeded her, but the Chinese chroniclers noted that "the people would not obey him. Assassination and murder followed.... A relative of Himiko named Iyo was made queen and order was restored."[6]

The reign of Himiko (who is not officially considered an imperial ancestor) was probably the apex for women's status in Japanese history.[7] From antiquity into medieval times, there was a perceptible decline of female status vis-à-vis males. Indeed, the nadir may well have been in modern times, because of the civil codes promulgated and in effect from the 1890s to 1945. Women were likely prominent in public life in early Japan because their sacerdotal power conferred them with political authority. In fact, historically both Korea and Japan have been characterized as matriarchal societies because women were presumed to have greater power as spirit mediums—the *Wèizhì* claims that Himiko "occupied herself with magic and sorcery, bewitching the people."[8] Since Amaterasu was gendered female, it was not a stretch to accept daughters of the "sun line" as rulers, and indeed, Himiko and Iyo were not Japan's last female sovereigns. The legendary *josei tennō* (woman emperor) Jingū was said to have conquered the Korean kingdom of Silla in the third century. Back in the world of reality, between 593 and 770 there were eight reigns under six women, two of whom occupied the throne twice: Kōgyoku/Saimei (r. 642–45 and 655–61); and Kōken/Shōtoku (r. 749–58, 764–70). Two more women ruled during the Edo period: Meishō (r. 1629–43) and Go-Sakuramachi (r. 1762–71). According to the 1889 and 1947 Imperial Household Laws, women may no longer succeed to the Chrysanthemum Throne.

For centuries after the arrival of patriarchal Confucianism, matrilineal or bilateral kinship relations, uxorilocal marriage (in which husbands either moved into their wives' homes or maintained separate residences, and offspring were raised in their mothers' homes), and equal distribution of property to daughters and sons endured.[9] During the early medieval Heian period (794–1185), one aristocratic family, the Fujiwara, used the uxorilocal marriage system to maintain kinship with and dominance of the royal family, by marrying Fujiwara daughters to each new crown prince, then raising their offspring in the mother's natal homes. Thus, for several generations the emperor had a Fujiwara mother, maternal grandfather, and consort.

The Heian period is also justly famous for the cultural prominence of women writers such as Murasaki Shikibu (ca. 973–ca.1014 or 1025), author of *The Tale of Genji*, Sei Shōnagon (ca. 966–1017), Izumi Shikibu (?976–?), and Lady Sarashina (1008–59). Their stories, poems, and diaries were regularly read at court and became canonical works of literature. One desperate male author is said to have used a female pseudonym to have his work read by his courtier peers, so great was the cultural standing of female writers. Court women also enjoyed a degree of financial and sexual autonomy that their descendants could scarcely imagine. They invested their wealth in provincial estates in a financial system not entirely unlike a stock market. They also had adulterous affairs, fornicating at will with few consequences more dire than the tittering gossip of their peers. Their stories and poetry were full of accounts of illicit trysts and the melancholy of postcoital farewells.

With the rise of *bushi* rule and the concomitant militarization of society in the twelfth through fifteenth centuries, both customary and legal limitations on female economic autonomy, sexual conduct, religious roles, and political power appeared. Warrior families increasingly saw the benefits of primogeniture—bequeathing entire estates to the firstborn son, rather than parsing them among children. This was partially a consequence of increasing violence that made protection of family lands a greater priority.[10] Younger brothers might be selected if the firstborn was a dullard, but fewer women inherited property and thus became more reliant on marriages than they had been before just to survive; hence, the origins of Japan's long, illustrious history of sexual commerce. Laws policing female sexuality also appeared in the scrolls: Buddhist priests—commonly stereotyped as lechers—were forbidden from visiting women without their menfolk present; penalties for female adultery became more severe, and chastity more highly prized.

It was not unheard of for *bushi* women to command their father's or husband's troops when necessary, but more often their roles in warfare were confined to protecting their homes and honor against rapacious enemy troops, which required at least some martial arts training. They also wandered blood-soaked battlefields after skirmishes, to find, clean, and blacken the teeth of the severed heads of enemies their menfolk had killed. If a head was expertly cleaned and made to appear as if it had once topped the neck of nobility, it could bring a higher price. Quality was as important as quantity.

One principle is tremendously important when studying the relative status of women historically: *class usually trumps gender*. The higher a woman's inherited or acquired status, the more constrained were her mobility, autonomy, and sexuality, and the higher were expectations that she live up to cultural ideals of femininity. In the seventeenth and eighteenth centuries, *bushi* girls learned from didactic texts to be submissive, meek, and chaste, and to suppress their "natural" inclinations toward silliness, gossip, frivolity, and jealousy. But few if any of these ideals were expected of commoner women, who therefore had much more latitude to do as they pleased. They worked in the fields, managed businesses, sat on village councils, and otherwise participated in the public sphere.

The abolition of formal status distinctions under the Meiji regime meant that women of all classes suffered legal discrimination together: civil law subjected women to their husbands' authority, punished female adultery with imprisonment, forbade women's political activity, and promoted the idea that women should be "good wives, wise mothers" (*ryōsai kenbō*), and little else. A new constitution promulgated under American occupation in 1947 conferred political rights and legal equality on Japanese women, something for which some three generations of feminists had been struggling.

(De)Merits of meritocracy

Throughout Japan's recorded history as a polity, there was a tension between two antithetical ideals: the attainment of status by Confucian meritocracy or by inherited social position. Under the reign of Suiko (554–628) and her nephew/regent Prince Shōtoku (574–622), the court introduced a Twelve-Level Cap-Rank system modeled on Chinese and Korean precedents, and a Seventeen-Article Constitution promoting Confucian ethics and Buddhist piety.[11] *Very* briefly in the eighth century, the government sponsored a civil service examination (Ch: *kějǔ*; J: *kakyo*; K: *kwagŏ*), the cornerstone of merit-based governance in China, to vet candidates for the imperial bureaucracy. It was not necessarily commonplace, but theoretically any male in China could sit for the exam and become an imperial official. Naturally, the sons of civil servants had educational and social advantages that enabled several generations from the same family to hold office. Yet if a boy in a poor rural hamlet seemed particularly gifted, a wealthy patron might sponsor him, or villagers pooled their resources to finance his education and rise to a position of prominence as a *jìnshì* (scholar).

However, although they professed the virtues of a state administered by men of wisdom, competence, fairness, and virtue, Japanese and Koreans never completely abandoned older family structures that privileged blood kinship and inherited status—in fact, under Korea's Chosŏn Dynasty, one had to have proper *maternal* pedigree just to sit for the exam. Heian court literature regularly attributed to heredity the virtues of a "person of quality"

(*yoki hito*). By that time it was customary for court ranks to be automatically passed down from those who earned them to their offspring, a pattern
that *bushi* administrators appointed by the *shōgun* were replicating by the
fourteenth and fifteenth centuries. Since both the royal and *shōgun* positions
were hereditary, why not?

Yet it was not unusual for people to blame government ineptitude on
nepotism and to call for a more merit-based appointment process. Over
the course of Japanese history many documents—law codes, official proc-
lamations, family codes (*kahō*), manifestos—earnestly reemphasized the
importance of merit, competence, trustworthiness, and virtue as the basis
for official appointments. Nonetheless, the idea that some people were simply *born* more meritorious than others never went away. The circular logic
that applied to the sovereign—who ruled because his divine provenance
made him inherently virtuous and wise, which made him most suitable to
rule—applied to courtiers and high-ranking samurai.

Confucian scholar Ogyū Sorai (1666–1728) attributed this mentality to "human sentiment" for what was old, but insisted that the "key to
fairly treating all mankind" was the meritocratic order of China's ancient
sage-kings.

> To try foolishly to preserve hereditary status by forever keeping those
> on top at the top and those below at the bottom violates the law of the
> universe, for it helps preserve from oblivion those at the top who have
> reached the point that they should give way. When men of talent and wis-
> dom are no longer at the top, it signifies the end of a regime, confusion
> and disorder will open the way for men of talent and wisdom to rise up
> and overthrow the dynasty ...
>
> If this [advice] were followed, the wise would always be on top, and the
> stupid would always stay at the bottom, in perfect accord with the uni-
> versal law; and thus the reign would go on forever.

Sorai's philosophy constituted a threat to the officially sanctioned caste system that theoretically ordered society under Tokugawa rule. "Why is it that
during a period of prolonged peace, men of ability are found only in the
lower classes, while men of the upper class grow increasingly stupid?" he
asked. "As far as I can see, men's abilities are developed only through hardship and tribulation. ... Therefore, in the Way of the sages, too, it is recommended that able men be advanced by bringing them up from below."[12]

Foremost among the grievances of the imperial insurrectionists who
overthrew the Tokugawa in 1867–68 was the favor given to lineage over
merit. They tended to be middle-ranking samurai who thought that men
of lesser talents were receiving undue attention and promotion. They "felt
an acute sense of status deprivation: they were part of the [*bushi*] elite,
yet their circumstances were straitened, and they could not depend on

office-holding to advance themselves."[13] By saying this, I do not mean to dismiss cynically the sincerity of their political convictions to imperial restoration or otherwise imply that they acted merely out of self-interest. Nonetheless, as we have seen, the appointment of inferior men to positions of power was a harbinger of dynastic decline in East Asian political cosmology, both a cause and an effect. The early abolition of formal, heritable status distinctions between *bushi* and commoners by the early Meiji regime signified a commitment to liberal Western ideals of meritocracy that paralleled those of Confucianism.

None of this is to suggest that lineage has lost all cultural importance in modern Japan, or in Korea, for that matter. To some individuals and families, having samurai or *yangban* (Korean aristocratic) heritage remains a source of pride—though that does not necessarily mean others are impressed by it. Although there were no automatic legal or economic benefits to it, in 1871 Japanese of *bushi* ancestry were categorized as *shizoku*, and everyone else as *heimin* ("regular people"). Those most disadvantaged by heredity in modern times are the so-called *burakumin* ("slum people"), descendants of the *eta* or *hinin* ("nonpeople") who traditionally performed necessary yet "dirty" work, such as undertakers, leather tanners, midwives (!), butchers, and collectors of "night soil" (urbanites' poo) for fertilizer. Though it is illegal, employers will sometimes refuse to hire people whose ancestors resided in *buraku* slums. Parents also sometimes check the backgrounds of their children's potential spouses to prevent "pollution" of their family line.

My purpose here has been to provide some kind of framework for understanding the cultural foundations and *longue durée* of Japanese history. Throughout the book I provide more historical context and narrative detail to situate the development of popular culture. I hope the reader will find the history of Japan as infectiously fascinating as I have lo these many years. After some three decades of study, I remain as curious and excited about it as ever.

CHAPTER ONE

The worst which has been thought and said? Defining popular culture

The term "popular culture" seems easy enough to define. An earlier generation of scholars was content to describe it as "what people do when they are not working; it is man in pursuit of pleasure, excitement, beauty, and fulfillment."[1] This statement is not untrue, but nowadays it is considered somewhat simplistic. As a scholar, my job is to make things more complicated than they appear to be, to politicize what seems innocently apolitical and to make the quotidian look strange. So that is what I shall do.

Since the 1960s what has interested humanists and social scientists most are the ways in which power is exercised, projected, and contested through cultural expression and leisure pursuits. In a media-saturated society, popular culture is both a potential means of social control at its most insidious when it seems the most innocuous, and also a possible vehicle for social revolt. Even the most trivial material is thus worth examining critically for its underlying presumptions, narratives, and messages, especially if it finds an audience. How does one undertake such analysis? Here are the crucial questions:

- Who creates and controls popular culture, and whom does it empower?

- Whose interests, autonomy, authority, or power does popular culture serve?

- What meanings, messages, or narratives does popular culture communicate, from whom and to whom?

- How is popular culture disseminated, and how does the medium of dissemination affect the message(s) and response(s)?

- How do audiences and consumers receive, understand, interpret, and respond to those meanings, messages, or narratives? Do they conform to or subvert these in actual thought and behavior?

Although they do overlap, there are two broad usages of the concept of popular culture: aesthetic and sociological. In either case the term is *relational*: it only has meaning in relation to something else. Japanese has several terms for popular culture (which I have provided in parentheses below) that are somewhat more precise but also loaded with implicit populist and nationalistic ideological presumptions.[2]

As aesthetic category

In the aesthetic usage, *popular* is a descriptor that distinguishes it from other forms of culture according to its aesthetic merit: by definition popular culture is supposedly the antithesis of "capital-A Art" in an implied hierarchy of artistic value. The following commonly used binaries express this difference:

Art ≠ entertainment

Tasteful ≠ kitschy

Highbrow ≠ lowbrow

Timeless ≠ forgettable

Complex ≠ simplistic

Edification ≠ escapism

Solemn ≠ frivolous

Meaningful ≠ vacuous

Connoisseurs ≠ dilettanti

Unique ≠ mass-produced

One task of cultural studies has been to discover how aesthetic hierarchies came to exist and who deserves credit or blame for creating them. One such "who" was British writer Matthew Arnold (1822–88). He insisted that Art (or capital-C Culture) appealed to and uplifted hearts and minds, whereas the entertainments and leisure pursuits popular among the urban working classes aimed a bit lower: at the stomach and genitals.

Arnold famously defined Culture as the "pursuit of our total perfection by means of getting to know, on all the matters which most concern us, the

best which has been thought and said in the world." As "the study of perfection," Culture "leads us ... to conceive of true human perfection as a harmonious perfection, developing all sides of our humanity; and as a general
perfection, developing all parts of our society."[3] Engagement with "the best
which has been thought and said in the world"—canonical literary, artistic,
theatrical, and musical masterpieces—has an ennobling effect on individuals and society at large; it thus "has a very important function to fulfil [sic]
for mankind." But Arnold was contemptuous of working-class amusements,
particularly in the United States, where his ideas were influential among
the middle class and the wealthy nonetheless. Indulging their "natural taste
for bathos" and mistaking it for "the sublime" leads people to ruin.[4] Like
his intellectual descendants, British literary critics F. R. Leavis (1895–1978)
and Q. D. Leavis (1906–81), and Spanish philosopher José Ortega y Gassett
(1883–1955), Arnold fretted over challenges to "traditional authority" and
its taste-making function. The Culture they advocated had little chance of
surviving in a marketplace catering to the majority's boorish sensibilities,
which justified creating nonprofit, government-subsidized museums and
concert halls immune to that marketplace.

Paul DiMaggio and Lawrence Levine (1933–2006) describe the "sacralization of culture" in the late-nineteenth-century United States as partially
a nativist response to a flood of immigrants from Southern and Eastern
Europe. Nonprofit institutions such as art museums, theaters, opera houses,
and symphony centers created standards of dress and decorum that effectively took Shakespeare, Bellini, and Mozart out of venues with diverse—and
occasionally rowdy—audiences, and fostered a church-like atmosphere in
which loud declarations of praise or ridicule, food, and beer were forbidden
(only cough drops survived the purge). The opera house had become "less
a center of entertainment than a sacred source of cultural enlightenment."
Whereas in the mid-nineteenth century, audiences from diverse backgrounds
enjoyed Shakespearean theater and operatic performances, within a few
decades such things were beyond the economic and (presumably) intellectual capacity of lower-class people to appreciate.[5] As the aesthetic "'Other'
of high culture," popular culture thus reinforces social distinctions; this is
where aesthetic and sociological definitions of popular culture overlap and
mutually reinforce one another.

One lesson such inquiries have taught us is that the aesthetic regard for
a particular form of expressive culture can and does change over time. In
his day Shakespeare was considered popular culture, and continued to be
so into the nineteenth century, even in the United States. Many canonical
musical compositions that are revered today were panned by critics when
they debuted. There is a tendency to presume that the passage of time simply adds luster to a work, but historians of performing, literary, and visual
arts have been able to trace the evolution of a work's critical reception.
More often than not, a composition, play, novel, or pictorial work benefits
from the advocacy of identifiable individuals—critics, patrons, or artists

themselves—with discernible agendas, who reevaluate its artistic worth or influence on later works, keep it in the public view, or curate and present it in a new light. In other words, *people* rather than *time* imbue particular works with aesthetic value and set them above other comparable works. The result is that sometimes yesterday's pop becomes today's Art; hence, aesthetic value or status is rarely stable or predetermined.

Japanese woodblock prints are illustrative in this regard, because they are considered Art today, although they were mass produced, purchased, and expendable in their original context. German philosopher Walter Benjamin (1892–1940) argued that an authentic, original artwork possessed an "aura" and "authority," which "technical reproduction" diminished.[6] Although Benjamin acknowledged the duplicability of images via woodcuts and lithography in earlier times, this did not appear to undermine his assumption that works of Art are, by definition, singular and aesthetically superior to mass-produced cultural products such as movies. Again we see that the value ascribed to expressive culture changes across time and space according to how it is used. Japanese consumed prints in very different ways than did late-nineteenth-century European painters, who collected them, displayed them in galleries and museums, and found inspiration in them for their own work. By contrast, when they got tired of looking at them Japanese used woodblock prints to wrap fish.

John Storey argues that aesthetic value is not something intrinsic to an object itself, but is a way of seeing, hearing, pondering, or otherwise experiencing it.[7] There are multiple levels of engagement or appreciation in most mass-mediated cultural products. According to my students, many people who listen to hip-hop pay no attention to its lyrical content, while others treasure its occasional poetic artistry and the musicianship of a rapper's "flow" or phrasing. It's likewise possible to see something profound or moving in J. R. R. Tolkien's *Lord of the Rings* books without ever noticing or accepting their allegorical Christianity—indeed, most fans probably do so.

Allow me to illustrate Storey's point by analyzing Christopher Nolan's *Dark Knight* trilogy of Batman films (2005–12). Most fans probably enjoy them as action movies with quintessentially good and evil characters, in which Batman disembowels Gotham City's criminal underbelly. I read the films as a meditation on the nature and consequences of well-intended, self-sacrificial yet ham-fisted heroism—some commentators even consider the trilogy as an allegory for the US "war on terror," and particularly its foolhardy military invasion of Iraq in 2003.[8] Nolan demonstrates how unclear and fraught any imaginable solutions to Gotham's plight might be. Batman himself becomes part of the problem rather than its remedy: he uses violence and intimidation to subdue the violent and intimidating. His doing so with mystery, deception, and a sizable arsenal makes his opponents all the more desperate and, in the language of the films, escalation ensues. The futility of Batman's mission is dramatized when he interrogates the Joker in the second film and has the epiphany that his physical strength, wealth, and combat and detective skills cannot yield the results he wants. "You have nothing to threaten me with," The Joker taunts him. In the third film, we find that the pacification of Gotham was the result of a morally and legally question-able ordinance that was itself built on the lie Batman and James Gordon concocted about the death of district attorney Harvey Dent. Both recognize Dent's public crusade as a "white knight" without a mask, who uses the law rather than violence to subdue crime, as less ethically objectionable than the Dark Knight's approach. Their lie is intended to protect Dent's reputation, so that his murderous spree as Two-Face remains unknown to the general public. However much we may wish to root for him, and however slick his ninja moves, Nolan's Batman is a morally ambiguous figure whose choices and end-justifies-means calculations are not beyond reproach. We are left to wonder whether Gotham's fate would have been less turbulent had Batman not intervened. Bruce Wayne, Lucius Fox, and Alfred Pennyworth all openly ponder this dilemma throughout the trilogy.

In temporarily assuming the mantle of Bat-dork, my point is that popular culture can have the depth, complexity, profundity, and artistry usually asso-ciated with Art or Culture. From this perspective, Western concert music (generically called "classical") is not a priori superior to popular music, nor is the work of painter Jackson Pollock inherently better or deeper than that of cartoonist Bill Watterson (creator of *Calvin and Hobbes*). Popular culture is capable of stimulating thoughts and emotions that are not vapid, depend-ing on the level of engagement, just as Art can be self-indulgent and vacuous.

I am no "aesthetic relativist": like most people I have specific personal standards and strong opinions about what is good or bad in any form of creative expression. For instance, though as a bassist I see their value for practicing, I loathe drum machines in a finished musical product. It strikes me as charlatanism. The musical worth of a song with a programmed rhythm track is diminished, even—especially—by artists I like (*cough* Prince, God rest his soul). Many a friend has foolhardily attempted to per-suade me that the level of musicianship required to program beats is com-parable to actually playing drums. Yet I must acknowledge that my opinions are just that—opinions—and are intellectually indefensible and objectively untenable to someone who finds aesthetic value or meaning in something I reject or abhor.

As sociological category

As a sociological concept, popular culture (*minshū bunka* in Japanese) desig-nates the entertainments, diversions, and creative pursuits produced for and consumed by nonelites. Aesthetic value is less important in this approach, which focuses more on how cultural activities reflect the broad Marxian distinction between the bourgeoisie and the proletariat in modern industrial capitalism. However, aesthetic value or taste is not completely irrelevant.

People consume culture based on what they can afford, what their education or background has prepared them to comprehend and appreciate, and what their social peers dig, thereby reifying and reinforcing class identities and boundaries.[9] French sociologist Pierre Bourdieu (1930–2002) argued that "communities of taste" cohere through consumptive behaviors that serve as signifiers of social distinction: a person is purportedly what s/he reads, views, wears, listens to, eats, and buys. Consumption, or—to use Bourdieu's famous phrase—the accumulation of "cultural capital— is thus a form of self-fashioning that distinguishes individuals as members of particular status groups. "Taste is what brings together things and people that go together ... Taste is a matchmaker; it marries colours and also people, who make 'well-matched couples,' initially in regard to taste."[10]

A complicating factor in sociological concepts of popular culture is that they have been used to describe both the orally transmitted folk culture (*minzoku bunka*) of rural people, *and* its conceptual antithesis, the industrially produced mass culture (*taishū bunka*) of urban laborers (Japanese use the term "townspeople's culture"—*chōnin bunka*—referring specifically to people who lived in early modern cities and castle towns such as Ōsaka, Edo, Kanazawa, Sakai, and Kyōto).[11] Folk culture is considered the collective property of rural communities, integrated into the daily life of the people, with no identifiable author and no value as a salable commodity. Mass culture, by contrast, is theoretically produced for profit, is bound by labyrinthine copyright restrictions, and is separated from work, religious, and social life—indeed, it is an escape from those. Think of the difference between a work song communally sung by farmers to rhythmically regulate their labor, and a popular song written by a known composer and sold as mass-produced sheet music or as a recording, for revenue split among the composer, the performer, and the publisher or recording company. Although such distinctions do not always stand up well to critical scrutiny, popular-as-folk and popular-as-mass generally refer to the spatial locations of the producers and consumers alike, in rural and urban settings, respectively.

Early sociologies of popular culture assumed too easily a Marxian "two-tiered" structure of dominant and dominated classes, inhabiting official and unofficial cultural realms. More recently, scholars have argued that this model is oversimplified at best, essentially lumping prosperous urban merchants into the same category as farmers and presuming their cultural lives were more alike than either's were with the governing elites.[12] In the case of Japan, neither elites nor commoners stayed within the prescribed boundaries of their respective status groups when expressing or amusing themselves. While humanists and social scientists who advocate a two-tiered framework may miss complicating nuances that make the tiers fuzzy around the edges, those who abandon it entirely risk underestimating or understating the political tyranny and economic exploitation with which the elite few oppressed the subordinate many.

Defining popular culture sociologically is difficult also because of the subtle yet meaningful difference in the use of the word *popular* within the Anglophone world. In the United Kingdom—long a hotbed of scholarship on popular culture—the word is more closely related to the Latin *populus* (*jinmin, minshū, shomin*), generally designating those who do not govern or have privileged status. In British society, where hereditary status has until recently been of great significance, popular culture would mean the culture of those who were not among the aristocracy or royalty. It thus leans toward the sociological concept, although aesthetic distinctions are also implied.

For most Americans, however, to whom aristocracy is alien (we seem to prefer plutocracy), *popular* means something that has broad appeal and that "lots of people like" (*ninki ga aru, mori agaru, sakan, zokumuki, hayaru*). Many of my students have argued that a particular movie or band is "not popular culture" because it never caught on with a sizable audience. It does not matter to them that one action movie flop such as *Pacific Rim* conforms to identical formulae as a blockbuster like *Transformers*, or that a successful band plays in the same punk-thrash style as a scuffling one. What matters is, do they sell? This is not necessarily to say that one of these uses of popular is superior to another, but clearly the British definition is the more inclusive of the two, in that it encompasses subcultures, niche markets, established formulae, and financial flops, regardless of popularity or economic return.

A final complicating factor in defining our object of study is the fact that, as a concept, popular culture has a history. It is a relatively recent idea, dating back no further than the late eighteenth century in Europe. It evolved as a sociological concept in tandem with the rise of nationalism and "the discovery of the people." Its meaning as an aesthetic category took shape only in the late nineteenth century, reflecting the class anxieties of educated elites whose authority the emerging industrial working classes supposedly threatened.[13] Therefore popular culture's meaning and the significance attached to it have changed over the course of two centuries.

Pop, politics, and power

As it has developed conceptually over time, popular culture has also accumulated ideological baggage. The status or ideological orientation of the observer determines whether the "lowborn" pedigree and artistic simplicity of popular culture are considered positive or negative. Some people romanticize popular-as-folk culture: they regard it as participatory rather than passively consumed, and produced by a community for itself, rather than for a paying audience. Since the *populus* (*minshū, shomin*) itself is implicitly and collectively responsible for cultural production, popular culture is thus an authentic expression of nonelite sensibilities, anxieties, and aspirations, woven into the very fabric of social life. Moreover, it is (or can be) a vehicle for resistance against oppression. It is by definition a *counterculture*: an inherently subversive and irreverent inversion of elite values, a space where nonelites and oppressed populations can define and heroicize themselves, even making a virtue of their low station.

In the 2003 comedy *School of Rock*, self-important musician Dewey Finn proclaims, "Dude, I service society by rocking! I'm out there on the front lines liberating people with my music." Dewey tells his prep-school students that authentic rock and roll is the means for defying the establishment, embodied in the ubiquitous, shadowy figure of The Man. "If you wanna rock, you gotta break the rules! You gotta get mad at The Man!" Responding to his fourth graders' bewildered little faces, he says, "Oh, you don't know the Man."

> He's everywhere. In the White House, down the hall … [Principal] Ms. Mullins, she's The Man. And The Man ruined the ozone, and he's burning down the Amazon [rain forest], and he kidnapped [the orca] Shamu and put her in a chlorine tank! Okay? And there used to be a way to stick it to The Man, it was called rock 'n' roll. But guess what? Oh no. The Man ruined that, too, with a little thing called MTV!

For Dewey and his minions, real rock—in its purest, noncommercialized form—embodies and expresses popular resistance to oppression by corporate and political elites. Adorably earnest, Dewey proclaims, "We're going to start a revolution!"

By contrast, those who regard popular culture as synonymous with mass culture claim it is the product of industrial techniques of manufacture and dissemination—courtesy of The Man. Popular culture thus conceived is not actually produced by the *populus* but rather by a culture industry motivated only by profit and the preservation of elite privilege and power. It is thus the very antithesis of folk culture: even if a cultural form originates among the nonelite or socially marginalized, the culture industry appropriates, repackages, and mass markets it, thereby neutralizing or trivializing its subversive potential. Cultural commodities are consumed passively by clueless masses who have essentially surrendered to this industry both the prerogative and the means to initiate cultural production. Moreover, since cultural commodities are produced for profit and therefore must appeal to the broadest possible audience, there is a concomitant homogenization of cultural products, an unwarranted exaltation of the trivial, and aesthetic degradation. Art and iconoclasm can no longer thrive, for "[t]he mass crushes beneath it everything that is different, everything that is excellent, individual, qualified and select."[14] Hence, Dewey Finn's righteous rage at M[an]TV.

Theories generically labeled "postmodern" or "poststructuralist" provide another set of questions and tools for exploring power relations in popular culture. So-called highbrow or elite culture is readily available via the same media as so-called popular forms; what were once "inaccessible" avant-garde techniques are now widely used in popular music, television ads, and action movies. The social and aesthetic distinctions between elite, popular, and folk expressions thus seem increasingly porous and less analytically useful. "There are no longer any agreed and inviolable criteria which can serve to differentiate art from popular culture," Dominic Strinati asserts, since "art becomes increasingly integrated into the economy both because it is used to encourage people to consume through the expanded role it plays in advertising, and because it becomes a commercial good in its own right."[15] Moreover, cultural theorists have exposed the ways in which artistic canons serve the interests of those in power, whose class, race, gender, nationality, or sexual orientation confer unearned privileges on some at the expense of others.

Yet exposing socioaesthetic hierarchical distinctions as fabricated and bogus does not necessarily diminish their operational power in social life or "negate their influence."[16] Their persistence also allows strategic inversions: for instance, ghetto pedigree or "street cred," racial identity, economic impoverishment, social marginality, and in some cases a criminal record are *assets* for legitimate participation in hip-hop counterculture. As we shall see below, unearned socioeconomic privileges and cultural capital are not always positive traits in popular culture, where antiestablishment and countercultural stances are also appealing and marketable. If beauty is in the eye and ear of the beholder, so is cultural capital.

In the study of popular culture the object of analysis has shifted as well from production to consumption. A key question is, who dictates the terms and content of popular culture, the producers or the audience? Who is responsive to whom? Early twentieth-century mass culture theorists of the Marxist Frankfurt School insisted that the industrial manufacture of culture served the interests of the corporate elite, manipulated popular taste, and induced apathy among the supine masses, who were too distracted by Betty Boop, baseball cards, and lindy hopping to make revolution.[17] Ah, the paradox of the communist intellectual: criticizing the capitalist elite for telling the working masses what to think and how to act, while simultaneously telling the working masses what to think and do themselves.

Subsequent scholarship has shown greater faith in the masses, however, assuming that consumers have "agency" and arguing that cultural texts are open to multiple, even seditious, readings and uses. For instance, Levine has argued that methods of industrial production and dissemination do not necessarily invalidate cultural products as "authentic" expressions of popular sentiment. Since mass cultural products are read in diverse ways and put to different uses by consumers, they constitute the "folklore of industrial society," which can even be deployed to contest the dominance of those who produced them. "Modernity dealt a blow to artisanship in culture as well as in material commodities," Levine concedes. "But to say this is not to say that, as a result, people have been rendered passive, hopeless consumers. What people *can* do and *do* do is to refashion the objects created for them to fit their own values, needs, and expectations."[18] In this conception, "The [commercial] production of mass cultural forms is judged to be intrusive and insistent in intent, but unpredictable and incomplete in its results." Rather than caving to the interests of political and corporate elites, consumers constitute a "guerrilla band operating furtively within a state."[19]

But T. J. Jackson Lears questions Levine's confidence in the consumer's sovereignty. Mass media culture restricts "the boundaries of what the less powerful can do or can even (sometimes) imagine doing ... Each human subject is born into a world filled with chains of signifiers: the expressive forms in which social and cultural power is constituted ... The chains are not unbreakable: they can be constructed and reconstructed to meet the needs and desires of the individual subject. But they *are* chains."[20]

Levine and Lears engaged in sort of a glass is half-full or half-empty dispute about the closest thing to a consensual theory of popular culture in use today: Antonio Gramsci's concept of hegemony. A founding member of the Partito Comunista Italiano, Gramsci (1891–1937) wrote some of his most insightful material while imprisoned in fascist Italy. He sought to explain why the proletarian masses had not yet overthrown global capital, after a century of oppression and exploitation by industrial capitalism. Why had the global workers' revolution not transpired? His answer was hegemony, a "compromise equilibrium" whereby dominant elites maintain control over subordinate or "subaltern" groups, not through force or coercion but via a negotiated "ideological consensus" to which mass media and cultural pursuits contribute.

Hegemony entails minor concessions to the tastes and interests of the subordinate masses, although it "cannot touch the essential ... the decisive function exercised by the leading group in the decisive nucleus of economic activity."[21] By making capitalism seem like the only fair, reasonable, and "natural" economic order, in which potentially anyone can prosper, corporate and political elites get less prosperous people to buy into an arrangement that is not particularly beneficial to them. In exchange, small compromises that do nothing to endanger the perpetuation of this arrangement give those less advantaged by it a sense of control, power, and freedom of expression that Marxists dismiss as "false consciousness."[22] Benjamin observed a similar dynamic at work in fascist societies: "Fascism sees its salvation in giving these masses not their right, but instead a chance to express themselves."[23]

Hegemony is not unlike the idea of "rituals of rebellion" developed by social anthropologist Max Gluckman (1911–75), who observed carefully managed expressions of hostility toward leadership in African tribal communities. He argued that controlled expressions of animosity actually promoted social cohesion and kept tensions from boiling over into violent conflict.[24] In like manner, the capitalist culture industry makes commodities with antiestablishment messages available to consumers who want to "stick it to The Man." The culture industry thus profits and endures through self-excoriation.

In a brutally cynical yet dispiritingly astute essay, Tom Frank criticizes revolution-through-consumption as meaningless.

> Marx's quip that the capitalist will sell the rope with which he is hanged begins to seem ironically incomplete. In fact, with its endless ranks of beautifully coiffed, fist-waving rebel boys to act as barkers, business is amassing great sums by charging admission to the ritual simulation of its own lynching.[25]

I wonder if Argentinian revolutionary Che Guevara (1928–67) spins in his grave while Smirnoff uses his image to peddle vodka and skateboarders wear T-shirts bearing his face.[26] Do they advocate the violent overthrow of global capitalism and summary executions of oppressive *propietarios*? Not likely. For them, Che is a long-haired, rebel motorcyclist with whom angst-ridden youngsters think they identify. The very capitalist system Guevara sought to demolish thus profits from his decontextualized, depoliticized visage.

One of my favorite examples for teaching hegemony in class is the hit television show *American Idol*, in which amateur singers compete to become the top singer and win a recording contract. The show has a narrative structure that replicates and updates the old Horatio Alger rags-to-riches stories of late nineteenth-century America. The protagonists are "regular folks" with varying degrees of talent—and not a little of the show's appeal is watching self-deluded yet untalented singers embarrass themselves on national television by singing off-key before a panel of expert judges (as I often say, in the age of unscripted "reality television" it's better to be humiliated on television than not to be on television at all). The narrative shows that the cream rises to the top, an affirmation of American meritocracy. In the later rounds of the contest, viewers vote to select who will advance and "become the next American Idol." The voting process affirms and rewards viewers in two ways: their vote actually does count and make a difference *here*, if not in the dysfunctional political process, and it empowers them to circumvent the gatekeeping recording industry by selecting the singer most appealing to the people. The conclusion is that "real people," rather than record company "suits," recognize and reward performers for their talent and determination. Thus, the democratic process works, reflecting and validating the collective will and tastes of the public, and the American mythos is thereby affirmed. The theory of hegemony acknowledges the sense of agency and efficacy the viewers possess, while pointing out that neither the music industry nor the fundamental system of capitalist democratic meritocracy *American Idol* embodies is in any danger of collapsing. Viewers' participation indicates their investment and faith in the ideological premises on which that system rests.

Hegemony therefore allows us to conceptualize popular culture "as a 'negotiated' mix of what is made both from 'above' and from 'below,' both 'commercial' and 'authentic'; a shifting balance of forces between resistance and incorporation."[27] Less beholden to rigid, ideologically loaded social categorization and aesthetic prejudices, popular culture becomes a phenomenon whose paradoxical nature is its defining trait. As a "compromise equilibrium," popular culture embodies a continual struggle for "sovereignty" and meaning between consumers and producers. It simultaneously provokes new, sometimes revolutionary thoughts and behaviors, just as it encourages frivolity and indifference. It is also the arena in which competing constituencies debate matters of great material and spiritual import. Popular culture initiates and sustains discussions on gender norms, inequities of wealth and status, tolerance, national identity, sexual morality, violence, political and civil rights, and social justice, matters that are not or cannot be directly addressed via formal political processes, legal channels, or grievance procedures. Popular culture has therefore become our primary means for "discussing" the things that matter most to us in ways that can be enlightening or sophomoric, complicated or simplistic, truthful or misleading.

To summarize the working definition of popular culture used throughout this book, the following can be said:

1 Popular culture consists of cultural spectacles, amusements, and products—literature, plays, movies, pictorial art, music, dances, athletics, and so on—intended to reach either as large and broad an audience as possible, or specialized niche markets, using technologies of mass reproduction and dissemination.

2 Popular culture is generally regarded as inferior or deficient compared to some other stratum of culture on an assumed hierarchy of aesthetic value. Though intellectually specious, this hierarchy by which Art is distinguished from entertainment retains power as an operational discourse in social life by which some people assert power, superiority, or status over others. But the boundaries between high/elite Culture or Art and popular entertainment are not impenetrable. Both realms regularly pilfer from the other to enhance prestige or marketability.

3 Popular culture is a primary mechanism for social control and ideological indoctrination, but does not always have the desired effect, since consumers, fans, or audiences are capable of actively manipulating meanings for their own purposes. That is, popular culture is one of the primary realms in which we observe the Gramscian model of hegemony: the struggle between corporate or governing elites and nongoverning or subaltern classes for autonomy, control, and meaning, within the parameters of a broad ideological consensus. As a manifestation of hegemonic social relationships, popular culture often substitutes for more direct

conversations about values, justice, anxieties, identities, inequality, historical and social change, and other weighty matters.

Getting to Japan

The narrative of "inventing popular culture" is Eurocentric: it focuses exclusively on ideas about popular culture as aesthetic and social categories that emerged in Europe and North America with the onset of the Industrial Revolution. Yet I contend that early modern Japanese had well-developed, indigenous aesthetic and sociological concepts of popular culture, which not only paralleled but predated those of European invention. Certainly, after Japan opened its borders to trade and diplomacy with the United States and European countries in 1854, Western ideas about aesthetic hierarchy, the ennobling benefits of Art and Culture, and the deleterious effects of the lower classes' diversions and amusements had a profound impact on Japanese intellectuals and artists. But well before this, there was an established vocabulary for articulating hierarchical notions of aesthetic value and the cultural differences between governing elites and commoners.

One example is the distinction between *ga* (or *fūga*, elegance, refinement) and *zoku* (vulgarity, coarseness). The first is used in a term for the ritual music and dance of the imperial court, *gagaku* (elegant music), believed to be the world's oldest extant orchestral music. It was imported from Tang China via the Korean peninsula (Ch: *yǎyüè*; K: *aak*) starting in the fifth century, as part of a larger package of accoutrements intended to promote the power and prestige of the nascent Japanese imperial state. *Zoku*, in contrast, is used in the term *zokkyoku* (vulgar songs), which designates the popular vocal music (accompanied by the *shamisen*) of the Edo period (1600–1868) and folk songs (*min'yō*) of Japanese commoners.

Before the 1870s there was no overarching concept of "music" that covered all organized sound, but rather distinct forms of aural expression specific to status groups and communities.[28] In other words, *gagaku* and *zokkyoku* were conceptually different because their respective constituencies differed in status and therefore their aesthetic value was presumably unequal. Moreover, in East Asia Confucian scholar-officials generally believed that music, specifically, both indicated and promoted moral conduct, ritual decorum in social relations, and harmony within the realm. Following the ancient Confucian text *The Record of Music* (*Yüèjì*), and possibly the more proximate Korean *Model for the Study of Music* (*Akhak kwebŏm*, 1493), early modern Japanese thinkers "preferred to condemn or praise a musical genre's imputed moral or social value; in short, its political effect."[29] Not unlike Arnold and other elitist critics of popular culture, Edo-period officials and scholars believed that exposure to "proper" music had an edifying impact on those who heard it, while commoners' "obscene" *zokkyoku*, by definition, had the opposite effect, turning listeners into sex-crazed lunatics.

In a famous essay on traditional Japanese aesthetics, Donald Keene identifies four general principles that are broadly applicable to several art forms, most of which were the near-exclusive province of courtiers and warriors of high rank, such as poetry, monochrome ink painting, *nō* theater, tea ceremony, ceramics, and gardens. These principles are suggestion, simplicity, perishability, and irregularity (or asymmetry). To some degree, these principles and the art forms that embodied them were infused with spiritual significance, mostly from Buddhist teachings but also occasionally from Shintō sensibilities and attitudes about spirits inhabiting the natural world. "Japanese taste did not stay frozen throughout the centuries," Keene cautions. "Nor were aesthetic preferences unaffected by social class and education." He notes that none of these four principles do justice to the "flamboyance" of kabuki or "the garish, polychromed temples at Nikkō."[30] Familiar aesthetic terms such as *yūgen* (mystery, profundity, applicable to *nō* theater), *aware* (melancholic appreciation of the transience of all things, prominent in early medieval literature such as *Tale of Genji* and *Tale of the Heike*), *wabi* (elegant poverty, as in tea ceremony), and *sabi* (rusticity, expressed in haiku) are barely discernible in the *chōnin* (townspeople) culture of the Edo period. Indeed, *chōnin* culture was unapologetically absorbed with scatology, sex, spectacle, and dissipation.

That said, *chōnin* developed their own alternative aesthetic vocabulary that lent a sense of sophistication and depth to their own diversions. One such term was *tsū* (connoisseur), which admittedly was less a principle of beauty than a form of praise for a man who not only kept up with the latest trends but also had a deep knowledge or expertise that enabled him to finely critique artistry and perceive subtleties that others would miss. A *tsū* could explain the qualitative differences between performances of a single puppet play by two different narrators or express a preference for one pictorial artist over another. The *tsū*, in other words, was the aesthete and tastemaker of early modern popular culture, someone whose refined taste and sensitivity suggested that even the amusements of commoners had some expressive heft, sublimity, and artistry comparable to the profound, spiritually informed Art of elites. (I have been asked if *tsū* were the *otaku*/nerds of their day. No doubt in the hallowed halls of geekdom, there are esteemed personages to whom less well-versed fanboys/girls turn for informed opinions, recommendations, and deep thoughts about the coolest anime, J-Pop songs, and video games, but to my knowledge, in their day *tsū* were "cooler" to outsiders than *otaku* are now. My condolences, dear readers.)

Another, far less translatable aesthetic ideal in *chōnin* culture was *iki* or *sui*, a concept so complex that philosopher Kuki Shūzō (1888–1941) devoted an entire book to its exposition.[31] Kuki argued that *iki*, a standard of chic in the early modern pleasure quarters (*yūkaku*) to which brothels, tea houses, and theaters were consigned, consisted of three qualities associated with archetypal figures: the coquetry (*bitai*) of the geisha; the valor (*ikiji/*

ikuji) of the samurai; and the resigned detachment (*akirame*) of the Buddhist priest.[32]

Nearly every scholar who has studied *iki* defines it somewhat differently, or at least emphasizes different aspects of it. One constant in these definitions is the idea of an elegant erotic gamesmanship. This is unsurprising, since nearly every aspect of *chōnin* culture pulsated with sexual energy. For Nishiyama Matsunosuke, *iki* was the aesthetic pleasure of an implicit yet unconsummated erotic attraction: "The aesthetic consciousness of *iki* was perfected within the world of the potential. *Bitai* arises when a man and a woman strive to achieve the imaginary goal of subjugating each other; but the essence of *bitai* requires that this purpose remain unachieved."[33] Hiroshi Nara summarizes it as "urbane, plucky stylishness."

> A man or woman in pursuit of iki would employ a certain cool, elegant, and flirtatious demeanor, backed by pluck, to win over the object of desire ... Iki became such a rarefied, creedlike code of behavior that it was said to be detectable in every facet of life, including patterns of speech, choices in food, furniture, and other household items, not to mention courting behavior and clothing colors and patterns.[34]

Iki thus aestheticized the controlled, stylish pursuit of sexual relationships, in sharp contrast to the boorish libertinism that usually reigned in the pleasure districts. Although quite distinct from elite sensibilities, *iki* was nonetheless symbolic of commoners' capacity for the refinement and self-regulation usually associated with the warriors who ruled them.

The existence of the various terms and standards of taste described above, and their association with particular status groups, indicates the presence of a hierarchical concept of culture resembling that which developed in the West in the eighteenth and nineteenth centuries. However, this was but one of the conditions in early modern Japan conducive to the formation of popular culture as we know it today. From the seventeenth century, the first under the Pax Tokugawa, a number of social and economic conditions provided the necessary basis for it:

1 a growing urban populace, increasingly literate and with both sufficient time and financial resources to spend on leisure pursuits;

2 new technologies enabling the mass production and dissemination of various kinds of literature and pictorial materials;

3 a commercial infrastructure of publishing houses, theaters, lending libraries, and communities of specialized artists and entertainers that comprised a "culture industry" and rendered imaginative works and performances into commodities for sale;

4 an obsession with novelty, fashion, and chic, which encouraged the accumulation of cultural capital and the self-fashioning of identity

through the consumption of the latest commodities or participation in the coolest activities;

5   a climate of celebrity worship, in which popular actors, writers, painters, and musicians had established fan bases, endorsed products, consorted with warrior aristocrats, and were objects of public scrutiny and gossip—all of which belied their official status as outcastes or *hinin* (nonpeople);

6   unprecedented access to information and material items from the outside world, which were incorporated in various ways into cultural life and fostered a sense of what might be called a "protonationalist" consciousness among Japanese.

Similar trends of urbanization, rising literacy rates, and mass-produced commercial culture were visible in parts of Ming China, Europe, and to a lesser degree in the Ottoman, Saffavid, and Mughal empires, but it may be that seventeenth-century Japan had a more firmly established commercial culture industry, and a fully conceptualized notion of popular culture as we understand it today, earlier than any other country on earth.[35]

CHAPTER TWO

Floating worlds—the birth of popular culture in Japan

In 1603, Kyōto, Japan's ancient imperial capital, was abuzz. Having completed the decades-long process of pacifying the realm initiated by his allies Oda Nobunaga and Toyotomi Hideyoshi, Tokugawa Ieyasu was appointed *sei-i taishōgun* (barbarian-subduing generalissimo) by Emperor Go-Yōzei (1571–1617). Over a century of civil war was now over, and the remaining regional warlords (*daimyō*) swore oaths of loyalty to their new leader. Setting up a new military government (*bakufu*) in Edo (present-day Tokyo), Ieyasu oversaw the creation of a federation of semi-autonomous *daimyō* who governed provincial domains (*han*). He distributed these territories strategically, placing closer to Edo those who had served him before his decisive victory at Sekigahara three years earlier, and scattering further away those who had seen the light a bit later. A final battle against Hideyoshi's heir, Hideyori, awaited in 1615, but in 1603 it appeared that the realm had achieved a peace and stability unknown for generations.

But Ieyasu's investiture was not the only event that set the denizens of Kyōto atwitter. In the dried-up riverbed at Shijōgawara a shrine maiden (*miko*) from provincial Izumo, who had come to the capital to collect alms for her father's shrine, attracted audiences with her peculiar dances. Izumo no Okuni (1574–ca. 1640) adapted and modified folk and sacred dances from Shintō and Buddhism to sexy them up. She recruited and trained local prostitutes and other outcastes to form a troupe that performed comical skits about illicit trysts; moreover, she irreverently cross-dressed as a man to satirize warriors and the Portuguese Christian missionaries who still had a presence in Japan.[1] Some historical records refer to her performances as *yayako odori* (puzzling dances), but the name that stuck was kabuki, possibly from the verb *kabuku*, which means to tilt, slant, or "behave oddly."[2]

Despite the risqué irreverence of her shows, Okuni performed at the imperial palace in 1612. The performance revolted neo-Confucian scholar Hayashi Razan (1583–1657), who tutored Ieyasu and his three successors.

> The men wear women's clothing; the women wear men's clothing, cut their hair and wear it in a man's topknot, have swords at their sides and carry purses. They sing base songs and dance vulgar dances; their lewd voices are clamorous, like the buzzing of flies and the crying of cicadas. The men and women sing and dance together.[3]

Hayashi's critique focused specifically on the gender-bending aspects of kabuki, which, in his mind, subverted the ideal neo-Confucian social order he and Ieyasu were at pains to construct. They envisioned a world in which people knew their place, fulfilled requisite duties accordingly, observed ritual decorum, and conformed to prescribed standards, including normative gender roles.

It was less the content or burlesque style of her productions, however, than the after-party that gave kabuki a reputation as a licentious art, suitable only for brothel districts. Female and male performers doubled as prostitutes; performances gave them an opportunity to advertise their wares, so to speak, which members of the audience could purchase later in the evening. Warriors were among the most enthusiastic customers, which meant that lethal drunken violence frequently erupted as they competed for access to their favorites. Samurai were not the intended target audience, but their unruly conduct had profound effects on kabuki's subsequent evolution. Donald Shively (1921–2005) famously argued those effects were "artistically beneficial."[4]

Though sketchy, Okuni's story nonetheless illuminates several fundamental characteristics of the popular culture of the Edo period: bawdy eroticism; carnivalesque masking, that is, switching status, gender, and ethnic identities in performance; socially marginalized entertainers such as actors, geisha, and *sumō* wrestlers attaining celebrity status; broad appeal that transcended prescribed caste distinctions; and government surveillance and intervention to maintain decorum and "public morality." It would be an overstatement to claim that Izumo no Okuni invented popular culture in Japan, yet her career as an entertainer certainly anticipated many of its defining features. The art she created is barely discernible in the kabuki one sees at Tokyo's National Theater nowadays. But this mysterious woman's influence helped shape and define an ethos that endured well after the last Tokugawa shogun relinquished his position.

Proper places

Theoretically, society under Tokugawa rule was organized by a heritable, hierarchical, and (ideally) endogamous caste system defined by occupation and social utility. Adapted from ancient Chinese Confucian and Legalist thought, this framework placed intellectual scholar-officials (*shi*) at the top, over farmers (*hyakushō* or *nōmin*), who provided the foodstuffs and raw materials for the entire realm, and craftspeople or artisans (*kōjin*), who rendered those materials into useful commodities. Merchants (*shōnin*), said to produce nothing but personal wealth by selling the products of others' labor, occupied the lowest position. Unlike China and Korea, in Japan the *shi* were warriors (*bushi* or samurai). The ideographs for *bushi* combined the military and the intellectual, an apt description for armed men whose peacetime occupation was civil administration. They were expected to balance martial training with intellectual cultivation, earning their place at the apex of the social order by maintaining peace, administrating, and setting moral standards for those under their stewardship. In the seventeenth century the *bakufu* issued guidelines for warriors, cultivators, and townspeople, going so far as to tell them the appropriate fabric for their clothing—only samurai could wear silk, for instance. The fact that "reminder" edicts were repeatedly issued suggests that compliance was spotty.

Scholars debate the degree to which this ideal social structure reflected the reality of Edo-period society. Many people did not fit tidily within the four categories: the imperial family and courtiers; Buddhist clergy; and so-called "nonpeople" (*hinin*), who performed a variety of essential yet "polluting" tasks (midwives, undertakers, leather tanners). Within each official stratum, moreover, there were gradated subcastes and considerable variation based on wealth or family reputation. Regional deviations could also influence how people of different statuses interacted with one another. The most important functional distinction was between warriors and everyone else, but by the latter half of the Edo period even that had become shaky. Material wealth grew in importance as a signifier of real status, a trend that did not go unnoticed at the time. Around 1800, prosperous commoners in France and the North and South American colonies led "bourgeois revolutions" for political rights and independence. Their counterparts in Japan simply purchased *bushi* status, strutting proudly in their silk garb. "Breaking caste," to borrow a phrase from India, and the predominance of money over moral idealism were among the most grating social problems to samurai intellectuals and government officials in the late eighteenth and early nineteenth centuries. Many of them directly blamed popular culture for this disruption of the social order.

The social hierarchy was reflected in a presumably parallel ranking of cultural products and activities of descending aesthetic value. Theatrical and dance performances, visual arts, literature, and most other forms of amusement were aimed at particular status groups, and rarely would anyone have considered them to be comparable in technique, theme, or aesthetic merit. Confucian intellectuals insisted that the arts should edify, instruct and refine individuals' and society's moral character, and that any content that did not "reward virtue and punish vice" (*kanzen chōaku*) was deleterious to public morality and customs (*fūzoku*).

The boundaries between the "high-class" (*jōhin*) culture of warriors and courtiers and the "low-class" (*gehin*) culture of urban commoners were real, but not insuperable. As we saw in Okuni's story, *bushi* enthusiastically partook of townspeople's entertainments, initially with enough shame to compel some of them to conceal their identities with broad-brimmed straw hats. By the late eighteenth century, however, *daimyō* and their families brazenly appeared at theaters and cavorted afterward with star kabuki actors. Conversely, prosperous townspeople demonstrated their erudition by singing and dancing parts from *nō* plays, whose spartan production values and sober spirituality were supposedly suited to *bushi* tastes. Playwrights for kabuki and puppet theater made conspicuous intertextual allusions to Chinese, Japanese, and (sometimes) Korean history, lore, and literature, which could only have appealed to *chōnin* if they were at least somewhat conversant in elite culture.

Thus people at the top and the bottom of the social hierarchy used participation in the other's culture to accumulate and display cultural capital. To the dismay of *bakufu* authorities, some of the most elite warriors in the realm thought slumming with the rabble was cool, while wealthy *chōnin* elevated their own status by dazzling their peers with fluency in the "respectable" arts. The next chapter explores in more depth the impact and significance of these transgressions in the history of early modern Japan.

From castle towns to cities

The paradoxical phrase "creative destruction" applies well to the sixteenth-century era of Warring States (*sengoku*). Despite the pervasive violence, Japan's population actually grew, after a centuries-long decline in medieval times. Sovereign local *daimyō*, acting with impunity while an impotent, impoverished imperial court and *bakufu* in Kyōto floundered, created innovative forms of social control and administration, encouraged economic growth, and otherwise tried to promote the "public good" (*kōgi*) within their domains. It was hard out there for a *daimyō*, who lived under constant threat from neighboring rivals and his own retainers. The warrior's cardinal virtue of loyalty to one's lord was laughably irrelevant in this age when samurai were doing what they did best: killing each other.

Yet *daimyō* also laid the foundations necessary for the development of popular culture. When they built the impressive castles that inscribed their majesty and authority on the landscape, they actively recruited artisans and merchants to settle nearby and supply the material needs of the warriors who lived in and around these fortresses. Before the creation of castle towns (*jōkamachi*), there were very few places in Japan that could be called "cities": the current imperial capital Kyōto; its predecessor Nara, which was the political center from 710 to 784 and had since become the headquarters of the six dominant Buddhist sects; the autonomous, merchant-run port city of Sakai, the center of weapons manufacturing during the Warring States period; and another port city, Nagasaki, which was briefly a Jesuit colony in the 1580s. But Edo, Ōsaka, Kanazawa, Nagoya, Kagoshima, and a few other decent-sized cities began as castle towns, populated by *chōnin* who provided local samurai with all they needed to produce the only thing they could: the corpses of other samurai.

Oda Nobunaga, the man who subjugated eastern and central Japan, was an advocate of "free markets" (*rakuichi*), by which he meant commerce not controlled by local guilds (*za*) or discouraged by barriers and levies. He offered *za*-free commercial markets as incentives to attract craftspeople, peddlers, and entrepreneurs to castle towns under his own or his vassals' control; he exempted them from the need to provide horses for officials and from debt moratorium decrees (*tokusei rei*); and he welcomed newcomers.[5] A 1577 order stated,

> People coming from other domains and other towns, once they establish domiciles in this town shall be treated equally with those who have been in this town before. No objection shall be raised with regard to their former affiliations with other lords.[6]

Most provincial castle towns were of modest size, but the small handful that became major urban centers would play increasingly important roles in governance, manufacturing, commerce, and culture as Tokugawa rule solidified. In 1615, Ieyasu—who had formally abdicated as *shōgun* in 1605 to guarantee the succession of his heir, Hidetada—issued a decree allowing but one castle per *han*; all other auxiliary castles were to be demolished. With an end to war, there was no longer an incentive to maintain and pay for such large forces anyway. The effect of this decree was to concentrate urbanization in the vicinity of the remaining provincial castles.

The three major cities were noticeably different in character, and their heydays as cultural centers were staggered. Kyōto had been the imperial capital since 794 and the seat of the Ashikaga *bakufu* from the fourteenth to the sixteenth century. In addition to the imperial family and the court nobility (*kuge*), it was home to thousands of craftspeople who provided both the material needs and the luxury items royals and aristocrats required to loaf around and write bad poetry. Its prestige as the cultural center of the realm endured into the Edo period.[7] The Tokugawa kept a mansion at Nijō where the *shōgun* could lodge when visiting the court, so Kyōto continued to grow, prosper, and rebuild after the devastation it endured in late medieval times. Ōsaka was the commercial center, the so-called "kitchen of the realm," a city with a small percentage of *bushi* but bustling with merchants. Less tradition-minded than Kyōto, Ōsaka was a more dynamic place where what we now call "economic development" transpired. A greeting still used by some Ōsakans, *mōkari makka*, literally means "Are you making any money?" Ōsaka and Kyōto together constituted what was called Kamigata or Kansai, and it was here that many of the distinctive diversions of *chōnin* culture developed and thrived.

Edo's character was wholly different, primarily because as the political center it was dominated by warriors. From 1635 to 1862, most *daimyō* were required to spend half their time in their home domains and half in Edo. Their wives and children—including the all-important heir—resided in Edo permanently, essentially hostages guaranteeing the loyalty of the warlord to the *shōgun*. *Daimyō*, their retainers (*hatamoto*), and *bakufu* officials thus comprised a large proportion of Edo's population, while most of the commoners were migrants or their descendants, charged with supplying a captive market of unproductive people with material necessities. In the first half of the Tokugawa period, then, Edo was considered rather square compared to Kamigata. However, by the latter part of the eighteenth century this had changed, in part because creative people from Kamigata relocated there.

Improper places

Edicts from on high had other implications for urban planning. To curtail the spread of prostitution in Kyōto, Edo, and Ōsaka, in 1617 *shōgun* Hidetada ordered the creation of licensed pleasure districts (*yūkaku*), to which a limited number of officially approved brothels, theaters, and bathhouses were restricted. Far from city centers, sometimes in undesirable, swampy environs, and surrounded by walls, the pleasure districts were a concession to what government officials believed to be the intrinsic moral depravity of *chōnin*. Hardly an endorsement of debauchery, this policy was rather a recognition that recreational fornication was going to happen anyway, and was better put under government oversight than allowed to occur surreptitiously in the streets. Ieyasu said as much himself in instructions on governance for his descendants:

> Courtesans, dancers, catamites, streetwalkers, and the like always come to the cities and prospering places of the country. Although the conduct of many is corrupted by them, if they are rigorously suppressed, serious crimes will occur daily, and there will be punishments for gambling, drunken frenzies, and lasciviousness.[8]

The numbers, sizes, and designs of theaters and brothels were limited by the licensure system, so it was not as if any enterprising individual could just pay a fee and set up shop. Failure to abide by the regulations would result in the revocation of one's license and its transference to more responsible hands. Issuance of licenses thus did *not* create a steady revenue stream for the *bakufu* or municipal governments, nor was it intended to. Oversight of sexual commerce remained an important governmental function even into modern times, eventually expanding beyond licensure to health inspections to contain the spread of venereal diseases. Despite fires, periodic shutdowns, and World War II air raids, many Edo-period *yūkaku* continued operating until licensed prostitution was abolished in 1958.

The most well-known *yūkaku* were associated with the three major cities: Edo's Yoshiwara was established by Hidetada's 1617 decree; Ōsaka's Shinmachi followed in 1623; and Kyōto's Shimabara opened in 1640. Smaller-scale pleasure districts operated in provincial towns. In the eighteenth century, as a distinction between regular prostitutes and artistically accomplished geisha began to crystallize, the latter were relocated to "flower towns" (*hanamachi*). Kyōto's Gion, Kanazawa's Kazuemachi, Nagasaki's Maruyama, and Edo's Shinbashi drew a higher-class, more sophisticated clientele to be entertained in private gatherings by geisha singers, instrumentalists, and dancers at teahouses (*ochaya*) and restaurants (*ryōriya*). Geisha were skilled conversationalists, flirters, and flatterers as well as musicians, poets, and dancers. The greater their artistry, the more selective they could be about potential sexual partners; that is, unlike all but the highest-ranked prostitutes (*tayū*), they were not obliged to sleep with just anyone who paid. Their erotic *potential*, then, is why geisha embodied what Kuki Shūzō called *bitai* (coquetry). It was in *hanamachi* that one developed an *iki* sensibility.[9]

Scandalous as it may seem to modern readers, the red-light districts of early modern Japan were the sites where the earliest popular culture—the amusements and diversions of the *chōnin*—emerged. Despite the *bakufu*'s best efforts to contain the bacchanalia within the walls of the designated demimondes, its influence leaked out to the broader society, slowly at first, but with increasing force by the last century of Tokugawa rule. In 1729, Confucian scholar Dazai Shundai (1680–1747) complained that "our kabuki plays of today put on licentious and unrestrained matters which … cater to vulgar sentiment … There is nothing worse than this in breaking down public morals."[10]

The pleasure quarters and its inhabitants—female and male prostitutes, actors, dandies, and rakes—were the settings and the subjects of popular fiction, pictorial art, popular songs, kabuki and puppet plays, and meticulously detailed travel guides. Susan Griswold finds in eighteenth-century fiction (*gesaku*, literally "low works") an obsession with the tangible and material, in stark contrast to the idealism of the regime. Pleasures of the body—uninhibited and experimental sex, gluttonous feasting, dancing, drunkenness, and even farts and bowel movements—seemed to dominate *chōnin* imaginations and tastes. "Bodily imagery in both verbal and illustrated texts signified a different kind of social reality with an inverted scale of priorities for the Edo townsmen," Harry Harootunian observes. "It was an order that had as its head the genitalia or anus and as its heart the stomach."[11]

Aside from their impact on the tastes and cultural sensibilities of early modern Japanese, *yūkaku* were liminal spaces, "betwixt and between" the "structural realm[s]" of social relations, where the rules of the regular world were either inverted or did not apply at all.[12] In Edo especially, the city with the densest concentration of warriors, *bushi* were drawn to Yoshiwara like possums to persimmons. They were required to surrender their swords, the most visible emblems of their privileged status, at the gates, lest deadly drunken brawls occur. Once inebriated and naked, samurai somehow seemed less dignified and imposing. Their sometimes meager government stipends were often insufficient for carousing, gambling, drinking, attending theaters, or a romp in the futon. In *yūkaku* samurai were the squares; the prostitutes, actors, rakes, and big tippers were the cool kids, wearing the latest fashions and hairstyles, conversant in the most popular songs and trends, and throwing the most money around. Under such circumstances, I imagine a scenario in which a wealthy, magnanimous *chōnin* might buy a round of drinks for some broke samurai, a patronizing gesture of condescension that demonstrated the irony of their respective fortunes.

This temporary liminality fits well with the euphemism *chōnin* coined for the pleasure districts: *ukiyo*, or "floating world," a term adapted from Buddhist cosmology to signify the ephemerality and illusory nature of human existence. "Its essence," Howard Hibbett writes, "was an unreflective enjoyment of the moment—a moment valued for present pleasure, but to be savoured with discrimination."[13] To enter the *ukiyo* was to fall into a dreamlike state in which to experience life as it *really* was without the facade of insincere decorum and idealistic self-denial, yet with the poignant awareness that the sensation would eventually, inevitably end with the sunrise. It was as if one could only truly attain enlightenment about the nature of existence by indulging in sentimentality and the appetites of the body.

Print culture

The technological basis for *chōnin* culture, that which most distinguished it from rural diversions, was woodblock printing. To some extent every aspect of urban entertainment, including the performing arts, relied on the mass production and dissemination of printed material.[14] No longer reliant on hand-copied manuscripts (which acquired fetishized prestige value as a result), seventeenth-century Japanese simply had much more to read and view than their forebears had. Moreover, textual material was in vernacular Japanese, unlike manuscripts traditionally written in classical Chinese (*kanbun*), classical Japanese (*bungo*), or epistolary Japanese (*sōrōbun*).[15] Visual materials were both more realistic and more playful than either the austere, Zen-informed ink-brush painting of medieval times or the ostentatious grandeur of Hideyoshi's heyday. The accessibility of both the substance and content of printed matter for commoners was without precedent.

Both woodblock (xylographic) and movable type (typographic) printing technologies were used in East Asia from the time of China's Han Dynasty (206 BCE–220 CE), predominantly for the reproduction of Buddhist sutras and Confucian texts. Movable type (using ceramic and wooden blocks) was invented during the Sòng Dynasty (960–1279); Koreans pioneered the use of metal blocks in the thirteenth century under the Koryŏ Dynasty (918–1392), about a century before Johannes Gutenberg's printing press. Japanese acquired two presses in the sixteenth century, one looted from Korea during Hideyoshi's invasion of that country (1592–98), and the other brought by Portuguese Jesuit Alessandro Valignano (1539–1606) to print Christian tracts. The final prohibition of Christianity in 1639 may be one reason Japanese stopped using the press. Typography was not much more attractive, since the logographic nature of written Chinese required the carving of literally thousands of blocks. Movable type was therefore less practical and more expensive than woodblocks, onto which text and images were carved and inked, and paper pressed.[16]

Therefore the oldest method of printing remained predominant, although Japanese made significant improvements to xylographic technology that enabled the production of monochrome illustrated books (*ehon*) and eventually of brilliantly multicolored images (*nishiki-e*). Today, regardless of their subject matter, these pictures are generically known as ukiyo-e (pictures of the floating world), because the iconic figures of the *ukiyo*—courtesans, kabuki actors, and geisha—were favorite subjects. The term applies both to paintings and to woodblock-printed pictures featuring images and personages from the demimonde.[17]

As in late imperial China and parts of Europe, the rise of mass printing, vernacular texts, and a literate, voracious readership had a profound impact on the commercial economy and the variety of reading material available. Commercial publishing houses were established by the early eighteenth century, using an assembly line method for producing both pictures and texts. An artist or writer—the individual whose name graced the final product—would typically be under exclusive contract to a publisher and would start the process with an original drawing or text. Carvers, calligraphers, and printers would then take over to finish the work. Although the accumulation of substantial personal libraries was a point of pride among some of the wealthier *chōnin*, those who could not afford to purchase books could pay a small fee at innumerable lending libraries (*kashihon'ya*) to get their hands on a bestseller.

To the bafflement of Euro-American visitors in the mid-1800s such as Ernest Fenollosa (1853–1908), Japanese considered ukiyo-e to be about as valuable as calendars from a petrol station. Japanese were equally flummoxed by Westerners who snatched up these disposable prints and revered them as artistic masterpieces. Fenollosa himself donated a sizable collection of ukiyo-e to the Boston Museum of Fine Arts and published an exhibition catalog extolling their aesthetic merits, creating a narrative of stylistic development, and constructing a canon of the most notable painters and printmakers in the genre. While acknowledging the mass production of the woodblock images, he still presented them as Art, subjecting them to serious technical analysis—they indeed had a profound impact on European art history, inspiring *japonaiserie* craftwork and the Impressionist movement. Fenollosa also characterized ukiyo-e as a "special organ of expression among the common people."

> Its artists, sprung up mostly from the ranks of the people, confined their subjects to the occupations and recreations of their class. Every change of fashion in the gay life of the capital at Yedo [*sic*] was faithfully followed in their drawings; and thus the Ukiyoe, unlike the hieratic and idealistic schools of earlier days, has the charm of being a complete mirror of Japanese life.[18]

Fenollosa must not have seen paintings and prints that were less a "complete mirror of Japanese life" than a mirror of Japanese interest in supernatural fantasies and grotesquerie that would sicken Quentin Tarantino. Mysterious apparitions, phantoms, and creatures known collectively as *yōkai* were among visual artists' favorite subjects. Shape-shifting (*bakemono*) humans whose moods transformed them into hideous monsters, trickster critters like foxes (*kitsune*) and raccoon dogs (*tanuki*), ghosts of the dead, demons (*oni*), water sprites (*kappa*), and goblins (*tengu*) provided spooky thrills to viewers. Printmaker Kitao Masayoshi (1764–1824), producer of a two-volume picture book (*kibyōshi*) entitled *Record of the Appearance of Monsters* (1788), noted in its preface that "what we call *yōkai* in our world represent feelings of fear that arise in our hearts."[19] Michael Dylan Foster concurs that interest in *yōkai* was "characteristic of wider cultural concerns." He links this to concepts of "transformation and transmigration [that] lie at the core of Buddhist theology." Belief in *yōkai* helped commoners understand and explain calamities and reflected their wariness of "deceptive appearances and instability of form."[20]

So prodigious was the print culture of the Edo period that publishers could profitably tap into niche markets. This included, as early as the late seventeenth century, a notable population of literate women readers, who constituted a "recognized segment of the commercial market for books." It was less remarkable that female *bushi* and courtiers were literate than that commoner women were, although literacy rates varied wildly across the archipelago. One of the most well-known—and notoriously misogynist—texts directed at *bushi* girls was *Onna daigaku* (The great learning for women, 1729) attributed to the prolific Confucian moralist Kaibara Ekiken (1630–1714), the very existence of which "takes women's literacy for granted." Like *Onna daigaku*, many works for women readers were didactic texts (*jokunmono*) from China that prescribed appropriate female conduct and comportment, or biographies of women noted for their moral virtue and humility.[21] But women also read Japanese and Chinese fiction, poetry, and travel literature. There was also a sizable number of sex manuals directed at courtesans of the pleasure quarters. In addition to visual evidence of women reading, there are records of men's annoyance with wives and daughters who neglected household duties and serious study because they were immersed in their books.[22]

Using the rich Mitsui Collection of printed material at the University of California, Berkeley's C. V. Starr East Asian Library, Mary Elizabeth Berry describes early modern Japanese as insatiable consumers of information.[23] Travel guides, maps, playbills, histories, descriptions of foreign lands, regional ethnographies, songbooks, biographies, sex manuals, and a plethora of other nonfiction works constituted what she calls a "library of public information" from which emerged a "common social lexicon" accessible to people of all status groups.[24] Two centuries before Yelp!, Japanese published critical guides (hyōbanki) about everything from restaurants and overnight inns to stage performers and courtesans. Such guides promised to make dilettanti into savvy tsū (connoisseurs), at a time when what we now call "cultural literacy" was prized.

Printed matter formed the foundation on which other aspects of chōnin culture were built. It was also how the ethos of the floating world crept out of its walled container. "Pains had been made to keep the two worlds distinct: the Yoshiwara was a good hour's journey outside of Edo," Timon Screech remarks. "Through pictures they leaked."[25] The handful of canonical figures who are household names in Japan, and whose work has been translated into foreign languages, displayed in galleries and museums worldwide, and taught in college-level humanities classes, represent but a small fraction of the Edo-period cultural scene. Among them are printmaker/painters Furuyama Moroshige (dates unknown), Hishikawa Moronobu (1618–94), Suzuki Harunobu (ca. 1725–70), Katsushiga Hokusai (1760–1849), and Utagawa Kuniyoshi (1797–1861); writers Ihara Saikaku (1642–93) and Ejima Kiseki (1667–1736); humorists Hiraga Gennai (1728–80) and Jippensha Ikku (1765–1831); and playwrights Chikamatsu Monzaemon (1653–1725) and Namiki Sōsuke (1695–ca. 1751). They are revered as important artists nowadays, but remember that they were members of a commercialized culture industry who returned time and again to dependable formulae and subject matter that had proven marketability. Chikamatsu contributed many plays to the faddish repertoire of "love suicide" dramas (shinjūmono); Moronobu was a pioneering pornographer whose erotic "spring pictures" (shunga) were among the first in the genre; the polymath Gennai wrote an essay entitled "A Discourse on Flatulence" (Hōhiron, 1777), which stated profoundly, "Careful reflection shows that humans are microcosms of the universe. Heaven and earth thunder; humans fart."[26]

Printed porn

Anyone surrounded by magazines in a supermarket checkout line, watching *American Pie* or *Two and a Half Men*, reading *Fifty Shades of Grey*, or seeing Miley Cyrus twerking with her tongue out, whether they approve or not, must concede that contemporary popular culture represents and feeds an obsession with sex. Some people yearn for a time when media were more reticent about sexuality—or at least when sexual material was consumed secretly by lechers who had enough sense to be ashamed of it. The Internet has made pornography so easily obtainable that many psychologists, social scientists, and activists insist it distorts real-world sexual behavior and relationships. Popular culture provokes and provides a forum for discussions about standards of sexual morality, indecency, modesty, sexual exploitation and objectification, gender inequality, definitions of childhood, adolescence, and adulthood, and a host of other issues that seemingly have little to do with sex.

But the lewdness of early modern Japan's *chōnin* culture proves that there were indeed no "good ol' days" of sexual discretion or restraint. The animistic folk religions collectively known as Shintō encouraged fertility and sexuality, and many a festival (*matsuri*) celebrated copulation: the annual Himenomiya Hōnen (Inuyama) and Kanamara (Kawasaki) festivals, in which massive pink vulvas and phalluses are the central ritual objects, are but two surviving examples.[27] Premodern Japanese attitudes toward sex were complex and varied dramatically according to social status. Generally speaking, attitudes were more permissive than in Christendom, the Jewish diaspora, and the Islamic world. This was especially so among commoners, where most "marriages" were what we call "common law" or "shacking up." There were no religious sacraments related to marriage (the Shintō wedding is a modern creation), divorce was common, and lifelong commitment, if ideal to some, was exceptional.[28]

Clergy in all but a few Buddhist sects took vows of celibacy that made them objects of ridicule when violated. This happened frequently enough that from medieval times there were laws proscribing monks from visiting a private home if the man of the house was out. For many monks, celibacy meant the avoidance of women but not of acolytes (*chigo*) or each other. As was the case with samurai—who supposedly replicated monastic practices—pederasty was the most prominent clerical practice, spawning a genre of literature known as "acolyte stories" (*chigo monogatari*) celebrating the joys of boys.[29] Despite no explicit doctrinal injunctions against the practice, many laypeople smirked at these men who preached detachment yet were so attached to sex. Were it not for Buddhist monastics, there would be far fewer dirty jokes in East Asia.

Among *bushi*, especially those of high rank, control of female sexuality and an insistence on chastity were important, if for no other reason than to ensure the paternity of heirs. Marriages were primarily alliances between families (which is why the Tokugawa *shōgun* had to approve unions between the children of *daimyō*), with the principal aim of perpetuating the patriline. Romantic love and emotional attachment between spouses were nice, but not prerequisites. Sex was usually problematic only if it interfered with one's responsibilities; excessive sexual attachment to one's spouse thus might be as censurable as to a backdoor lover. This is not to say that there was no expectation of monogamous fidelity whatsoever, which is one reason why jealousy was considered a peculiar weakness of women, and why exposed adulterous relationships among elites generated scandal. But rather than an absolute cultural taboo regarding premarital, extramarital, or same-sex relations, discretion, reputation, propriety, and priorities were more significant. The emphasis was more on sexual *discipline* and *decorum* than on morality. The parent-child bond was prior to that between spouses or lovers, something the stereotypical East Asian mother-in-law never allowed her son's bride to forget.

Nevertheless, early modern Japan had its share of prudes. Although unburdened by Judeo-Christian-Islamic doctrines about chastity, adultery, and modesty, Tokugawa authorities fretted over a population that seemed to be in a "permanent state of sexual excitement."[30] Chagrined that public morals or customs (*fūzoku*) were befouled by sexual frivolity and scatology, several generations of officials issued stringent reform edicts to rein in debauchery. With varying degrees of discretion, publishers continued to produce and sell pornographic "spring pictures" (*shunga*) and erotic illustrated books known as "pleasing color books" (*kōshokubon*) or "pillow books" (*makura ehon*), with graphic, depictions of contorted sexual positions, exaggerated genitalia, and the occasional peeping voyeur. *Shunga* could be kinky: orgies, pederasty, bestiality, women penetrated by demons or octopi—the sheer variety boggles the mind. Google *The Octopus and the Shell-Diver* (*Tako to ama*, 1814, known in English as *Dream of the Fisherman's Wife*) by Hokusai if you do not believe me.

Like woodblock prints generally—and for that matter, performance art of the Edo period, as well—*shunga* are a form of popular culture that have crossed the threshold into the venerated realm of Art. This is in part because the same master painters who created the canonical masterpieces produced *shunga*, as well. But it is also just because they are *old*, and their titillating powers have therefore theoretically waned. They seem to be more comical than a turn-on to modern viewers. Art historians such as Screech, however, emphasize the importance of acknowledging their *use* or function at the time they were made, sold, purchased, and passed around. That is, he opposes the notion that *shunga* are "categorically separate from solitary-use pornography."[31] Since *shunga* were usually published and disseminated as books rather than single sheets, they were essentially the early-modern Japanese equivalents of *Hustler*, *Penthouse*, *Club International*, and *Asian Babes*. Unlike today's antiporn crusades,

Edo-period Japanese authorities were not concerned about pornography's deleterious impact on social views of women and gender equality, but as in our contemporary discourses, there was moral panic about other negative psychosexual effects. Again, their worries are best characterized not as puritanically "antisex" but instead about the possible prioritization of sex over social obligations and duties.

There were softer-core alternatives available, particularly in literature. Ōsaka author Ihara Saikaku, whose name is synonymous with the Genroku-era "golden age" of *chōnin* culture (1688–1704), wrote a series of "floating world books" (*ukiyo zōshi*) narrating the carnal exploits of female and male protagonists. Saikaku's novels and short stories were not nearly as sexually explicit as *shunga*, and frequently concluded with some sort of karmic consequence for his characters' dissipation. However, Saikaku was less a convincing moralist than a realistic observer of the occasional sexual and materialistic excesses of *chōnin*. His readers likely enjoyed reading about the debauchery itself more than its repercussions. In the 1680s he published a series of novels and anthologies devoted to these themes: *The Life of an Amorous Man* (1682), *Son of an Amorous Man* (1684), *Five Women Who Loved Love* (1685), *The Life of an Amorous Woman* (1686), and *The Great Mirror of Male Love* (1687).[32]

Saikaku's material was erotic, but more suggestive than explicit. *Amorous Woman*'s narrative arc resembles the roughly contemporaneous *Moll Flanders* (1722)—since the titular protagonists reflect on their lives with regret and repentance—more than the graphic *Fanny Hill* (1749). *Great Mirror* also is almost entirely devoid of sexual detail per se, but is a collection of sentimental short stories about romantic love between samurai, kabuki actors, adults and youth, and *chōnin* men (there seems to be precious little in the historical record about sexual relations between women). Same-sex relationships between men (*nanshoku*, literally "male colors") were quite common and did not impugn their masculinity at all. If anything, they augmented it. Most such men had procreative relations with women as well, but some of them expressed not only a preference for men—with whom relationships were supposedly less "complicated"— but outright antipathy toward women. The modern-day image of natural affinity between gay men and heterosexual women does not apply to these "women haters" (*onnagirai*). One of Saikaku's protagonists was "passionately addicted to pederasty [*shudō*] and did not waste a thought on women." In another story a man chases away from his house a woman seeking shelter from the rain:

> Then Hayemon in fury seized a bamboo cane and drove the woman away, crying: "Get out of here, you vile female! You witch, you very poisoner, begone!" When the terrified woman had run away, he purified the place with salt and clean sand. It is an ancient Japanese custom to spread salt

and sand to purify a place which has been polluted. Without doubt there was never in all the great town of Yedo [sic] a fiercer enemy of women.[33]

Some aficionados insisted that "the way of young boys" (wakashudō or shakudō) was a superior, more refined romantic relationship than one between women and men.[34] A famous vernacular story (kanazōshi) entitled Tale of a Bumpkin (Denpu monogatari, ca. 1624–44) features a dialogue between a connoisseur of boy love and the titular bumpkin, unversed in the delights of shudō, who preferred "the way of women" (onnamichi).[35] "We say the Way of Youths is refined because it's usually preferred by high-ranking samurai and priests," the shudō advocate says. "Really, a youth's elegant form, when he's dressed in beautiful clothes … is like the willow tree bending in the wind … His charms, even the way he smells, are so intoxicating!" The bumpkin responds with his image of the boy-lover: "His face is blacker than the 'old man' noh [sic] mask, and his neck and forehead are grimy. He doesn't cut his nails, and his hair is as reddish and wild as that of an orangutan … His [head is covered] with stinking boils." The bumpkin adds that shudō was a cruel, exploitative practice:

> But while you're fucking them, they knit their eyebrows, and screw up their mouths in pain—that's real pathos for you! Afterwards they don't treat you so nice. They suffer from hemorrhoids and walk bow-legged. When their parents inquire, "Why do you walk as though you were being stuck with a bamboo cane?" they can't explain what's ailing them. They just blush with embarrassment. Pitiful! Then they contract incurable diseases, which even the springs of Arima and Totsukawa can't cure … Their lovers might apologize afterwards, but the boys get no pleasure out of these encounters.

This passage is rare evidence of an attitude resembling our modern views of child molestation and its perpetrators and raises some important questions. Is the psychological trauma of childhood sexual abuse transhistorical—that is, universally experienced by children regardless of time, place, and culture? Or is it historically contingent to a time when societal attitudes treat sexual relations between adults and children as aberrant and inhumane? The young men who catch the eyes of older suitors in Saikaku's romanticized Great Mirror tend either to be flattered by the attention or repulsed by love-struck individuals rather than by the idea of sex with older men itself. But Tale of a Bumpkin gives us pause about whether such relationships were universally accepted or deemed harmless to the boys involved. It was but one of many Edo-period texts that debated the merits of heterosexual relations and same-sex pederasty, further evidence that chōnin culture was marked by both sexual candor and lively discussions about competing standards of taste.

Puppets and players

The print culture of the Edo period paralleled and contributed to the development and propagation of performing arts. *Chōnin* loved the theater, and with the advent of itinerant provincial theatrical troupes, their country cousins also developed a taste for it. Moreover, *chōnin* created new genres of vocal and instrumental music, some of which accompanied theater performances, others of which stood alone. Their popularity made both theatrical and musical arts objects of occasionally severe censorship by the *bakufu* and local authorities, yet this was undermined by lax enforcement, performers' clever avoidance strategies, and *bushi* enjoyment of what for them technically were forbidden fruits.

Puppet theater (*ningyō jōruri* or *bunraku*) was more popular than kabuki, at least until the 1760s. Stanleigh Jones writes that "in the forty or so years following the death in 1725 of the great puppet playwright Chikamatsu Monzaemon the puppet theatre held a nearly vice-like grip on the enthusiasm of Japanese playgoers." Puppetry even influenced the dynamic physical movements and gestures of kabuki actors. "Indeed," Jones adds, "Kabuki's indebtedness to Bunraku today is such that if it were deprived of those plays taken from the puppet theatre it would probably lose something on the order of half or more of its standard repertoire."[36]

Puppetry had been performed for centuries by troupes that toured the provinces. Prior to the astonishing advances in puppet technology in the eighteenth century, older puppets were crudely made. As the craftsmanship of the puppets, the virtuosity of puppeteers and chanters (*gidayū*), and the literary quality of puppet plays evolved from the late 1600s into the next century, *bunraku* delivered thrills comparable to those of effects-laden cinematic blockbusters nowadays. Chikamatsu wrote for puppets that were manipulated over the head by a single puppeteer (*tezukai ningyō*), but by the 1730s the puppets had become so large and intricate in their movements and expressive capabilities that they required three puppeteers: the master, whose face was visible and who manipulated the head and right arm, and two apprentices, whose faces were hidden by black hoods and who moved the left hand, legs, and feet. In contrast to many other puppetry traditions, the three puppeteers are not hidden from the audience, but their presence fades from consciousness as one becomes absorbed in the movement of the puppets.

Besides the attraction of the puppetry itself and the dramatic stories—either contemporary (*sewamono*) or historical (*jidaimono*) tales—audiences were drawn by famous narrators and *shamisen* players. *Gidayū* performances involved highly stylized narration, singing, and all characters' voices. It was an exhausting task, so two pairs of narrators and accompanists would usually tag-team in the course of one play.

Ōsaka was the unquestioned capital of mainstream *bunraku*, boasting two major theaters, the Takemoto-za (1684–1767) and the Toyotake-za

(1703–65). The latter burned down twice, in 1761 and 1763, and eventually converted to a kabuki theater. Ōsaka-style puppet theater thrived another decade or so in Edo, although most of the repertoire remained the Ōsaka classics. However, Edo had its own tradition of puppet plays, which originated in 1635 when Yūki Magozaburō established the Yūkiza and received recognition from the *bakufu* as one of five licensed theaters in Yoshiwara and later Asakusa. Yūkiza specialized in string puppets, or marionettes (*ayatsuri ningyō*), and in some of its productions the marionettes interacted with live actors onstage. In general, marionettes were more often seen in street carnivals (*misemono*) or variety halls (*yose*); however, Mari Boyd describes Yūkiza as less hidebound and more innovative than standard *bunraku*, adapting new technologies and puppeteering methods, and even including in its performances contemporary sociopolitical content reflecting the liberal ideas circulating in the 1920s. The school survives to this day under the supervision of the twelfth-generation master (*iemoto*) carrying the Yūki name.[37]

From around the mid-eighteenth century until the early Meiji period (1868–1912), kabuki reigned supreme. Although nearly all *chōnin* arts were affected to some degree by government censorship, kabuki was profoundly transformed by it, as the next chapter recounts. Suffice to say for now that this theatrical form—involving song, dance, stylized movement, instrumental music, and increasingly daring special effects—had by the late seventeenth century evolved from a female-dominated genre to one in which only males could participate, in the process creating a tradition of female impersonation that is world renowned. Nō actors had long performed female roles, but in kabuki transgendered performance became a specialized art, to the extent that some have said—absurdly, in my view—that men could play women better than women could: "Actresses become plausible only when they play their parts, not by miming women, but by imitating *onnagata*." Another major shift due to government pressure was the (very) gradual separation of kabuki from prostitution, a connection that endured well after Okuni's time and that proved stubbornly resistant to persistent *bakufu* reform campaigns.[38]

Compared to the standard that earns a performer an Oscar or Tony award nowadays—namely, naturalism, the ability to inhabit a character and suspend audience disbelief—kabuki acting was judged by very different criteria. Although actors had some artistic license, most aspects of kabuki were stylized to such an extent that perhaps only a true *tsū* could discern between individual performances. There were conventions for character types and specific roles. The actor did not "disappear" within a role to replicate reality so much as his artistry became the focal point. The makeup, dazzling costumes, dynamic music, and occasional acrobatics clearly distinguished kabuki from the real world.

Nevertheless, the subject matter and character types of kabuki plays were much closer to the real lives, emotions, and challenges of *chōnin*. Both kabuki and *bunraku* put commoners on the stage. Yes, there were warriors, spirits, and magical critters as well, but to some extent *chōnin* audiences could see glimpses of their own lives. Compared to *nō*, a more spartan, metaphorical, mystical type of theater set somewhere between the tangible and spirit worlds, kabuki and *bunraku* were more grounded in a recognizable reality, albeit a reality that was decidedly unrealistic. Also unlike *nō*, kabuki especially could get salacious, mawkish, obscene, and gruesome. Playwrights, actors and theater owners, intent on keeping audiences agog, continually pushed the envelope in the last decades of Tokugawa rule, brashly inviting trouble for themselves.

Shively's comprehensive examination of the "social environment" of kabuki draws particular attention to the cult of celebrity that accrued around actors. Anyone in our time who has met a celebrity and requested a selfie with her/him would understand how awestruck *chōnin* and even high-ranking *bushi* felt when in the company of a star performer. When he strode onto the *hanamichi*, or "flower road," an extension of the stage that projected out into the audience, the actor gave viewers a greater sense of intimacy with him and affirmed his connection to *chōnin*. Even though by law actors worked and resided in the "evil places" (*akusho*) of the pleasure districts, their fans—including even *daimyō* and their wives—came to *them*, as if in homage. *Daimyō* also hosted actors in their own mansions, demonstrating inappropriate degrees of friendship and intimacy. It was, of course, unseemly for samurai to aspire to the same standard of cool as lowly rakes, dandies, spendthrifts, and elite harlots. The exposure of the Ejima-Ikushima affair (1714)—a secret, nine-year romance between the lady in waiting for the *shōgun*'s mother, Ejima, and kabuki star Ikushima Shingorō—brought down the heavy hand of the *bakufu*. Ikushima's theater was closed and razed, reducing the number of Edo's kabuki theaters from four to three, all of which were shut down for three months. Officials issued strict new guidelines for performers' conduct and for the architectural design of theaters.[39] Several subsequent *bakufu* sumptuary edicts (*ken'yaku rei*) tried to separate *bushi* from these celebrity outcastes, but the repetition of such moral reform efforts says much about their efficacy.

Theater provided much, but not all, of the musical and dance repertory of the Edo period. The musical realm was yet another that undermined the stratified society that neo-Confucian ideologues cherished. "If the Pax Tokugawa gave birth to ideals that fragmented the musical world along social lines," Gerald Groemer contends, "it simultaneously engendered forces rendering it increasingly difficult to enforce and sustain a divided musical culture." The social intermingling that occurred in the cultural marketplace "meant that people and music of all sorts now interacted at places and in manners that conservatives could only see as unbearably promiscuous." Given the cultural and demographic realities of the Edo period, "the possibility of a coherent notion of 'Japanese music' was becoming increasingly real," although its actual articulation would wait until the Meiji period. That is, music became more a shared culture across status groups than a marker of station, as neo-Confucians believed it should be. Commoners chanted *nō*; warriors sang and danced kabuki; female geisha performed *gidayū* libretti; rural folks learned city songs; sighted people entered the musical profession that had once been the province of the blind.[40]

The three-stringed lute called the *shamisen* was to Edo-period music what the electric guitar is to popular music today. A plucked string instrument with a resonator similar to that of a banjo, *shamisen* was adapted from the Chinese *sānxián* and imported to Japan via the tributary Ryūkyū kingdom (now Okinawa). In the seventeenth century it became the primary instrument in both kabuki and *bunraku*, and accompanied street singers, bards, and geisha in teahouses. Officials described the *shamisen*'s sound as "lascivious," the same charge critics of jazz in the early 1900s made against the saxophone.

A bewildering number of distinct styles of music were performed and heard, each with its own structure and conventions. One important distinction was between narrative songs and so-called "long songs" (*nagauta*), which were "lyric" or more directly emotional, sometimes suites of short songs (*kouta*) with no story.[41] There was a long tradition of narrative songs dating back to medieval times, performed by sightless bards playing the *biwa* (a lute derived from the oud, brought from Persia via the ancient Silk Road). One of the few *za* that survived Nobunaga's suppression was Tōdō, a guild of blind musicians subsidized by the Tokugawa *bakufu*, which performed for pay and offered musical instruction to neophytes. With the popularization of the *shamisen*, that instrument usurped much of the *biwa*'s function to accompany narrative singing.

Another important distinction in Edo-period music culture was between elite and folk songs "that seemed more resistant to change," and *hayariuta*, popular songs that came and went as times and tastes changed. Sometimes new lyrics would be set to extant melodies to create a new piece. By the mid-1800s musical "cognoscenti" had emerged, so "it had become an embarrassment for a 'man of taste' not to be able to sing, and sing well, up-to-date popular music styles."[42] The widespread printing and distribution of song sheets and *shamisen* method books made it possible for nearly anyone to participate in a vibrant musical culture.

Chōnin were surrounded by music, which was not limited to the pleasure districts. Walking the streets of Ōsaka or Edo, one was likely to hear a number of singers and instrumentalists performing, or songs used to advertise products, report news or attract customers. The earliest variety halls (*yose*) that emerged in the early 1800s mixed musical entertainment with comedy, dance, and acrobatics. Musicians and dancers were hired to play in private homes and parlors. During the Edo period more women learned and performed instrumental and vocal music than at any point in Japan's history to that point; some became teachers with male pupils. Many officials regarded this as a violation of their "no women onstage" law and labeled female musicians immoral. Indeed, they were often performing a repertoire similar to that of geisha in the *yūkaku* or *hanamachi*.

What made Edo-period music culture distinctive was its participatory nature. This was facilitated by wide availability of the materials to make music, the sheer ubiquity of music in everyday life, an expanding market and new incentives for professionalization and the absence of any real, enforceable obstacles to prevent status groups and the sexes from transgressing their respective boundaries. Moreover, music was part of a tripartite structure that constituted *chōnin* culture, which included print culture and theater. That is, there were extensive codependent and mutually beneficial connections between print, plays, and music, sometimes described as "commingled media."[43] Printed materials publicized performances and performers, and made theatrical and musical texts widely available; music and theater gave the publishing industry an inexhaustible supply of textual and pictorial material to sell; music was inseparable from both kabuki and *bunraku* and made it possible for amateurs to participate vicariously in theatrical culture; and theater provided much of the repertory for purely musical and dance performances. Indeed, it is difficult to imagine any one element of this tripartite structure thriving without the other two.

A whole new world

Despite decades of scholarship to the contrary, some still describe Japan under Tokugawa rule as "isolationist." In 1639 the *bakufu* sharply curtailed interactions with foreign countries and banned Christianity, which had thrived beyond all expectations for almost a century. Japanese returning from abroad were executed. Yet relations continued with Chinese and Dutch traders in Nagasaki, with diplomats from neighboring Chosŏn (Korea), and with the Ryūkyū kingdom and Ezo (Ainu) on Japan's southern and northern frontiers, respectively. In foreign relations, as elsewhere, efforts to concentrate all control in the hands of a few high-ranking officials were undermined by their own actions, and commoners had opportunities through popular culture to encounter foreigners. In fact, popular culture provided numerous ways for Japanese to reimagine their place in a world that had rather suddenly become much larger and more diverse than earlier generations had realized.[44]

Tokugawa officials had understandable reasons for wanting to control relations with foreign polities, merchants, missionaries, and peripheral ethnic communities. In 1543, at the height of the Warring States period, Portuguese merchants aboard a Chinese vessel arrived at Tanegashima, and Japanese first encountered firearms. Thereafter individual *daimyō* sought a military and economic edge by establishing trade and diplomacy with Europeans, and through them, Southeast Asians. Catholic missionaries also made their way to Japan. Portuguese Jesuit Francis Xavier (1506–52) learned the hard way that going straight to the court or Ashikaga *bakufu* would get him nowhere in his proselytization efforts: "We tried earnestly to speak with the king … When we learned that his subjects did not obey him, we made no further efforts to obtain this permission to preach in his kingdom."[45] Cementing ties with local *daimyō* was the best way to spread the Gospel. When the Tokugawa came to power, Ieyasu and Hidetada reined in such higgledy-piggledy diplomacy, deputizing outlying vassals to communicate with borderland polities and peoples: the Shimazu clan with Ryūkyū; the Matsumae with Ezo; and the Sō with Chosŏn. The *bakufu* dealt directly with the Dutch East India Company (VOC) factory at Nagasaki.

Besides the pragmatic value of controlling diplomacy and overseas commerce, the Tokugawa used interactions with foreigners to augment their own legitimacy, majesty, and authority at home.[46] Over the course of two centuries several processions of foreigners marched to Edo in full public view, impressing on the populace that foreign kings were paying "tribute" to their ruler: eighteen Ryūkyūan envoys from 1610 to 1842; annual (quadrennial after 1790) VOC gift-bearing missions; and twelve Chosŏn embassies from 1607 to 1811. The first two were unambiguously tributary, but not the Koreans': they viewed their missions as a way to preserve friendly relations, not to "serve the great" (K: *sadae*; J: *jidai*) as they did with the Ming and Qing Chinese dynasties. Moreover, Chosŏn steadfastly refused to accept reciprocal Tokugawa envoys. Historians usually attribute this to protocol,[47] but surely Koreans had no desire ever to see samurai on their soil again after the devastation of the invasions of the 1590s. The first three Chosŏn embassies were to normalize relations and repatriate abductees, but they could do nothing to control Japanese perceptions of their visits.

In any case, the foreign embassies are prominent examples of the impact that contact with the outside world, however limited and intermittent, had on popular culture in the Edo period. With their rich print culture and carnivalesque proclivities, *chōnin* could not resist appropriating what they witnessed into their playtime. In fact, Korean historians and municipalities have celebrated the cultural impact of the Chosŏn embassies (K: *t'ongsinsa*; J: *tsūshinshi*) on Japan as the first "Korea Wave" (K: *hallyu*; J: *kanryū*), a term that refers to the popularity of Korean pop music, television programs, movies, and tourism in Japan, Taiwan, China, and Southeast Asia in the early twenty-first century (see Chapter 9).[48]

Ronald Toby notes that Chosŏn embassies became a staple subject of visual culture. High officials and commoners alike commissioned paintings, illustrated scrolls, and votive pictures to keep visual records; publishers and ukiyo-e artists printed depictions by the thousands to sell. Older paintings and prints were copied later (with variations that are conspicuous now), suggesting a sizable demand for images, even when the last embassy had been a generation or two earlier.[49]

FIGURE 2.1 *Kano Masunobu (1625–94), Illustration of Reception of the [1655] Chosŏn Envoys (Chōsen kokushi kantai zu byōbu), folding screen, British Museum, Wikipedia Commons (https://ja.wikipedia.org/wiki/朝鮮通信使#/media/File:Korean Embassy1655KanoTounYasunobu.jpg)*

Aside from the visual spectacle of processions, Korean musical displays also fascinated Japanese of all statuses. *Records of Journeys across the Sea (Haehaeng ch'ongjae)*, an anthology of official travelogues by envoys to Edo from 1655 to 1811, contains a handful of accounts of musical encounters with Japanese elites and commoners.[50] An 1802 administrative handbook recounts embassies traveling with as many as eighty musicians and dancers (*sodong*). Instrumentalists were divided into chamber orchestras (*p'ungaksu*, strings and winds) and marching bands (*ch'wigosu*, winds and percussion).[51] Every important moment, from the arrival of boats at Tsushima and points along the Inland Sea coast, to each time the Chosŏn king's letter to the *shōgun* changed hands, involved music and dancing and was observed by spellbound Japanese commoners and *bushi* alike.

Required to provide lodging, food, and entertainment, *daimyō* regaled their guests with sumptuous banquets and routinely requested musical performances. On some occasions the envoys obliged; other times they refused on grounds of protocol. The account of the first mission in 1607 claims that Japanese requests for music were "rude" and that envoys did not want their musicians performing in a squalid marketplace.[52] The record of the 1682 embassy to congratulate Tokugawa Tsunayoshi (1646–1709) for his succession as *shōgun* describes a battle of wits between Japanese officials and Chosŏn diplomats regarding musical performances: "We [Japanese] like to listen to Chosŏn's music, especially the sound of *p'iri* [bamboo oboe] and *puk* [barrel drum]. Why did you reject the official's request for your band to come and play the music? Please follow what he wants, as he will come to make the same request sooner or later."[53] Such incidents indicate Japanese interest in Korean music, as well as a not-so-latent desire to get the envoys to submit to Japanese demands. However, they also suggest Koreans' resistance to taking orders, and their longstanding belief that in terms of protocol and Confucian decorum, Japanese were pretty unsophisticated.

On other occasions, however, Korean envoys gladly presented music, not only for arrivals, official banquets, and ceremonies but also for large audiences of Japanese commoners. "Because I do not like bustling banquets such as the Japanese officials hosted," an envoy on the 1719 mission wrote, "I went out to the street and set up a wooden stage. As I let the musicians play p'iri and two dancers [kwangdae] dance, a crowd gathered around."[54] Korean sources often mentioned the enthusiastic responses of Japanese crowds for whom they performed. "Today, the musicians from my country went outside the gate to play string instruments, while the young dancers danced on the street," a 1748 delegate recorded. "Japanese men and women gathered to watch, laughing occasionally—their laughs are not that different from those of our countrymen."[55]

Generally speaking, Koreans were less impressed by Japanese music and dance: "All their voices are weak and the sounds fast," a 1711 envoy noted.[56] But typically their disapproval was on the grounds of propriety—as good Confucians, they denigrated Japanese music for its failure to embody the moral principles enshrined in the Chinese Yüèjì (see Chapter 1). One envoy was scandalized by a performance by ten young male dancers at a banquet hosted by the daimyō of Tsushima, the island between the Korean peninsula and Kyūshū where the embassies landed first.

> They went out and came back with their dresses changed again. Five of them dressed as prostitutes [ch'angnyŏ] ... while the other five dressed like young boys, boasting a debauched character. When they marched in procession to enter the room, the glamorous dresses glittered like sunshine ...

> Suddenly they changed their dances to act out the romance between men and women. They made seductive gestures, smiling at each other. The Japanese official ... asked me, "This dance imitates Japanese prostitutes' gestures and appearances. Are the prostitutes in Chosŏn similar to these?" I answered, "Even though the dresses are different, their gestures are not that different." The Japanese official asked again, "Do you enjoy this kind of entertainment?" I answered, "There are no men who have a heart made of cast iron or rock. Even though I like it, I try to restrain myself." He laughed aloud. When they tired of watching the performances, I said, "I don't care to watch these obscene entertainments anymore." The Japanese officials ordered them to stop the performances.[57]

Chosŏn ambassadors, like all civil servants in Korea and China, had passed a series of grueling examinations on Confucianism to earn their positions. They served a monarchy that presumed to have created a neo-Confucian order that surpassed China's—after all, if the Ming Chinese were such good Confucians, would they have suffered humiliating conquest by the Manchurian barbarians in 1644? Japanese scholars sought audiences with their Korean counterparts, either out of a sincere desire to learn from them or simply to claim such an encounter as a credential.[58] In a discussion on music during the 1719 mission, an envoy remarked that Japanese music lacked the "ritual propriety" (Ch: *lǐ*; K: *ye*; J: *rei*) idealized in Confucian musical aesthetics and sounded rather more like Buddhist chant. "All of these performances indicate that Confucianism is not prevalent in your country," he told his host. The Japanese official replied, "That is absolutely true. We can even say that there is no Confucian culture left in my country."[59] Some Japanese were quite willing to concede Korean superiority in Confucian erudition and to accept music as evidence of that.

The impact of the Korean embassies on Japanese visual and performance culture is most conspicuous in the ways that Japanese commoners incorporated them into their religious and recreational life. Especially in communities along the so-called "Korean Road" (*Chōsenjin kaidō*) by which the embassies traveled to and from Edo, Japanese created shrine festivals and other carnivalesque occasions during which they masqueraded as Koreans. They paraded through their communities in homemade faux *hanbok* (Korean costume), horsehair hats, flags, and shoes, singing "Korean" songs, playing "Korean" instruments and dancing "Korean" dances (*tōjin odori*).[60] In Edo even the *shōgun* would emerge from his palace to observe the Hie Shrine Sannō festival, which gave these spectacles a subversive edge. The *shōgun* himself was more accessible to foreign dignitaries than to his lowly subjects, so by "masquerading as Koreans, as aliens not constrained by the rules of Japanese society, but privileged to see, or be seen by, the shogun, the *chōnin* of these wards might have been asserting their own moral claim to equivalent high status."[61] In some communities—such as Tsu (Mie prefecture) and Kawagoe (Saitama)—there has been a revival of festivals, parades, and dances in which masking as Koreans continues.[62]

Historians generally agree that people in the Edo period were more likely to identify themselves as residents of a particular village or *han*, as members of a specific family or clan, or as someone in the occupational status groups (warrior, farmer, artisan, merchant) than as "Japanese." The Meiji state of the nineteenth century went to great lengths to persuade people that they were subjects of an imperial nation-state known as "Japan," with the attendant loyalties to emperor and country and responsibilities for national service. But several scholars have argued recently that the availability of information on Chinese, Korean, Ryūkyūan, Dutch, and Ezo dress, manners, music, dances, hairstyles, literature, and material culture contributed to a nascent sense of quasi- or protonational identity in early modern Japan, based on an "other" with whom a Japanese "self" could be contrasted. Articulations of difference took many forms: a mental displacement of China by Japan as the "center" of civilization; a belief that living in the "land of the gods" (*shinkoku*) gave Japanese intuitive knowledge of "the Way" of morality well before they encountered Confucius; distinctions in mannerisms that made non-Japanese seem exotic and barbaric; and visible phenotypical differences, such as hair, clothing or skin color (but without a concept of "race").[63]

Printed ethnogeographic taxonomies (*bankoku jinbutsu-zu*) of the world's people—equivalents of *National Geographic*, if you will—were one vehicle by which notions of Japan as a distinctive polity and civilization formed and proliferated. Hair was one convenient marker of difference in pictorial imagery of foreigners, mostly because both the Tokugawa and Qing Chinese states inscribed their dominance on their male subjects through tonsorial laws. The requirement that Japanese men shave their pates (leaving the sides long and binding the hair in an oiled topknot, *chonmage*) and that Chinese adopt the Manchurian hairstyle (shaving the entire head above the temple and braiding the hair from the crown in a long ponytail, *biànzǐ*) made hair politically symbolic of submission to these respective states' authority. The Tokugawa also forbade facial hair, which had been a common emblem of masculinity and "belligerent intent" during the medieval and Warring States periods.[64] Toyotomi Hideyoshi, famously incapable of growing a passable beard, pasted a custom-made one to his chin.[65] So when Koreans visited, sporting beards and long, untrimmed hair, they were called *ketōjin* (literally "hairy Chinamen"). Chikamatsu had several opportunities to use this epithet in his most famous play, *The Battles of Coxinga* (*Kokusen'ya no gassen*, 1715). The story is based on the historical Guóxìngyé (1624–62), a military leader and pirate of mixed Japanese and Chinese parentage who headed a resistance campaign from Taiwan and the Philippines against the Manchurian Qing dynasty. At one point, the hero exclaims, "Gathering an army around me, I shall counterattack Tartary [Manchuria] and twist the Tartars by the pigtails on their shaven pates."[66] Similarly, the Ezo/Ainu of the realm's northern frontier (northern Honshū and Hokkaidō) were depicted in numerous pictures and travelogues with bushy beards and hairy bodies, which signified their barbarism.[67] The Dutch were labeled "red-haired barbarians" (*kōmō no banjin*) with long noses like goblins (*tengu*).

The "red-hairs" and their predecessors—the Portuguese, Spanish, and English, who had been evicted from Japan in 1639—had an impact on popular culture with their novel technologies, material culture, medical knowledge, and food. Portuguese brought *pão* (bread, *pan* in Japanese) and the prototype for deep-fried *tenpura* to Japan in the sixteenth century. From the late 1500s Christian converts and even Hideyoshi wore crucifixes, while the bodhisattva of mercy, Kannon, was depicted in icons as Mary. By the nineteenth century, clocks, magic lanterns (image projectors), telescopes and magnifying lenses, replica Dutch East Indiaman ships (*spiegelretourschip*), and other items were included in street fairs and outdoor bazaars (*misemono*). Perhaps the most famous example of European influence on Tokugawa Japan was the use by a handful of artists of linear perspective in woodblock prints, which became known as *uki-e* (floating pictures), after the 1730s.[68]

It will be apparent in subsequent chapters just how profound and transformative Euro-American influence was on all aspects of Japanese society, particularly so in popular culture. Nonetheless, it is worth noting that from its inception as a recognizable phenomenon, popular culture in Japan did not develop in complete isolation from the outside world. If not as sustained, intense and conspicuous as it would later be, foreign influence as presented in the media and culture of play of the Edo period made the world "bigger" and more diverse in Japanese popular consciousness.

CHAPTER THREE

Delicate dancing—early modern Japan's culture wars

In 1804, renowned ukiyo-e artist Kitagawa Utamaro, master painter of *bijinga* (pictures of beautiful women), was imprisoned and then sentenced to fifty days of house arrest, in manacles. His publisher was fined. Utamaro was charged with impugning the dignity of the long-dead warlord Toyotomi Hideyoshi, Tokugawa Ieyasu's predecessor as military suzerain of the reunified realm, with Utamaro's triptych painting of Hideyoshi (sporting his signature pasted-on mustache) lounging merrily with his five concubines. Considering Hideyoshi's grandiose indulgences, it was hardly libelous. Nonetheless, authorities deemed it a violation of the *bakufu*'s prohibition on the depiction of political figures. When Utamaro died in 1806 many said it was because his enthusiasm for making art, and thus his reason for living, had been crushed.[1]

"Censorship was not a joke in the Tokugawa period," Hibbett asserts. "If it lacked the modern efficiencies to be introduced by the Meiji government, it appears to have made up for this by creating an atmosphere in which strict regulation was unnecessary."[2] Discretion was a necessary survival skill for artists, performers, publishers, and proprietors; blatant subversion would put them out of business—or worse. Unfortunately, the difference between discretion and subversion was not always clear, and could change. We cannot be sure of either his thinking or his motives, but Utamaro may not have realized that naming Hideyoshi—who had no kinship whatsoever to the ruling Tokugawa—would elicit such a response. Many other historical personages had been identified by name in books and plays, oftentimes as surrogates for contemporary figures. Like beauty, discretion and subversion were in the eye of the beholder, who would not necessarily share his predecessor's sensibilities.

The attitude of Tokugawa authorities and neo-Confucian ideologues toward *chōnin* culture combined self-assured paternalism with a sense of dread. The regime's policies may seem unimaginably harsh and draconian today, but they were so for a reason. Hideyoshi, Ieyasu, his heir Hidetada and their contemporaries had never known a time of peace and stability; neither, for that matter, had their parents, grandparents and in some cases great-grandparents. Memories of the Warring States haunted generations of Tokugawa rulers, who feared nothing more than a return to the chaotic violence, treachery, and disorder of that time. Add to this the seductive appeal to high officials of the neo-Confucian cosmological order, and we may understand, if not necessarily sympathize with, the highly structured, eternally paranoid system they imposed.

Early modern Japanese administrators and intellectuals found sufficient evidence in popular culture to affirm their already low opinion of urban commoners. The original basis of that culture in prostitution, transvestism, scatology, and playful impropriety was not lost on them. In what kind of world would people hang portraits of famous courtesans in their homes, laud female impersonators and puppeteers as geniuses and shamelessly read the sexual vitae of loose women and rakes? What sorts of people sold their daughters to brothels;, blew their inheritances on gambling, drinking, and whoring; and then enjoyed reading stories, hearing songs, and watching plays depicting and occasionally celebrating those same actions? Only excess and gluttony satisfied their ravenous appetites for physical pleasure; moderation, discipline, sobriety, propriety, and self-cultivation seemed beyond their capacity.

For *bakufu* officials and private intellectuals, the depravity of *chōnin* culture was not a minor irritation but a serious menace to the social fabric their forebears had so carefully woven. They also predicted dire political consequences for allowing commoners to do what came most naturally to them, namely, to gratify every physical desire rather than refine their moral potential. Yet in a bizarre circular logic—not unlike that underlying colonial ideologies of assimilation—many Tokugawa elites thought commoners incapable of proper moral action, but also condemned them for not exerting any such effort ... even though it was theoretically beyond their capacity.

This is the mentality with which commoners had to contend. Yet if there was one thing cultural entrepreneurs and their clientele did well, it was either responding to *bakufu* censorship and sumptuary edicts or evading them altogether. They were unfailingly resourceful, ingenious, and manipulative when it came to negotiating with flinty officials who had lost all patience with them. Granted, if we pay attention to dates, we see that sometimes these negotiations could take a decade or more to yield an outcome acceptable to all parties. There were times when either particular theaters or brothels were closed for extended periods, or entire *yūkaku* shut down or relocated—always farther away and accessible only inconveniently.

Nonetheless, like careless parents, the *bakufu* and local magistrates were inconsistent in their discipline and "erratically repressive" in their rule (it did not help that some of them were addicted to *ukiyo* delights, as well).[3] It may seem that *chōnin* had little recourse to protest government harassment and interference, and in some cases that was true. But there was also a virtuosity to cultural entrepreneurs' entreaties that enabled them not only to continue doing what they had been doing but also to push the envelope further. I have yet to read an Edo-period history that argues that, for instance, kabuki became more wholesome over the long term. Whatever short-term concessions were made to suit *bakufu* demands, they did not endure, and the tendency was always toward darker, more salacious, more violent, and more scandalous material.[4] The successor Meiji state was far more effective taming kabuki, but also had to deal with several new cultural media, with which it had mixed success at best.

Did *chōnin* culture indeed constitute a revolt against Tokugawa authority or the neo-Confucian ideology on which it was based? Was it, as some scholars contend, a true counterculture in which official ideas and behaviors were patently rejected and inverted? Did the *bakufu* have legitimate fears about its political survival? Conversely, was a merchant's son engaged in political subversion when he drank and gambled away his family's fortune? Was a Shimabara courtesan undermining Tokugawa authority by giving her body to a paying customer? Was a pornographer drawing *shunga* thumbing his nose at The Man? Was a blacksmith's wife threatening Japanese civilization when she read a salacious novel or learned *bunraku* songs on the *shamisen*?

A number of scholars do indeed detect political import, if not always intent, in these gestures. That is, even in the absence of a consciously defiant, insubordinate rage against the machine, such acts collectively transformed the social and political order of the Edo period. Put another way, the argument goes, *not caring* about what neighbors or authorities thought of one's behavior, or just slyly hiding it, were "political" inclinations and acts with ramifications beyond the individual. Yet how subversive could these attitudes and actions be, if elites expected commoners to be doing such things and were predisposed to regard them as incapable of self-restraint anyway?

There is no "right" answer to these questions; they are historical interpretations and as such open to debate. My view is that the Edo period is a supreme example of Gramsci's theory of hegemony (introduced in Chapter 1), but one that is far more complex than a duel of wits between warrior elites and lowly commoners. For one thing, *yūkaku* were teeming with *bushi* of various ranks, whose appetites for debauchery were limited only by their stagnant salaries. For another, there were samurai intellectuals who *did* believe commoners had the capacity for moral action and self-perfection. There were also commoners who sincerely embraced the *bakufu*'s neo-Confucian ideology, cultivated it within themselves and their households and were staunch apologists for the hierarchical social order that disadvantaged them. Some of the harshest critics of the *ukiyo* were themselves *chōnin*, while some of the most ardent advocates for the dignity and humanity of rural and urban plebs were *bushi* educators and philosophers. The social fabric of early modern Japan was in fact a crazy quilt.

Navigating censorship

The classic example of *chōnin* entrepreneurs adapting to government restrictions was seventeenth-century kabuki. A century after Okuni's big debut in Kyōto, she would not have recognized the art attributed to her; in fact, she would not even have been allowed onstage to perform it. I refer readers to Shively's oft-cited article for a narrative of the delicate deliberations between the *bakufu* and theater owners and performers. From that piece I have made a table of some of the most significant edicts that affected kabuki. The list is by no means exhaustive; Shively stated there is "no comprehensive collection," but "there are well over a hundred" in extant sources.

Shively's inescapable conclusion was that the *bakufu* won some battles but lost the war. Theater owners either petitioned officials for leniency, claiming financial hardship, or flagrantly violated each law in part or full. "The *bakufu* lost ground on almost every front: the increasingly substantial construction of the theaters, the luxurious teahouses, the elaborate staging, the use of wigs and rich costumes, and the introduction of 'subversive' subject-matter into the plays. The appeal of *kabuki* to all classes could not be checked."[5]

Although Shively did not apply it explicitly, the theory of hegemony allows us to see the compromise equilibrium achieved in this centuries-long contest of wills: the *bakufu* "lost ground" indeed, but without imperiling its authority. It made strategic concessions that pacified theater owners, performers, and fans, while never surrendering its authoritative prerogative to make such concessions in the first place. Neither did the petitioners challenge or deny the *bakufu* that authority. When Shively concluded that government pressure was "artistically beneficial" to kabuki, he was tacitly acknowledging this, too: to a degree, authorities achieved their aim of "cleaning up" kabuki and distinguishing actors from prostitutes. Had he known this history, Gramsci could scarcely have found a better case study for the operation of hegemony.

There are few detailed records of the negotiation process, but it likely resembled that described by Irwin Scheiner in an influential article on how rural peasants brought concerns and demands to their local lords. Farmers thought of their relationship with *bushi* authorities as a "covenant," deftly invoking the Confucian philosophical principles of benevolent governance to which administrators were expected to adhere. That is, peasants knew what they were "owed" for their obeisance to *daimyō* and their deputies and "had the capacity, language, and organizational ability to create a new world view when the old was inconsistent with reality." Peasants understood

Year	Objective	Repetitions
1629	Ban female prostitutes (*yūjo*) from stage; end of "women's kabuki" (*onna kabuki*)	1630, 1640, 1645, 1646
1636	Ban silk, brocade, and "rich materials" for costumes and curtains	1649, 1650, 1655, 1662 (in 1668 "authorities were making concessions on this front also"), 1794
1642	Ban female impersonations; 1644 repeal allowed it as long as gender distinctions of actor roles were obvious to audience	
1648	Ban homosexual prostitution	
1648	Actors not allowed to leave theater quarters	1655, 1661 (2x), 1662, 1668, 1671, 1678, 1689, 1689 (3x), 1689, 1695, 1697, 1699, 1703 (2x), 1706 (4x), 1709
1649	Ban screens and blinds in box seats (used to conceal high-ranking samurai from view)	"repeatedly"
1652	Ban "youth's kabuki" (*wakashū kabuki*) and child prostitution; twelve Edo kabuki and puppet theaters closed for one year; reduce attractiveness of *onnagata* by requiring shaved pate (*sakayaki*) and removal of alluring forelock (*maegami*)	
1653–54	Ōsaka theaters closed for one year due to sword fight	
1657	Edo theaters moved to new location after Yoshiwara fire	
1657–69	Kyōto theaters closed	
1664	Ban hair wigs used by *onnagata* to conceal shaven pates; caps and scarves allowed	

Year	Objective	Repetitions
1664	Ban plays depicting "contemporary persons," preventing political and social criticism or satire	1703, due to puppet play on Akō Vendetta (*Night Attack at Dawn by the Soga*), staged two weeks after offenders' suicides; 1794
1665	Ban glamorous depictions of prostitutes, romanticization of pleasure quarters	
1671	Actors banned from visiting guests in teahouses, backstage or box seats	"essentially unenforceable"
1679	Ban drumming on mornings when performances were staged, to draw audiences	1684
1689	Ban "unauthorized" actors from stage	
1694	Limit of twenty actors per theater	
1706	Female dancers prohibited from visiting private mansions outside pleasure districts	
1707	No performances on days when *shōgun* left his palace	Rescinded in 1716
1707	Ban (outdoor) performances on windy days, to prevent fires caused by torches	
1714	Closing of Yamamura-za, due to Ejima Affair, leaving only three theaters in Edo	
1718	Permanent roofs (wooden shingle and tile) permitted on theaters, to allow performances on rainy days	
1723	Ban "love suicide" (*shinjū*) plays (also applied to *bunraku*)	
1827	Salary caps for star actors (initially instituted by agreement between three Edo theater owners in 1794, but soon broken)	1842

two fundamental principles of Confucianism: hierarchical relationships were based on reciprocity, and words and reality must be consonant under the principle of "rectification of names" (Ch: *zhèngmíng*; J: *seimei*).[6] Loyalty and deference to authority were contingent on the wisdom, benevolence, and mercy of its rule, and verbal guarantees should be borne out in deeds. Peasants also brandished the Confucian assumption that the peace and harmony of the realm hinged on the virtue and justness of the ruler (*jinkun*); this gave complainants some serious leverage in negotiating with *daimyō* who wanted neither their counterparts nor the *shōgun* to question their competence. Scheiner argues that peasants "lived in a world of conditional loyalties, established duties, and mutual obligation" and felt no compunction about refusing to pay taxes or follow orders "if justice was not given or aid refused."[7]

Yet theater owners or brothel proprietors had neither the moral authority nor sense of entitlement that "honorable farmers" (*onbyakushō*) had. From the *bakufu*'s perspective these "stupid people" (*gumin*) traded in smut and filth, cared more for profits than moral propriety, and violated established laws with impunity, yet pleaded insatiably for even more concessions. Nonetheless, the entrepreneurs of the *ukiyo* doubtless knew what to say and how to say it, with humility, deference, self-deprecation, and flattery. They deployed what James Scott calls a "public transcript," a "stereotyped, ritualistic" rhetorical strategy that hewed closely to "how the dominant group would wish to have things appear" (the public transcript exists in opposition to the "hidden transcript" among the governed, which expresses their discontent, cynicism, and bitterness toward authority).[8] That is, their pleas reinforced authorities' self-conception as righteous, benevolent, and therefore legitimate rulers. Suppliants could appeal to precedents of magnanimity, such as the patronage of kabuki by the third and fourth *shōgun* and several *daimyō*, prior invitations to perform kabuki on the Tokugawa palace grounds, the reversal of previous decisions or the rationale behind Ieyasu's instruction to permit profligacy in designated places. They were not without resources, nor were they stupid. Add to such virtuosic bargaining skills the fact that even some of the highest-ranking men and women in the warrior aristocracy were avid fans of kabuki, and its persistence under such a stern regime seems less mysterious.

Some of the most severe restrictions on popular culture—affecting theater, music, *sumō*, and publishing—were part of three major reform campaigns (*kaikaku*) initiated by the *bakufu*: the Kyōhō (1716–45), Kansei (1787–93), and Tenpō (1830–43) reforms. Designed to rationalize administration and achieve financial solvency, each also included measures to reestablish standards of public morality and proper station officials believed had been abandoned due to the evident depravity of popular culture.[9] One passage in the Kyōhō edicts reads, "Whereas, among material heretofore published by houses of edition there have been books on sexual matters [*kōshokubon*] some of which are not conducive to good mores, and all of which are constantly changing, these are no longer to be produced."[10] The Tenpō were more comprehensive, closing over a hundred *yose* in Edo, leaving a mere fifteen; relocating Edo's three theaters and shutting down several in Ōsaka; pushing hundreds of unlicensed prostitutes into the pleasure quarters; forbidding full-color woodblock prints of the *ukiyo* and its people; and reiterating salary caps and dress regulations for performers. Acclaimed actor Ichikawa Danjūrō VII (1791–1859) was singled out and banished from Edo for his ostentatious lifestyle, his luxurious home destroyed.

The most consistent censorship standard the *bakufu* rigorously enforced was the 1664 proscription on any reference to "contemporary persons" or events. Criticisms and even depictions of the Tokugawa or *daimyō* families, official policies, and recent incidents in the news were forbidden. Playwrights, authors, and visual artists circumvented this policy multiple times by identifying roughly similar personages or circumstances in the medieval Kamakura (1185–1333) and Muromachi (1336–1573) periods, and using "theatrical surrogates" to tell a contemporary story disguised as *jidaimono* (historical plays).[11]

For instance, one of the most sensational incidents of the Edo period was the Akō Vendetta (1701–03), in which forty-seven samurai successfully avenged their lord by assassinating his nemesis. The writers of the most well-known *bunraku* and kabuki version set their play *The Treasury of Loyal Retainers* (*Kanadehon Chūshingura*, 1748) in the fourteenth century, with historical figures assigned as ciphers to the incident's principal figures.[12] Another example was Chikamatsu's satire of Tokugawa Tsunayoshi, mocked as "the dog *shōgun*" (*inu kubō*) because of his over-the-top prohibition on the killing of any living thing, especially dogs. As humane as this policy may sound, it caused much hardship for people, as well as an explosion in the population of stray dogs, over twenty-four years. Five years after Tsunayoshi's death, and after his successor repealed the "laws of compassion for living things," Chikamatsu staged a play in (safely faraway) Ōsaka that substituted Hōjō Takatoki (1303–33), a regent in the Kamakura *bakufu*, for the "dog *shōgun*."[13]

Of course, audiences were hip to what story was really being told—so, too, were *bakufu* censors. They were not fools. They may have been erratic in their enforcement, and even hypocritical in their attitudes toward *chōnin* culture, but they also picked their battles, which is key to maintaining the compromise equilibrium in hegemonic relationships. However, while many scholars characterize playwrights' placement of current events in historical settings as an ingenious evasion of the spirit of Tokugawa law, it can be seen another way: as a way to appease the *bakufu*.

Chikamatsu is emblematic of the sophistication with which a balance could be struck in remaining deferential to authority while fomenting critical thought about the premises on which it rested. A recurrent tension associated with his narratives is that between socially assigned obligations and public duties (*giri*) and human emotions, the private desires of the heart (*ninjō*). Unsurprisingly, in most such narratives *giri* wins and the puppets make a bloody mess onstage committing suicide, to restore honor, to demonstrate sincerity, or to liberate a loved one to take some bold action without inhibition. The inevitable victory of *giri* has led some to characterize Chikamatsu (who was of *bushi* heritage) as a propagandist for the martial values of loyalty, self-sacrifice and moral action on which the warrior regime based its authority.

Andrew Gerstle presents two important caveats to this viewpoint, which by no means make Chikamatsu a dissident, but do suggest a sensitivity to nuance rivaled perhaps only by his contemporary Saikaku. First, Chikamatsu was a pioneer of *sewamono*, plays in contemporary settings with *chōnin* protagonists. Wealthy merchants, dissolute rakes and gamblers, prostitutes with hearts of gold, criminals, wives and mothers either stalwart and loyal, or jealous and cruel, populated these plays, which were either set in the *ukiyo* or haunted by its aura. These were seriously flawed characters, hardly paragons of purity and virtue, suffering karmic retribution onstage.

Gerstle presents Chikamatsu as someone with a unique perspective, who was outside of the status system—a man of *bushi* background with unusual empathy for commoners—and located in Kamigata, far from the center of power in Edo. Writing at the height of the Kyōhō reforms, Chikamatsu was involved in a broader discussion about the nature of personal honor, heroism and the relationship of the individual to the state. Orthodox and neo-Confucian intellectuals were contemplating the capacity of *all* individuals, regardless of gender or status, for moral self-cultivation and action. "Chikamatsu is consistent that honor is open to everyone—prostitutes, clerks, thieves, widows, not just male samurai."[14]

In this, the playwright was hinting at the "moral egalitarianism" suggested in the work of his contemporaries Ogyū Sorai and Kumazawa Banzan (1619–91), who favored meritocracy over lineage. "To try foolishly to preserve hereditary status by forever keeping those on top at the top and those below at the bottom violates the law of the universe," Sorai wrote. "When men of talent are no longer at the top, it signifies the end of a regime." Miyake Sekian (1665–1730), dean of Ōsaka's Kaitokudō merchant academy, likewise claimed that "With ceaseless effort, ordinary humans can rise to become sages." The 1758 version of the academy's principles stated that "Students will interact with one another as colleagues without regard to high and low or rich and poor."[15] In short, there was a philosophical strain in Edo-period Confucian discourse that questioned the assumption of the innate moral superiority of male *bushi*. Although he certainly featured heroic samurai in a number of his historical plays, in his *sewamono* Chikamatsu created commoner characters of both sexes who, though weak in many respects, cared about and acted out the moral principles generally considered to be distinguishing characteristics of the warrior caste. Gerstle argues that since "theatre was far more widely and deeply influential on popular morality than Confucian treatises," Chikamatsu's subtle advocacy of moral egalitarianism was his way of exposing and making intelligible to his audiences what would otherwise be an abstract and marginal strain of Confucian thought, of which they might otherwise be unaware.[16]

Yet Chikamatsu did not object to the values of selflessness, personal sacrifice and heroic honor, so much as show his audiences what the consequences of pursuing those values to their logical conclusions could be. This is the second caveat Gerstle introduces about the playwright's muted critiques of Tokugawa society. "His genius ... is not in a systematic exposition of the nature of heroic honor but in the depiction of the complex and often devastating effects of such a system on individuals from all levels of society." Moreover, "those who face tragedy are not from the highest ranks of whatever social group they are in."[17] The upshot was that Chikamatsu's worldview was pretty bleak. He was certainly not alone among Japanese writers who took the Buddha's first noble truth ("Life is suffering") as a fundamental premise, but he was adept at showing individuals entangled in complex webs of obligation to family, commerce, lovers and the state, which prevented them from being who they were as individuals. It might be unusual for a real people to find themselves in such tragic circumstances and conflicting commitments, but, Chikamatsu submitted, it was plausible.

We have a substantial record of sumptuary edicts, crackdowns, reprimands, arrests, fines, exiles and other efforts by local authorities and the *bakufu* to rein in the excesses of *chōnin* culture. But on balance cultural entrepreneurs and creative people had incentive to police themselves and were keenly aware that an infraction by one person, publisher or theater could hurt entire industries. Despite some high-profile incidents of noncompliance and retribution, there were longer stretches of calm and acquiescence. The most effective censorship is that which is least visible.

Putting on airs

We have seen numerous examples of *bushi*—from lowly retainers to *daimyō*—indulging in the amusements of the *chōnin* and augmenting their own cultural capital with conversancy in the hippest fashions and trends of the lowborn. *Daimyō* particularly risked disgrace and even the forfeiture of their *han* for conspicuously patronizing the demimonde.[18] Even so, this hazard was somewhat mitigated by the fact that their peers, and sometimes even *bakufu* officials, were deep into it, too. In important ways, however, commoners mimicked their superiors, embracing their value system, developing fluency in elites' culture and even organizing themselves as *bushi* did.

Chōnin culture was déclassé not only for warriors but also for farmers. Being of relatively high official status and the very foundation of the economy, peasants were held to a higher moral standard than *chōnin* were. Edicts of 1619 and 1643 admonished rural people to work hard, avoid frivolity and luxury and use their time off from farming productively. Such injunctions explicitly spelled out how farmers should organize their days in particular seasons; what they could eat, drink and wear; and where they could and could not reside.[19] Yet although the stock image of the pathetic, downtrodden Japanese farmer is not without some basis in reality, improvements in agricultural practices, technologies and productivity, with little concomitant rise in tax obligations, meant that several rural communities had time and money for activities other than work. Anne Walthall shows that some peasants—especially so-called *gōnō* (wealthy peasants)—had access to the literary and even performance art available to *chōnin*. Much of their own diversions were focused on religious rituals and festivals (*matsuri*), which involved drinking, dancing and singing, with musical accompaniment (in the case of fertility festivals, "hookups" were not uncommon). Rural communities also enjoyed visits from touring kabuki and *bunraku* troupes, yet sometimes they either made or purchased puppets and costumes for their own performances. They dedicated spaces within their communities to erect stages and performance halls. Walthall argues that agrarian people modified plays to suit local tastes and sensibilities, being "unmoved" by tales of *chōnin* avarice and lechery. Local amateur performances were not due to a lack of access to professional troupes but "because they wanted to act."[20]

In cities, their physical proximity to one another blurred the lines somewhat between *bushi* and *chōnin*. Samurai could and did find brides among the wealthier merchant families, augmenting their sometimes meager stipends with their in-laws' fortunes. Conversely, prosperous merchants prepared their daughters with education and etiquette to snag a *bushi* husband. Regardless of its murkiness and disadvantages, *bushi* status was still symbolically valuable to many commoners. As early as the seventeenth century, David Howell notes,

> peasant officials, privileged merchants, and other commoners who had rendered meritorious service or financial assistance [were rewarded] with the right to carry two swords and publicly use a surname. This practice ... did no violence to the status order; if anything, it reinforced it by affirming the inherent desirability of the warriors' status privileges without pretending that the commoners so rewarded had become genuine samurai.

Toward the end of the Edo period, as many *daimyō* found their revenue streams insufficient for their expenses, they offered *bushi* status as an incentive to receive financial contributions from wealthy commoners. For the latter, it was a win-win situation: they had samurai status but not samurai obligations for service.[21] However, there were some who found *bushi* status to be burdensome and contrary to their interests. The founders of the Mitsui, Sumitomo and Mitsubishi companies had *bushi* pedigree, but they (or their ancestors) determined that they would have more autonomy and more economic opportunities if they renounced it. In these three cases, at least, they were right.

Yet even *chōnin* who did not become *bushi* advocated and practiced warrior ideals in their own households and communities. They lived at a time when armed philosophers were articulating the "way of the warrior" (*bushidō*) to confront what was no less than an existential crisis among samurai: what was their purpose in peacetime? Yamaga Sokō (1622–85) candidly conceded that "the samurai eats food without growing it, uses utensils without manufacturing them, and profits without buying or selling. What is the justification for this?" he asked rhetorically. "Within his heart he keeps to the ways of peace, but without, he keeps his weapons ready for use. The three classes of the common people make him their teacher and respect him. By following his teachings, they are able to understand what is fundamental and what is secondary."[22]

Treatises by armed intellectuals like Yamaga, Miyamoto Musashi (1584–1645), Daidōji Yūzan (Taira Shigesuke, 1639–1730), and Yamamoto Tsunetomo (1659–1720) emphasized unquestioned loyalty to one's lord, unhesitating action in the face of death, austere self-discipline, personal honor, and even grooming and hygiene. The ultimate aim of *bushidō* was to control the circumstances of one's death and, for lack of a better expression, to "die pretty." The cause for which one was fighting was secondary to carrying out one's duty and facing death without thinking.[23] In his 1716 book *Hidden among Leaves* (*Hagakure*) Yamamoto presciently lambasted the corruption of samurai by popular culture, about a century before such denunciations became hysterically apocalyptic:

> During the last thirty years customs have changed; now when young samurai gather together, if there is not just talk about money matters, loss and gain, secrets, clothing styles, or matters of sex, there is no reason to gather together at all. Customs are going to pieces ... This new custom probably appears because people attach importance to being beautiful before society and to household finances. What things a person should be able to accomplish if he had no haughtiness concerning his place in society![24]

The inventors of *bushidō* pined, if not for war, then for a stoicism and readiness that samurai presumably exhibited in times of war. Their emphasis on loyalty suited Tokugawa politics, but by projecting it backward into the Warring States period, when military expediency was paramount, they revealed their historical ignorance and naïveté.

Edo-period merchants developed a similar, parallel creed, "the way of the merchant" (*shōnindō*), that emphasized personal integrity, frugality, beneficence, customer service and the honorable reputation of the family business. Like *bushidō*, these were *ideals* for conduct rather than reflections of reality, but their very existence represented a gentle yet firm pushback against the negative stereotype of the avaricious, unscrupulous, unproductive merchant. They were, in essence, a display of the dignity and ethical conduct of which *chōnin* were capable. Treatises of *shōnindō*—which often came in the form of instructions to one's descendants—closely resembled the house laws that Warring States *daimyō* used to corral their retainers, and which the Tokugawa in turn issued to *daimyō* as the Law for Military Houses (*Buke shohatto*) in 1615.[25] Here are some examples from prominent merchant houses of Ōmi province:

> When peddling in another country, treasure all its people, without regard to your own personal affairs and think not of making personal profit. —Nakamura Jihei of Gokashō, *Kakin* (Family Precepts), mid-eighteenth century

> A merchant's duty is to reach [a state of] presence or absence [*umu*] through riches, receive their benefits, and set up an inheritance. —Nakai Genzaemon of Hino, *Nakai seiyō* (Essential Rules of Nakai), ca. eighteenth century

> A merchant's mission is in managing the duties of all people through the existence/non-existence [*umu*] of all things; to vainly pursue one's own desires is to err in his essence, diverges from the hearts of the gods, and will result in one's destruction. —Nishitani Kohei and Uchiike Sanjūrō, Ōmi Hachiman, mid-nineteenth century

> Commerce is a bodhisattva's work; respect for the way of commerce is to sell and buy anything that is beneficial, to provide the world's insufficiencies, and match the heart of the Buddha. —Itō Chūbei of Toyosato, *Zayūmei* (Desk Motto), early nineteenth century[26]

Buddhist compassion and Confucian ethics permeate these merchant house codes, but generally speaking their main emphasis was on economic prudence and frugality. They notably discouraged entrepreneurship and expansion; rather, *preservation* of family wealth and the bequeathing of an estate to future generations were the primary filial obligations of heirs.[27] Saikaku emphasized this in *The Eternal Storehouse of Japan* (1688), offering advice on becoming wealthy in the burgeoning commercial economy, with "the objective... to create a prosperous family line."[28]

But *shōnindō*, like virtually everything, was fodder for satire. Ejima Kiseki, himself the son of a Kyōto shopkeeper, delighted in telling tales of the dissolute "wastrel—the 'spoiled young master.'" However, readers likely paid less attention to the unsubtle moral lessons of these stories than to the salacious process of dissipation itself: occasionally, "vice remains unpunished." One of Kiseki's "character studies" begins with the proverb "A father slaves, his son idles, and the grandson begs."[29] The reader is left to wonder whether this is a sincere lament for generational regression, or whether it means frugality and financial good sense will come to naught anyway, so why bother? Who is the greater fool, the abstemious father whose self-sacrifice and endless labor build a business, or the profligate son who uses daddy's money to actually enjoy life? In *Eternal Storehouse*, too, Saikaku denounced "the worship of money and advocate[d] an honest, frugal, and steady lifestyle" rather than reckless pursuit of endless wealth.[30] The accumulation of a vast fortune, in fact, was almost guaranteed to produce degenerate descendants.

The explication above explains why some of the harshest critics of the popular diversions of the pleasure districts were themselves *chōnin*. Some sought to adhere to the moral and commercial ideals of *shōnindō*. Others were content to experience the *ukiyo* vicariously through literature, songs or pictures, while others spurned it completely, acutely aware of how its excesses and very existence contributed to the negative image of all nonwarriors. If *bushi* officials believed *chōnin* absolutely must have such a place to debase themselves, many—perhaps most—townspeople felt otherwise. Heads of family businesses could be disgraced if someone spied a son, daughter, apprentice or employee in the pleasure quarters. Upright *chōnin* apparently felt far greater shame in such situations than samurai patrons of the *ukiyo* did. Urban commoners believed gambling, drinking, and whoring were the biggest threats to the maintenance of the family treasury, and indeed innumerable books and plays depicted such circumstances.

Some *chōnin*, disgusted by *ukiyo*, found other ways to amuse themselves, partaking in cultural pursuits that had traditionally been monopolized by courtiers and high-ranking warriors. For instance, by the mid-seventeenth century, *Tale of Genji*, *Tales of Ise*, *Sarashina Diary* and other works of classical poetry, fiction, diaries, and travelogues that had previously circulated only among the civil and military aristocracy in manuscript had been printed as illustrated vernacular books (*kanazōshi*)—sometimes for satirical purposes. They became popular primarily, though not exclusively, among women readers. Sites mentioned in these books became favorite tourist destinations at a time when travel became an increasingly prominent leisure activity.[31]

Despite its artistic reputation, *Genji* was not a universally admired text among Edo-period intellectuals, who detested the serial dalliances between the Shining Prince and a bevy of female lovers. To some critics, it seemed little better than contemporary *kanazōshi* erotica and romances marketed to women. Nonetheless, *Genji*'s author, Murasaki Shikibu, was lionized as an "ideal woman" in most biographies, even by people who derided her masterpiece. If the novel's female characters were models to avoid emulating, the author herself was an exemplary woman whose story fit well within the burgeoning library of didactic literature for women and girls.[32] The harm to feminine virtue by reading *Genji*, therefore, was attenuated.

One of the elite arts most frequently appropriated by commoners was *nō*, particularly its songs, instrumental music, and dances. *Nō* was so highly respected that it enjoyed the active patronage of the *bakufu* and *daimyō*, who provided rice stipends to masters of the art, a privilege reserved only for *bushi*. Like most elite arts, *nō* had its origins in a popular theatrical form once known as "monkey music" (*sarugaku*) performed by itinerants in early medieval times. The acknowledged founders or refiners of the art—Kan'ami (1333–84) and his son Zeami Motokiyo (ca. 1363–1443)—enjoyed the patronage of the Ashikaga in Kyōto. Its Zen-influenced austerity and concern with inspiring spiritual enlightenment and profundity (*yūgen*) in its audiences made *nō* a source of edification. *Bushi* who learned its songs, dances, and instrumental accompaniment were considered culturally accomplished.[33]

By the Edo period commoners embellished their cultural capital with proficiency in one or more aspects of *nō* performance. Nishiyama cites a record from Kasuga village, near Ōsaka, where the scion of a sake brewer household was able to support himself teaching *nō* songs (*utai*) after his family's fortunes declined. He says this indicates "that during the Genroku period *utai* was sufficiently popular to allow a professional *utai* teacher to make a living in such villages." Amateurs performed in private homes and temples, gave lessons to neighbors, and, despite a long tradition of secretive oral transmission within closed communities, *nō* texts were widely published so that aficionados could learn them. Among old-schoolers this was not a welcome development; they tried to identify and excommunicate anyone who leaked these secrets to the general public.[34] Nonetheless, wealthy peasants and merchants had become some of *nō*'s most conspicuous patrons by the end of the Edo period.

Like top-flight *nō* performers, popular entertainers typically learned from their predecessors and taught their successors through a relatively closed system of stylistic schools called *iemoto* or *mon*. *Iemoto* refers both to the individual founder or patriarch of a distinctive style (*ryū*) and to the "household" of pupils and descendants to whom he transmitted that style. Female-headed *iemoto* were rare until the twentieth century, but developed out of necessity since by that time much of the interest in learning and teaching traditional arts such as instrumental music, dance, tea ceremony, cuisine, and flower arranging (*ikebana*) came from middle-class women.

Modeled on patriarchal, patrilineal, and hierarchical samurai households (*ie*)—which was the cornerstone of modern civil law from 1899 to 1947—artistic *iemoto* were lineage systems for intergenerational transmissions of *ryū*, based on real and fictive kinship relations. I say "fictive" because who counted as "family" in Japan was far more flexible than in either Korea or China, where consanguinity (blood relations) was an almost inviolable principle. After primogeniture (bequeathing an estate to a single male heir, preferably but not necessarily the oldest son) became the legal norm among warriors, Japanese with no sons began adopting adult male heirs via marriage to a daughter. These "male brides" (*mukoyōshi*) were usually the younger brothers of designated heirs in other families, and they took their in-laws' surnames. This was a holdover from matrilocal marriage patterns in antiquity and early medieval times, when kinship was traced either bilaterally or matrilineally. It offered a high degree of flexibility based on individual households' circumstances. When changes in medieval law basically made women ineligible to inherit some or all of their parents' estates, adoption of their husbands into their natal families became a regular compensating practice. Even today, when women can legally inherit estates, adult adoption is not uncommon.

Virtually every artistic *iemoto*, some of which date back to medieval times, at some point resorted to this practice in the absence of a talented or cooperative heir in the bloodline. Despite being treated as lowborn social outcastes, kabuki actors, puppet theater *gidayū*, and musicians created their own *iemoto* in replication of *bushi* households, *nō* performers, and other occupational groups.[35] Their unique *ryū* were transmitted via master–disciple relationships centered on repetitive mimicry and sometimes lectures on aesthetic philosophy. Successful disciples took the family name (*yagō*) and became representatives of the *ryū* accredited to teach the style to others. Ideally, relationships between pupils were cooperative rather than competitive, and everyone was expected to treat the *iemoto* master (*sōshō*) with complete deference.

One example is the Yūki marionette *iemoto* mentioned in Chapter 2. Another is the Naritaya *mon* of Ichikawa Danjūrō, the stage name of a kabuki actor, which has been passed down for twelve generations since the early 1700s.[36] The original Danjūrō (1660–1704) established conventions for acting and dancing in heroic tough-guy roles (*aragoto*). Unfortunately, life imitated art, as Danjūrō I died in an act of violence, stabbed to death in his dressing room by a fellow actor. To earn his coveted mantle, successors were expected to excel at playing *aragoto* roles in eighteen canonical plays handpicked by Danjūrō VII. The most recent actor, Danjūrō XII, died in 2013, and at this writing has yet to be succeeded.

It is unclear whether the adoption of samurai household organization was an effort to earn respect for performers from their *bushi* overlords, to advocate for artists' concerns or simply to build communities of common interest. But if it added a mystique and luster to them and their artistry, *iemoto* also functioned like other credentialing or professional groups to distinguish legitimate from fraudulent practitioners. Association with an *iemoto* enhanced one's reputation by tapping into the charismatic aura of the original founder. Every traditional art form has more than one *iemoto*, each claiming to be the art's most sublime representative. The mimicry of this form of professional organization by subaltern artistic communities was not really a subversive practice that endangered the authority or prestige of the warrior aristocracy. It actually reinforced *bushi* dominance while conferring cultural capital on the entertainers who chose to organize themselves in this manner.

The adoption of *iemoto* by performers in the floating world was paralleled by an extremely complex ranking system among prostitutes. There were over four hundred terms for "prostitute" in the Edo period.[37] Ranks (*kaku*) had been adopted by the ancient Yamato state from Tang China to designate administrative posts, which were usually assigned to traditional aristocrats.

In the Heian period *kaku* became hereditary, which was of course completely antithetical to the meritocratic ethos ranks were supposed to reflect. Rank and official post (*shoku*) remained important in warrior society and determined even the clothing a samurai could wear.

The glamorous ranking system used by women of the pleasure quarters was at stark odds with the ignominy attached to the actual work. The vast majority of girls and women who staffed brothels were sold into indentured servitude by rural peasants and sometimes *chōnin*, who received cash advances that then became debts their daughters were obliged to work off. It would normally take years for a woman to repay such a debt, by which time she would likely decide to stay in the pleasure district, fearing ostracism in the outside world. Women of unusual beauty, artistic talent or popularity who attracted big-spending clients could be ranked highly and priced accordingly. The most prestigious was the *tayū*, who was "treated as a celebrity" and "an increasingly exclusive product that few could afford." With a *tayū*, "the artistic emphasis on the pleasures of social and cultural intercourse made the sex act almost incidental."[38] Just being in the presence of a superstar prostitute spoke volumes about a man's influence, financial resources, and discriminating palette.

Politics of pleasure

Many, perhaps most, historians today have populist inclinations and sympathies. Since the rise of social history in the 1960s, they have made arguments that "restore agency" to subalterns. This means thinking of commoners as agents, rather than objects, of historical change. It entails highlighting attitudes and actions that demonstrated defiance and resistance to oppression and injustice, and finding evidence that the downtrodden did not internalize notions of their own inferiority. It is an inherently politicized interpretive framework, which does not necessarily make it illegitimate. Where it is not a predetermined state ideology (as in socialist states like the USSR and People's Republic of China), it has been a productive enterprise that sensitizes us to the dignity, intelligence, and sense of self-worth of unnamed historical actors.

In the last two or three decades, this "history from below" approach, with its celebratory view of rebellion and defiance against authority, has been occasionally criticized for romanticizing class conflict or overreaching in its interpretations. One of the major risks of this type of populist social history is the projection of the historian's wishful thinking onto events and people of the past. But an equally serious danger is that, by emphasizing the heroism and consciousness of the subaltern, we understate the severity of the violence and structural oppression they faced.

A number of Japan scholars have portrayed *chōnin* culture as a self-conscious, countercultural thumb in the eye of the ruling warrior regime.

Hibbett writes, "the theatre was both an escape from life and a criticism of it." Nishiyama deems "antiauthoritarian sentiments," a "spirit of resistance," and an "attitude of defiance" to be fundamental characteristics of Edo *chōnin*. "The impulse to create, to enrich leisure time with cultural pursuits, to imitate the life-style of the upper class, ignored governmental prohibitions and undermined the status system," Walthall contends. "In this way cultural pursuits became acts of resistance to the established order." Griswold detects a "secessionist spirit" in the materialism of eighteenth-century popular fiction (*gesaku*).[39] For these scholars, the very act of seeking personal physical gratification or momentary release was "political" because the objectives of Tokugawa orthodoxy were self-restraint, self-cultivation, and self-sacrifice in the line of preassigned duties to society.

Yet as I hope this chapter has demonstrated, the *bakufu* and commoners reached a compromise equilibrium whereby the latter confirmed the former's authority through the appeal process and (usually) following the rules, or at least breaching them discreetly rather than flagrantly. Without dismissing the notion that "the personal is political" altogether, it is safer to conclude that the interests of theater, teahouse, and brothel proprietors, and of performers, courtesans, and their patrons, were financial, indulgent, and fleshly. *Chōnin* who disdained the pleasure quarters hoped both to make profits and to demonstrate the social utility and moral dignity of their professions. If there was one overarching aspiration uniting all *chōnin*, it was the desire for more *personal autonomy*, but within the parameters of warrior rule. It was not until the mid-nineteenth century that a new political order became imaginable, and even then it was so mostly among reformist *bushi* rather than commoners. Peasant rhetoric of "rectifying the world" (*yonaoshi*) was less revolutionary than it was advocacy for the existing order to operate as it should, with reciprocity—deference in exchange for benevolence—at its core.

This charge to benevolence was not easily dismissed by the *bushi* aristocracy. It was a more powerful check on capricious tyranny than one might imagine. There were many incidents of despotic cruelty, no doubt, and the personality or beliefs of a particular *shōgun* or *daimyō* could determine how much or little latitude commoners had for autonomous action. Nonetheless, as a general rule the *bakufu*, like its subjects, chose its battles. Flagrant violations had to be punished to keep face and reinforce its authority. But lesser offenses could be overlooked, and skillfully executed entreaties—especially those based on financial losses—heard and sometimes granted. Contempt for *chōnin* decadence was tempered by samurai indulgence in *ukiyo* diversions and by the intimacy between the two classes that proximity in urban spaces and regular financial transactions made unavoidable. *Bakufu* efforts to squelch popular culture were thus compromised, but then could be rationalized as compassionate benevolence for people who did not know any better than to be disreputable.

That said, in the end I think popular culture was consequential to the fate of the Tokugawa, if for no other reason than that its perceived degeneracy in the early nineteenth century portended "dynastic decline" to contemporary observers. In East Asian political cosmology the rise and fall of dynasties were theoretically the consequences of the ruler's moral conduct or lack thereof. Dynastic degeneration was foreseeable through disruptions in the natural world as well as in government corruption and inattention to administration and the plights of the people. Earthquakes, floods, famines, rural unrest, and deteriorating public morale and morality were the omens; endless austerity measures and ineffectual reform policies were the death throes of a regime. Few Japanese thought it was coincidence that two major earthquakes occurred in 1854, the same year the "barbarian-subduing generalissimo" had to accept the humiliating terms of a trade treaty with the American barbarians. A quake of similar magnitude rattled Edo less than a year later.[40] *Chōnin* popular media covered these events, with pictures of giant catfish (*namazu*) thrashing around beneath the earth's surface, and long-nosed foreigners and their "black ships" encroaching on Japanese shores. Print media, especially, but also songs, plays and carnivalesque eruptions of peasants chanting "Ain't it great?!" (*ee janaika*) announced the end of an era to people throughout Japan, as they tried to imagine what the future held.

CHAPTER FOUR

Popular culture as subject and object of Meiji modernization

On January 4, 1868, a fifteen-year-old boy, scion of the world's oldest abiding monarchy, became official head of state of Japan. Less than a year after succeeding his father, Kōmei (1831–67), to the chrysanthemum throne, Mutsuhito (1852–1912) proclaimed to the realm and the world,

> The Emperor of Japan announces to the sovereigns of all foreign countries and to their subjects that permission has been granted to the Shōgun Tokugawa Yoshinobu to return the governing power in accordance with his own request. We shall henceforward exercise supreme authority in all the internal and external affairs of the country. Consequently the title of Emperor must be substituted for that of Tycoon [*taikun*], in which the treaties have been made. Officers are being appointed by us to the conduct of foreign affairs. It is desirable that the representatives of the treaty powers recognize this announcement.[1]

The new sovereign adopted the reign name Meiji (enlightened rule), setting the tone for a sweeping, decades-long transformation of Japanese government, society, and culture. *Bushi* activists from western Japan, who regarded overthrow of the Tokugawa as the only feasible solution to "troubles within, dangers abroad" (*naiyū gaikan*), rallied around slogans such as "revere the emperor, expel the barbarian" (*sonnō jōi*) and "restore imperial rule" (*ōsei fukkō*). But once in power, their objectives quickly evolved to "rich country, strong military" (*fukoku kyōhei*) and "civilization and enlightenment" (*bunmei kaika*), by any means necessary. That is, the same "men of purpose" (*shishi*) who had once assassinated *bakufu* officials for signing humiliating "unequal treaties" with Western countries as well as foreign ambassadors and traders, now endorsed opening Japan's borders to those same countries, their technologies, ideas, institutions, and world-views. Sakuma Shōzan (1811–64) coined yet another phrase in this slogan-saturated milieu, "Eastern ethics, Western science" (*tōyō no dōtoku, seiyō no gakugei*), that would eventually become the guiding ethos of the new regime.[2] The intent was to modernize the military, economy, laws, and political system, while retaining the fundamentals of Confucian ethics and the Shintō mythistorical basis on which imperial rule rested.

The new government announced remarkably liberal intentions in its five-article Charter Oath of April 7, 1868:

By this oath, we set up as our aim the establishment of the national wealth on a broad basis and the framing of a constitution and laws.

- Deliberative assemblies shall be widely established and all matters decided by open discussion.
- All classes, high and low, shall be united in vigorously carrying out the administration of affairs of state.
- The common people, no less than the civil and military officials, shall all be allowed to pursue their own calling so that there may be no discontent.
- Evil customs of the past shall be broken off and everything based upon the just laws of Nature.
- Knowledge shall be sought throughout the world so as to strengthen the foundation of imperial rule.

These principles, especially the one calling for deliberative assemblies, would later vex the Meiji oligarchs, former *shishi* from the Satsuma, Chōshū, Tosa, and Hizen *han* in the west. Common people (*heimin*) and former samurai (*shizoku*) alike took them at their word and agitated for two decades to see that promise honored.

The *bakufu* had its defenders. Over three thousand people died in the Boshin War (1868–69) between the new imperial government and Tokugawa loyalists. Incidentally, one of its last battles involved a rare documented example of female *bushi* in combat. Nakano Takeko (1847–68) of Aizu domain, a trained martial artist, led a small female brigade (*jōshitai*) wielding bladed staffs (*naginata*) against imperial forces. Nakano killed five or six imperial soldiers before being shot dead, but, significantly, her head was not taken by the enemy.[3] I mention this because the woman warrior (*onna musha*) is an iconic, staple figure in contemporary Japanese popular culture, whose influence has extended across the Pacific to Hollywood.

The Meiji Restoration's impact on popular culture was monumental. The arts, entertainments and diversions of commoners were significant objects of modernization campaigns. As in the Edo period, censorship and reform of popular culture were significant endeavors to the new government. The Meiji oligarchs had little more regard for commoners' culture than their Tokugawa predecessors had. Yet they exploited popular media to create an aura of majesty around the new emperor, whose ancestors had been nearly invisible, politically irrelevant figures. The emperor was to be the focal point of a novel concept: nationalism. People who had previously identified themselves as members of a particular status group or domain were now admonished to think of themselves as *Japanese*, part of a national community that extended from one end of the archipelago to the other, united by a common spiritual connection to the sovereign. In James Huffman's estimation, "no single institution did more to create a modern citizenry than the Meiji newspaper press," comprised of a "collection of highly diverse, private voices" who facilitated sometimes heated discussions on the reformist state and Japan's precarious place in a hostile world.[4] Hence, popular media was charged with making people into Japanese imperial subjects and members of a national community.

Yet the reciprocal impact of popular culture on Meiji modernization was equally pronounced. Older media such as woodblock-printed broadsheets and pictures, theater, street singing, and *yose* converged with newer media such as newspapers, political cartoons, magazines, naturalistic novels, and New School (*shinpa*) kabuki to encourage greater political consciousness and involvement among common people. The operations of government were more transparent than ever before and were both reported and critiqued in news media whose readership expanded rapidly and exponentially. If popular culture served the interests of the nascent imperial state, it also provided means for critiquing it and holding it accountable. Through popular culture people learned about and shared the liberal ideas of the European Enlightenment, and concepts of human rights and representative government, of education and industrial capitalism, of gender equality and companionate marriage, of foreign affairs, imperialism, and war. English polymath Herbert Spencer's (1820–1903) application of Charles Darwin's concept of "survival of the fittest" via "natural selection" to human societies and international relations (later dubbed Social Darwinism), became an article of faith in Japanese thought.[5] Common people used the media to hold the government to promises it made in the Charter Oath: to treat all imperial subjects as equal before the law and to give them a constitution and representative government. Nearly every subject conceivable was broached, with the significant exception of imperial sovereignty. As rebellious as political liberals could be, there was broad popular consensus that the emperor was inviolable. Discontent targeted the oligarchs who stood between the sovereign and his subjects. Lèse-majesté was a taboo the Meiji generation largely declined to violate; their children and grandchildren would be bolder.

Continuities

By any measure, the initial policies of the Meiji government to foster national integration were earthshaking. From December 1871 to September 1873, half of the oligarchs who comprised the government embarked on a world tour of the United States, Europe, and British colonies in the Middle East and Asia. Fortuitously, their journey was well timed, coinciding with ongoing processes of national integration in three countries on their itinerary: the United States (Reconstruction), Germany (*deutschen Einigung*), and Italy (*il Risorgimento*). The so-called Iwakura Mission—named for the court noble Iwakura Tomomi (1825–83) who was the expedition's nominal leader—closely examined education, administration, commerce, manufacturing, agriculture, court systems, transportation, law enforcement, and, naturally, militaries that they could use as models for building a modern infrastructure in Japan.

The Meiji government implemented a number of policies to end what they regarded as the political, social, linguistic, and cultural fragmentation of the nascent nation-state. In 1871 it abolished feudal domains, reducing over 200 *han* to 77 prefectures. To ensure the cooperation of former *daimyō*, some were appointed as prefectural governors or titled nobles. The hereditary occupational status system was replaced by a European-style peerage system (*kazoku*), consisting of former courtiers and *daimyō*. The only distinction remaining was between *shizoku* (former *bushi* and nobility) and *heimin* (commoners), but this conferred no legal privileges or disadvantages to either group in terms of education, employment or entrepreneurship. If anything, the most impoverished *shizoku*—deprived of their rice stipends in 1877—faced greater economic challenges than *heimin*, because they were accustomed neither to productive labor nor commerce. They could not eat residual prestige.

In 1872 the government mandated compulsory schooling for all boys and girls, which local communities were to fund. Abolition of border restrictions, investments in industry and freedom to choose one's occupation fostered economic liberalization, entrepreneurship, and capitalization. The 1873 Conscription Act was among the most controversial measures: it ended the hereditary *bushi* privilege to monopolize weapons, which angered many samurai, and peasants protested against what they called the "blood tax" (*ketsueki*), which took their healthiest workers from the fields. Land tax reform in 1873 bestowed deeds and titles to farmland to individual households, making them, rather than entire villages, taxable units. Academics trained in the Western discipline of linguistics were ordered to formulate a "national language" (*kokugo*) to eliminate mutually unintelligible regional dialects ("educated middle-class Tokyo speech" was said to be singularly "qualified for this honor").[6] Not until 1889–90 would the oligarchy honor its promise to promulgate a constitution and establish a national parliament (*kokkai*, or Diet), although deliberative assemblies had convened earlier at the prefectural and municipal levels.

Amid all of this dizzying change, however, there was also much continuity, as aspects of Edo-period life persisted. Among these was the popular culture of Japan's urban working classes, petit bourgeoisie, and provincial rural communities. Though legally classified as sex workers in 1872, geisha continued to sing, dance, and strum the *shamisen* for high-paying customers; audiences continued to flock to *yose*, kabuki theaters, red-light districts, and *sumō* wrestling matches; street carnivals and spectacles (*misemono*) continued to draw sizable crowds with foreign novelties, exotic animals, and other curiosities.

This continuity was itself bothersome to the "civilized and enlightened" elite, whose scorn for popular culture and the "feudal past" only intensified when Japan was under Western scrutiny. Persistent cultural decadence was one indicator of Japan's inferiority compared to Western civilization. One of the most important objectives of the Meiji government was to renegotiate the unequal Ansei treaties it had signed with

FIGURE 4.1 *Musumegidayu. From J. J. Dubochet, "Amusements d'étudiants: au yosê, ou salle de declamation," L'Illustration, October 14, 1905 (http://www. gutenberg.org/files/36596/36596-h/36596-h.htm).*

the United States, Britain, Russia, France, and the Netherlands in 1858. Japan had surrendered its tariff autonomy, opened new trading ports, given Westerners increasing rights to roam at will and eventually permitted Christian proselytization. To terminate these agreements, Japanese believed they must earn the respect of Western countries by committing to modernization. Popular culture thus became an index of how deeply this "civilization and enlightenment" project had penetrated the grassroots level. For the first few decades of the Meiji era, it did not inspire confidence among the governing class.

Yose, misemono, and nishiki-e (colored woodblock prints) were among the most tenacious cultural forms that survived the Meiji tumult. The first of these were similar to North American vaudeville theaters; they featured comic storytelling (rakugo), narrative singing (rōkyoku or naniwa bushi), and comedy dialogues (manzai) and increasingly admitted female performers into their ranks. Since women had been mostly absent from stages for over two centuries, audiences found their presence titillating, even if there was nothing overtly erotic about their performances. Tokyo's 1877 yose regulations lifted a ban on female gidayū that had been implemented during the Tenpō Reforms of 1830–43.[7] In the 1880s there was a dramatic increase in the number of women who performed in this manner, many of them former geisha with some formal artistic training.

At yose "virtuosi turned their art into a commodity that could be sold at a premium," Nishiyama says, and "could achieve great popularity" in major cities. He characterizes yose as "communal" spaces, where the "mode of reception of these arts did not change; nor did the fundamental nature of the arts themselves."[8] Taking this a step further, yose may be regarded as conservators of chōnin performance art into the modern period. For instance, toward the end of the Edo period audiences for puppet theater had dwindled, its theaters closed, and its performers lost their jobs. Well before the Meiji Restoration they found employment at yose, where, even without puppets, the texts and songs continued to draw audiences. Therefore, one could argue that twentieth-century efforts to revive bunraku were at least somewhat indebted to the men and women gidayū who kept that component of the art alive and in circulation. The same could be said for rakugo comic storytelling, which remains one of the most popular traditional performing arts among contemporary general audiences.

Topping yose in terms of variety, misemono were open-air street shows, bazaars or exhibits that had drawn commoners and warriors alike throughout most of the Edo period, with increasing frequency after 1800. Originating as fundraising sideshows at temple and shrine fairs, misemono ringmasters eventually went independent, setting up shop in heavily trafficked areas such as the Asakusa district and Ryōgoku Bridge in Edo/Tokyo, or tourist and pilgrimage sites in Ise, Ōsaka, and Kyōto. Andrew Markus argues that much can be gleaned about nineteenth-century society and culture from misemono, even though they could be "generally crude, frequently

FIGURE 4.2 *Itō Seiu, Meiji jidai no yose, 1958, Edo-Tokyo Museum, Wikipedia Commons (https://commons.wikimedia.org/w/index.php?curid=38500839).*

vulgar, liberally dosed with commercialism and rapacious hucksterism." Their transitory nature enabled *misemono* to push the envelope of taste and propriety, even under the stringent Tenpō regulations: "only when an exhibition showed signs of permanence did it incur the risk of official censure."[9]

The variety of entertainments one could see at *misemono* for a small admission fee included Korean equestrian troupes; exotic plants and animals such as tigers, camels, elephants, and fragrant dead whales; Dutch gadgetry and "fancy craftsmanship"; top-spinning; acrobats; impersonators; dancers; magicians; illusionists; puppeteers; wrestlers (a 1769 match featured "one sighted woman wrestl[ing] eight lascivious blind masseurs simultaneously"); spring-driven giant moving dolls (*karakuri ningyō*); peep shows; strongmen and human prodigies such as hermaphrodites, a hirsute girl known as the "Bear Boy", and a 244-cm- (eight-foot-) tall man from China. People with deformities were presented as "karmic acts" (*ingamono*), whose abnormalities were supposedly consequences of sins from former lives. Because of *misemono*'s resemblance to Western tent shows and circuses, Japanese performers and prodigies were among the first from their country to travel abroad, just as Euro-Americans brought their acts—including blackface minstrel shows—to Japan.[10] Ultimately, however, *misemono* did not persist as long as *yose* did, since the "puritanical legislative fervor" of the Meiji government chipped away at the most tasteless and inhumane aspects of the carnivals. By the 1880s, Edo-style *misemono* had virtually disappeared.[11]

Despite the introduction of photography by a Nagasaki merchant in 1848, woodblock printing remained a dominant visual medium in Meiji Japan, at least until the first decade of the 1900s. One of its most important functions was journalistic. Although landscapes, customs, personages, historical subjects, and sometimes current events had long been subjects of woodblock prints, in Meiji times there was an explosion of visual depictions of the modernization process. Illustrated broadsheets helped Edo residents learn about, interpret, and make fun of the traumatic confusion swirling around their city as it was occupied by troops from Satsuma and Chōshū and transformed into the new imperial capital, rechristened Tokyo. One cartoon depicted the battle between imperial and Tokugawa armies at Toba-Fushimi (January 27–31, 1868) as a war of farts, in which imperial flatulence proved the mightier wind.[12]

It is significant to note that, whereas Tokugawa law forbade images of political elites aside from formal portraiture, prints from the Meiji era depicted the oligarchs in deliberation on controversial issues (such as Saigō Takamori's ill-fated plan to attack Korea in 1873). Even the august sovereign himself was the subject of such prints; he was shown greeting foreign dignitaries, conferring with the oligarchy, promulgating the constitution and overseeing military plans in the war with Qing China (1894–95). As Takashi Fujitani's brilliant study of imperial pageantry contends, putting Emperor Meiji in public view was part of a deliberate strategy to inculcate both reverence and affection for his person and his position. In the twentieth century, Meiji's son and grandson were comparatively less visible in public media, as a variety of formal and informal taboos accrued. But initially, when many Japanese (outside of Kyōto, at least) were only vaguely aware of an emperor to whom they should be attached, his public visibility was crucial.[13]

Woodblock prints are essential visual records of the Meiji transition: we learn what Japanese artists and publishers thought was important enough to document. In them we see the new railroads and trains, telegraphy, brick buildings, men and women with Western dress and hairstyles playing violins and pianos, and other conspicuous changes to Japan's physical and social environments. Assassinations, political rallies, riots and uprisings, and military conflicts were all described in immaculately detailed images. Robert Eskildsen contends that commercial print media exaggerated the significance of the 1874 Taiwan Expedition, Japan's first military engagement overseas with conscripts. Putatively to punish aborigines who had murdered Ryūkyūan seafarers, the expedition was an opportunity for Japan to demonstrate to the world the progress and prowess of its modern military, to highlight the carelessness and fragility of Qing control of Taiwan, and to assert

Japanese sovereignty over Ryūkyū (whose monarchy would be abolished in 1879 to facilitate its annexation as Okinawa prefecture). The media, however, portrayed the conflict in much grander terms, as a conflict between "civilization and savagery." "Irrespective of the government's motives, but by no means antithetical to them, commercial sources ... made it possible to assert that Japan had begun the process of civilizing the aborigines."[14] Media spin on this small military operation equated modernization with imperialist action overseas.

Woodblock images and illustrated broadsides (*kawaraban*) thus endured and were to some degree repurposed in the Meiji era, enabling Japanese to witness the profound transformation of their country and to envision its place in the modern world. As late as the Sino-Japanese War in the mid-1890s, woodblock printing would remain the technology of choice for visual reportage. Naturally, the prints were for sale. Pictures depicting military engagements sold like hotcakes, slowly building popular support for the conscript forces whose creation had once been described as a "blood tax." Not until the Boxer Rebellion in Beijing and the Russo-Japanese War did photography and moving pictures become the preferred media for reporting military operations.

Changes

The Meiji government proactively tried to modernize and sanitize the culture of the working classes, but this was not exclusively a state project. Performers and proprietors in the cultural industry themselves formulated and initiated reform agendas, for three broad purposes: to remain economically viable in a rapidly changing commercial environment; to stay abreast of the times out of sincere belief in the Meiji ideals of civilizational progress and enlightenment; and to achieve a social legitimacy and respectability that had long eluded them, by demonstrating their commitment to the national good, treaty revision, and service to the emperor.

One area in which the Meiji state vigorously intervened was music. Initially, at least, official interest in modernizing music—which meant embracing "international" (Western) standards of tonality, aesthetics, orchestration, rhythm, presentation, and the like—was pragmatic rather than artistic. More specifically, the military applications of music made the deepest impression on Japanese. In August 1863, Kagoshima in Satsuma *han* faced a British naval bombardment in retaliation for the murder of a British national and the wounding of two others. Eleven months later a multinational force (Britain, France, the Netherlands, and the United States) fought Chōshū *han* for control of the Shimonoseki Straits. These battles were accompanied by martial music, which to the astonishment of the Japanese seemed to enhance the fighting spirit of their opponents. Consequently, military fife and drum bands were in place as early as 1866, two years before the Restoration and six before the Conscription Act. The presence of nine Satsuma and six Chōshū natives in the oligarchic circle surely made a difference. They realized that no genre of indigenous music could conceivably arouse the passions and courage needed to slaughter opponents. This was an irredeemable flaw.

Hence, initially it fell to the military to train musicians in Western music and instruments. Western music also was essential to the "ceremonial style of governance" that embellished the majestic aura cultivated for the sovereign.[15] A Korean envoy reported that Western music was featured at diplomatic banquets as early as 1877.[16] But the 1872 law mandating compulsory schooling also made music education a standard curricular subject: vocal music (shōka) in elementary schools and instrumental music (sōgaku) in middle school. Yet even in this case, Ury Eppstein remarks, Western music (yōgaku) was introduced to Japan "without attracting to itself any attention beyond its immediate auxiliary function." Even in schools "the attitude remained basically unchanged." Music was part of a package deal, in that it was but one aspect of Western modernity that Japanese believed would be a cornerstone in their own efforts to construct a modern nation.[17]

But in 1872 qualified teachers and appropriate materials were lacking. Enter Izawa Shūji (1851–1917), head of a normal school in Aichi prefecture, whose own musical expertise and experience were limited to one of the early military bands. In 1875 he was part of a delegation of teachers whom the Ministry of Education sent to Massachusetts for three years to observe classrooms and teaching methods. Under the mentorship of music educator Luther Whiting Mason (1818–96), Izawa set about compiling songbooks for use in Japanese schools. Izawa's 1879 report to the Ministry emphasized the ancillary benefits of music education:

> [M]usic refreshes the mind of schoolchildren, provides relaxation from the efforts of hard study, strengthens the lungs, promotes health, clears the voice, corrects pronunciation, improves hearing, sharpens thinking, pleases the heart and forms character … [This] can be observed in the civil conduct of all the various European and American countries.[18]

Izawa's first songbook, published in 1881, was mostly comprised of Western folk and children's songs from Mason's anthologies, with Japanese lyrics. But soon thereafter the emphases of Izawa's pedagogical theory changed to "character formation" and a "compromise" between elements of yōgaku and so-called "national music" (kokugaku). A shift in Japanese educational philosophy in the 1880s compelled him to pitch musical education as a means of inculcating morality (shūshin) and nationalism.[19] Much like its predecessor, the Meiji government firmly believed music should instill public morality and a sense of duty to the state. In articulating his vision Izawa reiterated the longstanding contempt for the popular or "vulgar" music (*zokkyoku*) most people continued to favor, an opinion worthy of Matthew Arnold:

> The popular music of Japan was neglected by the educated, [and] remained for many centuries in the hands of the lowest and most ignorant classes of society. It is against the moral and social welfare of the community. It is against the progress of the ethical education of society. It is against the introduction of good music into the country. In foreign relations it damages the prestige of the country.

The compromise Izawa proposed involved composing monophonic (single-line) songs with nationalist sentiments and *yonanuki* pentatonic scales (five-note major or minor scales without the fourth and seventh scale degrees), to be sung in unison in schools. The preference for unison rather than polyphonic singing (with two or more parts) was neither unintentional nor insignificant when one objective was national cohesion. Eppstein concludes, "As Japanese national pride began to assert itself and doubts about the wisdom of importing things Western wholesale began to be expressed, so the formerly despised Japanese music was rehabilitated and defended."[20]

Nevertheless, within a generation the new professional middle classes, at least, had become more familiar with Western musical traditions, tonalities, and harmonies, and almost completely alienated from indigenous musical traditions.[21] By the early twentieth century, in common parlance "music" meant *yōgaku*. Among other things, this was the result of the adoption of tempered scales, even in traditional Japanese music (*hōgaku*). Before the early Meiji period, performers of the *koto* (zither), *shamisen*, *biwa*, and various wind instruments used *relative* instead of *fixed* intonation. For instance, the frequency of a C# (277.18 Hz above middle C) in one performance might be slightly different in another. Strings on chordophone instruments like the *shamisen* would be tuned relative to each other; ensemble musicians would likewise tune their instruments to one another. But they might be "out of tune" relative to equal tempered, twelve-tone scales used in Western music. In the Meiji period even instrumentalists who did not perform foreign *yōgaku* started tuning according to the Western "equal temperament juggernaut" that was then becoming the global standard of tonality. "The globalization of equal temperament," James Millward writes, "which changed the very notes heard around the world not only in European but in most non-European music as well, is a profound yet hitherto largely unremarked result of European expansion since 1500, akin to redefining the color red or standards of female pulchritude [beauty]."[22]

Aside from changes in music itself, the people who performed it did so in an entirely new environment, in which their art was more thoroughly commodified and the old distinctions between *zokkyoku* and elite styles no longer had legal basis. All idioms were lumped together as *hōgaku*, which conceptually was the antithesis of *yōgaku*. By the early twentieth century it had in fact become an institutionalized distinction: *iemoto* transmitted indigenous music and conservatories taught Western concert music.[23] Like samurai who lost their stipends in 1877, musicians were on their own in the new free market, and failure to master the required skills or adapt to that market meant professional death. A master chamber musician accustomed to performing in salons or private mansions might have to hold her nose and play *zokkyoku* for paying customers in a tavern or *yose*.

Unsurprisingly, under the Meiji regime kabuki was in for another round of reform. But in this case, there was more synergy between the government's concerns and the interests of theater owners and performers, who—again in a classic hegemonic interaction—were not at all antipathetic to "civilization and enlightenment" and the destigmatization of their art and social standing. In 1886 prominent figures in the kabuki world joined forces to create the Society for Theater Reform (Engeki Kairyōkai). The Society's agenda centered on abolishing "old customs" that inhibited the modernization of society and culture offstage. Closely aligned with the Meiji regime's national objectives (one member was the son-in-law of the prime minister), the Society represented one of the foremost examples of self-reform in the cultural world of Meiji Japan.

Given the long-standing official contempt for kabuki, it is surprising that it was one of the first art forms selected for presentation to foreign dignitaries. In the summer of 1879 Germany's Prince Heinrich (1862–1929, younger brother of Kaiser Wilhelm II) and former US president Ulysses S. Grant (1822–85) were both treated to performances starring Ichikawa Danjūrō IX (1883–1903) at the Shintomi-za, owned by Morita Kan'ya XII (1846–97).[24] Morita took advantage of the obsolescence of Tokugawa licensing regulations, relocating his theater from Asakusa to central Tokyo in 1872. He also broke with his counterparts in the "three theaters" (*sanza*) consortium to initiate "free market competition" between them.[25]

Takahashi Yuichirō regards the opening of Shintomi-za as a "historical node" at which "the introduction of a new theatre architecture, a new mode of theatregoing, and efforts to attain respectability" as Art fundamentally transformed kabuki. During the Edo period theatergoers behaved much like nineteenth-century American audiences: they chatted, ate, drank, and sometimes interacted with actors onstage. The "sacralization" of culture in the United States, which made attending operas and plays like going to church, paralleled the "new mode of theatregoing" Takahashi observes in Meiji-era kabuki. At the Shintomi-za's grand opening in June 1878, Danjūrō IX made a speech admitting that "*kabuki* had degraded itself by playing to the tastes of the populace, by portraying their manners and neglecting to honor righteous principles." Moreover, he said, "the opening of the new theatre put an end to *kabuki* as good-for-nothing amusement." The government officials in attendance approved; the traditional patrons of kabuki, the urban merchants and artisans, were conspicuously absent.[26]

Government directives coincided with Danjūrō's almost remorseful remarks at the opening ceremony. Kabuki was basically beholden to the same moralistic guidelines of the Tokugawa regime: everything about kabuki, from the content of plays to the actors' offstage comportment, should reflect and encourage moral virtue and the triumph of good over evil (*kanzen chōaku*). "The new rulers saw the theatre as a pedagogical tool that could be used to correct the tastes and manners of the people." As "the only form of theatre in Japan that could compare in size and complexity with Western opera," kabuki was chosen as a representative art to exhibit to Euro-American visitors. This also entailed substantial modifications to theater design and amenities to make those visitors comfortable. The transformation from pop to Art meant that defining elements of the kabuki experience required substantial modification.[27] By 1887 kabuki at places like Shintomi-za was sufficiently respectable to show the Meiji emperor.

Smaller theaters (*koshibai*) continued to attract petit bourgeois patrons and laborers in their work clothes, who enjoyed tobacco and tea while they watched. It was at this level that kabuki performers and theater proprietors took the most radical step of all: putting female performers (*onna yakusha*) back onstage. The best remembered of these was Ichikawa Kumehachi (1846?–1913), whom Danjūrō IX took as an apprentice in 1888. Loren Edelson deems Danjūrō IX "the logical choice of actors to break precedent and perform onstage with a woman," because as demonstrated in his aforementioned speech at the Shintomi-za, "he had been on the cusp of innovation and reform in the kabuki world for a decade already" and had begun training his two daughters in kabuki dance. Danjūrō insisted that "Only a real biological woman ... could 'compete with the spirit of the far-away Western theater that captures the truth.'"[28]

Oddly enough, his first female disciple begged to differ. In her essays on theories and techniques of kabuki acting, Kumehachi admonished other female actors that "Just because a woman was a woman did not mean that she knew the least thing about how to play an *onnagata*. To become a woman on the kabuki stage was a matter of learning how to act in a way that did not necessarily reflect her own innate characteristics of femininity."[29] In other words, men playing women set the standard to which women playing women should aspire. Typical.

For two decades before she became a formal member of the Danjūrōs' Naritaya artistic "family," Kumehachi had been a busy kabuki actor, performing both female and male roles at small theaters and in the private residences of *daimyō*. Nor was she the only *onna yakusha*, just the most famous. This indicates that, as soon as the 1629 prohibitions ended, second-tier kabuki performers, at least, took initiative to change the conventions of the art on their own, waiting neither for government guidance nor the top-tier actors and theaters to nudge them in "civilized and enlightened" directions. It would be somewhat of an overstatement to say that there was

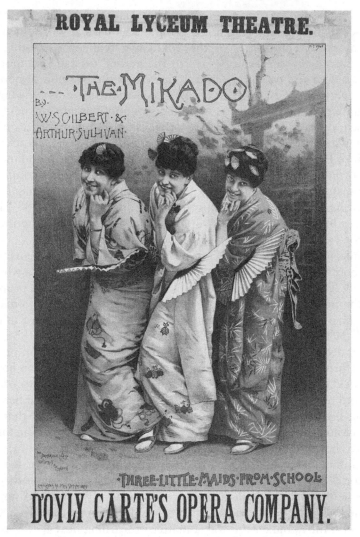

FIGURE 4.3 *"Three Little Maids from School," poster for The Mikado by W. S. Gilbert and Arthur Sullivan, D'Oyly Carte's Opera Company, Royal Lyceum Theatre, Edinburgh. Printed by The Strobridge Lithographer Co., 1885. National Library of Scotland: http://digital.nls.uk/74592382. -*

a fully formed feminist ideology behind this, but there *was* an oft-stated desire for more realism on the kabuki stage. That may have helped justify women playing roles formerly monopolized by *onnagata*, but not the revival of Izumo no Okuni's tendency to cross-dress as a man.

Clearly, the kabuki world had a complicated relationship with the realism of Western drama that had become the gold standard in theater by the end of the Meiji era. But if the impact of Western culture on Meiji Japan is indisputable, so is the contemporaneous reciprocal impact of Japanese prints and craftwork on Western visual, literary, decorative and performance arts. A fad for *japonaiserie* (Japanese-themed or influenced arts and crafts) swept Europe and North America, most prominently in Impressionist painting, inspired mostly by *nishiki-e*. Édouard Manet (1832–83), Edgar Degas (1834–1917), and Oscar-Claude Monet of France (1840–1926), and Vincent Van Gogh (1853–90) of Holland collected cheap *nishiki-e*, the basis for the artistic movement known as *Japonisme*.[30] Van Gogh once conceded, "All my work is based to some extent on Japanese art."[31] In England, Japan's biggest impact was on furniture design and the decorative arts. Western fascination with Japanese culture found musical expression in two operas, W. S. Gilbert and Arthur Sullivan's *The Mikado* (England, 1885) and Giacomo Puccini's *Madame Butterfly* (Italy, 1904).[32] Ironically, Euro-Americans were enamored of the Edo-period popular culture that Meiji officials, cultural entrepreneurs, and entertainers themselves wanted to reform, redeem, or abolish to appear civilized and enlightened; they recast Japanese pop as gallery- and theater-worthy Art. Late-nineteenth-century *japonaiserie* was the first of several recurring waves in the West, anticipating the global impact of J-Cult on media culture at the turn of the millennium.[33]

Agit-pop

Man is free. …
Man's freedom does not allow a dearth of rights… .
The people of Japan must claim their rights;
If we do not, then our companion is shame… .
Rise up, be prosperous and go forward.
A political system of constitutional freedoms
Is the pressing need of today… .
Become enlightened people and
Let's make brilliant the majesty of our country. —Ueki Emori (1857–92), "Country Song of Popular Rights" ("Minken inaka uta," 1879).[34]

In 1968 the indefatigable scholar Irokawa Daikichi made one of the most significant discoveries in the field of modern Japanese history. In the remote mountain village of Itsukaichi, in the storehouse of the Fukasawa family, he found a cache of documents dating back to the Edo period. One of those documents was a 204-article constitution drafted by schoolteacher Chiba Tokusaburō (1852–83), the product of extensive discussions between villagers who had formed a learning and debate society. Although a couple of similar documents had been discovered elsewhere, Irokawa found evidence that in communities surrounding Itsukaichi there were as many as sixty comparable study/discussion groups. Translations of books by liberal philosophers and political theorists such as Jean-Jacques Rousseau, John Stuart Mill, John Locke, and Herbert Spencer were in villagers' libraries and informed the Itsukaichi draft (Spencer's ideas on natural rights directly inspired Ueki's song). Irokawa was struck by the level of sophistication, initiative, and political consciousness the draft constitution demonstrated: mountain villagers were participating seriously in the creation of a new political order and civil society, based on both Western social-contract theory and indigenous communal models of local governance.[35] They expected a degree of local autonomy from the central government, while recognizing the need for a state strong enough to resist further imperialist incursions.

The defection of Itagaki Taisuke (1837–1919) from the Meiji oligarchy to found Japan's first political parties is regarded by some as the spark that ignited the Freedom and People's Rights Movement (*Jiyū minken undō*, 1874–84).[36] In many ways, however, we can see its seeds in the government's foundational document itself. Whereas once historians thought of Meiji modernization as a remarkably peaceful, consensual process, nowadays scholars emphasize its disruptive, coercive, contentious, and occasionally violent nature. Some government officials could be pitiless toward people and communities negatively affected by economic and social development. In 1892, in a terse response to protests that copper mine waste in the Watarase River had decimated surrounding farmland, an Agriculture and Commerce ministry official snorted, "the public benefits that accrue to the country from the Ashio mine far outweigh any losses suffered in the affected areas."[37]

Yet it was far more complex than a rulers-versus-ruled dynamic, for there were oligarchs who were themselves impatient for elected assemblies, a constitution, and the participation of an informed public. The devil was in the details of implementation. The more people clamored, the more concerned the state became with maintaining order than with honoring liberal promises it had once made with conviction.

Again, popular culture was at the forefront, expressing disaffection with the government and proposing alternative visions for domestic politics and international diplomacy, therefore drawing greater state scrutiny and censorship. Popular culture is a powerful index of how deeply the Meiji state's early professions of political liberalism penetrated the populace. Here we briefly examine three popular media—political cartoons, street singing (*sōshi enka*), and New School (*shinpa*) theater—that were heavily involved in disseminating information and ideas that, if not openly seditious, nonetheless struck the oligarchy as threatening enough to merit surveillance and suppression.

Political satire was nearly impossible to get away with under Tokugawa rule. It taxed the metaphorical skills of illustrators and writers to be as discreet and clever as they needed to be to pull it off, while still being intelligible to their audiences. The political cartoon was thus a novel art form in the Meiji era, but it was one that Japanese illustrators were astonishingly quick to master. Japanese were, of course, not unfamiliar with "humorous pictures" (manga), but European-style editorial cartooning was introduced by British soldier Charles Wirgman's (1832–91) monthly *Japan Punch* (1862–87) in Yokohama. An "eccentric, engaging, polyglot" personality, Wirgman was prominent in the treaty port press, settling in Yokohama until his death, marrying a local woman and having a son with her. He tutored Japanese artists in Western-style oil painting and cartooning, and one of his pupils was the prolific and influential Kobayashi Kiyochika (to whom we will return in later chapters).[38] *Japan Punch* demonstrated Wirgman's keen observations of the occasional excesses and absurdities of modernization on the ground.

Japanese publishers and artists immediately took to the medium of visual satire and commentary. The unprecedented visibility of government officials (in contrast to the shadowy figures who occupied the *bakufu*) made it easier to skewer policies and the men who made them. Editorial cartoonists maintained what Peter Duus calls "democratic surveillance" to keep the government accountable to the public.[39] Initially, at least, it was open season on everyone beneath the emperor; indeed, many Japanese might have become familiar and disillusioned with their leaders primarily through the cartoon medium. But political leaders were not the only fodder for cartoon satirists: they also provided multiple perspectives on the process of modernization on the streets. Foreigners were caricatured as long-nosed oafs and bullies; so-called "high-collar" sophisticates were depicted as monkeys in Western attire, a derivative affectation; and increasingly wealthy capitalists and landowners looked like rapacious scoundrels.

A new press code in 1875 targeting small-scale newspapers provided incentive for publishers to emphasize visual over verbal satire.[40] This helped Kitazawa Rakuten (1876–1955) become Japan's first professional cartoon satirist, drawing on traditions of "humorous pictures" and Western-style multipanel cartoons. The most long-lived satirical magazine was founded by the disenchanted former home minister Nomura Fumio (1834–90): from 1877 until 1892, when its editorial board decided to make it purely "entertaining," the *Marumaru chinbun* was the leading comic magazine devoted to political and social satire. Its "adversarial" editorial stance spoke for "political outsiders" and "sought to shape a political critique of the regime." Catfish—whose subterranean gyrations were blamed for earthquakes—became visual metaphors for government officials, because of their wispy-thin whiskers.[41]

Even the abstract, high-minded ideals of the early Meiji era were ripe for satire. Among these was the concept of progressive civilization articulated by the era's leading public intellectual, Fukuzawa Yukichi (1834–1901). A former *bushi*, Fukuzawa became the foremost exponent of the Meiji ideals of "civilization and enlightenment."[42] Though he never held government office, his ideas were influential and reflected in official policies encouraging economic entrepreneurship, legal and social egalitarianism, compulsory education for girls as well as boys, and the quest for knowledge "throughout the world so as to strengthen the foundation of imperial rule." Yet as a committed political liberal who insisted that "the spirit of [intellectual] independence" was the foundation for civilization, he was by no means a government mouthpiece. He wrote prodigiously, translated numerous foreign texts, founded Keiō University, and took students from Korea and China who hoped to bring Meiji-style progress to their own countries. His *Outline of a Theory of Civilization* (1885) conceived of human societies as progressing through a continuum from savagery to semicivilized to civilized.[43]

One cartoon I regularly share in class might be read as either an endorsement or a satire of Fukuzawa's schema. It depicts three men: one is dressed in a top hat and Western clothing with a dog on a leash; one sports a Western hat, shoes, and umbrella, but wears traditional trousers (*hakama*); and the third wears complete samurai garb with the *chonmage* top-knot hairdo. The first man is labeled "enlightened person" (*kaika no hito*), the second "half enlightened person" (*hankai no hito*), and the third "unenlightened person" (*fukai no hito*), drawing attention to how clothing, shoes, hairstyles, and puppy dogs, or the lack thereof, supposedly "make the man." A common theme in Meiji political and social humor was the superficiality of "civilization and enlightenment" as displayed, or in this case *worn* in public. One possible interpretation is that most Japanese had not in fact forsaken "feudal" mind-sets of the repudiated past, but had simply donned the veneer of modernity without allowing its fundamental spirit to permeate their souls.

But political liberals, activists, and sympathetic cartoonists were more likely to support the government than ridicule it when the issue was the sanctified person of the emperor or the integrity of the nation-state in the face of imperialist aggression. Cartoons "served to naturalize the idea of the Japanese nation," no less than other media such as the *shōka* that Izawa composed for schoolchildren.[44] Though elusive in other areas, on the importance of nation-building, the sanctity of the emperor, and the seriousness of external threats, there was broad ideological consensus.

Another form of popular culture intended to raise political consciousness, harass government officials, and satirize the silliest manifestations of "civilization and enlightenment" was street singing by men known as *sōshi enkashi*. Today *enka* is a genre of sentimental popular music enjoyed by the postwar generation (see Chapter 8), but in the 1880s it referred to ballads with social and political commentary. *Sōshi* refers to politically engaged, pugnacious young male student activists—"punks" may be an apt translation— who habitually blew off classes to quarrel and agitate for political reform.

Enka singers were occupational descendants of Edo-period *yomiuri* (read and sell), who had strolled streets and country back roads shouting and singing news of current events or ephemera. "No event, even a thunderclap or the ... birth of triplets, was intrinsically too insignificant to be made meaningful if subject to sufficient exegesis and literary or musical stylization." Although *yomiuri* made their livings selling single-page, woodblock-printed broadsheets, oral performance was essential to their work: "printed material was rendered as a type of strolling musical concert that lent a strength to the uncertain facts ... and to produce an effect that appealed to the emotions of the audience."[45]

Street singer Soeda Azenbō's (1872–1944) fascinating memoir provides an account of *sōshi* who stood on street corners singing satirical songs and trying to raise onlookers' political consciousness. Michael Lewis describes Azenbō as an example of Gramsci's "organic intellectual, whose ideas, usually formed outside established educational institutions, become widely propagated and at times challenge the dominant social and political order." His songs were distributed via song sheets (the *enka* singer's primary source of income) throughout the country, "sung by tenant farmers in rural hinterlands and factory hands in Tokyo and Osaka ... [H]e embedded in his songs contemporary views on class conflict, gender relations and racial attitudes toward international rivalries." Although it is impossible to assess his actual impact on social consciousness, "Ordinary people valued Azembō's [*sic*] music because it was of them and for them."[46]

Azenbō was not wedded to any particular ideology, refusing to be associated with socialist groups. But in his early work he pointed out the irony and destructive consequences of modernization for commoners and urged the government to take greater heed of the people's suffering. Like most other liberal activists, he was also a fervent nationalist.[47] In the age of high imperialism, it was hard not to be. Azenbō was attracted to street singing in the late 1880s by three *sōshi* he saw in the naval town Yokosuka who were preaching and singing nationalist songs. "The young men wore braided hats pushed back to the rear of their heads and white *obi* bands wrapped around and around their waists. They passed a thick stick from hand to hand, one to another, as they altered between chatter and song." Their song expressed indignation toward Western imperialism:

How hateful to consider Asia's prospect
Civilization spreads steadily month after month
Yet even Japan blessed by the bountiful fortunes of war
Cannot rid itself of the foreigners' laws
Cannot restore control of its own taxes
The red-bearded louts rudely rampage
And one step away, Korea
Time after time, the people there bow down childlike
Terrified before the powerful birds of prey... .
In the end, it is the East
Trampled beneath the power of the West
And of those crushed
Not one has gained equality
Resentment and indignation fill our breasts
To be the England of East Asia

This is the duty our country has accepted.... .
The flag of the Rising Sun shall shine forth
Our nation's flag from the summit of the Himalayas. ...[48]

Clearly, Meiji liberalism was an ideological mess: people bemoaned the injustices of imperialist aggression toward Japan yet aspired to imperial power themselves.

Azenbō recalled that the songs he heard "suddenly and fundamentally transformed my childish view of life," and he joined a Youth Club to become a *sōshi enkashi* himself. He was soon recognized as a natural, although he admitted that most *enka* "were just shouted and roared out tunelessly." His songs addressed everything from treaty revision and election fraud to politicians' sexual indiscretions and the abolition of licensed prostitution, from the maltreatment of Japanese immigrants overseas to the celebration of victories and individual heroism in wars. *Sōshi enka* lyrics likened politicians to prostitutes, since both were for sale. Some songs took a puritanical tone, admonishing young men to practice sexual continence: "Lecherously, they pour their gaze over the young woman ... The sin is not with the temptress / But falls to the tempted philanderer / Family wealth, money, whatever there is / What will be left afterward won't fill a thimble" ("An Air for a Girl Singer," by Yokoe Tesseki). Singers were certainly committed to message songs, but they could not afford to ignore the demands of their audiences. They thus had to write songs that were sufficiently clever and provocative, while addressing issues about which listeners actually cared, in order to sell enough song sheets to support themselves.[49]

Activist singers sometimes moonlighted as actors in the New School of drama.[50] *Shinpa* was an artist-initiated effort for theater reform (*engeki kairyō*), an offshoot of the aforementioned synergistic campaign by the government, proprietors, and performers to rehabilitate kabuki. However, *shinpa*'s didacticism served a different, more subversive purpose. Founders Kawakami Otojirō (1864–1911) and Sudō Sadanori (1867–1907) envisioned an agitprop populist theater for the Freedom and People's Rights movement, to push liberal agendas and consciousness-raising. *Shinpa* melodramas raised issues "on the proper function of drama and fiction in contemporary society, a debate that essentially revolved around what kind of theatrical realism would prevail."[51]

Conceived at a December 1888 theater reform conference in Ōsaka organized by Sudō, *shinpa* is frequently characterized as a transition between kabuki and Western-style New Theater (*shingeki*). It retained the dramaturgical, oratorical, choreographic, and musical conventions of kabuki, so it was accessible to most spectators. As kabuki veterans, *shinpa* actors' style was hyperbolic and not much more realistic than kabuki's. But *shinpa* troupes commissioned newly written plays or adaptations that addressed topics of contemporary interest, just as political cartoons and *enka* did. Plays were sometimes written specifically for the stage, or adapted from Japanese novels and occasionally William Shakespeare. Referring to its Korean derivative (*sinp'a*), Kang Yŏnghŭi claims scenarios told stories of "antimony," situations in which protagonists faced inescapable crises generated by antiquated values and practices.[52] For example, *shinpa* frequently depicted women facing no-win situations due to unrelenting patriarchy, or regular people suffering poverty or injustice.

One of *shinpa*'s important hallmarks, compared to the later realist *shingeki*, was that it relied less heavily on translations of Western repertoire. *Shinpa* dramas were most often written in kabuki-style Japanese and therefore expressed more indigenous sensibilities. Another innovation was that *shinpa* put actresses onstage alongside *onnagata,* both to heighten realism and to make a feminist statement. Among these, Kawakami's geisha wife, Sada Yakko (1871–1946), was the most famous. Sada impressed audiences in Chicago, New York, London, Berlin, and at the Paris World's Fair during an 1899–1901 tour, earning acclaim as "the Sarah Bernhardt of the Japanese stage."[53] A patronizing American profile of "little Mme. Yacco" reported that "kisses and embraces" from strangers were the "personal courtesies" she "found to be the strangest of all the customs in this new country. But she is becoming quite accustomed to them now."[54] But Sada was hardly the cute little doll the American press made her out to be. She expressed the liberal political and feminist agenda that distinguished *shinpa*, telling one reporter, "I shall never forget how the American women are cherished by the men, and when I return to Japan I hope to have at least a little influence in making my countrywomen a more important factor in the life of the nation."[55]

Shinpa proved to be influential in early Japanese film as well as in modern Korean theater and Chinese "civilized dramas" (*wénmíngxì*), which also mixed elements of older, indigenous theater with newer, Western ones. *Shinpa* actors were among the first to appear in Japanese narrative movies. In the 1900s they also appeared in so-called *rensageki* (chain dramas) or *kino* dramas that used both live actors onstage and filmed images projected onscreen. Another example of "commingled media," *rensageki* was eventually criticized by Pure Film advocates, who believed movies should be self-contained, not reliant on other supplementary media to tell their stories.

Although its heyday seems to have passed rather quickly in retrospect, and the more realistic—and derivative—Western-style new theater assumed a higher profile and prestige value, "From the perspective of popular audiences, *shinpa* occupied a much more important place than *shingeki*."[56] Treated mostly as a footnote in studies of kabuki and *shingeki*, *shinpa* has nonetheless continued to exist as a fringe performance art, still melodramatic to be sure, yet not as political and polemical as in its earliest incarnation. Along with political cartoons and *sōshi enka*, *shinpa* demonstrates the mutual impact that the broader Meiji modernization project and popular culture had on one another.

Andrew Gordon characterizes the Meiji Restoration as a "revolution from above": the transformation of Japanese society was indeed nothing short of revolutionary, but it was not initiated by nonelites as the French Revolution was. It was led by *bushi* of middling rank who had rebelled against the Tokugawa and rallied around the emperor, whose prerogative to rule trumped that of the *shōgun*.[57] They then became the core of a new government cabal that oversaw sweeping changes of the structure and characteristics of practically every aspect of Japanese society. But within less than a decade of their victory, they lost either sight or control of the liberal agenda with which they began their nation-building project. The oligarchy was unable to contain or completely suppress the sociopolitical consciousness and aspirations of *shizoku* and *heimin* who took seriously the objectives stated in the Charter Oath.

Popular culture was integral to both the regime and the agitators for Freedom and People's Rights. It was a primary conduit for the state's goal of creating an emperor-centered national identity, a goal that had clearly yielded results by the 1890s, but it was also an important vehicle for expressing the discontent, disillusion, and restlessness of a broad swath of society intent on making the "revolution from above" serve their interests better. Historians disagree about whether the promulgation of the Meiji Constitution in 1889 was the result of the unrest of the 1870s and 1880s or whether the oligarchy simply decided either that the time had come to fulfill that particular promise from the Charter Oath or that the document was yet another tactic for achieving international repute and treaty revision. The constitution itself proved to be a disappointment to liberal activists, not so much because it placed sovereignty in the emperor as because the right to stand for office or vote in elections was so tightly restricted, yielding a Diet that was skewed toward moneyed interests and the hereditarily privileged. The franchise was limited to men twenty-five or older who paid ¥15 per annum in land or income taxes—a mere 1.25 percent of the population could thus vote or run for office. Women had no political rights whatsoever, which was admittedly the international norm at the time (New Zealand was the first country to grant women the franchise, in 1893).

Popular culture in the Meiji period was inarguably thoroughly commercialized and still served escapist functions for most of the population. Nonetheless, its broader political significance as described here should not be underestimated. It proved to be a primary forum or arena for struggles between the modernizing state and the population that paid for, benefited from, and suffered through its aggressive and ambitious agenda. It provided the best chance the general population had of taking at least partial rein of the "revolution from above."

CHAPTER FIVE

Cultural living—cosmopolitan modernism in imperial Japan

She was Japan's Nora Helmer, the homemaker who abandons her children to "become a reasonable human being" and "think things out for [her]self" in Henrik Ibsen's play *A Doll House* (1879).[1] Matsui Sumako (1886–1919), the first actress to take the stage in a Western-style *shingeki* play, had a remarkable affinity with Nora and other women she portrayed.[2] Onstage and off, Matsui earned notoriety playing outspoken, independent women and vixens and for being one herself. "Passion and derangement ... marked her acting," Phyllis Birnbaum writes, "and she became known for her portrayals of forthright, headstrong heroines who cried a lot." By all accounts, Matsui was "rude" and "pushy"; entire casts refused to share the stage with her because of her violent tantrums; she had a nose job to correct a "flaw" that initially kept her off the stage; and she was a two-time divorcée, the sexually audacious lover of many an artist and intellectual, and the mistress of the very married Waseda University professor and *shingeki* director Shimamura Hōgetsu (1871–1918). When he died of Spanish flu while she was at a rehearsal, Shimamura's coterie made Matsui the scapegoat. Three months later this paragon of *jikaku*, "self-awakening"—the cornerstone of modern life—hanged herself.[3]

She was Japan's It Girl, he her suave sheik. Clara Bow and Rudolph Valentino: Modern Girl (*moga*) and Modern Boy (*mobo*)—pejoratives or plaudits, depending on the observer. They both worked in an office, she as a secretary, he as an accountant. Despite parental disapproval, they went on dates to see the latest Charlie Chaplin comedy or some cinematic swashbuckling by Douglas Fairbanks; to watch a baseball game or play a little tennis; to catch a musical revue with bare-legged dancers and jazzy bands; to stroll Ginza's neon-lit promenade, arriving finally at a café, to read magazines and detective stories, smoke cigarettes, and dish on some celebrity gossip, while Tin Pan Alley and jazz tunes played on a phonograph. Their chat was littered with English, French, and German words. Her hair was bobbed, his greased with pomade. To their parents' generation, he was too foppish, she much too flirtatious; she a little bossy, he clearly whipped. Her drop-waist dress was loose and her high-heeled shoes rounded out her exposed calves. He was debonair yet intoxicated by her painted lips and rouged cheeks. They were more conversant about the fashions and trends among their counterparts in New York, London, Berlin or Paris than about tea ceremony, rice farming or filial piety.

A police officer side-eyed them disapprovingly. His widowed cousin in the countryside had lost her farm and was now sharecropping on it. His nephew was in the army, fighting bandits in China. And these citified brats seemed to have bottomless pockets, purses, and passions for lollygagging. Their self-involved, pompous prattling sickened him, for the benefits of this so-called "modern life" were not shared equally by all. Secretly, the officer hoped the couple would caress or kiss each other so he could use his discretionary authority to arrest them for "disturbing public morals." That did seem to be their purpose in life.

Icons of modernity

The opening paragraph is a true story, the subsequent vignette a plausible scenario, based on broad stereotypes of *moga* and *mobo*. Matsui foreshadowed the *moga* phenomenon by some years, making her name in the 1910s when the New Woman (*atarashii onna*) was the topic of conversation in print media and lecture halls throughout Japan.[4] Matsui shared the social consciousness and devotion to artistic expression of the New Woman, and the self-indulgence and sexual candor associated with *moga*. She was a pioneer, but not necessarily a role model later self-awakened women cared to emulate, for she embodied some of the worst qualities the general public attributed to feminists.

Mobo and *moga* were icons of modern life in the 1920s and 1930s; what they consumed and how they played was what *made* them modern. Like other figures who inspire moral panics, their prominence in mass media was out of all proportion to their actual numbers. But what they symbolized was far more culturally significant and controversial than their meager numbers would suggest. The stereotypically effete *mobo* flouted conventions of masculinity, embodied in the militarized "imperial male" (*teikoku danshi*), rugged farmer, industrial laborer, decisive patriarch, or self-made entrepreneur. Few observers regarded this faddish, "flashy" fellow with slicked-back hair and bell-bottomed trousers as anything more than a "hooligan."[5] However, far more ink was devoted to the *moga*'s transgressions, suggesting they were considered a greater social threat than her paramour's.

FIGURE 5.1   *Ginza "modern girl" and "modern boy," ca. 1930, Old Tokyo: Vintage Japanese Postcard Museum, 1900–1960—Ginza Crossing, ca. 1910–1940 (http://www.oldtokyo.com/ginza-crossing/).*

Japan's *moga* were a localized manifestation of a global phenomenon in the interwar years, modern girls identified by "their use of specific commodities and their explicit eroticism."

> Adorned in provocative fashions, in pursuit of romantic love, Modern Girls appeared to disregard roles of dutiful daughter, wife, and mother. Contemporary journalists, politicians, social scientists, and the general public debated whether Modern Girls were looking for sexual, economic, or political emancipation. They also raised the possibility that the Modern Girl was little more than an image, a hollow product of clever advertising campaigns in the new commodity culture.[6]

The *moga* was more than a "hollow image" to many Japanese. She "cut a terrifying figure" who had "grave intentions behind her up-to-date look."[7] Tanizaki Jun'ichirō (1886–1965) helped fashion this image in his 1924 novel *A Fool's Love* (*Chijin no ai*). The Pygmalion-like narrator grooms the teenaged Naomi to become the Westernized woman of his dreams, but she becomes an uncontrollable, sexually aggressive *moga*, and he a cuckold.[8]

   The bodies of women have historically been metaphorical sites of struggles over modernity and tradition: "debates in favor of and against measurements of progress … have relied on the control or liberation of the female body as a major technique."[9] Social change is most visually conspicuous in women's attire, hairstyles, education, work lives, manners, sexual behavior, and public comportment. Certainly, machines, skyscrapers, electricity, locomotives, automobiles, financial institutions, and mass media are emblematic of modernity, but rarely generate as much apoplexy as the length of women's dresses or hair, their beauty regimens, relations with men and involvement in the public sphere. Women have embodied the preservation or abandonment of traditions. Like their counterparts elsewhere, Japanese *moga* instigated moral panic and discussions about cultural purity, foreign influence, gender norms, and modernity itself. "To talk about the Modern Girl," Miriam Silverberg (1951–2008) asserted, "was also to talk about modernity."[10] New Women and *moga* thus became lightning rods and ciphers for Japanese modernity—and modernity, some believed, was a condition that must be overcome.

Documenting modernity

"Eroticism and nonsense and speed and comic-strip humor of current events and jazz songs and ladies' legs." This was how future Nobel laureate Kawabata Yasunari (1899–1972) described modern life in *The Scarlet Gang of Asakusa* (*Asakusa kurenaidan*, 1930), the story of a loosely formed theatrical troupe with "hopes of staging something spectacular—or what it would consider spectacular." Instead of being "truly aspiring artistes," the troupe "want to scandalize everyone at least once with ... displays of outlandish and unexpected originality."[11] Guided through the neon lights and jazzy din of the Asakusa entertainment district by this gang of "delinquent youths," the bewildered, disoriented narrator feels as if he has entered a high-speed erotic playground, whose lurid, foreign-born diversions attract the eyes, ears, nose, and genitalia.

The Japanese intelligentsia was well attuned to changes in mass media, thought and mannerisms (*fūzoku*), closely monitoring and investigating their causes and effects. As in the Edo period, *fūzoku* was a ubiquitous term in public discourse about popular entertainment and its social effects. It seemed as if, like a damsel repeatedly prone to distress, *fūzoku* were always imperiled by new diversions or cultural products. Social scientists acting as "ethnographers of modernity" meticulously documented such changes in mannerisms/*fūzoku*, producing reams of statistical and qualitative data that remain useful to historians of interwar Japan.[12] Their interpretations of that data occasionally reveal ideological biases, yet these surveys are almost unfailingly sophisticated, methodologically transparent, and insightful. Careful social scientific inquiries about popular entertainment (*minshū goraku*) in the 1920s and 1930s indicate that modern life and media culture inspired not only anxiety but also genuine intellectual curiosity and philosophical reflection.

One of their insights was that an undifferentiated "mass" (*taishū*) of people was illusory. Ōbayashi Sōshi's (1894–1944) study of Ōsaka amusement districts in 1920 highlighted both the diversity of audiences/consumers and the responsive marketing of the culture industry to specific "class [sub] cultures." He concluded that the entertainment industry was neither "pandering to popular tastes, nor attempting to manipulate them," but actively "cater[ing] to the different audiences it hoped to capture."[13] Similarly, Gonda Yasunosuke (1887–1951) regarded "the pleasures of the people" as an index of both social differences and "changing conditions." Through "modernologio" ("study of the modern," in Esperanto), Kon Wajirō (1888–1973) observed what he called the "moving present," the transformation of Tokyo mannerisms in the aftermath of a massive earthquake in 1923: "If you take one step outside the door, you see the spectacle that I will make as my object."[14] These social scientists' intense focus on the quotidian everyday was appropriate for a time and place in which both the culture industry and consumers defined modernity in terms of tangible objects and pleasurable amusements: attire, hairstyles, living spaces, phonograph records, films, sporting facilities, and radios.

Not all observers were so dispassionate. "Modern life's center of gravity is in the senses," writer Ōya Sōichi (1900–70) declared. He associated modern mannerisms with a "modern stratum" of society that had succumbed to frivolity. "Modern life is a type of consumptive economics, the aim of which is to satiate the senses," with "no 'ideals' … [or] 'morality.'"[15] Sound familiar? The attentive reader will notice that Ōya's critique echoed elite attitudes toward popular culture in the Edo period, but that a different understanding of time and history informed it. From the Meiji era onward, Japanese had embraced a notion of progressive time, in which modernity was the antithesis of tradition, society became more rational and scientific, technological innovation and capitalist development were unambiguously beneficial, and the future was an improvement on the present, which was itself an improvement on the past. Modernity was an inexorable force that moved societies through stages of development from savagery to civilization. That did not mean everyone liked all of its effects. For Ōya and others, material progress entailed moral and culture regress. Obviously, this is not a pattern humanity has abandoned, as everything from music to video games is said to foretell civilization's doom.

Moga and *mobo* were the principal perpetrators. They were the beneficiaries of Japanese industrialization and capitalization, the daughters and sons of nouveaux riches (*narikin*) who financially prospered from Japan's World War I economic boom. As European countries switched to total-war economies, demand for imports of munitions and consumer goods from the United States and Japan increased dramatically. Although a bust soon followed, in the 1920s *narikin* retained enough wealth to fuel an expanding commercial economy based on consumption. Hence, Ōya suggested, modern or cultural lifestyles had a clear correlation with socioeconomic class and urbanism.

Historians usually affirm Ōya's argument. Tessa Morris-Suzuki notes that *bunka* (culture) entailed the consumption of the "novel and the foreign" among "the 'higher strata' of social existence," and that its "most tangible symbol" was the suburban family home or "cultural residence" (*bunka jūtaku*).[16] Jordan Sand describes *bunka* as a "floating signifier" and "narrowly bourgeois" concept that implied cosmopolitanism, alertness to novelty and convenience, and efficient, economical, and sanitary domesticity.[17] Ōya and others dismissed all this as superficial obsession with American middle-class lifestyles. But because it widened the gap between the prosperous urban professional/clerical class and the petite bourgeoisie and urban and rural manual laborers, it was noteworthy nonetheless.

A number of neologisms described this cultural milieu: "modern life" (*modan raifu*); "cultural lifestyle" (*bunka seikatsu*); "modernism" (*modanizumu*); and "erotic grotesque nonsense" (*ero guro nansensu*). These terms represent "vernacular modernism," Japanese inflections of a global cultural movement that welcomed and celebrated change, innovation, and the disavowal of tradition in culture and the arts. Vernacular modernism is "a provincial response to modernization and a vernacular for different, diverse, yet also comparable experiences."[18] Interwar Japanese modernism emphasized a "culture of play" informed by global cultural trends rather than by rigid native traditions. This culture of play required near-constant "code-switching," a linguistic concept for "shifting between languages" and inserting "loan words" into one's speech. This is a useful metaphor for Japanese modernism because "it emphasizes agency and flexibility while challenging the idea of cultural 'borrowing' and replacing it with the idea of cultural strategizing," through which the user could "maintain more than one social identity."[19] Code-switching demonstrated modernites' cultural capital, cosmopolitanism and fluency in modern trends. When deciding how to amuse themselves, *mobo* and *moga* had more choices available to them, and from more diverse points of origin, than any generation ever had: cafés, radio, phonograph records, dances, fashion, food, print advertising, graphic design, detective novels, grotesquerie, spectator sports, cartoons, mass magazines, and recreational shopping at department stores all comprised this modern culture of play.

Though based on consumptive behavior, modernism in Japan and elsewhere was paradoxical: it manifested as an orderly, nontraditional, rational domestic, and professional life, but also as decidedly irrational erotic grotesque nonsense, unorthodox mannerisms/*fūzoku*, and sensuality. A product of the existential crisis generated by the mechanized carnage of World War I, global modernism was partially a cultural critique of modern industrial civilization itself. Ambivalence toward technological progress and reason compelled artists and intellectuals to celebrate the more authentic, subconscious self, unhealthily repressed by civilization. Thus primitivism, which idealized primordial modes of living and fetishized African, Polynesian, and Mesoamerican art, and jazz, was integral to modernism. Unconventional aesthetic and social norms, disseminated by new electronic media technologies, led to new modes of representation: Dada, cubism, abstract expressionism, montage, collage, bricolage, stream of consciousness and atonality (represented in Japan by the quasi-terrorist Mavo artists' collective).[20] Although many modernists disdained commercial popular culture, the two realms affected and influenced one another. George Gershwin's *Rhapsody in Blue* was one of several formal compositions that borrowed elements from popular music, and Dadaist collage was used in popular magazines and advertisements.

If the cataclysm of the Great War inspired modernism in Europe, the Great Kantō earthquake of September 1, 1923, had a comparable effect in Japan. What the tremors left standing fires consumed, razing Tokyo and Yokohama. The disaster's effects on cultural life were profound: the destruction of film studios and the popular Asakusa Opera (1919–23); the migration of filmmakers and entertainers westward to Ōsaka and Kōbe; and the reimagining and rebuilding of Kantō urban environments as ultramodern spaces. The earthquake made the capital region a virtual blank slate on which visionary urban planners, architects, government officials, and private business interests could make an imprint. By the late 1920s, when much of the rebuilding had been completed, the capital region displaced more populous Ōsaka as the locus of the latest entertainment media. In this sense, the Kantō earthquake was creatively destructive.

The awakened "I"

In the Edo period, *chōnin* diversions indicated a latent desire for greater personal autonomy and release from the strictures of neo-Confucian orthodoxy. But since there was no coherent ideological rationale behind it, calling this "individualism" is not really historically appropriate. In the culture of modernism there was a comparable desire simply to be left alone by the state, to indulge the senses and to "self-awaken," but this was in a context of fully formed global political movements, ideologies, and visions that celebrated individualism as a core tenet. The liberty and subjectivity of the self-awakened individual was at the very core of controversies surrounding New Women, *moga*, *mobo*, radicalism, and iconoclasm. "We must mutually reflect on this: the moral thought of Japanese people conforms far too much to the life of society," street singer Soeda Azenbō mused. "We are too bound by external standards. This causes the individual personality to contract and wither. In turn, this causes the withering and contraction of society itself."[21] Azenbō, Fukuzawa Yukichi and others considered individualism socially beneficial.

Confessional, first-person "I Novels" (*shishōsetsu*) by Natsume Sōseki (1867–1916) narrated the individual's struggle with societal expectations and constraints (echoing the proverbial *ninjō-giri* conflict). The literary magazine *Shirakaba* (1910–23), published by a coterie of writers known as the White Birch Society, promoted individual liberty and dignity through literature. In the 1910s liberal scholars such as Minobe Tatsukichi (1873–1948) and Yoshino Sakuzō (1878–1933) tried to resolve the inherent tension between the sanctified emperor-centered state and the individual self. In his 1911 lectures on the Meiji Constitution, Minobe insisted that individualism had made Japan a world power and would continue to be in the national interest.[22] Twenty-four years later, Minobe was defending his views before the Imperial Diet, while protesters outside accused him of lèse-majesté. In the 1930s and 1940s, individualism (*kojin shugi*) was roundly condemned as the source of all evils.

Yet before then it was the bedrock of modern life. Popular culture from post–World War I Europe and the United States gave Japanese visions of individual autonomy and subjectivity to emulate. Individualism was also encouraged by distinctive political and cultural conditions of "imperial democracy" in the years between Emperor Meiji's death in 1912 and the early 1930s. During the reign of the mentally impaired Taishō emperor (1912–26), Japanese struggled with the inherent contradictions between an emperor-centered polity and a political order in which "individual freedom and human rights" were recognized and protected.[23] Elected politicians replaced the old Meiji oligarchs in cabinet posts, making voting more consequential in governance. Politicians, bureaucrats, and the military "accepted some degree of democratic participation, but they supported empire and the emperor as foundations of the political order."[24] In the 1910s and 1920s there were parallel efforts to expand the Diet's legislative powers and secure voting rights for more people, while pacifying labor unrest and eliminating political radicalism, socialism, and anarchism.

Relatively open, public debates about political and labor rights, feminism, and a host of other controversial issues transpired. One of the most representative and high-profile examples of mass media's intervention in such discussions was the pioneering feminist journal *Bluestocking* (*Seitō*, 1911–16), named after a literary society of educated women in eighteenth-century England.[25] Founded by Hiratsuka Raichō (1886–1971) and other alumnae of Japan Women's University, *Bluestocking* carried essays, fiction, poetry, and some visual art. Who was the New Woman? Who was she *not*? Could a woman be "self-awakened," politically engaged and a "good wife, wise mother"? These were among the questions with which *Bluestocking* contributors and readers wrestled. Other publications fostered discussions and debates about the role of arts and entertainment in promoting the rights of laborers, social revolution, and anti-imperialism (*rōdō geijutsu*). Having established the magazine *Literary Front* (*Bungei sensen*, 1924–34), socialist writers organized as the Nippona Artista Proleta Federacio (NAPF, pointedly using the international auxiliary language Esperanto for its official name), and occasionally interacted with leftist artists and activists throughout East Asia as well.[26]

Imperial democracy exemplifies well the hegemony concept that is this book's primary framework: through political action, cultural expression, and consumption, ordinary Japanese agitated for greater autonomy in their personal lives, yet without, for the most part, demanding the dismantling of the emperor system, and in the 1910s and 1920s, at least, governing elites grudgingly tolerated organized labor, feminist expression, expanded voting rights, and erotic grotesque nonsense in media culture. For its part, the entertainment industry constantly adapted to evolving standards of political acceptability and fickle popular tastes, trying to stay both profitable and out of the crosshairs of government censors. Like the culture industry of the Edo period, its defining characteristic was its opportunism.

Yet the contradictions of imperial democracy became painfully obvious in May 1925. On the fifth, the Diet removed property restrictions and thereby expanded voting rights to all men aged twenty-five and up.[27] Seven days later, it approved the Public Security Preservation Law, whose two provisions made it illegal to discuss, organize or agitate for changes to both the emperor-centered *kokutai* (national body) and the system of private property. This law authorized the creation of the Special Higher Police, charged with rooting out "thought crimes" (*shisō hanzai*), a category of infractions that only expanded in ensuing years. The law was revised and invoked repeatedly until 1945 to suppress thousands of Japanese—and also to shape the content and form of interwar and wartime popular culture.

The remainder of this chapter examines three examples of interwar popular culture that expressed and promoted the sensibilities of cosmopolitan modernism, individualism, and the paradoxes of imperial democracy: cinema; popular music and social dancing; and spectator sports. With their emphasis on cultured everyday life, consumption of these enabled Japanese to imagine they were part of a cosmopolitan "culture of taste." When dancing the foxtrot, watching a Buster Keaton film or enjoying a ball game, Japan's self-styled mods were cognizant that their counterparts around the world were doing the same things at the same time. This cosmopolitanism also made them rods attracting nativist lightning: as the clouds of war gathered, conservative nationalists demonized the values and mannerisms on which "cultural living" was based—individualism, materialism, consumerism, sensual pleasures and internationalism. These critics' mantra was "Make Japan great again."

Cinematic modernity

Imagine going to the movies and finding live *shinpa* actors onstage, gesticulating and speaking in quasi-kabuki style. When the plot takes the action "outdoors," the actors step behind a screen onto which their filmed images are projected. Or visualize going to the theater to view a bill consisting mostly of newsreel footage from the Boxer Rebellion (1900) or the Russo-Japanese War (1904–05). On another visit, one might see a silent American or French film that would make no sense if it were not for a well-dressed, charismatic narrator (*katsudō benshi*) standing off to the side commenting and handling the characters' dialogue.

This is what theatergoers would see in Japanese movie theaters in the first two decades of the twentieth century. Komatsu Hiroshi states that the difference between Japanese and Western cinema was not the medium but the "representational mode." In its earliest days, "there was a mixture of native and Western ideas and modes ... [that] had to coexist, yet they also tended to counteract each other."[28]

Early moving pictures in Japan were not self-contained or autonomous, but rather augmentations of older indigenous genres of performance art. This was in the tradition of commingled media, in which various arts were melded to enhance their expressive power. Historians tend to concur that early Japanese cinema retained the characteristic interdependence of various media (instrumental and vocal music, dance, acting, and the printed word) in Edo-period popular culture. "The Japanese audience perceived film as a new form of theater, and not (as in, say, the United States) a new form of photography." Hence until well into the 1910s, "Japanese filmmakers clung to the idea of the film frame as stage."[29] Indeed, the oldest extant Japanese film is a scene from the kabuki play *Maple Viewing* (*Momijigari*, 1899), intended to document the acting styles of Danjūrō IX and Onoe Kikugoro V (1844–1903). Japan's first film star, the "round-eyed" Onoe Matsunosuke (1875–1926), was a former kabuki actor who brought heroic samurai from stage to screen. *Benshi* became the modern incarnations of puppet theater *gidayū*. Film also infused *shinpa* with much-needed novelty just as Western-style *shingeki* began its ascent as the theatrical mainstream. However, film historian Aaron Gerow regards early film more as a variation and continuation of *misemono* than of theater, the emphasis of which was on visual spectacle, supplemented by music and narration.[30]

Unfortunately, precious few of the hundreds of Japanese films produced from the 1900s to the 1920s have survived: few prints were made in the first place, and the highly volatile nitrate film stock simply deteriorated or combusted in Japan's humid climate; films were also destroyed in the 1923 earthquake and Allied airstrikes of World War II; and during the US occupation Tōhō and Daiei studios deliberately destroyed a handful of negatives and prints of movies made after 1931, "presuming that these films were 'not appropriate to be shown.' "[31] Therefore film historians must rely almost exclusively on print material (synopses, scripts, reviews, press accounts), oral histories, and memoirs in order to reconstruct the first three decades of Japanese cinema. Nonetheless, there is abundant evidence testifying to the uniqueness of early Japanese film culture, some of which involved engagement between this most modern of media with older expressive modes.

The first cinematic blockbusters were the near-weekly movies that reported and promoted Japan's David-and-Goliath conflict with the Russian empire in 1904–05. Eighty percent of the films shown in those years were actual footage or faux "documentaries" about the war, using miniature boats and cigar smoke. Many of these were actually produced overseas.[32] This enormously expensive war tested the patience of many Japanese, so these films were important vehicles for managing home-front morale and stirring up nationalism—a strategy that worked all too well, it turned out. I will have more to say about early war films in Chapter 7. For now, it is important to recognize that initially the cinematic experience in Japan was more distinctive, more suited to Japanese tastes and interests and less derivative of foreign models than it would later be.

By the late 1910s many more foreign and domestic films were available for viewing, boasting new narrative and cinematography techniques, longer running times, and famous actors making and breaking romances, committing or avenging crimes and performing feats of derring-do or slapstick. American screen idols were models for modern mannerisms, fashions, and hairstyles. Live stage actors were gone by then, but *benshi* remained, serving one or more of three broad functions: performing narration and voice acting; providing commentary, interpretation, and comic banter (*mandan*); and "react[ing] to the film" as the "chosen representative of the audience."[33] The profession was exported to Japan's overseas colonies, where practitioners were known as *pyŏnsa* in Korea and *benzi* in Taiwan (more on them in Chapter 6).[34]

Around 1910, silent film narrators appeared on the covers of movie magazines and "functioned as a commercial attraction that enticed audiences to visit playhouses." So popular were *benshi* vocal performances that they were recorded and sold as 78-RPM SP (short play) records. Sometimes audiences would see a film two or three times just to compare the distinctive artistry of *benshi* virtuosi. Intertitles and sound were not only unnecessary but inhibited the *benshi*'s creative license; thus, "silent films were already regarded as talking pictures by the audience."[35]

So potentially powerful was their influence, yet so low was their social standing, that after 1917 *benshi* required licenses from the police. Like kabuki actors a generation earlier, the desire for a modicum of social respectability motivated narrators to acquiesce to such regulation. The profession was open to women, but in a survey conducted during their heyday (1927–31), only 2.64 percent of the nearly 7,000 narrators throughout Japan were female.[36] *Benshi* were so popular that nascent movie studios signed them to exclusive contracts, and when they organized to protect their collective interests they had considerable leverage. Some film histories imply that their collective action impeded the development of Japanese cinema as a self-standing medium, in part because their presence delayed the advent of talkies. But, Donald Richie says, "this line of thought is valid only if one believes that the development of narrative was a 'natural' development of the film and that there were no other alternatives. Actually, as Japanese film itself indicates, there were."[37]

Narrators tended to specialize in one of three types of film: domestic historical or contemporary dramas, or Western movies. Ironically, *benshi* were most necessary for explicating foreign films, yet it was the increasing popularity of American and European movies and actors after 1915 that altered and diminished their role. "The object of the audience's applause shifted from the *benshi* to actors," narrator Nishimura Rakuten (1902–83) conceded in 1917. "I have decided that, when an actor's facial expression was highlighted, I would hold my tongue." Although they continued to be star attractions in the 1920s, by the mid-1930s talkies eventually made *benshi* obsolete; "the subordination of the *benshi* to the film industry and Japanese government made them more easily replaceable."[38] There are *benshi* revival performances one can view on YouTube, but it is no more like the original experience than kabuki at the National Theater in Tokyo is like that staged at Edo's Morita-za.

We—or maybe just I—may think early Japanese cinematic culture sounds cool, but at the time its distinctiveness compared to that of other countries was no source of pride among some prominent filmmakers and critics. In the mid-1910s these sticks-in-the-mud objected to the distinctive commingled approach that paired movies with live performances. They were advocates for what they called self-contained "pure films" (*jun eigageki*) like those made overseas.[39] Gerow describes the Pure Film movement as "less an effort to establish the motion picture as a pure art form in opposition to commercial cinema than to introduce the filmic innovations of Hollywood and European production, considered to be the best examples of the cinematic medium, into the Japanese industry." The movement's intervention constituted no less than an "epistemological break in early knowledge about cinema," to revolutionary effect: "Japanese film culture in the 1910s and early 1920s witnessed a major shift in the basic understanding and social definition of cinema that exceeded changes in film form."[40]

Pure Film advocates welcomed the formation in 1920 of new studios Shōchiku and Taikatsu, which, unlike the more established Nikkatsu (founded in 1912) and Tenkatsu (1914–19), vowed to completely sever cinema's connection to theater. "The main purpose of this company," Shōchiku's manifesto proclaimed, "will be the production of artistic films resembling the latest and most flourishing styles of the Occidental cinema; it will distribute these both at home and abroad; it will introduce the true state of our national life to foreign countries; and it will assist in international reconciliation both here and abroad."[41] Reformers did not want derivative filmmaking but rather a distinctive "national product within an international market." This required, among other things, excision of live performance (including *benshi* narration) from Japanese cinema so that it could more easily be exported into the burgeoning global film market.[42] Yet it is worth considering that the persistence of *benshi* into the mid-1930s was a form of resistance to the Pure Film movement's agenda. That is, well after domestically produced "pure films" began to appear in theaters, audiences still appreciated the *benshi*'s performance enough to carry the tradition into its fourth decade, regardless of what film theorists thought best.

Almost a century before anime became one of Japan's most prominent cultural exports, Daisuke Miyao contends, animated films were the most promising vehicles interwar Japan could offer as a distinctive, export-worthy national cinema. For one thing, both the subject matter of animated films and the techniques for producing them drew from traditional Japanese culture and craftsmanship. For instance, Ōfuji Noburō (1900–61) mined native folklore for content and used traditionally crafted paper (*washi*) and folding and cutting techniques to create paper and silhouette animation (*chiyogami anime*). But the reformers, with rigid ideas about what constituted cinematic artistry, missed this potential. "Japanese animated films met many of the criteria of the Pure Film reformers," for whom "the essence of cinema lay in its ability to depict the world with greater realism than other art forms." But realism was not animation's strong suit, so Pure Film advocates completely overlooked its potential as a novel contribution to international cinema.[43]

Few films actually made it to the international market in the interwar period, and Japan therefore remained a marginal presence in world cinema. One reason was that, because of the *benshi*'s residual popularity and clout, and the expense of the technology involved, Japan's film industry was slow to produce sound films. The first talkie—Gosho Heinosuke's (1902–81) *The Madam and the Wife* (*Madamu to nyōbō*, 1931)—did not actually set the industry standard until the mid- to late-1930s. The movie featured a jazz band led by an archetypical *moga*, and thus was one of several depictions and commentaries on the liberating—and corrupting—effects of modern life.[44]

Despite domestic film's relative technological deficiencies, production values improved enough that audiences for domestic films steadily increased in the late 1920s and 1930s, challenging the dominance that imported movies had enjoyed since the mid-1910s. Between 1928 and 1938, at a rate of about seven hundred films per year Japanese film production surpassed that of any other country.[45] Even without explicit connections to stage plays, domestic films tended to be defined in much the same ways as kabuki and *bunraku* were, as contemporary (*gendaigeki*) and historical or period films (*jidaigeki*). Arguably, the latter category was the more popular among general audiences, and its exoticism would eventually pique the interest of foreign critics and cinephiles.

One of interwar Japan's biggest movie stars, Bandō Tsumasaburō (1901–53), made his reputation as a cinematic samurai in a huge number of historical *chanbara* (swordplay) films. He was also a producer, the first screen star to start his own production company and seal a deal with an American studio to remedy Japan's technological deficiencies. His most famous work—*Orochi* (*Serpent*, 1925, dir. Futagawa Buntarō)—is considered an early example of filmic commentary on contemporary politics. Just as Edo-period playwrights set potentially censorable political commentary and satire safely back in medieval settings, *Orochi* did the same to criticize the treacherous political climate in which the universal manhood suffrage and Public Security Preservation laws were passed nearly simultaneously. The opening title card read,

> Not all those who wear the name of villain are truly evil men. Not all those who are respected as noble men are worthy of the name. Many are those who wear a false mask of benevolence to hide their treachery and the wickedness of their true selves.

What seems to be a fairly innocuous general statement was too on the nose for government censors, who clipped about one-fifth of the film and required some reshooting. Predictably, the buzz merely increased *Orochi*'s appeal to audiences. The extended sequence in which Bandō's hero fends off probably a hundred sword-wielding opponents may merely have thrilled most viewers, but its metaphor of the haplessly beleaguered individual valiantly resisting overwhelming social forces spoke to the aforementioned tensions between individualism and statism under imperial democracy and indicated the potential thematic depth of *chanbara* films.

Another example of a filmic commentary on contemporary social issues is Mizoguchi Kenji's (1898–1956) 1936 melodrama *Ōsaka Elegy* (*Naniwa ereji*), one in a series of movies the director made to highlight the discrimination and cruelty women faced in modern Japan. Besides being a sort of visual record of the hypermodern city of Ōsaka, the film traces a young woman's transformation into a *moga* outcast. As portrayed by the prolific actress Yamada Isuzu (1919–2012), Murai Ayako—a telephone operator in a corporate office—feels responsible for repaying money her father had embezzled from his former employer. She is eager to marry her coworker Nishimura, but when he cannot provide the money Ayako needs she reluctantly becomes the mistress of her employer, who pays off her father's debt (as an adopted heir, this lecherous twit was really spending his *wife's* money). Then Ayako's brother comes home needing money to pay his university fees. Again she becomes a mistress to another older admirer, making the transition to full-blown *moga* in dress, speech, and saucy mannerisms. She is eventually arrested for solicitation, having taken the money from her second sugar daddy without delivering the goodies. When she is released Nishimura and her family scorn her, despite her filial motives. At the end of the film, on the famous Dōtonbori bridge, she describes herself as a "stray dog."

In the broader context of Mizoguchi's oeuvre, *Ōsaka Elegy* easily fits among his "women films" (*josei eiga*) in which female protagonists face no-win scenarios, and the male characters are either dirty old men or spineless, pusillanimous young ones. It is less a celebration of modern urban life than an exposé of the "incompleteness" of Japanese modernity. Despite the neon-lit glamour of Ōsaka's landscape, traditional male entitlement, unjust filial obligation, and the subordination of women persist. This is a perfectly valid interpretation, but not the only plausible one. It is just as likely that more conservative viewers read this film as a satisfying karmic tale in the "reward good, punish evil" (*kanzen chōaku*) tradition, in which a woman is corrupted by big-city ways, becomes a shameless harlot, and gets what she and all *moga* deserve. By depicting the moral ambiguity of modern life, *Ōsaka Elegy* potentially yields polar opposite readings depending on the viewer's perspective.

Since the 1950s *Ōsaka Elegy* and the works of other early Japanese directors such as Kaeriyama Norimasa (1893–1964), Murata Minoru (1894–1937), Shimazu Yasujirō (1897–1945), and Naruse Mikio (1905–69) have passed from the realm of popular culture to that of Art, in part as a result of the international attention Japanese cinema earned after *Rashōmon* (1951) took first prize at the Venice Film Festival. As a consequence, canonical films by auteur filmmakers have all but monopolized Japanese film studies. There is far less scholarship on a host of popular musicals, period films, and contemporary dramas that drew bigger audiences than the canonized movies did. To be fair, this is partially a consequence of the deterioration and destruction of possibly hundreds of reels of "lesser" films, but it is also due to traditional biases in film studies against work less "deep" or technically innovative than silent classics such as Kaeriyama's *The Glow of Life* (1919) and Murata's *Souls on the Road* (1921), Naruse's gloomy "working class dramas" (*shomingeki*), or Mizoguchi's "women films." "[T]he dominant narrative of Japanese film history has been structured around the auteurs," Mitsuyo Wada-Marciano writes, and thus "has narrowed the scope of [film] history."[46] She represents a new generation of film scholars exploring cinematic experiences of spectators and discourses about film and venturing into the realm of noncanonical cinema to reconstruct a richer portrayal of interwar film culture.

Musical modernity

Seldom does a song capture the zeitgeist of a specific time and place as well as the hit record/movie theme "Tokyo March" ("Tokyo kōshinkyoku") did in 1929. Its lyrics spoke of "Dancing to jazz, drinking liquor into the wee hours"; having "secret trysts in chic Asakusa"; going to movies, department stores, and dance halls; and riding mass transit. "Tokyo March" gave the general public a peek into the fashionable, hormone-drenched world of the *mobo* and *moga* as they flitted about Japan's capital with jazz in their ears and boozy amorousness on their faces. The song was the first time that most Japanese heard the word "jazz" (*jazu*) and associated it with a frivolous, urbane lifestyle. When the new national radio network (founded in 1926, later known as NHK) refused to play the record on the air during its brief popular music programs, the song predictably earned more notoriety, selling some twenty-five hundred copies.[47] But "Tokyo March" also generated concern, as the mannerisms of modernites—spelled out gratuitously in the lyrics—gained more exposure than ever.

The impact of recording and broadcast technologies on the creation, performance, and enjoyment of music cannot be overstated. Neither can it be explicated in full here. Suffice to say that electronic media did not supplant live performance so much as promote and augment it. They transformed music into a capitalist commodity, with an entire business infrastructure devoted to identifying talent and recording, advertising and selling product, with the explicit aim of hitting as big and as frequently as possible. Why kid ourselves? Emotive self-expression was tangential. These technologies did not create the professional performer, but certainly widened the gap between professionals and amateurs, musicians and listeners, concert music and popular song. Most people consumed music by purchasing radios and records rather than instruments. Before radio and phonographs, the primary medium for distributing, selling, and purchasing music was print: full scores for piano, guitar, mandolin, violin, and other instruments, or simple song sheets such as those Soeda Azenbō and other street singers sold. Now professional-grade music could be enjoyed in private rather than exclusively in public spaces.

Christine Yano discerns a profound transformation of musical production in interwar Japan. Before the late-1920s, "songs originated outside record companies, became popular, and then were recorded and sold by record companies" to exploit their established popularity. This was the process by which "Katusha's Song" became Japan's first hit record. Composed for the mercurial actress Matsui Sumako to sing in the play *Resurrection*, "Katusha's Song" entranced audiences as the production toured Japan's major cities in 1914. The score was published and Matsui's recording released *after* the song hit. However, with the 1929 release of "I Long for You" ("Kimi koishi"), "the process reversed," and record companies set up assembly-line structures of songwriters, arrangers, studio bands, contracted singers, promoters, and connections with cinema and radio to get product out on the street. The production of popular music—"primarily vocal music written by a known composer, disseminated through mass media, sold in the form of recordings or printed sheets"—was therefore industrialized to yield a salable commodity.[48]

Azenbō lamented this change as he observed it transpiring: "We needed good songs ... Good songs required good composers. We needed artistic merit. I thought we should be able to expect those things from the ranks of professionals in the business. Now, late in life, I realize that such poets are under exclusive contract to the record companies. My dream of a world of creative musical professionals has ended up being just that: a dream." Azenbō "lost interest in using the music ... to express only anger, taunts, mockery, and curses ... I wanted to sing from the bottom of heart.

I wanted to sing of the hearts of our people; the way the masses lived, the way I lived." He desired no less than "the return of my artistic conscience," but the new modus operandi of the popular music industry thwarted him.[49]

Among the peculiar characteristics of interwar popular music, there are three I would like to highlight here: its detailed yet confusing genre categories, inscribed prominently on records' center labels; its cosmopolitan character; and its utility for social dancing. Aside from *shōka*, the word for vocal music in school songbooks, the most general term for popular music was *ryūkōka* (an alternate pronunciation of the Edo-period term *hayariuta*, designating songs that circulated widely). The term *kayōkyoku* was "coined to avoid the vulgarity some considered to be inherent in 'ryūkō-' (be in vogue or broadly favored)." For several decades the two words were used "interchangeably," but eventually *ryūkōka* fell out of use because, ironically, "it sounded outmoded."[50] Like *shōka*, *kayōkyoku* melodies were usually based on pentatonic major or minor *yonanuki* scales (lacking the fourth and seventh scale degrees), and featured either Western or Japanese instrumentation, or a mix thereof. Today *kayōkyoku* generally refers to "nostalgic melodies" (*natsumero*) of the Shōwa period (1926–89, the reign of Emperor Hirohito), as "oldies" is used for American radio formats that focus on baby-boomer music.

"Jazz songs" (*jazu songu*) constituted a subgenre of *ryūkōka*, and initially, at least, these were American popular songs that were rerecorded with translated lyrics. The first big hit of this sort was Futamura Teiichi's (1900–48) "My Blue Heaven" b/w "Song [Sheik] of Araby" (1928), which was released simultaneously on *two* record labels! The most popular *jazu songu* singers were actually native-born Americans whose parents had emigrated from Japan at the turn of the nineteenth and twentieth centuries. So-called nisei (second-generation) performers such as the multitalented Alice Fumiko Kawabata (1916–2007) had the advantage of singing in fluent English and Japanese, with the nuanced rhythmic phrasing of American jazz singers. When racial discrimination prevented these entertainers from breaking through in their homeland, Japanese companies delightedly recruited them. *Jazu songu* recordings also featured ensembles that moonlighted in dance halls. Modeled more on Paul Whiteman's "symphonic jazz" than on the "hot" styles of Louis Armstrong, Duke Ellington, and Jelly Roll Morton, *jazu* featured relatively little instrumental or vocal improvisation.[51]

"New folk songs" (*shin min'yō*), another important subgenre of *ryūkōka*, were either traditional folk songs that had been arranged for Western orchestration and structures, or newly composed songs that *sounded* "folkish." Examples include jazz arrangements of "Yagi bushi," "Harusame," and "Ryoshū," by Sugii Kōichi (1906–42), and "The Mountain Temple Priest," by Hattori Ryōichi (1907–93).[52] However, songsmiths and arrangers did not draw exclusively from the well of Japanese folksongs. *Shin min'yō* also included folkloric material from other countries, including "Aloha 'Oe" and "My Old Kentucky Home."

This segues nicely into a description of a second major characteristic of interwar popular music: its voracious cosmopolitanism. Western popular music provided a basic foundation for much of Japan's in this period. In *kayōkyoku* pentatonic melodies and lyrics' content and language were the most identifiably Japanese elements, but the rhythms, orchestration, and harmonies were derived from the West. However, the worldly nature of *ryūkōka* did not end there. Japanese consumers had access to a global smorgasbord of music, including Italian operas, French chansons, Argentine tango, American jazz, Hawaiian hula, and Cuban *rumba*, of which lyricists, composers, arrangers, and performers took full advantage.[53] Although some musicians were identified with particular genres, the flamboyant and versatile diva Awaya Noriko (1907–99) voiced chansons, tango, Hattori's "Japanese blues," *jazu songu*, and an early *shin min'yō* rendition of the Korean song "Arirang."

The internationality of interwar Japan's commercial music market is indicative not only of the listening public's catholic tastes but also of how early the music industry itself was globalized, earlier than even the movie industry.[54] In Japan, this was most conspicuous with the influx of foreign capital from overseas—which, again, outpaced what transpired in cinema—to produce and promote commercial recordings. In 1927, US companies Columbia and Victor and Germany's Polydor set up branch offices in Tokyo to produce domestic recordings. Until a forced consolidation process in the early 1940s, there were also several native firms, three of which (Orient, Taihei, and Teichiku) were based in Kansai (Kyōto, Nara, and Hyōgo prefectures). The recording industry in the early twentieth century was thus far less geographically centralized than it is nowadays, when all the major labels are in Tokyo.[55]

There were several places in imperial Japan at which one could hear live bands playing popular music: movie theaters, music revue halls, department stores, and hotel ballrooms. Revues and follies were controversial—as they were in the United States and elsewhere—because of the spectacle of young women in short dresses baring their legs and showing their bloomers in suggestive kick-dance routines. "[T]hese dancers are just fourteen- or fifteen-year-old children. The oldest must be around twenty," a character in Kawabata's *Scarlet Gang* explains. "[T]hey don't wear stockings, 'going stockingless' it's called, and show off their bare legs on purpose, you know. They don't use white makeup on their arms and legs, either. When it's hot you can see the red bumps—mosquito bites."[56]

Theatrical revues were an important vehicle for the dissemination of popular music, both native and foreign. The most popular musical revue was the all-female Takarazuka troupe, based in a resort city in Hyōgo near Kōbe and Ōsaka, which remains popular today. Most programs consisted of adapted musicals, operettas, plays, and literature from the West, Japan, and China, and the occasional original production, with kick-line dance finales. "From 1914 Takarazuka became a significant site of Japanese musical modernity," Alison Tokita contends, "where Western music entered Japanese life and developed a localized form."[57] Like kabuki actors, individual Takarasiennes specialized in male (*otokoyaku*) and female (*musumeyaku*) roles and underwent extensive training in singing and dancing in the company music school. The ardent jingoism of Takarazuka's founder, Hankyū Railroad magnate Kobayashi Ichizō (1873–1957), may have deflected the kind of censure a cross-dressing revue might otherwise have attracted. No doubt that sounds odd, since cross-dressing and the mutability of gender were long-standing characteristics of Japanese popular culture. But we must remember that they were never universally accepted, especially by self-appointed custodians of public morality, nor were the concerns and anxieties of interwar Japan identical to those of early times. As already noted, with the appearance of New Women and Modern Girls, incertitude and moral panic about gender and sexuality were among the most irksome social issues in public discourse. To some observers, women seemed to be transgressing every last boundary of their socially acceptable stations, and this is what made modernity so vexing.

The music venues that were most irritating to law enforcement and stewards of public morality were the commercial ballrooms that began sprouting up like obstinate weeds in the late 1920s. Like so many facets of interwar Japanese modernism, dance halls emerged first in the Ōsaka–Kōbe nexus and caught on later in the newly reconstructed Kantō metropolis in the late 1920s. From their inception, police, municipal, and prefectural oversight dogged the ballrooms, where dancing involved the unorthodox practice of male and female bodies swaying in perpetual contact. "If a man and a woman danced with their arms around each other," Tanizaki wrote in *A Fool's Love*, "people assumed that they were having an improper relationship and started to spread the word. Reactionary newspapers wrote groundless articles that gave social dancing a bad name, and so most people had made up their minds that it was unwholesome."[58] Western-style social dancing existed in Meiji times, but only among elite statesmen in the ballrooms of the Rokumeikan, a building that housed foreign dignitaries in Tokyo, and which symbolized the adoption of Western mannerisms in the Meiji period. By the 1910s and 1920s stylish urbanites took to the foxtrot, rumba, tango, and Black Bottom, generating as much apoplexy as twerking does today. Marxist philosopher Tosaka Jun (1900–45) wryly noted the government's zeal to protect public morality through dance hall regulations while still sanctioning licensed prostitution.[59]

Ōsaka in the mid-twenties boasted stylish and garish dance halls such as Paulista, Parisian, and Union, in which young women were employed to dance with paying male customers, who purchased tickets at the door, which they exchanged for each dance. Orchestras were encouraged to play many short pieces so that tickets would keep moving. Fraternization between customers and "taxi dancers" was strictly verboten, which, of course, made it more tantalizing. The Ōsaka dance halls closed in mourning for the Taishō emperor's death in December 1926, but not long enough to suit municipal and prefectural officials, who cracked down with stricter regulations and eventually shuttered all of the commercial ballrooms one year later. Other dance halls opened along the Hanshin Railway to Kōbe in neighboring Hyōgo prefecture, but most musicians immigrated back to the rebuilt capital region, where newer facilities "sprung up like bamboo shoots after a rain," as Tanizaki put it. Having once referred to Ōsaka as the "America of Japan," Ōya Sōichi was not pleased to witness "the Ōsaka-ization of Tokyo." But a 1937 survey counted thirty-nine commercial ballrooms outside of metropolitan Tokyo, not including seventeen others in colonial territories abroad, in Taiwan, Korea, Manchuria, and the Japanese concession in Shanghai.[60] The imperial state and law enforcement gave up on this whack-a-mole game until 1940.

Popular music described and commented on modernity and fostered nationalist consciousness in imperial Japan. Discourses on *ryūkōka*, jazz, and social dance were proxies for broader discussions on national cultural identity, gender values, public behavior and mannerisms, and Japan's level of engagement with the outer world.[61] Official attitudes toward popular music and dancing mirrored the country's drift away from the cosmopolitan ethos of the 1920s to the estrangement from the international community that followed the 1931 military intrusion in Manchuria.

Sporting modernity

Naturally, when Japanese opened their country to trade and diplomacy, they noticed physical differences between themselves and foreigners. Abundant photographic evidence from the mid-nineteenth century demonstrates that on average Japanese were of shorter stature than Europeans and Americans. People in government, military, and educational circles thus considered the physical "improvement" of Japanese bodies a priority. This was one of the rationales for consuming meat and dairy, and also for physical education, calisthenics, and competitive sports. This does not mean that Japanese had no competitive games before. Obviously *sumō* had been around for centuries, as had various martial arts and a kickball game (*kemari*) that aristocrats had played in early medieval times.

Considering its perceived importance to homeland security, it is unsurprising that a bunch of committed Social Darwinists set such store in physical fitness. Hence, kinesiology and physical education were on the long list of things about which Japanese sought knowledge in the West. But sport was not just imported through official channels. The small foreign settlements in treaty port cities such as Yokohama and Kōbe had sport enthusiasts and athletes in their midst, who taught local Japanese baseball, tennis, association football (soccer), and cricket, and formed recreational leagues for regular play.[62] Foreign advisers (*oyatoi gaijin*) such as Horace Wilson (1843–1927), Archibald Douglas (1842–1913), and Japanese who had studied abroad encouraged sport teams as extracurricular school activities. Competitive sport was another essential aspect of a modern, civilized society. However, traditional concepts of mind/body fitness remained influential in modern Japan: echoing a number of samurai philosophers, Meiji-era minister of education Mori Arinori (1847–89) stated, "If the body is strong, the spirit will advance without flagging. Physical training is an indispensable element for character training."[63]

Yet clearly, participating and spectating are two different things. For most Japanese, aside from physical education in school, sport became a form of recreation to observe rather than play. Spectating came to involve much more than simply attending a game: new electronic media enabled audiences to see newsreel highlights in movie theaters, read newspaper sport sections, and listen to remote radio broadcasts either at home or in public spaces.

The cultural impact of high school, collegiate, professional, and international competition was multitudinous, creating fan communities and rivalries, while initiating discussion on broader social issues. Intellectuals debated the effects of "the almost ravenous consumption of sports, particularly by students and the intelligentsia," with some insisting that sport "fostered passivity among the masses, masked class conflicts and served as a means of ideological control by the state." The intensity of fans' emotional attachments to individual athletes and teams—often reflected in coordinated cheers and songs—concerned some observers.[64] The value of sport for encouraging nationalism was lost on neither leftist nor rightist commentators. As Japanese athletes engaged more frequently in international competitions, the nation's prestige was at stake.

Robin Kietlinski points out that the success of Japanese female athletes internationally often neutralizes conventions of femininity. "Preconceived notions about the appropriateness or acceptability of a certain sport or athlete seem to melt away—at least for a while—when that athlete represents Japan well against international competition … [T]his phenomenon has helped to slowly chip away at firmly entrenched notions of what is or is not acceptable for Japanese women."[65] But this came too late for Japan's first female champion. In the 1920s, the heyday of *moga*, women began to participate more in competitive sports at all levels. By 1928 Hitomi Kinue (1907–31) became the first Japanese to win a medal, taking silver in the 800 meters at the Amsterdam Olympic Games—she and the German gold medalist both broke the standing world record. Initially the public was elated, and Hitomi appeared in several media. When the titular girl in the 1931 animated short *Chameko's Day* (*Chameko no ichinichi*) daydreams about her, we see live footage of Hitomi doing the long jump.[66] Her cameo in this prescriptive little film, in which Chameko models how good little Japanese children should behave, indicates that some considered Hitomi a role model.

But Hitomi was also besieged by prurient, prejudicial media scrutiny, which mirrored the vitriolic discourses about modernity and femininity. An interviewer for *Women's World* (*Fujin sekai*) queried, "So, since [54 kilograms] is about the same weight as most men, haven't people said that they are doubtful that you are really a woman?" "I'm embarrassed," Hitomi responded. The interviewer continued, "This may be a bit rude but the shape of your chest and hips really isn't like normal Japanese women, so it seems like you are more like a Western woman ... So are you physically becoming more masculine? ... Is it true that very intense physical activity can cause gynecological abnormalities?"[67] Like other forms of popular culture, spectator sport thus reflected Japanese ambivalence about modernity and its impact on femininity and national identity.

In the interwar period baseball (*yakyū*) was the most popular spectator sport. Although baseball had been introduced to Japan in the early Meiji era, between 1913 and 1929 its popularity boomed, mostly as a result of the expansion of collegiate leagues and sponsorship of high school and middle school tournaments by newspaper and railroad companies. Kōshien, the National High School Baseball Invitational Tournament, began in 1914 and continues to be a national event every spring, comparable in popularity to that of high school (gridiron) football in Texas. One of baseball's most ardent supporters was a Christian socialist professor of economics at Waseda University, Abe Isō (1865–1949). Abe had prevailed in a 1910 press debate in the *Ōsaka Asahi* about the possibly baneful influence of baseball on schoolchildren. Citing Fukuzawa Yukichi's support for the game, Abe insisted it promoted self-discipline, sportsmanship, and internationalism, and was moreover an important complement to didactic education (*tokuiku*). "He was convinced that team sports, as exemplified by baseball, were the best way to instill the spirit of fair play and cooperation required of citizens in the coming social order."[68] At a Big Six tournament in 1926, Abe served as "expositor" for Crown Prince Hirohito, whose presence signified imperial support for the game. Sayuri Guthrie-Shimizu argues that, from the early Meiji period until the American occupation (1945–52), baseball created informal transpacific networks between Americans and Japanese that operated underneath formal diplomatic channels and constituted cultural common ground.[69] An eighteen-game November 1934 tour by an all-star team of Major Leaguers—including Babe Ruth, Lou Gehrig, and Lefty Gomez—managed by Connie Mack warmed Japan-United States relations momentarily, before Japan's military invasion of Republican China chilled them.[70]

Although association football was much less popular than baseball, enthusiasts and players organized and competed internationally in the interwar period. In 1921 the Japanese Football Association (JFA) was founded to organize tournaments for company and collegiate teams, and sponsored the first Emperor's Cup national tournament. The JFA became an affiliate of the Fédération Internationale de Football Association (FIFA) in 1929. In 1935 the JFA Cup tournament was inaugurated, allowing teams from the colonies to compete. After the first cup was taken by a team from Seoul, the JFA made the controversial decision to include two Koreans on their national side for the 1936 Berlin Olympic Games.[71] The squad's best showing in international competition occurred in Berlin, when it defeated Sweden in the first round—after which the side was thumped by Italy 8–0 in the quarterfinals. Despite poor performances, Japan's participation in football on the world stage was yet another indicator of the cosmopolitanism that marked interwar popular culture.

Professionalization of sport helped foster a culture of spectatorship, but without undermining the popularity of collegiate and school sport, which was relatively more stable and had nostalgia value among alumni. After a couple of failed efforts in the 1920s, the Japanese Baseball League (1936–49) was established, its teams associated with corporate sponsors rather than cities. *Sumō* was less popular than baseball as a spectator sport in the interwar period, but its indigeneity and tradition made it a potent nationalist symbol. Professionalization of wrestlers (*rikishi*) was a slow process that began in the Edo period, when organized bouts were used to raise funds for public works projects, charity, and Buddhist temples. Wrestlers—usually unemployed samurai—were paid a portion of the proceeds. Originally itinerants, in the seventeenth century they began wrestling for paying spectators in urban centers, so that by the mid-1700s *sumō* "became almost exclusively an urban entertainment," with seasonal tournaments in the three main cities.[72] Greater organization in the Meiji period resulted in the formation of the Japan Sumō Association and the creation of a championship system.[73] Its directors were retired wrestlers, who organized tournaments, regulated, ranked and paid *rikishi*, and oversaw referees (*gyōji*). Shintō purification rites of throwing salt and gesticulating to get the attention of spirits (*kami*) were of course retained, and the referees dressed as Shintō priests, maintaining the ritual element of the sport that distinguished it from imported ones. Radio broadcasts of tournaments (*basho*) and newsreel highlights helped expand the audience for *sumō* in the 1920s and 1930s, but it was perhaps the implementation of a statistics-based ranking system and a tournament structure producing an undisputed champion at the end that heightened the drama and intensified popular interest in wrestling.[74]

In the process of transforming *sumō* from a "bawdy, marginalized entertainment into purified symbolic acts for the nation, the military government, and the emperor," it "assumed greater cultural significance" than it had ever possessed.[75] The same could be said of other martial arts (*budō*), which were modernized hybrids or novel fabrications used more for spiritual discipline than for combat readiness. Okinawan karate was remade by Andō Itosu (1831–1915) and Funakoshi Gichin (1868–1957); *jujutsu/judō* by Kanō

Jigorō (1860–1938); *kendō* (fencing) by Sakakibara Kenkichi (1830–94); *kyūdō* (archery) by Honda Toshizane (1836–1917); and *aikidō* developed by Ueshiba Morihei (1883–1969). "*Budō*, of which Kōdōkan judo was the prototype," Inoue Shun contends, "was originally conceived as a hybrid cultural form produced by modernizing 'traditional' practice. With the rise of militarism and ultranationalism, however, *budō* was reinvented as a counter to Western values and to infuse Japan's modern sports culture with 'Japanese spirit.'" Their modern provenance notwithstanding, the militarist regime of the 1930s and 1940s promoted *budō* as "timeless" traditions that were the antitheses of "individualistic" imported sports.[76]

William Kelly identifies "two processes" of "sportification" and "samurai-ization" in the early twentieth century: *sumō* and other *budō* "were reshaped into rule-governed physical competitions; at the same time, new Western sports ... were spiritualized with newly articulated Japanese values," such as the invented tradition of *bushidō*. "[T]his is merely the sports version of *wakon yōsai*, the selective adaptation of Western practices and their ideological domestication with Japanese 'spirit.'" This was not a peculiar Japanese practice, however, since in the United States and the United Kingdom sport was "imbued with a moralizing ethos" and nationalism.[77] Kiku Kōichi critiques the widespread theory of *bushidō* and modern sport as "two different modalities," in which rules-governed sporting competition and "an indigenous, pre-modern playing mentality" constitute a paradox peculiar to Japan. Instead, he sees an affinity between *bushidō*'s core emphasis on self-regulation and modern sport's role in the "civilizing process" and the creation of "obedient bodies" in service to the nation.[78]

Another trend, reflecting the individualist ethos that flourished in interwar Japan, marked modern sport as well: the "sports-star" system in which individual athletes became media celebrities. Athletes such as Hitomi Kikue, *sumō*'s Hitachiyama Taniemon (1874–1922), and pitcher Sawamura Eiji (1917–44) "shot to sports stardom" because of carefully crafted public personas as "self-made" individuals with "exceptional skills, bodies, and character" that embodied Japanese values of filial piety, dedication to their sport, and service to the nation. Sawamura's heroism was embellished by his death as a soldier in World War II.[79]

Cinema, popular music, social dance, and spectator sport developed in a cultural milieu in which the meanings, benefits, and drawbacks of modernity; the integrity of national cultural identity; the instability of gender norms; and the effects of individualism were hotly contested. The typical dyad of tradition versus modernity, or of a "double life" in which one bounced from one pole to another, does little justice to the complex vernacular modernism that affected the urban Japanese culture of play and the (re)invention of their lifestyles.[80] Many intellectuals, on the political right and left, openly scorned the superficial veneer and derivative materialism of modern life, arguing that attitudes, customs, and civic involvement, not commodities and diversions, were the proper indices of modernity. As Japan's military encroached into continental Asia in the 1930s, the materialism and frivol-ity associated with modern life became targets of critics and policymakers, whose goals included deploying popular culture to "spiritually mobilize" the entire populace and to "overcome modernity" as a divisive factor in Japanese society.[81]

CHAPTER SIX

Entertaining empire—popular culture as a "technology of imperialism"

In the age of modern imperialism (ca. 1870–1919) Japan was both victim and perpetrator. European powers competed with one another to secure "free trade" rights from weaker states and colonize broad swaths of the planet. Empires have been around for centuries, of course, but most historians agree that "new" or "high" imperialism was qualitatively different in terms of how empires were assembled and administered, for what purposes and to what effects. When the earnest scramble for colonies in Africa and Southeast Asia intensified in the 1870s, Japan had already surrendered to American gunboat diplomacy and a subsequent rush of European states whose treaty demands infringed significantly on Japan's sovereignty. Recall that eliminating the noxious unequal treaty regime was a priority for the Meiji state, behind nearly every major policy initiative.

Fundamentally speaking, imperialism is a *relationship*, but one of inequality in which one party (typically a nation-state) imposes its will on another (which may or may not be an organized polity). Colonialism is a type of imperialism involving the seizure, either through negotiations or military conquest, of a territory for the express benefit or national interests of the imperial power (metropole). It is "a relationship of domination between an indigenous (or forcibly imported) majority and a minority of foreign invaders," in which "the colonizers are convinced of their own superiority and of their ordained mandate to rule."[1] But as Japan, Qing China, Ottoman Turkey, Siam, Chosŏn (before 1905), and Qájár Persia, among other polities, discovered, one need not actually be colonized to be bullied by imperialists. Unequal treaties, forcibly opened trade ports, unilaterally imposed tariffs,

Christian missions and churches, and white people's boots on the ground were mortifying enough.

The construction of the Japanese empire, which lasted a half century, from 1895 to 1945, can be easily explained within the context of the times—indeed, explained much more compellingly than Belgian King Leopold's (1835–1909) claim to the African Congo can be. No less than Japan's homeland security was at stake. Although Japanese avoided outright colonization, and had the advantage of witnessing Qing arrogance and miscalculation lead to its humiliating defeats by European states, they still learned a hard lesson in international relations: to be modern and preserve sovereignty, one had to have wealth, industry, military might, and colonies on which to prey.

The Japanese empire bore similarities to others, but remained singular in a number of ways. Japan was similar in the following respects:

1   Japan was engaged in a zero-sum, Social Darwinian competition for resources, markets, military dominance, and national prestige.

2   Japanese justified their imperial expansion and aggression with claims of racial superiority, fitness to rule, and altruistic rhetoric akin to the "white man's burden" and *mission civilisatrice.*

3   Much like the French, the Japanese ideal of colonial rule was assimilation (*dōka*), making colonized peoples "Japanese," while still withholding some of the privileges that entailed. Yet whereas the French allowed colonials to become full citizens, with representation in the Assemblée Nationale, Japanese never extended such benefits to their colonial subjects.

"The colonial project as a whole was shot through with anxiety on the part of colonizers about how to assimilate the colonized without granting equality or implying cultural equivalence," Jordan Sand writes, "as well as anxiety on the part of the colonized about how to gain equality without the cultural erasure of assimilation."[2]

However, unlike other empires,

1   Japan's was parochial—clustered around the home islands as buffer zones—to secure its borders from imperial predations;

2   contrary to V. I. Lenin's model in *Imperialism, the Highest Stage of Capitalism* (1916), when it began cobbling together its empire, Japan's industrial capitalist economy was still in its early developmental stages and thus not anywhere close to the "highest stage" at which empires were considered economically beneficial; and

3   with the doctrine of "Pan-Asianism," Japanese claimed cultural and ethnic kinship to the peoples they subjected to imperial rule, a claim no Dutchman would make in relation to Indonesians.

Apologetics for empire pitched Japan not as an "isolated archipelago, but rather as a continuum with the continent of Asia and the Pacific region" and "stressed resemblances and analogies, rather than differences" between Japanese and Pacific Asians. "These new paradigms of knowledge justified empire as a territorial unification of areas originally one but later divided." Robert Tierney describes the Japanese empire as a "triangular structure," because it consisted not simply of a "dyad composed of colonizer and colonized" but also included the West as "the (implicit) third party." This enabled imperialist proponents to claim that "Japanese resembled or were closer to the people they colonized" than to white imperialists, and that the imperial relationship between Japanese and Pacific Asians was qualitatively different from, say, that of the British and Indians.[3]

But Japanese imperialists' worst enemies were themselves. Specifically, the arrogant brutality of the military throughout occupied territories during World War II made Chinese and Southeast Asians realize that Japanese motives were not as altruistic as claimed. Wartime expediencies and matériel needs always trumped Japanese support for national independence movements and respectful, mutually beneficial partnerships. Unfortunately for continental and Pacific Asians, another of the Japanese empire's distinctive traits was the contrast between its altruistic ideals and the callous cruelty with which it was actually assembled and preserved. It is truly difficult to exaggerate the imperial military's methodically sadistic conduct. Even having studied it for decades, new disclosures can still nauseate me.

Until the 1980s, studies of imperialism centered on its political, strategic, and economic causes and effects, but in the last few decades scholars in literature, history, and other disciplines have undertaken cultural analyses of empire. The principal inspiration for this trend was the publication of Edward Said's (1935–2003) pioneering study *Orientalism* (1978). His fundamental argument, based primarily on literary texts about the Near/Middle East, is that European cultural representations of "orientals" were dehumanizing and thus an assertion of (imperialist) dominance over them. The privilege and ability to create such representations, and to generate ethnographic and historical "knowledge" about the colonized "other," was a prerogative monopolized by the powerful. As instruments for asserting dominance over subjugated peoples, cultural representations were neither innocuous nor innocent politically. In scholarship and the arts, Orientalism reflected and contributed to prejudiced imperial mind-sets: orientals became simplistic stereotypes, projections of European fantasies, and the obverse of everything "Occidental."[4]

Said's argument is not without significant limitations or weaknesses, but its implications remain enormous. French people who had never set foot in Algeria or Indochina, Britons who had never fired a weapon at a Zulu or Hindustani, Belgians who had never cut off a Congolese child's hand, were participants in imperialism when they consumed insidious orientalist representations in their fiction, art, stationery, music, theater, and cinema.

Their mental images of colonized peoples were distorted, prejudicial and lacking in empathy. Even children's literature and cartoons such as *Histoire de Babar le petite éléphant* (France, 1931), *Tintin au Congo* (Belgium, 1930–31), *The Jungle Book* (England, 1894), and *Tarzan of the Apes* (USA, 1914) depicted undifferentiated caricatures of "savage" peoples, requiring the civilizing influence of white imperialists.

Popular culture thus disseminated imperialist ideologies among people of all ages. Lenin argued that the seizure of empires served the interests of capital, but that governments and capitalists exploited nationalist hubris and mass media to build support for imperial expansion among the working classes. If imperialism did not serve their *economic* interests, the proletariat could be persuaded via expressive culture and propaganda that it served *other* interests instead. The rise of electronic mass media coincided neatly with the new imperialism, providing a platform for its masterminds to dress it "in the brightest colors" for mass consumption.[5]

Compared to their counterparts in British and French studies, Japan scholars were relatively slow to explore the impact of empire on culture and the significance of culture to empire. In 1984 one of the most respected senior historians of Japan stated, "There were no Japanese Kiplings, there was little popular mystique about Japanese overlordship and relatively little national self-congratulation."[6] Since the millennium there has been a flood of correctives, involving not just historians of Japan but also scholars in other disciplines who work on China, Taiwan, Korea, and Southeast Asia. Andre Schmid has urged scholars to treat the empire not as a side topic but as an integral part of the national history of modern Japan. Moreover, Schmid admonishes historians not to think of the empire as a consequence of Japan's modernization but as a component of that process.[7] That is, Japan assembled its empire while still under the unequal treaty regime and struggling to industrialize, enforce its educational policies nationwide, foster emperor-centered nationalism, and strengthen its military capabilities. "In essence," Louise Young writes, "the processes of state building and empire building became intertwined in Japan."[8] Japanese subjects also required convincing that an empire was worthy of their sacrifice, treasure, and blood.

As in the prior implementation of a neo-Confucian order overseen by warriors, and the sacralization of the monarchy, a new hegemonic negotiation ensued, to build an ideological consensus that imperialism was essential to Japan's very survival and destiny. But as the empire's borders expanded, new constituencies were brought into this negotiation: millions of colonial subjects—Ainu, Okinawans, aboriginal and Han Taiwanese, Koreans, Manchus, Chinese, Mongolians, Polynesians, Southeast Asians of every nationality, and hundreds of ethnic minority groups—had to determine whether their own interests were better served buying into or resisting Japan's imperial order. As an arena for these negotiations toward a compromise equilibrium, popular culture was essential.

Building an empire

Japanese motives for empire were rooted in security concerns that few could deny were plausible. When they saw that Britain was willing to go to war to keep supplying illegal opium to Chinese junkies, and that the US Navy was prepared to empty cannons to initiate commercial and diplomatic relations, Japanese understood immediately the ruthlessness of imperialism.[9] In the next two decades practically all of monsoon Asia—with the exceptions of Japan, Siam, and China—had become either colonies or clients of Western imperialists, and those exceptions were still beholden to humiliating infringements on their sovereignty. To the extent that there was a master plan at all, Japanese envisioned empire as an assemblage of buffers cocooning the home islands. The nearby world was threatening and that is one reason that Japan's overseas empire was nearer to the metropole than others—that, and the fact that there was so little territory left to colonize.

To secure the archipelago's frontier borders, sovereignty was asserted over Ezochi (renamed Hokkaidō) and the Ryūkyū islands (Okinawa), both of which became prefectures in the 1870s. In 1895 Taiwan became the spoils of war after Japan's decisive military throttling of Qing China. Japanese aspired to make it a model colony through scientific management of human and natural resources and thorough ethnographic investigation of the indigenous highlands people who had become a minority on the island after centuries of Chinese migrations. The aborigines were more resistant to imperial rule than Han Chinese were, and pacification took a decade. The Treaty of Shimonoseki that ended the war with China also granted territorial concessions for Japanese enclaves in Tianjin and Hangkou, and by the 1910s Japanese settlers (mostly prostitutes and businessmen) constituted the largest ethnic community in the Shanghai International Settlement. Imperial Japan's economic and military footprints in mainland China would only grow larger in the early twentieth century.

But throughout the Meiji period, Japanese officials and military strategists fixated most on the Korean peninsula as key to their security. The Mongol Empire had attacked Japan from the peninsula twice in the thirteenth century. The first time the Meiji oligarchy discussed attacking Chosŏn was in 1873, but for a perceived breach of protocol toward the emperor, not for strategic purposes. As factionalism in the Chosŏn royal court worsened and Western demands for trade and diplomacy intensified, Japanese policy makers came to fear that Korea was destined to become *somebody's* colony, likely China's or Russia's. Initially Japanese hypocritically imposed the unequal Treaty of Kanghwa (1876), then began meddling in fractious Chosŏn court politics, hoping to bring to power a faction of progressive Koreans whom Japanese could guide through the modernization process to transform them into stable, dependable allies. As this scenario became less plausible, Japan fought two wars, against China (1894–95) and Russia

(1904–05), ostensibly to preserve Korea's independence, but for de facto control of the peninsula. Japanese diplomats coerced the Korean king's advisers to sign a protectorate treaty in 1905, and then in 1910 abolished the 518-year-old Yi dynasty and annexed the peninsula.

Korea was Japan's last formal colony. After World War I, the League of Nations assigned to Japan governance of the South Seas Mandate (the Marshall, Caroline, and Northern Mariana Islands), Pacific islands previously under German rule. Japanese essentially administered these as a colony (called Nan'yō) unchallenged. From the 1931 Manchurian Incident, imperial expansion took the form of "nation-building" in nominally sovereign client states (Manchukuo and the Reorganized National Government of China), or military "liberation" and occupation of Euro-American colonies (Dutch East Indies, Philippines, Portuguese Timor, Burma, Malaya, Hong Kong, and Singapore). In the 1930s and 1940s expansion was considered part of Japan's "divine mission" to release Asians from the shackles of Western imperialism and unify them under the banner of Pan-Asian brotherhood. It was anti-imperialist imperialism, if you will.

Nearly everywhere Japanese forces and settlers went, they purposefully introduced locals to Japanese language and culture. In the formal colonies these were intensive policies; in client states and occupation zones, depending on who was in charge, what resources were available, and cost-benefit analyses, such efforts could be either zealous or lackadaisical. Cultural imperialism, the imposition of the imperialists' language, manners, religion, arts, and values on the colony, was a hallmark of modern empires. One of the most important insights of new imperial studies, however, has been that colonies had corresponding cultural impacts on their metropoles. Visual, musical, cinematic, literary, and theatrical iconographies of exotic, distant lands—the conduits for Said's orientalism—saturated the popular culture of imperial states and became important indices of the racial and cultural distinctions between colonizers and their subjects. This was no less true of Japanese popular culture, particularly in the 1920s and 1930s, when colonial exotica permeated adult and children's literature, popular music, theater, tourism, postcards, and other media. Empires were endlessly entertaining.

Popular culture and the colonial modern

Export of Japanese media products to the colonies was a synergistic venture between private capital and the imperial state: the state provided relatively stable, captive markets with an expanding urban middle class to consume entertainment commodities, while the culture industry provided products facilitating the proliferation of Japanese as the national language and the creation of cultural trends, attachments, and communities of taste binding metropole and colonies together. The urban consumer cultures of colonial Taiwan and Korea were a complex, cosmopolitan mixture of European,

American, Japanese, and native elements. Michael Robinson explains, "The bilingual nature of emerging popular culture, [and] the influence of Japanese and Western popular culture," disseminated via migrant laborers and new communications technologies, "militated against a simple dichotomy between a national and an Other identity."[10] The target demographic for this consumer culture were the Korean, Taiwanese, and Shanghainese counterparts to Japan's *moga* and *mobo*.[11]

Scholars of East Asia use the shorthand term "colonial modernity" for describing "a particular articulation of the universal notion of 'modernity' in the colonial context" in Japanese colonies and occupied territories in the 1920s and 1930s.[12] Japanese regimes and corporations exported media technologies and cultural content of Western origin to the colonies for the consumption of colonized people, to transform them into loyal subjects. However, colonized populations often used new media, technologies, economic and labor systems, and diversions to further their *own* interests. Thus colonial modernity was another example of hegemony: it was modernity conceived, refashioned, and lived by people under colonial domination, sometimes conforming to and sometimes obstructing the imperial state's agendas.

The conditions of colonial modernity produced a new social stratum generically known as the colonial (or nationalist) elite, who pursued new opportunities for social advancement, novel forms of identity and higher standards of living through consumption of Japanese popular culture. Whether through established socioeconomic privilege, personal moxie or serendipity, they earned educations, professional credentials, and linguistic and cultural proficiencies to operate within the parameters of colonial society. Colonial elites provided the white-collar labor required to administer, conduct business, and develop the colonies, but some became leaders of national independence movements. They also were the primary audience for popular entertainment.

The growth of mass media in Japan coincided almost exactly with the wars against China and Russia and the expansion of its empire to include Taiwan, Karafuto (southern Sakhalin), and Korea (see Chapter 7). The wars and acquisition of colonies were perfect fodder for print media, popular song, and film; they also opened opportunities for media companies to cultivate new markets. On June 17, 1925, the Government-General of Taiwan began radio broadcasting in Taipei, to commemorate the thirtieth anniversary of Japan's takeover of the island—this was over a year before the consolidation of Tokyo, Ōsaka, and Nagoya local broadcasters into what would become state-run NHK in the metropole. In 1927 NHK opened a fourth network affiliate (JODK) in Keijō/Kyŏngsŏng (Seoul). Initially on the air for about six hours a day, its Korean-language programming was one-third of that in Japanese. For Japanese settlers, that was too much, for Korean listeners not enough. In 1933 the network started broadcasting two signals, one in each language. In addition to news and morning calisthenics, broadcasts consisted of soap operas, lectures, traditional music, and some popular music. Book, magazine, and newspaper publishers; movie studios and theaters; and recording companies also slowly but deliberately established branches in the frontier markets of Taiwan and Korea. Publishing houses provided printed matter for Japanese settlers, and eventually on a smaller scale for locals in their vernacular languages.

The silent film narrator is exemplary of how culture imported from the metropole was reconfigured in colonial settings. Korean *pyŏnsa* and Taiwanese *benzi* required skills similar to the Japanese *benshi*'s—extemporaneous eloquence, charisma, and wit—as well as some knowledge of the West and Japan to explain and comment on imported films. Therefore, *benzi* and *pyŏnsa* tended to be of higher-class, better-educated backgrounds than *benshi* were. Very few were fluent enough to perform for Japanese or mixed audiences. Yet the *pyŏnsa* and *benzi* were not simply Japanese transplants; rather, they demonstrated the refraction of imported culture that characterized colonial modernity. They had the power to shape audiences' experiences and interpretations of the films they watched. This made them subject to police surveillance.

Recall from Chapter 5 that municipal officials and law enforcement in Japan worried that *benshi* had too much influence over theater audiences and the potential to disrupt public morals, and that therefore they were required to register with local police. The concerns of colonial police in Taiwan and Korea were less about mannerisms/*fūzoku* than about anti-Japanese nationalism. Their fears were not groundless. *Benzi* and *pyŏnsa* risked arrest by using their platforms to ridicule or criticize Japanese rule. In 1912 a *pyŏnsa*'s "passionate oration" sparked a riot between Japanese and Korean viewers at a Seoul theater. Watching a filmed bout between a Western boxer and Japanese *judō* master Maeda Mitsuyo (1878–1941), the *pyŏnsa* encouraged Koreans to root for the boxer. When Maeda prevailed, pandemonium ensued, with Japanese and Koreans hurling chairs, food, and seat cushions at one another. Another incident involved Korea's first blockbuster film, *Arirang* (1926), directed by and starring Na Ungyu (1902–37), and conventionally described as an expression of nationalist outrage. The film is lost, but a surviving script shows little evidence of such intent. Instead, it was *pyŏnsa* Sŏng Tongho's (1904–?) commentary that transformed *Arirang* into a nationalist statement. Similarly, when narrating *Ben Hur: A Tale of the Christ* (1925), Sŏ Sangp'il (1901–?) likened the slave revolt to the Korean independence struggle.[13]

Benzi were required to follow a preapproved script, with occasional improvised comment, for which they were scolded or arrested if they used foul or politically sensitive language. Unbeknownst to authorities, the Taiwanese word "dog" (*tákáu*) sometimes referred to Japanese; hence, "whenever the word 'dog' was uttered, it became a poignant moment rich with mutual recognition of the colonial structure shared by the *benzi* and their audiences. Those moments of linguistic play were potential forms of subaltern subversion, undermining the *authorship* of the films, and, by extension, the authoritarian hold the colonial regime had on the meaning of film texts."[14]

No less than cinema, the establishment of a commercial music industry was an essential aspect of colonial popular culture. It followed closely the Japanese trajectory described in the preceding chapter: commodification and corporatization of musical production and consumption that exploited advances in recording and broadcasting technologies; new contexts for live musical performance and appreciation, including commercial ballrooms; pop stardom for singers (and occasionally instrumentalists); and entirely new taxonomies distinguishing genres of musical product. There were interesting variations in the colonies, however, some of which were unintended consequences of official policies or Japanese corporate practices.[15]

Some of the most prominent purveyors of pop music in colonial Korea came from a profession legally classified as sexual labor. These were *kisaeng*, courtesan-entertainers somewhat analogous to Japanese geisha in that they were highly trained musicians, vocalists, calligraphers, dancers, poets, and conversationalists employed to entertain men at banquets and private parties. The distinction between them and geisha before the twentieth century was that *kisaeng* were government employees, recruited and trained as young girls for service at provincial- or state-level functions in the Chosŏn period. A series of reform measures issued by the Chosŏn government in 1894–96 (the Kabo Reforms) released *kisaeng* from government servitude, requiring them either to find work or start their own businesses in the entertainment sector. *Kisaeng* were among the first entertainers to perform at the state-sponsored modern theater, Wŏn'gaksa, and to take the stage in mixed-gender performances of the new *ch'anggŭk* operas.

The Japanese colonial government ordered the creation of "licensing academies" (K: *kwŏnbŏn*; J: *kenban*) to train and credential future *kisaeng*. Although beholden to the colonial state's regulatory standards, the women themselves ran *kwŏnbŏn* and trained *kisaeng* to be versatile enough to respond to cultural trends and to work in a variety of venues. A Korean businessman might request "Tokyo March," or an off-duty Japanese policeman could ask for an excerpt from a *p'ansori* libretto or court dance (*chŏngjae*). Some elder *kisaeng* stressed the importance of maintaining or adapting Korean singing and dancing traditions, while others ensured their pupils could sing narrative ballads from the geisha repertoire, or knew the latest popular songs (*kayo* or *yuhaengga*).[16]

So, although known as carriers of artistic traditions, during the colonial period *kisaeng* stepped out of their usual workplaces (teahouses, inns, and private parties) to stand at the vanguard of popular entertainment as self-employed entrepreneurs, performing for general audiences instead of their regular highfalutin clientele.[17] Traditionally known as "whispering flowers" (*haeŏhwa*), in modern times they became "broadcasting flowers" whose

FIGURE 6.1 *Gesang [sic] school (kwŏnbŏn), P'yŏngyang, postcard, 1904, Willard Dickerman Straight and Early US-Korea Diplomatic Relations Collection, Cornell University Library, Wikipedia Commons (https://ja.wikipedia.org/wiki/妓生).*

voices could be heard on recordings and radio, in concert halls and singing competitions, and at ceremonial events. For instance, in early May 1927, when the *Tong-a ilbo* newspaper celebrated the grand opening of its new office building, *kisaeng* from the Chŏnju *kwŏnbŏn* provided the entertainment, performing traditional dances, Western-style vocal songs (*ch'angga*) and folk songs (*chapga*).[18]

Not everyone was pleased about their new public visibility and audibility. In addition to lingering prejudice carried over from earlier times, the legal designation of *kisaeng* as sex workers (underlined by the continued use of the Chinese ideogram for "prostitute," *ji/ki*, in their job description) meant that many Koreans were appalled to hear their voices on the radio or otherwise witness their prominence in the media.[19] Their inherent eroticism worked both ways, however, inspiring prurient interest in both Koreans and Japanese and helping propel some individual *kisaeng* to celebrity. Like female pop stars today, sex appeal was an important element of their popularity—which is not to say that *kisaeng* twerked in public.

Of course, *kisaeng* were not the only people recording, broadcasting or performing music in colonial Korea. Japan's major record labels established branch offices and studios in colonies, hired local scouts, and sponsored singing competitions to identify new talent. A 1935 magazine article estimated that sales had reached 1,200,000 records a year, a third of which were Korean vocal music by native pop singers.[20] The modern "star system" that had emerged by the 1930s stirred public interest in celebrity gossip about pop stars such as the prolific Ch'ae Kyuyŏp (1906–49) and *kisaeng* Wang Subok (1917–2003). It also sparked fierce, cutthroat competition between the six record labels to sign new talent to exclusive contracts. One A&R man for Polydor put Wang into hiding to keep her from signing with Columbia. The Korea branch manager from Okeh "went to great lengths" to woo Yi Nanyŏng (1916–65) before she could commit to Taihei: "One night all of the employees of Okeh dressed in disguise and surrounded Taihei, and even engaged in a car chase." When Hwang Kŏmsim (1922–2001), unfamiliar with the rules of exclusive contracts, signed with both Okeh and Victor, the companies sued each other to land her.[21]

Diversity of musical styles reflected deeply rooted Korean regional identities. The peninsula-wide dissemination of these styles by Japanese-sponsored electronic media and modern live performance venues gave most Koreans their first exposure to that musical variety. In May 1936 the Chŏnju *kwŏnbŏn* hosted a recital in Seoul in which its pupils sang various provincial songs, and in May 1938 the *Chosŏn ilbo* newspaper sponsored a two-day Korean Regional Entertainment Competition, in which thirty female singers (including *kisaeng*) performed songs and dances from southern, western, and central provinces.[22] This diversity apparently irritated some more close-minded listeners and stirred debate about which regional styles best represented Korean national music (*kugak*). Nonetheless, recordings and radio broadcasts also encouraged Korean national identity, as Yano contends popular music did in Japan. "Though *yuhaengga* was a newly invented cultural production by modern Koreans," Ming-Jung Son says, "it also provided a cultural space in which Koreans re-articulated their traditional cultural identity while reflecting on modern values" and crafting "modern personas."[23] Aggressive assimilation policies precluded neither Koreans' appreciation of their own performing arts traditions nor the development of vernacular versions of modern popular music.

The Governments-General of Taiwan and Korea exercised tight censorship control over popular media in both colonies. They issued regulations for movies, books, magazines, newspapers, and recorded music that subjected them all to prepublication inspection. To be fair, almost identical regulations were in force in Japan, although in the colonies officials were particularly focused on content that expressed anti-Japanese nationalism. Nonetheless, it was possible for colonized East Asians to use popular culture for nationalist purposes or to critique either specific colonial policies or Japanese rule generally. Sport provided one such outlet, since by its very nature it was not censorable. In Taiwan, "baseball … became an instrument of nationalist assertion, indigenous self-respect and anti-imperial expression in the face of Japanese attempts to use the game as a means of political hegemonic control, militaristic purpose and cultural integration." As had been the case in the metropole, "military-style" athletics were promoted primarily through compulsory physical education in the school system, not only to "'build a physically well-developed body" but also to teach Taiwanese to "obey the rules." Some school officials worried that team sports in the colonies would stimulate nationalist sentiment, so they recommended individual sports such as gymnastics. For a time, participation in team sports was thus a privilege for Japanese settlers, and "Taiwanese" squads consisting only of Japanese nationals played in international competition. The officials' predictions were not wrong: when a multiethnic team whose starting nine were two Han Chinese, four aborigines, and three Japanese who qualified for and played in the prestigious Kōshien high school tournament in 1931, Taiwanese were elated and more young people took up the sport.[24]

Recall from Chapter 5 that a Korean football team took the 1935 JFA Cup and two of its players were added to the Japanese national side for the 1936 Berlin Olympics. Yet this was hardly the most notorious incident of Korean sport nationalism. At the same Olympiad two Korean marathoners representing Japan, Son Kijŏng (1912–2002), and Nam Sŭngnyong (1912–2001), took gold and bronze medals, respectively. Discreetly concealing the Japanese flag on his uniform with his laurel branch, Son bowed his head solemnly as the Japanese anthem *Kimigayo* was played at the medal ceremony. The *Tong-a ilbo* was more brazen, printing an altered image in which the Japanese flag was totally erased from Son's uniform (though, curiously, not from Nam's). Eight newspaper staffers spent nine months in prison for that little stunt.[25] Koreans' public delight about the medals irritated Japanese authorities. In its *Annual Report* the Government-General—like all tyrants, oblivious to irony—fumed, "The victory of the Korean marathon racer at the Olympic Games at Berlin in August of [1936] was seized as a sign of the superiority of the Korean race, arousing almost fanatic excitement, fanned by certain Korean Nationalists, which did much to harm popular tranquility. The minds of the people have now however gradually settled down aided by the careful guidance of the authorities."[26]

The introduction of mass-mediated popular culture to the colonies served a number of Japanese imperialist purposes: it enabled Japanese settlers to stay connected with trends and fashions in the metropole; it was useful for propaganda among native populations, to inform them of their obligations as subjects of the Empire of Japan and to bind them more closely to the metropole; and it offered virtually unlimited economic opportunities for the corporate culture industry (publishers, movie studios, and recording companies) to infiltrate new markets, attract new consumers, and make millions of yen. These goals were mostly realized, and the modern girls and boys in colonial cities such as Taipei, Harbin, Seoul, Shanghai, and Pusan were indeed drawn to Japanese entertainment and diversions as the most up-to-date in East Asia.

But popular culture also served the interests of colonized people, giving them new opportunities to participate in a cosmopolitan culture that appealed to them, and also new avenues toward economic advancement and fame, as film narrators, pop stars, actors, and athletes. With the exception of *benzi/pyŏnsa*, these avocations were open to women, giving them at least some degree of economic autonomy and control over their own destinies. *Kisaeng* were among those who took greatest advantage of these opportunities and openly advocated for themselves in the face of stigma and prejudice, using stage, screen, radio, and records to take control of media representations of themselves. In addition to such opportunities for individual advancement, popular culture gave colonial subjects tools for expressing collective national identities, which faced all but total obliteration in the face of Japanese assimilation campaigns. The successes of individual Koreans and Taiwanese as witnessed in the mediascape were taken as national victories and a thumb in the eye of their imperialist oppressors.

Colonial kitsch

People nowadays would be horrified—I hope—by the images that used to appear on picture postcards at the turn of the nineteenth and twentieth centuries. French and Dutch grandmothers might find in their mailboxes images of bare-breasted Algerian harem girls or Afro-Surinamese men in loincloths, respectively. Their American counterparts might receive a postcard depicting the mutilated body of a lynched black man, hanging from a tree in the Jim Crow South. And Japanese grandmothers plausibly received images of Taiwanese aborigines, posing with one or more severed heads.[27] What did people say when sending "colonial porn" to a beloved matriarch? "Wish you were here, Nana!"?

In the age of high imperialism, colonial sex, violence, and exotica were standard fare in popular media, which disseminated orientalist stereotypes of savagery, backwardness, and inferiority supposedly justifying imperialist intervention and its civilizing influence. Even the primitivist strain of modernism (see Chapter 5), which glorified and glamorized the simple, primordial barbarism of colonized people, bore orientalist poison. The latest scholarship on Japanese "cultures of empire" brings to our attention the prominence of colonial visual and aural imagery in interwar popular culture. Nayoung Aimee Kwon calls this "colonial kitsch," referring as an example to a 1938 Japanese theatrical production of the venerable Korean *p'ansori* tale *Ch'unhyang*; its producer considered it an introduction to Korea's cultural essence for Japanese audiences. Jennifer Robertson's provocative suggestion that the all-female Takarazuka Revue was a "technology of Japanese imperialism" can be applied to film, popular music, literature, and graphic arts as well.[28]

It is equally important to recognize the semi- or unofficial nature of so much imperial and wartime propaganda. With reference again to Takarazuka, Robertson says, "The relationship between the revue theater and the state was more a matter of mutual convenience and opportunism than of seamless consensus or total state control over forms of popular entertainment."[29]

（付發店画井板昌節参）　NRCK OOT IN ABORIGINES, FORMOSA.　首戯人蕃生

FIGURE 6.2 *Nrck cot in Aborigines, Formosa (Seibanjin kakushu), postcard,*
1911. Image courtesy Special Collections and College Archives, Skillman Library,
Lafayette College, and the East Asia Image Collection (http://digital.lafayette.edu/
collections/eastasia/).

Revue founder Kobayashi Ichizō, equally passionate about both Japan's
imperial mission and box office receipts, embodied the nationalist entrepreneur who profited from Japanese imperial expansion by integrating state
ideology into entertainment. Certainly, the imperial state had strong views
about what sorts of imagery and messages were *not* appropriate, and was

unsparing with the rod of correction; it was also unreserved suggesting what messages it expected to see in the media. Nevertheless, compared to the more intrusive top-down approach of the contemporaneous Nazi and Soviet regimes, the private sector did much of the Japanese imperial state's propaganda work. Profits, fears of crackdowns, and genuine patriotism were sufficient motivations for the culture industry to promote imperialism. Regardless of their own individual purposes, ideologies or opinions, by "providing publicity," filmmakers, cartoonists, songwriters, actors, novelists, and their media sponsors "indirectly supported state aims" and made money doing it.[30]

As far back as the Edo period, depictions of foreigners in visual, aural, and performance art were methods whereby Japanese could define the parameters of their own ethnic, cultural, and national identities (this is by no means a peculiar Japanese practice). In modern times the seizure of colonies and display of their peoples to both domestic and international audiences provided Japanese with regular opportunities to articulate both their own distinctiveness through the exhibition of difference, as well as to demonstrate to their own great power tormenters Japan's modernity, military prowess, and commitment to the "civilizing mission."

In the era of high imperialism it was common practice for imperial powers to organize ethnological exhibits in which live human beings from their empires were paraded before gawking audiences. The greater the variety of peoples and the wider the gaps in culture, civilizational development, and race, the more impressive and popular such displays were. At the 1904 Louisiana Purchase Exposition, for instance, several North American Indian tribes; Philippine Igorrots and Negritos; Patagonians from Argentina; Zulu, Swazi, and Ndebele villagers from British South Africa; and Mbuti pygmy Ota Benga (1883–1916) from the Belgian Congo were on display as "living exhibits."[31] Japan's exhibit featured nine Ainu, recruited from Piratori and Sapporo by an American anthropologist to live in a faux Ainu *kotan* (village) in St. Louis for seven months: Sangyea, Santukno, and their daughter, Kin; Kutoroge, Shutratek, and their baby girl, Kiko; newlyweds Yazo and Shirake; and Bete Goro (whom the anthropologist considered too "Japanized"). Although deemed "far above the average of their race," the Ainu were among the Fair's most popular exhibits. One reporter rhapsodized, "the inmates of the little hut of thrushes, in their neatness, their gentleness and courtesy, offer a rare example of sweet and simple living ... Of all the people at the fair, none seem more truly God's own children than the Ainu of Japan."[32]

Of course, laying eyes on colonized people out of captivity or in their natural habitats was far more thrilling to metropolitan audiences. When a group of prominent aboriginals from Taiwan visited Tokyo in 1912 to observe conditions in the metropole, a police escort had to hold back throngs of gawkers in Asakusa who gathered around to get closer looks at the visitors' attire and tattooed faces. After the last aboriginal revolts

in Taiwan were quelled in 1923, a tourism infrastructure enabled sightse-
ers to view pacified indigenes in their own communities. Around the same
time, some Ainu communities sought to lure tourists through selective cultural preservation or recovery, reviving rites and customs such as the sacred
iyomante festival (involving sacrifice of a bear or owl), which the previous
two generations had been forced to abandon, and performing them for visitors. Imperialism indeed provided the basis for Japan's organized tourism
industry: the Japan Tourism Board was founded two years after the annexation of Korea, precisely to facilitate recreational travel to the peninsula.
Because of its voluntary nature, Kenneth Ruoff argues that Japanese traveling around the empire were engaged in self-administered "citizenship training" and indoctrination in imperial ideology.[33]

Picture postcards (*e-hagaki*) and the stamps used to mail them were
some of the most prominent media by which images of colonized people
circulated within the metropole and wider Japanese empire. Before photography became standard in newspapers in the early 1920s, postcards were
"the dominant source of photographic imagery from the colon[ies]."[34] Their
"everyday-ness" demonstrates how thoroughly ingrained the possession of
an empire was in Japanese consciousness. Aside from occasional shots of
modernized urban settings such as Seoul, Taipei, and Dàlián (Manchuria),
or of Japanese-built landmarks such as shrine complexes, their emphasis
was almost always on exotic subject matter: landscapes and people in native
costume engaged in quaint or primal customs. Paul Barclay notices that in
one collection he has examined, Han Chinese, 91 percent of Taiwan's population in the early 1930s, were subjects of only 23 percent of images. The
camera clearly favored the less populous, more exotic highland aborigines.[35]

As mentioned in Chapter 4, Japanese first encountered Taiwan indigenes
in 1874 when an expeditionary force attacked the Paiwan in retribution for
the slaughter of 54 Ryūkyūan mariners. Media coverage emphasized the
widespread practice of headhunting and (falsely) cannibalism among most
indigenous tribes, which symbolized their barbarity and required the civilizing influence of Japanese intervention. Ironically, headhunting had been
a centuries-old practice among samurai, who brought the severed heads of
enemy combatants to their commanders to prove their number of kills and
get paid accordingly. Moreover, after uprisings by Seediq indigenes in Wushe
(central Taiwan) in 1930–31, Japanese troops permitted other Seediqs to
behead surrendered rebels.[36] Although the civilizing of colonial subjects
was a common theme throughout Japanese imperial discourse, as the most
stereotypically exotic and "savage" (*banjin*) of the lot, indigenous Taiwanese
were the most intriguing and entertaining to general audiences.

Another favorite subject of colonial iconography was the *kisaeng*, who
became the most potent human emblem representing Korean tradition.
Most images of *kisaeng* I have seen do not picture them in their work
clothes and elaborately braided and curled hairstyles, but rather in simple
clothing that emphasized their rusticity compared to geisha—whether this

added to or detracted from their appeal depended on the observer. One postcard features a *kisaeng* with a geisha, but the caption only mentions the Korean, referring to her as a "natural beauty who harmonizes seamlessly" with the Korean landscape. As a feminine symbol for the colonized peninsula, the *kisaeng*, "whose purpose in life was to gratify her patrons," represented demure, dutiful compliance, "everything many Japanese wished their Korean subjects to be."[37]

In 1931 the Chinese Northeast, Manchuria, became another important pillar of the empire, but as a "client state" rather than as a colony. The Imperial Japanese Army—which took military control of the region in defiance of orders from Tokyo—claimed the action as a "liberation" of indigenous Manchurians, Han Chinese, Koreans, Mongolians, and Japanese settlers from the incompetent rule of Chiang Kai-shek's (1887–1975) Nationalist government. The interwar international community and the League of Nations frowned upon the naked seizure of colonies, so the foundation of the State of Manchukuo in 1932 under the leadership of the last Manchurian Qing emperor, Puyi (1906–67), was touted as national "self-determination."[38]

Throughout the 1930s, Manchukuo became a fixture of popular culture in the metropole. Indeed, in the wake of the global depression after 1929, "the entertainment and publishing world looked upon the outbreak of the Manchurian Incident as manna from heaven."[39] Visual culture focused generally on rural folk who represented the "five races under one union," including Japanese agrarian settlers working to convert Manchuria's vast grasslands into productive arable farmland. Other images included Manchukuo's cutting-edge architecture, urban planning, infrastructural and agricultural development, and foreign capital investment, all of which surpassed those in the metropole. Japanese were told and shown by the South Manchurian Railway (SMR, 1906–45) Corporation's propaganda that Manchukuo was a blank canvas onto which Japanese could paint modernity in its most vibrant colors.[40] A Manchukuo/SMR exhibition of the Golden Temple of Jehol at the 1933–34 Chicago World Exposition was a desperate effort to persuade the world of Manchukuo's sovereignty, but came off as just another colonial display.[41]

Manchuria and Korea produced two of interwar Japan's biggest celebrities: Yamaguchi Yoshiko (1920–2014), an actress and singer who passed as Chinese under the pseudonym Lǐ Xiānglán (pronounced Ri Kōran in Japanese), and Ch'oe Sŭnghŭi (Sai Shōki in Japanese, 1911–69), a modern dancer and choreographer who rose to fame in the metropole with her adaptations of traditional Korean dances. Both embodied for the public the possibilities of cultural innovation and collaboration within Japan's New Order in Asia. They were "exotically familiar," different enough to be entertaining, yet since both spoke fluent Japanese they could be held up as tangible evidence of the wisdom and efficacy of colonial assimilation policies in Northeast Asia. It did not hurt that both women were stunning beauties who were neither threatening nor (openly) disaffected with Japanese rule. They thus stood in stark contrast to the recalcitrant colonial male icons: the feral aboriginal headhunter, the troublemaking "Korean malcontent" (*futei senjin*) and the marauding Chinese "bandit" (*bazoku, hizoku*) who sabotaged infrastructure and terrorized Japanese settlers in Manchuria.[42] At a discursive level, at least, Ch'oe and Yamaguchi's femininity mediated a relationship between Japanese and colonial "others" that frequently exploded into violence and reprisals when the menfolk got involved.

Ch'oe Sŭng-hŭi was born to an aristocratic family at the dawn of colonial rule in Korea. Despite widespread prejudice that "dance was something low and crude," performed by disgraceful *kisaeng* at drinking parties, she was entranced by the "linear rhythm of beautiful bodies flowing like water … like a delightful dream" at a performance by the Japanese modern dance pioneer Ishii Baku (1886–1962), and went to Tokyo at age fifteen as his pupil. Her star first rose after a 1934 Tokyo recital for which she choreographed and performed new material based on various Korean dance traditions. "I thought to myself: there is no one else of Korean birth intending to dance, so I must represent Korea, and create dances from the traditions of my homeland."[43] It was a brilliant move in a cultural marketplace favorable to colonial exotica.

Although her principal audiences were well-heeled urbanites, she also had a much wider following as a popular celebrity. In 1936, at the ripe old age of twenty-five, Ch'oe published an autobiography; starred in a semiautobiographical film, *The Dancing Princess of the Peninsula* (*Hantō no maihime*); and was featured in advertisements for cosmetics and other products. As Japan's global reputation sagged under the weight of its war with Republican China in the late 1930s, Ch'oe proved to be a propagandist's dream as a cultural ambassador: she was an assimilated ethnic Korean who could testify to the benefits of Japanese imperial rule and pan-Asian cultural ideals among skeptics abroad.[44] Because her work was a self-conscious synthesis of costumes, gestures, and movements from continental Asia, some lauded it as the first successful example of the sort of pan-Asian art they hoped would become the pillar of cultural life in the Japan-led New Order.

Yamaguchi Yoshiko was similarly bicultural: she was born to Japanese parents and raised in Manchuria, had Han Chinese godparents, and grew up speaking Mandarin in school. But when she shot to initial stardom neither Chinese nor Japanese audiences were aware of her true nationality. It was a dangerous charade, concocted by film producers, that almost cost Yamaguchi her life. After the Japanese surrender in 1945, the Chinese Nationalists arrested and charged her with treason (more precisely, *hànjiān*, betrayal of the Han Chinese racial state) for appearing in Japanese "national policy films" (*kokusaku eiga*). She was spared execution only by the retrieval of her Japanese birth certificate, which very easily could have been destroyed in the war.

FIGURE 6.3 *Sai Shōki [Ch'oe Sŭnghŭi] Dance Recitals program, November 28–30, 1940, Tokyo Takarazuka Theater (http://www.kiyo-books.jp/?p=143).*

Her 1938 debut as Lǐ Xiānglán /Ri Kōran occurred when the Manchuria Film Association, on the lookout for a bilingual beauty, signed her to appear in national policy films, the purposes of which were to foster affective bonds between Japanese and the peoples of Manchuria and to educate audiences about official aspirations for a New Order in Asia. Although several other singing actresses had donned Chinese costume and spoken phonetic "Chinese" onscreen, Michael Baskett affirms that "No single personality so perfectly exemplified the exoticism, mystery, and allure of a Japanified China" or "exuded authenticity" as Lǐ did. Her authenticity was strangely versatile, however, because her roles included characters from each of Manchukuo's "five races" (Japanese, Korean, Chinese, Russian, and Mongolian), making her a "powerful tool of propaganda," the very "fulfillment of the catchphrase 'Asia is one.' "[45]

Lǐ's most notorious contributions to imperial pop were her starring roles opposite leading man Hasegawa Kazuo (1908–84) in the "Continental Trilogy" about interracial romances: *Song of the White Orchid* (1939), *China Nights* (1940), and *Oath of the Burning Sand* (1940). In each of these "goodwill films" (*shinzen eiga*), intended for audiences in both Manchukuo and Japan, Lǐ played a spirited Chinese woman whose anti-Japanese nationalism crumbles when she falls in love with Hasegawa's dashing Japanese studmuffin. The films narrate the "gendered domestication of Chinese women," showing how "Chinese pride" makes Lǐ's characters initially oblivious to "the kind intentions" of the Japanese. These movies thus attribute resistance to "misunderstanding" and centuries-old notions of Chinese superiority, and subtly hint at what measures might be required to overcome this excessive self-veneration: "The irony of the goodwill film genre is that the non-Japanese characters were able to arrive at an understanding of the sincerity of Japan's intentions only through ... acts of physical violence."[46] When Hasegawa slapped Lǐ in the face in *China Nights*, Japanese aggression was recast onscreen as tough love. Was John Wayne emulating Hasegawa when he famously spanked Maureen O'Hara in *Flintlock* (1963)?

The theme song of *China Nights* represents yet another example of imperialist popular culture: the "continental melodies" (*tairiku merodi*) referencing China and Manchuria that proliferated from 1938 to 1941. These ditties were "evocations of continental Asia," produced and consumed to create a sense of "exoticism" or "pleasure in the foreign." They took a variety of forms, such as "scenery songs" (*fūkei mono*) with lyrical "images expressed by noun phrases, rather than complete sentences" to "create loose symbolic frames within which the foreign can be imagined," Edgar Pope observes. These were "Liminoid spaces where the listener can play with exotic images and sensations." Clothing, famous landscapes or buildings, ethnic implements or transportation (for example, Chinese junks), hairstyles, smells, sounds, tastes—all were potential signifiers of exotica in such songs.[47] Another way of evoking the continent was to orchestrate Asian folk songs for modern dance ensembles, as Sugii Kōichi did for King Records' Salon

FIGURE 6.4 *Li Xianglan. Wikipedia Commons (https://en.wikipedia.org/wiki/Yoshiko_Yamaguchi#/media/File:Li_Xianglan.jpg).*

Music Series. These late-1930s arrangements possibly served dual purposes. On the one hand, they tapped into contemporary popular interest in all things China that swept Japan, interestingly enough, as soon as the two countries went to war. On the other hand, they allowed dance musicians to appear compliant and accommodating toward the imperial state, at a time when commercial ballrooms, their primary workplaces, were under constant threat of shutdown (which indeed happened in 1940).[48]

Popular media brought empire home to millions of Japanese who would never venture outside of the home islands. Songs, postcards, travel guides, musicals, movies, and novels all exploited and stoked popular interest in the myriad peoples under Japanese colonial domination. The media culture magnified the revue-like presentation of the empire that appeared on Takarazuka stages as a "montage-like display and concatenation of different, even contradictory, images, lands, settings, peoples, and scenarios."[49] Popular culture had a paradoxical effect, distancing metropolitan Japanese from Koreans, Chinese, Taiwan indigenes, Ainu, and others by emphasizing their odd customs, exotic dress, and relative underdevelopment, but also fostering a degree of intimacy through pan-Asian rhetoric, possessive phrases such as *waga hantō* (our [Korean] peninsula) and individual celebrities like Ch'oe and Yamaguchi who were talented, attractive and cooperative. Popular culture gave a wider segment of the population a sense of involvement and investment in the empire, which became even more crucial as increasing numbers of families saw their sons, brothers, nephews, cousins, and fathers mobilized for military service in its furthest corners.

Imperialism as national service

Besides presenting entertaining exotica, popular culture admonished Japanese civilians to get more involved as "grassroots agents of empire."[50] Large-scale suasion campaigns by governmental and corporate entities like the Hokkaidō Development Commission (1869–82), the Manchuria Colonization Corporation (1937–45) and the SMR deployed visual, textual, cinematic, and aural media to recruit settlers from the poorest rural regions for relocation to Hokkaidō, Karafuto, Taiwan, Korea, and Manchuria. Ostensibly this would relieve population pressures in the archipelago and give migrants boundless opportunities for prosperity in territories in which they would automatically have privileged status by virtue of being Japanese.

Endlessly creative in devising ways for all Japanese to stay (or look) busy serving the imperial state, official propagandists and the entertainment industry were also adept at targeting specific constituencies by age, gender, occupation, and region through a variety of media. Domesticity and motherhood were frequently said to be the bedrock of imperial viability. Implicit in the official slogan "good wives, wise mothers" (*ryōsai kenbō*) was the concept of the domestic sphere as at least a semipublic space, in which the physical and spiritual nourishment of the emperor's future subjects took place. Indeed, colonial assimilation is equated with standard enculturation through childrearing in Koizumi Kikue's autobiographical story *Manchu Girl* (*Manshūjin no shōjo*, 1938), which depicts "motherhood as a means of enacting imperialism." Koizumi's decision to adopt her maid, Guiyu, "is seemingly motivated by maternal sentiment rather than imperialist desire," and thus Guiyu's assimilation as culturally Japanese is "naturalized" and "justified."[51] A 1941 cookbook for Japanese housewives living in Korea shows how concern with nutrition, food scarcity, economy, and settler identification with the homeland were invoked to make the private kitchen a location for the performance of "imperial citizenship." In its preface the cookbook exhorts, "Whether the meals of one million Japanese comply with national policies is critical to the management of the entire nation and can even determine its rise and fall."[52] When it came to imperialism and war, every aspect of Japanese life could—should—be marshaled to conform with "national policies" (kokusaku).

Children's literature also employed not-so-subtle persuasive tactics to involve youngsters in empire building. Stories, songs, and pictures of overseas conquest and settlement were intended to shape the imaginative lives of children. Statesman and scholar Nitobe Inazō (1862–1933) thought that children's stories should foster a thirst for travel and adventure that he believed was crucial for maintaining and expanding the empire. To address a "relative paucity of colonial prototypes and heroes," imperial ideologues sought to mine traditional folklore for role models and narratives, which had the advantage of being a "domestic resource" rather than an imported one. The "mobilization of folklore for empire served to show that Japanese imperialism was not simply an imitation of Western empires but an inalienable part of its cultural heritage."

It so happened that Japan's quintessential folk hero, Momotarō (the Peach Boy), was perfect for the task. In this folktale from Okayama, an old woman doing laundry sees a giant peach floating downriver toward her. She brings it home and with her husband breaks it open to find a boy, who exclaims that he was sent from heaven to be the childless couple's son. After a few years Momotarō befriends several talking animals—a dog, monkey and pheasant—who join him in the conquest of the Isle of Demons (Onigashima). He returns triumphantly to his parents' home, bearing the demons' treasures with him, so that his family can live comfortably. Since Momotarō's story involved the conquest of an island of ogres and the seizure of their treasures, and the legend was indigenous, Nitobe determined that it was the perfect allegory for imperial expansion. In his mind, the ogres were South Pacific savages who would benefit from the "missionary social work" of colonialism and its civilizing impact.[53]

Another character intended to enthuse boys about imperialist adventures in the South Pacific was Bōken (Adventurous) Dankichi, hero of an eponymous comic strip by Shimada Keizō (1900–73) that ran in the magazine Youth Club (Shōnen kurabu, 1933–39). Shimada confessed to having childhood fantasies of ruling a tropical island paradise with "neither money worries nor homework." The light-skinned boy-hero Dankichi colonizes a tropical island, subduing both its man-eating fauna and its black-skinned,

FIGURE 6.5   *Bōken Dankichi takes his subjects to the Hinomaru Jinja
(National Flag Shrine), Keizō Shimada, Lambiek Comiclopedia (https://www.
lambiek.net/artists/s/shimada_keizo.htm).*

grass-skirted, thick-lipped cannibal inhabitants. To tell his undifferentiated
subjects apart, he paints numbers on their chests. Tierney remarks that
Dankichi's lack of distinction drives home the point that "every Japanese
colonizer, no matter how mediocre, is superior to any member of the conquered people, no matter how outstanding, simply by virtue of being from
a conquering country … His adventures suggest that colonialism is simple,
fun, and above all, within the capacity of even the most ordinary and callow
Japanese."[54] It is sobering to consider that some boys who grew up reading
Bōken Dankichi fought in the Pacific War when they grew older, learning
firsthand that the seizure, pacification, and defense of insular colonies was
much more dangerous than it had been for Dankichi.

However, children's literature in the colonies often expressed local interests. As a college student in Tokyo, Korean writer Pang Chunghwan (1899–1931) was impressed by serialized adventure stories in children's magazines, which he said "develop good things that can't be taught in ordinary ethics textbooks ... [and] develop a strong and beautiful power" in young readers. The narratives of Pang's adventure stories for Korean children were premised on the perils and indignities of colonial status and lost sovereignty. If Japanese children could conquer overseas ogres, Korean children had demons with whom to wrestle at home. Their "geographical imaginations" sharply circumscribed, Korean children read stories about rescuing siblings or friends from human trafficking and other travails associated with Korea's subjugation. Pang's stories for *Orini* (a magazine published by the Ch'ŏndogyo religious community) emphasized Korean collaboration and self-reliance. Hyungjun Han writes, "The adventure story was not an end but a means. Through it, [Pang] sought to make the children of colonial Korea into a body brought together by the unifying principle of nationhood."[55] Of course, both Korean and Japanese adventure stories promoted children's efficacy and duties to nation, yet like other colonial-modern popular culture mentioned earlier, Koreans transformed a medium imported from Japan into an expression of their own feelings and interests.

Popular media emphasized repeatedly the obligation of all Japanese subjects, in the metropole and in the colonies, to engage actively and mindfully in the imperial state's grandest, boldest ventures. Age, gender, occupation, health or physical capacity did not preclude *some* form of national service. This is to say neither that the state had the capacity to actually compel the levels of involvement it sought nor that all Japanese subjects eagerly responded—if indeed they had, why would propaganda be necessary? But whether they participated in empire or not, most Japanese *consumed* it, and all but the most radical elements in society believed empire was beneficial both to Japanese and to colonized peoples. To be fair, some courageous, high-profile individuals condemned the most brutal pacification campaigns, particularly the crackdown on the March 1, 1919, national uprising in Korea, but even they believed that Koreans, Taiwanese, and other Asians were ill-equipped to govern themselves, and that therefore Japanese rule was a beneficent force for peace and stability in East Asia. Popular culture kept telling them what they wanted to hear.

Imperialism as self-remonstrance

Popular culture was indispensable for making imperialism seem palatable, thrilling, even noble and obligatory. Media messages repeatedly drew on pseudoscientific discourses of racial difference, human cultural evolution, and strategic interests to persuade metropolitan audiences of their own superiority and prerogative to govern "inferior" people in the national interest. Yet, in closing this chapter, it is worth noting another significant insight of new imperial studies: imagery and discourse about the colonial other could become a form of self-criticism in the metropole. We saw earlier that romanticized views of primordial societies and their simpler life ways sometimes underlined colonial mentalities. A backhanded compliment, to be sure, it was also a double-edged sword that could cut its wielder quite deeply. Indeed, part of being modern is the painful recognition of the loss of values and lifestyles that did not survive industrial modernization, the rise of nation-states and secular rationalization. In most developed countries, popular culture provides vehicles for nostalgia—indeed, it has become one of entertainment's most important functions.

The purported ethnological and cultural affinities between Japanese, Koreans, and other Pacific Asians lent a particular poignancy to some variants of Japanese imperialist discourse. Japanese could look at continental or insular Asians and say, "They're so backward compared to us," or gasp, "This is who we once were, but no longer are." The British claimed that people in India were stalled in an earlier developmental stage, but rarely would they identify with Indians enough to see primeval versions of themselves. For Japanese it was—or could be—different. As ongoing research on the "ethnogenesis" of the Japanese race continued into the early twentieth century, producing theories that Japanese were the product of mixing among South Pacific Malays, archipelago indigenes (Jōmon/Emishi/Ezo/Ainu), and Northeast Asian migrants, a sense of genetic connection seemed to have more scientific than merely sentimental bases. Japanese had always regarded modernization as a mixed bag. Even its most eloquent proponent, Fukuzawa Yukichi, had likened it to a communicable disease. The antitheses of modernity and civilizational maturity were, theoretically, purity and innocence; barbarity could be glossed as integrity, civilization as contamination.

Kim Brandt, Robert Tierney, and I have documented at length this "colonial nostalgia" in imperial Japanese history.[56] Here I would like to use a short piece of music criticism to make the point. Koga Masao (1904–78), the most successful and well-known writer of sentimental ballads in Japan, spent part of his childhood in Inch'ŏn and ascribed his signature melodic style to his immersion in Korean folk songs and "the reverberations of the Korean zither [kayagŭm]." His rendition of the Korean folk song "Arirang," voiced by diva Awaya Noriko and Korean crooner Ch'ae Kyuyŏp (using the Japanese pseudonym Hasegawa Ichirō) and accompanied by the Meiji University Mandolin Orchestra, became a hit record in the autumn of 1932. Later that year Koga published an homage to "Arirang" and Korean folk music generally, insisting that profound mysteries of the Korean psyche could be extrapolated from it. For the songwriter, "an eerie, overarching pathos" was the defining characteristic of Korean folk songs. Koga then compared Korean and Japanese folk songs, saying flatly, "Korean folk songs are superior to Japanese folk songs as musical art."

The technique of Japanese folk songs, and the aspects of Korean folk songs born from an extremely free soil, express the national characteristics of both countries. In Japanese folk songs, there is the great influence of the *shamisen* as an accompanying instrument … In Korea there are few instruments, and aside from pounding on stones in ancient times, or using the harp and drum, [Koreans] do not usually accompany singing. Because of this, the peasants sing when they meet for work, they sing when they are sad, and they sing if happy. It is through songs that they express and console themselves.

Koga used his appreciation of "Arirang" to lament the still-nascent industrial production of popular songs, which had fundamentally transformed the process of creating music, distinguished performers from listeners and separated song from life. Koga himself had participated in this transformation and made a fortune from it. In 1932 he said mass-produced Japanese music expressed contrived, inauthentic emotions, while Korean songs retained their sincerity, directness, and emotional purity. His own artistic goal was to retain the latter qualities in his own songs despite their existence as commodities.[57]

It makes no difference whether Koga was correct about the sincerity and purity of Korean songs compared to Japanese pop ditties: what matters is that his musical assessment inverted the conventional imperial hierarchy, so that Koreans had the advantage over Japanese. This is but one example of many throughout the colonial world, in which the more loudly proclaimed assertions of metropolitan superiority were countered by softly spoken reflections on the moral, social, and aesthetic disadvantages and costs of being modern and sitting on top of the world.

CHAPTER SEVEN

"Our spirit against their steel"— mobilizing culture for war

One of the many slogans of the Meiji era was *fukoku kyōhei*, "rich country, strong military," an acknowledgment that military might was one of the two pillars of national survival. In their roughly seven-decade history (1873–1945), the Imperial Japanese Army and Navy were involved in three all-out wars and a handful of smaller-scale campaigns and skirmishes that earned them both valuable experience and international respect. Japanese forces also participated in multinational operations: in 1900, they were in the Eight-Nation Alliance that entered Beijing to smash the Boxer Rebellion, a summer-long siege of foreign legations by rural insurgents known as the Society of Righteous and Harmonious Fists (Yihétuán); and the Siberian Intervention (1918–22) to aid White Russians in their civil war against the ascendant Bolsheviks. They joined the Allies in World War I, seizing German Micronesia and attacking the Kaiser's territorial concession in Qingdao, China (where the Imperial Navy launched history's first aerial assault from a seaplane carrier).

Each of Japan's three major wars—against Qing China (1894–95), against Imperial Russia (1904–05), and against Republican China, the United States, the Netherlands, Britain, Australia, and New Zealand (1937–45)—strained its military and economic capacity and took increasingly heavy tolls on its population. This is precisely why popular culture was so important to Japan's capacity to make war. In each case, Japan had notable material disadvantages that made victory a long shot. Official and unofficial propagandists used popular media to create and disseminate myths about the compensating spiritual resources of the Japanese military specifically and the population generally, which theoretically explained their victories and emboldened them to face future battles against overwhelming odds. Each war was imbued with noble purpose—usually some variation on "peace in Greater East Asia"—that Japanese could achieve despite material deficits, with recourse to their cultural heritage of *bushidō*, the Way of the Warrior.

In 1899 the polymath Dr. Nitobe Inazō wrote in English a book entitled *Bushidō: The Soul of Japan*, which some readers considered an explanation of Japanese military successes against China a few years earlier. Originating among the hereditary warrior caste, the "moral influence" of *bushidō* had infiltrated the entire Japanese population, Nitobe declared.[1] In reimagining *bushidō* as a comprehensive ethical philosophy, Nitobe was inventing what he claimed merely to be transmitting. Recent scholarship maintains that "all modern *bushidō* theories are later constructs with no direct continuity from pre-Meiji history, while it is precisely the claims to such continuity that make *bushidō* an invented *tradition*." The decades of the Sino-Japanese and Russo-Japanese Wars witnessed a "*bushidō* boom," as thinkers at home and abroad attempted to account for Japan's victories, and *bushidō* was enshrined as a foundational aspect of Japanese national identity.[2]

The myth of *bushidō* as a comprehensive codex with which all Japanese were genetically programmed was no less appealing to observers outside of Japan than to Japanese themselves. Indeed, in foreign accounts of Japanese troops' conduct and victories against the Qing and Russia, it is clear that many reporters had drunk the *bushidō* Kool-Aid and portrayed the Japanese soldier or sailor as the ideal military man. He was unfailingly obedient, tactically clever, meticulously observant of the rules of war and unflinching in the face of death, motivated above all by worship of his god-king in Tokyo. Minister of War Ōyama Iwao's (1842–1916) admonition to his troops in 1894 was widely reported in the international press:

> Our army fights for the right and in accordance with the principles of civilization. Our enemies are the military forces of the country with which we are at war, not the individuals of the country. Against the force of our foe we must fight with all resolution, but as soon as any of his soldiers surrender, are taken prisoners, or receive wounds, they cease to be enemies, and it becomes our duty to treat them with all kindness.[3]

In 1900, fighting alongside troops from seven other nations in Beijing, Japanese troops distinguished themselves.

> Not only did Japan send the largest contingent, but the *personnel* perhaps excelled more than that of any other nation ... [D]epartmentally, at any rate, the young Eastern nation outshone its European *confrères* ...

> It should be mentioned that the behaviour of the Japanese troops was exemplary, and that in this respect they could give points and a beating to nearly all the other troops engaged.[4]

Anticipating hostilities between Japan and Russia, the *New York Times* quoted military officials who insisted "the Japanese are the better soldiers," whose discipline was "most excellent" compared to the "industrious foragers" the Russians were known to be. "'If Japan can keep her armament and equipment on a par with her soldiers, she is a most valuable ally and a most formidable enemy." After Japan's attack on the Russian naval base at Port Arthur in February 1904, even "official utterances from Russian sources" became noticeably more "respectful to the Mikado's men." "The latter's right to consideration is now clear," another contemporary report stated, "and the proof lies not alone in the work they have done, but in the spirit and temper they have shown."[5] Western writers laid it on thick, heralding global fascination with *bushidō* as a quasi-mystical ethos celebrated in American films such as *Ghost Dog: The Way of the Samurai* (1999) and *The Last Samurai* (2003).

Such foreign accounts merely encouraged the Japanese media's emphasis on the power of spirit over material in wars of destiny. Popular culture in wartime recounted semitrue stories of battlefield valor by individual soldiers and sailors; of mothers, wives, and daughters on the home front who gave sacrificially not only their menfolk but their labor and their possessions to support the war effort; of journalists, photographers, and movie cameramen who braved seasickness, wintry conditions, capture, and mortar fire to report on the war's progress. Cartoons belittled caricatured enemies. Popular songs, performed on the streets, in recitals, and on recordings, stiffened Japanese spines for indefinitely lengthy periods of hunger, deprivation, service, and sacrifice. Children's story time included narratives of brave "older brothers" piloting aerial suicide missions, or sometimes taught kids how to build air raid shelters and put out fires. Each war encroached more deeply into everyday life.

By the late 1930s government and military officials came to see the realm of entertainment as another front in the war, deserving of significant attention and creative thought. How could the people be comforted and diverted from the hardships of their lives, without undermining their fighting spirits? How could the empire's war aims be couched and communicated to push civilians to superhuman feats of productivity and patriotism? How could the entertainment industry generally convince people to imagine themselves at the front alongside the troops themselves, fighting with the same desperation and commitment to promulgate the "imperial way" (*kōdō*) in Asia and the world? Far from being of negligible importance, popular culture was in fact considered an essential weapon in Japan's arsenal in times of war.

Sino-Japanese War (1894–95)

The Sino-Japanese War is surprisingly understudied in Anglophone scholarship, but people who witnessed it were convinced of its monumental importance. "Japan's first modern war," as Stewart Lone describes it, was closely monitored by the rest of the world, especially by major powers that had standing commercial or colonial interests in Pacific Asia.[6] The war was the culmination of more than two decades of diplomatic wrangling over both countries' relationships with Chosŏn, which had for centuries been the model "little brother" tributary state in the Sinocentric diplomatic order of East Asia. Having already made mortifying concessions to Western imperial powers, the Qing had no intention of releasing Korea from its orbit. Japanese, however, sought to render the peninsula as unthreatening as possible. Both Qing and Japanese interests were represented by feuding factions in the Chosŏn royal court: generally speaking, one side thought Korea's interests were best served by continuing the tradition of "serving the great" (*sadae*), while the other wanted to renounce fealty to the Qing and modernize their country as Japanese had theirs.

On December 4, 1884, the Korean court's pro-Japan faction—which included students of Fukuzawa Yukichi's—initiated what is now called the Kapsin Coup. It was a "fatal blunder" that was suppressed by the local Qing garrison, at the request of the court, within three days. The coup d'état did more harm than good to the cause of reform and modernization in Korea, hardening resistance among conservatives and binding them closer to the Qing.[7] Some of the conspirators escaped with Japanese assistance. The Japanese legation headquarters was torched and forty Japanese killed in retaliation. In April 1885 Qing envoy Lǐ Hóngzhāng (1823–1901) and Japan's Itō Hirobumi (1841–1909) negotiated an agreement whereby both countries would remove their troops from the peninsula and formally notify the other should either have cause to send them back in.

Nine years later, threatened by the Tonghak Rebellion, a major peasant insurgency in southwest Chŏlla province, Korean King Kojong (1852–1919) requested Qing military aid. The Qing claimed to have informed Japanese diplomats as per their agreement, while the Japanese retorted that the missive got lost in the mail and sent its own troops into the peninsula. Fighting between Qing and Japanese troops and Korea's Tonghak rebels took place primarily on the Korean peninsula, with naval engagements to its west in the Yellow Sea. Unfortunately, it would not be the last time that outside powers backing Korean factions would tear the peninsula apart.

Summarizing the Sino-Japanese War's impact on East Asian and global affairs, Sarah Paine argues it "changed perceptions in both the East and West, and these changed perceptions had a direct impact on the foreign policies of all parties engaged in the Far East." The "carving of the Chinese melon" began as soon as Qing vulnerability was proven, with European powers demanding further territorial concessions or "spheres of influence" for long-term lease—as long as ninety-nine years. Furthermore, "Western rivalries now played themselves out in Asia on a grander scale, giving regional issues a new international significance."[8] Japanese learned the bitter lesson that they would never be treated as equals in the international arena when Russia, Germany, and France issued "friendly advice" that Japan relinquish one of its spoils of war, China's Liáodōng Peninsula, which Russia was eyeing as its potential warm-water port in the Pacific.[9] The resentment created by this Triple Intervention stuck in Japanese craws into the 1930s and 1940s. Howls of indignation indicated that the war had accelerated the growth of Japanese nationalism: the China war thus marked the fulfillment of the Meiji nation-building campaign, or at least its first stages. Lone emphasizes the "sense of an extended community" that developed from the transport and training of troops conscripted from rural hamlets throughout the archipelago. Furthermore, he sees the war as the time of "transition in Japan to a mass media society ... with an increasingly literate population."[10]

The Sino-Japanese War set the pattern for "unbounded enthusiasm" for war in popular culture. Illustrator, painter, and woodblock printer Kobayashi Kiyochika (1847–1915), a student of cartoonist Charles Wirgman, produced more than seventy full-color triptychs and many more single-block prints and cartoon images during the ten-month conflict.[11] Although of *bushi* stock, Kiyochika is generally regarded as the last of the great traditional woodblock artists, but from a thematic standpoint he was an innovator. He was a prodigious documentarian of the Meiji modernization process. Before photography became the standard medium for reportage, the mass-produced, salable woodblock print remained the primary source of visual information about the dramatic transformation of Japan's landscapes and people under Meiji rule. Though he also drew satirical cartoons for comic magazines, Kiyochika's name is synonymous with visual depictions of the China war, whose major battles and heroic figures were his favored and bestselling material. In Kiyochika's images Japanese heroism is magnified by the harsh winter landscapes, turbulent seas, and torrential downpours in which soldiers and sailors fought. His visual ridicule of Chinese soldiers is merciless. Qing troops are portrayed as cowardly and incompetent, in stark contrast to the professionalism of Japanese soldiers. With their facial hair, Prussian-style uniforms and modern weaponry, Japanese appear to be fighting enemies from an earlier time, whose equipment, attire, and ponytails make them anachronistic clowns.

Contempt for Chinese and paternalism toward Koreans were widely expressed in the streets and popular media.[12] Street singer Soeda Azenbō recalled an altercation with a listener while prefacing one of his songs:

When I tried to give the explanation at the start of the *enka* someone among the crowd yelled out, "the chinks are weak. One Japanese can send ten of their kind flying." I countered saying, "Don't be afraid of a powerful enemy, but neither make light of a weak one ..." Immediately, someone shouted that I should not side with the Chinese and accused me of being a spy for the enemy. All of a sudden, the audience began to turn into a dangerous mob.

Generally speaking, however, *enka* singers' patriotism was beyond reproach. Azenbō's colleague Hisada Kiseki composed several songs that proclaimed Japan's altruistic war aims and celebrated deeds of derring-do performed by individual soldiers.

"War's Outbreak"
Our empire rich in benevolence and chivalry
To guide neighboring Korea
Toward the honor of becoming an independent nation
Totally and for all time
Maintaining the peace of Asia
And doing the opposite: China
Arrogant, disrespectful of Korea …
To punish this, war is declared
By great imperial mandate
In indignation we clench our fists, grind our teeth …

Enkashi also sang in tribute to individual soldiers at the Battle of P'yŏngyang (September 15, 1894):

As agile as a monkey he darts to the top [of the fortress ramparts]
This man who nimbly plunges over
Is our Harada Jūkichi
Squad leader Mimura follows
With a death-defying fighting spirit
The enemy soldiers beaten to desperate straits
Find their legs wobbly and in that instant
The fortress gate is pushed open
Our troops are beckoned in
And thanks to them Pyongyang falls
Past and present nothing can compare to such a feat …

Donald Keene observes that the heroes of the war were from "the humblest ranks," "first-class privates," and "unknown farm recruits" whose samurai-like valor and sacrifices proved the wisdom of a conscript force, since "even the humblest Japanese was courageous and loyal to the death."[13]

The indignity of the Triple Intervention inspired Hisada to write yet another *enka*, in which he fantasized about wreaking vengeance on the great power bullies:

The flag of the rising sun shines forth from Himalayan peaks
England, Russia, Germany, and France from behind the cloudy vastness
Issued forth their common goodly advice
When we recall the return of Liaotung
The cloudy vastness seems to close down over us

Japanese swords and Murata rifles
Marching and charging across the five continents
In a dream I saw all utterly destroyed.[14]

Theater provided yet another vehicle for celebrating Japanese heroism and ridiculing the Chinese enemy. *Shinpa* cofounder Kawakami Otojirō debuted his *Grand and Splendid Sino-Japanese War* (*Sōzetsu kaizetsu Nisshin sensō*) on August 31, 1894, a mere thirty days after the official declaration of war. It ran for forty performances. *Nisshin sensō* told a story of a Japanese journalist captured by Chinese for spying and brought before Qing general Lǐ Hóngzhāng, a favorite target of abuse in popular culture. The reporter lectures Lǐ—marked by his pigtail and "Confucius beard"—on his disregard for "the principles of international law."[15] After visiting Korea to check out the action, Kawakami wrote and staged another play in December, *Diary of Kawakami Otojirō's Observations of the Battlefront* (*Kawakami Otojirō senchi kenbun nikki*), for which he recruited Korean actor Chŏng Munam. He followed this with *Surrender at Weihaiwei* (*Ikaiei kanraku*) in May 1895, commemorating Japan's decimation of the Qing navy in the war's last major battle. These "war plays" staged in Tokyo, Ōsaka, Kyōto, and Yokohama helped popularize *shinpa* and establish its conventions. Their political liberalism did not curb the unabashed jingoism *sōshi enka* singers and *shinpa* artists expressed throughout the war.

The conflict encouraged the expansion of print, photographic, and filmic media. Photographer Kamei Koreaki (1861–96), scion of a military house who transitioned into the peerage, became Japan's first photojournalist embedded with troops. From October 1894 to May 1895 he followed the 2nd Army under Ōyama Iwao's command, producing some three hundred images.[16] Kamei's photographs captured many aspects of the war, from ordinary soldiers lolling on hillsides or riding ships to the front to scenes from naval engagements, and troops scaling the wall of a Qing garrison in Chŏnju. He also provided rare photographic evidence of the November 21–22, 1894, massacre at Port Arthur (Ch: Lǚshùn; J: Ryojun) on China's Liáodōng Peninsula, in which Japanese troops slaughtered thousands of Chinese civilians in retaliation for the mutilation and display of several Japanese. In addition to piles of corpses, he captured a poignant image of a Chinese woman fleeing Lǚshùn with her children.[17] His extensive travels to multiple fronts weakened Kamei's health; he died in July 1896, at the age of 36.

The image projector colloquially known as the "magic lantern" (*gentōki*), a transitional technology between still and motion photography, also became an immensely popular medium for people on the home front to experience the war visually. The Dutch had introduced the device to Japan before Commodore Matthew Perry's arrival, and it was included in *misemono* in the late Edo and early Meiji periods. Audiences for public exhibits—which, like American "tent shows," traveled throughout rural areas—swelled during wartime. Although there may have been some war footage taken, film was still a rare technology in the 1890s, so magic lantern shows functioned as newsreels did in the twentieth century.

The Sino-Japanese War demonstrates the mutually beneficial relationship between popular culture and wartime society. The war provided "content," if you will, for burgeoning mass media at the turn of the twentieth century. Conversely, popular culture built support for the war among the populace, feeding the fire of nationalism and a sense of superiority vis-à-vis continental Asia. Lone figures that "wartime censorship of the press appears to have been very light compared to later years," in part because the popularity of the war made it virtually unnecessary.[18] However, the mythistorical, emperor-centered ultranationalist ideology (*tennōsei*) and its attendant media taboos had not yet been fully articulated. The severest censorship was yet to come.

Russo-Japanese War (1904–05)

Japan's next war was qualitatively different in many ways: it put greater strain on the nation's economic and military resources; though generally supported by the populace, it elicited more overt dissent and suppression; and it generated considerably more angst among both Japanese and foreign observers. It was the biggest war to date in the modern imperialist era pitting white and nonwhite people against each other. Japan's eventual victory led to dire warnings of a "yellow peril," which intensified discrimination toward Japanese immigrants in the United States and threatened relations between the United States and Japan. Russia's defeat was a factor in the 1905 revolution that forced Czar Nikolai II to consent to a constitutional monarchy and deliberative assembly.

Perhaps most importantly, the war's outcome encouraged colonized peoples to challenge the white supremacist ideology that undergirded imperialist oppression. From the Philippines to Indochina and from India to Egypt, anticolonial nationalists were inspired by Japan's win and openly expressed hope that Japan would lead "colored" races in a global liberation campaign. "There is a moral for our countrymen to be drawn from this stupendous struggle and this beginning, let us hope, of the end," M. K. Gandhi reflected, referring to the *bushidō* mystique that purportedly explained Japanese successes. "The Japanese ... have shown unity, self-sacrifice, fixity of purpose, nobility of character, steel courage and generosity to the enemy ... The rise of Japan has shewn the world that if the 'white man' is to retain his supremacy, he must deserve it."[19]

Although "World War Zero" may be a hyperbolic—not to mention inelegant—descriptor, there is no question that the Russo-Japanese War had global significance, which people at the time recognized, and that it prefigured many of the characteristics of World War I: "Its origins were linked to the imperial expansion of the European powers, its battlefields were stocked with the weapons and munitions of the industrial revolution, and neither the civilian nor the military leadership was prepared for the war that actually occurred in Manchuria."[20]

In a scenario that foreshadowed the events of 1941, Japanese diplomats believed they had been backed into a corner and had no choice but to initiate hostilities. Yet in contrast to the almost universal denunciation of the surprise attack on Pearl Harbor in December 1941, international observers praised Japan's unannounced naval strike on the Russians' naval base at Port Arthur on February 8, 1904, as a brilliant tactical move. Newspapers worldwide carried cartoons of bearded Russian giants tormenting Lilliputian Japanese, indicating widespread perceptions of the war as a David-and-Goliath struggle, which the tiny Japanese would surely lose. Within weeks, however, it became apparent that Japanese were fighting with greater strategic intelligence and fervor than their antagonists. Russians appeared, at least, to take the war too lightly. When Russia's Baltic fleet was forced to embark on a seven-month, 33,000 km journey around the cape of Africa and through the Indian Ocean to the front, only to meet almost total annihilation within twenty-four hours by Japan's navy in the Tsushima Straits, a narrative of Russian incompetence and overconfidence took hold. The victory was fortuitous, because unbeknown either to Japanese at home or to most international observers, Japan's forces were on the ropes. Had the war dragged on much longer, the outcome might have been different.

US president Theodore Roosevelt (1858–1919)—a man hardly averse to war—won the Nobel Peace Prize for mediating a settlement between the belligerents. The Treaty of Portsmouth conceded practically everything the Japanese delegation wanted, including paramount interest in the Korean peninsula and takeover of Russia's Manchurian railroad. When they received news that neither indemnities nor additional Siberian territory east of Lake Baikal were among the spoils, Japanese rioted in Tokyo's Hibiya Park and then nationwide to protest the "humiliating" terms. The government's campaign to instill popular nationalism had succeeded all too well: the imposition of martial law "underlined the vulnerability of a political system that rested on a narrow balance of power between powerful political elites, excluding not only dissenters ... but also the people from the political process."[21] It also indicated just how much ordinary Japanese had suffered during the war.

As in the previous war, popular culture both expressed and stoked this fervent nationalism. Kiyochika's oeuvre grew substantially during the war. But *nishiki-e* renditions of Russians were significantly different compared to those of Chinese a decade earlier. The latter made Chinese objects of contemptuous fun, with little phenotypical resemblance to their Japanese adversaries. The Russia prints, however, emphasize physical resemblances between Japanese and Russians and, rather than ridicule the enemy, illustrate his formidability. An early print (February 1904) by Watanabe Nobukazu (c. 1872–1944) shows a meeting of military officers from both sides, probably negotiating a surrender after the battle of Port Arthur. The facial hair worn by Russians and Japanese alike and their identical skin pigmentation emphasize Japan's "Westernness," as *nishiki-e* from the previous war had, but *not* in contrast to the opponent. The czar was more likely to be skewered than Russians in general. One of Kiyochika's more bizarre cartoons, entitled "Ghosts from the Crushing Defeat," shows a distraught Nikolai in bed haunted by ghosts with mangled human bodies and battleships and cannons for heads. The caption—by former *Marumaru chinbun* writer Nishimori Takeki (1861–1913), using the pseudonym Koppi Dōjin (Master Skin and Bones)—reads,

> Russia's navy and army had not a single victory, despite suffering great defeats and ridiculous losses from the outset, and reported nothing but lies to their country to conceal these drubbings … Learning of these defeats for the first time, the czar said, "Hmm, there haven't been many victories in the information I've heard so far, but I didn't know we were losing so badly. Well, that's regrettable, but nothing can be done now. Sorry, but you guys just [have to] stay injured."[22]

By and large, wartime *nishiki-e* focused more on Japanese heroism and moral conduct. A print by Utagawa Kokunimasa (1874–1944) illustrates a Japanese Red Cross hospital in which military doctors provide care to injured Russians.[23] Indeed, the Japanese military earned praise from the global press for its humane and respectful treatment of POWs and injured enemy soldiers, generally following the 1864 Geneva and 1899 Hague Conventions meticulously. With the notable exception of the 1894 Port Arthur massacre, imperial forces neither killed many civilians nor foraged for food and supplies from them. The contrast with the Japanese military's conduct and disregard for international law after 1931 is staggering.

Despite prodigious output, *nishiki-e* sold much less well than those from the China war, which had sold in the tens of thousands. Photography and moving pictures supplanted the color print, as audiences demanded more realistic depictions of a "highly visualized war."[24] The Russo-Japanese War boosted attendance at movie theaters significantly, accounting for Japan's first cinematic blockbusters and feature films (with running times long enough to fill a program). The pioneering Yoshida and Yokota film companies dispatched camera crews to the front in March 1904. New documentary films (*kiroku eiga*), including some imported from France's Pathé, as well as from British and American companies, appeared on almost a weekly basis. Theater orchestras played martial music, and *benshi* provided patriotic commentary. Through this medium, millions of Japanese civilians could see for the first time conditions at the front and vicariously experience modern warfare.

FIGURE 7.1 *Kobayashi Kiyochika, Ghosts from the Crushing Defeat (Mecha make no bōrei), print #83, from Long Live Japan: A Hundred Victories, A Hundred Laughs (Nihon banzai—hyakusen, hyakushō), 3rd series, 1904. Waseda University Library (http://archive.wul.waseda.ac.jp/kosho/bunko10/bunko10_05481/), and Fine Prints: Japanese, pre-1915, Library of Congress, (http://www.loc.gov/pictures/collection/jpd/item/2008660178/).*

Daibō Masaki's research in film company catalogs indicates that more than eighty movies about the war, from the siege of Port Arthur to the Portsmouth conference, were released during and immediately after the war. British Pathé's *La Vigie de Port-Arthur* (The siege and surrender of Port Arthur; *Ryojun no kōfuku*, 1904), arguably the most valuable documentary and possibly eighty minutes long in its original form, was also shown in various abridged versions. British cameraman Joseph Rosenthal (1864–1946), who had previously filmed the South African Boer War, shot footage mostly of troop movements and naval training exercises rather than real combat.[25]

Not unlike history documentaries on television today, most Russo-Japanese War films mixed footage from the front with staged recreations. Audiences were not amused. Indeed, although many leading film scholars claim that realism was not of particular concern to early Japanese movie audiences, there is evidence indicating verisimilitude was, in fact, a selling point in war movies. "The films you are about to see are not filled with the eight hundred lies of charlatans and fortune hunters," a Kōbe *benshi* boasted to viewers. "Every foot was shot at the actual places sanctified by the blood of our countrymen. Therefore, when you see our soldiers marching into battle, I want you to shout *banzai* to cheer them on!"[26] Lone cites a letter to the local newspaper in provincial Gifu expressing anger when a film advertised as containing real battlefield footage had none: "no matter how rural you may think it here, don't make fools of us!" When another film used toy ships on a pond to illustrate a naval engagement, a newspaper writer fumed, "Childish flim-flammery of this sort convinces no one." "What we clearly see here," Lone concludes, "is a critical audience which knew what it liked and did not simply accept from some kind of militaristic zeal whatever was presented to it."[27]

Military songs (*gunka*) had been composed as early as the 1870s—recall the military's leading role in the Westernization of Japanese music—but became popular among the general public during both the China and Russia wars. By the late 1930s *gunka* almost dominated popular music. *Gunka* proliferated via songbooks, school classrooms and *enka* singers.[28] The most popular *gunka* was "Comrade in Arms" (*Sen'yū*), composed by schoolteachers Mashimo Hisen (1878–1926) and Miyoshi Kazuoki (1881–1963) for the Russo-Japanese War, which remained one of the most enduring *gunka* of the twentieth century.

Hundreds of leagues from our home country
In faraway Manchuria,
Illuminated under the red evening sun
Under the rocks of a hill, my dear comrade lies buried.
Sadly I recall the day before
That he bravely led the charge
Our foe was severely beaten back.
Will this brave warrior rest well here?

Ah, in the very midst of battle
This comrade who was next to me
Suddenly was struck down,
Along with the flag he bore.
Without a moment's thought
I rushed to his side.
Military discipline is harsh,
But how could I have just left him lying there?
"Hang on," I said, holding him,
Tending to his wounds with bullets still flying past us.
Just at that moment, our army's charge broke through
My comrade turned his face to the task at hand
"It's for the sake of our country, I'll be fine,
"Do not tarry here," he said, tears in his eyes.
Afterwards in spirit he may remain
But nothing would remain of him in body, I knew.
"Then shall I go," I said and left him
But thus we were to part for eternity.[29]

In contrast to military songs in other countries, Japanese *gunka* are known for focusing more on losses, sacrifices, and death than on victories, cheering, and macho posturing. Arguably this makes them more realistic about the horrors of war than, say, "La Marseillaise," "Battle Cry of Freedom," "The Invincible Eagle," "Over There" or "Panzerlied." But most Japanese today are turned off by the "inconsolably sad melodies and the image of inevitable death" ubiquitous in *gunka* lyrics.[30]

It is worth noting the profound disconnect between the noble sentiments expressed by professional songwriters who had never seen combat, and soldiers' diaries and letters from the front, which described their comrades' deaths as "cruel," "tragic," and "pitiful." Rural conscripts felt pressure to report battlefield fatalities as "honorable war deaths" (*meiyo no senshi*) regardless of the circumstances, even though they generally "did not identify with the cultural ideal" of their superior officers: loyalty unto death for the emperor.[31]

Not all wartime songs were so unrelentingly somber. To his later shame, Azenbō mercilessly mocked the enemy in his comic "Song of the Russian Army."

If you listen carefully to the Russian army song
Truly, you will laugh until water boils in your belly button
Advance, advance together all and one
We should be resigned to die as we advance
And when we encounter the enemy at that moment
Run away before you're injured
For such a tiny monthly wage? ...

Advancing may be our duty
But running away is our right
Everyone on your own, flee!
But not before raping the women
Stealing the treasure of others
These things we must not neglect
Military regulations be hanged!
Advance to the rear, retreat!
To the place where the enemy is not, advance![32]

The wars with China and Russia were somewhat of a quandary because they pitted Japanese against countries that had been fundamentally influential to their culture. Clearly, China's impact was the deeper, and Keene describes how Japanese opinion of that country tanked during the prior war. Less well known is the significance of Russia on post-Restoration Japanese culture—especially literature. Japanese Russophiles like Futabatei Shimei (1864–1909) translated Leo Tolstoy, Fyodor Dostoevsky, and Ivan Turgenev, and wrote *Floating Clouds* (*Ukigumo*, 1887), considered Japan's first modern novel, in a "Russian" style.[33] Leftists were sympathetic to anti-czarists and Russian socialists. The Commoners' Society (Heiminsha), a pacifist/socialist organization, had begun agitating against the war through its newspaper a year before a shot was fired. After the Port Arthur siege it maintained correspondence with Russian pacifists. In one of its first major acts of wartime censorship, the government shut down the newspaper on January 29, 1905.

But Russophilia and pacifism do not explain all cultural expressions of opposition or diffidence to the war. "Admittedly, patriotic fervor was prominent in the public sphere," Naoko Shimazu acknowledges, "but, beneath its veneer, war-weariness prevailed among the majority," which "derived from the practical socioeconomic problems that the war engendered." Despite censorship, it was not impossible for people to read broadsheets reporting the "wayward conduct of mobilized soldiers" that contradicted their domestic and international reputations—including a "major disturbance" in the brothel district of Hiroshima, the point of soldiers' embarkation for the front. Lone concurs with Shimazu, showing that Gifu prefecture was rife with "very public examples of disunity, discontent with elites and propaganda, a refusal to suffer in silence, sometimes lack of interest in the war and its aims, and a healthy satire and derision of those who made a public spectacle of their relations with the military."[34] Indeed, the war's most famous literary work was a protest poem by author and social activist Yosano Akiko (1878–1942), addressed to her younger brother, entitled "Beloved, You Must Not Die," in which she asked,

How could our great emperor,
whose wondrous heart is so deep,
not do battle himself

but still ask others to spill their blood,
to die like beasts,
and think those deaths a glory?[35]

As was the case in the previous war, there was a symbiosis between the Russia conflict and Japanese popular culture, albeit intensified. A government censorship apparatus was more well developed and proactive in the latter war, but again, the commercial culture industry required little overt guidance, remaining "unrepentantly profit-motivated" because patriotism sold well. The greatest expansion in the cultural industry was in cinema, music publishing, and pictorial magazines that featured "highly sanitized" photographs from the front.[36] As in the Sino-Japanese War, the *bushidō* mythos sufficed as an explanation of Japan's victories for both domestic and overseas observers, cultivated by press accounts of individual heroism by troops on the ground and at sea, and by patriotic women at home. Both wars, particularly that with Russia, remained culturally significant in public memory well into the 1920s and 1930s. "Articles in popular magazines in the 1930s, for example, show both a pride in Japan's physical capacity to wage war and a marked lack of any instinctive abhorrence for war in general," Sandra Wilson remarks. "Such attitudes are very difficult to imagine in a mainstream publication in countries like Britain or France, or even the United States, where the memory of war [World War I] was very different."[37] The defeats of the Qing and the czar fed a hubris that Japanese brought to their next conflagration, when they essentially took on the world.

World War II (1937–45)

For Japanese World War II was both defensive and "holy." They spoke of being encircled by the "ABCD" powers (Americans, British, Chinese, and Dutch) and of being choked by the US oil embargo. They claimed their destiny was to liberate Southeast Asia from Western colonial rule, and the Chinese from both the corrupt, inept, "comprador" Nationalist regime and a possible communist revolution, and in the process construct a regional economic autarky, which they would naturally lead.

World War II in the Asia-Pacific theater was partially a consequence of accumulated grievances against Japan's peer nations. Foremost among these were the racial double standards of international diplomacy and war. Western imperial powers rarely treated Japan as an equal. I mentioned earlier the Triple Intervention, in which Russia, France, and Germany joined forces to prevent cession of the Liáodōng peninsula to Japan. In the 1900s and 1910s there were multiple diplomatic rows over the racist attacks and indignities heaped on Japanese immigrants to Hawai'i, Canada, and the United States. And in 1919 US president Woodrow Wilson (1856–1924) and Australian prime minister Billy Hughes (1862–1962) opposed and shot down Japan's Racial Equality Proposal for the League of Nations Covenant. To accept it would have undermined American Jim Crow laws and the White Australia policy, and possibly encouraged more immigration from Asia. Neither man could abide such a thing. Then the 1921–22 Washington Naval Conference, which produced the first international arms control agreements, set ratios for battleships that disadvantaged Japan compared to the United States and the United Kingdom. Military commanders' blood boiled as the civilian government agreed to these terms.

Most Japanese felt humiliated by decades of such insults, but radicalized officers in the Imperial Army were in a position to do something about it. Embarrassing and undermining the civilian government was easy to do with weapons at hand. In September 1931, the Kantō (Guāndōng) Army, assigned to protect the South Manchuria Railway, blew up a section of it and accused Chinese troops in a nearby garrison of sabotage. They did so without the consent or foreknowledge of Tokyo. As described in Chapter 6, this became the pretext for military occupation of Manchuria and the establishment of a client state there. Throughout the 1930s Japan and Republican China engaged in several skirmishes, which broke out into full-fledged war in July 1937. In 1941, when the US government decided to stop shipments of petrol and scrap metal for Japanese to use against China, Japanese officials considered this an act of war and simultaneously attacked the Pearl Harbor naval base and Clark Air Base in the Philippines. Throughout the spring of 1942, Japanese forces effectively swept Southeast Asia clean of Western colonialism, replacing it with a subjugation the locals considered far worse.

Commercial media were complicit in the march to war. Throughout the 1930s they were unrelenting in their condemnations of the Chinese Nationalist regime and especially its leader, Chiang Kai-shek. His failure to corral communist rebels intensified the bellicosity of Japanese media discourse. Official records of the desperate November 1941 negotiations to avoid war with the United States indicate that domestic popular opinion constrained what the Japanese diplomatic corps thought feasible to bring to the table. Aware that the Japanese press had begun beating war drums, American negotiators despaired that their counterparts would ever agree to withdrawing troops from China and Indochine française. By emphasizing national survival, US and Chinese recalcitrance, and Japanese lives already sacrificed in battle, popular media made peace less likely.[38]

After half a century of reluctance to do so, scholars have recently become comfortable using the term "fascism" to describe Japan's 1930s, a decade that witnessed the militarization of culture, society, economics, and politics. Certainly, signing the Tripartite Pact in September 1940 aligned Japan with fascist Italy and Nazi Germany (each signatory wisely avoiding discussion of their partners' respective pretensions to racial superiority). Yet Japan had no counterpart to a mass party helmed by a charismatic male leader who diagnosed the nation's infirmities and prescribed a remedy involving abolition of civil liberties, corrosive individualism, and class conflict. Nor was there a (successful) coup d'état or structural change in the Meiji Constitutional government. Instead, active-duty military officers increasingly occupied cabinet posts and exploited the constitutional "independence of the Supreme Command" (tōsuiken), which the army and navy interpreted as giving them direct access to the throne with no civilian oversight.[39]

Japan historians use "fascism" most comfortably when describing wartime culture rather than political movements, because "culture is where fascism forms its ideological power."[40] There are indeed striking parallels with Robert Paxton's "minimal" conditions for fascism:

- a sense of national humiliation and victimhood that scapegoats perceived internal and external enemies;

- militant nationalism based on racial or ethnonational superiority;

- rhetoric about internal purification or "cleansing" through "redemptive violence";

- external expansion as national destiny.[41]

Fascist culture "exalted mindlessness and glamorized death," scorned "rational thought," and expressed "a passion for violence."[42] Even if Japanese did not fully embrace or identify with its European variants, Reto Hofmann affirms that "interwar Japanese culture and politics was steeped in fascism."[43]

Unquestionably, wartime Japan's popular culture was saturated with messages promoting service and glorifying sacrifice unto death. Yoshimi Yoshiaki argues that these messages were not merely government propaganda directed at a docile public, but reflected ordinary Japanese "popular consciousness" and "grassroots fascism." Without explicitly saying so, Yoshimi applies a hegemony framework: he argues that people from all walks of life invested heavily in imperial expansion into continental Asia, crafting their dreams and aspirations to accommodate national policy. Although people criticized specific policies and official messages and expressed general war-weariness, he counters the conventional notion that Japanese were duped into war and imperialism by a cabal of secretive leaders, insisting that fascist ideas and values permeated society much more deeply than most people openly acknowledged later.[44] Following Yoshimi's argument, then, wartime popular culture was not merely a tool of the state to propagandize the masses but to varying degrees spoke for, as well as to, producers and consumers alike.

Censorship (ken'etsu) was not the exclusive work of government officials. It was exponentially more sophisticated, constricting and invasive than in previous wars, but many in the culture industry self-censored adroitly. Article 29 of the Meiji Constitution—"Japanese subjects shall, within the limits of the law, enjoy the liberty of speech, writing, publication, public meetings and associations"—had a built-in proviso that authorized the imperial state to contravene such "liberty." Unofficial propagandists not only "enjoy[ed]" these liberties more than others but also recognized the profitability of commercialized patriotism. Artists and entertainers who considered the war unwise or immoral simply kept their mouths shut. It is often said that the only people who openly criticized the war were the socialists already in jail.

The Home Ministry (Naimushō) was the cabinet office responsible for issuing and enforcing censorship laws and regulation of amusements. Sometimes it applied nationwide regulations imposed by local municipalities within their jurisdictions, such as Ōsaka's 1927 dance hall ban (implemented nationwide in 1940). Starting with commercial print media in the Meiji period, government officials drafted and updated censorship laws for each new mass media technology or leisure activity, including film and theater scripts, novels, pictorial arts, recorded music, radio programs, and social dance. Prepublication approval became the norm, but if censors missed anything, civilian, military, and the Special High Police had authority to confiscate published items, break up a gathering and scold or arrest anyone they deemed was threatening public morality. The World War II–era censorship regime did not materialize out of the blue, but built upon an existing body of municipal, prefectural, and national laws and regulations that had accumulated over some eight decades.

In popular media, the emperor was rarely visible, yet omnipresent. Whereas Emperor Meiji's image was fairly prevalent during his reign, strict taboos about depictions of the august sovereign developed with the ascension of the sickly Taishō emperor, embellishing the throne's aura and mystique. The Shōwa emperor Hirohito (1901–89), whose reign began at the very end of 1926, was occasionally visible in newsreels, usually dressed in military uniform, but very few civilians ever heard his voice before his radio broadcast of August 15, 1945, announcing Japan's surrender. Unlike Benito Mussolini or Adolf Hitler, Hirohito's authority did not emanate from charisma, a quality of which he was entirely bereft.

Augmenting imperial luster was a year-long festival in 1940 commemorating the mythical 2600th anniversary of the founding of the "unbroken imperial line" (bansei ikkei). There were around twelve thousand associated events throughout the empire. Print media and department stores were essential instruments for promoting consumption of the celebration, through best-selling national histories and tourism to imperial sites in Japan and to the outer empire, particularly Korea and Manchuria. "Far from being displaced by nationalism and its mystical rhetoric," Ken Ruoff writes, "Japan's modern mass consumer sector was enveloped and also spurred on by the patriotic atmosphere."[45]

Japan's wartime government frequently delegated or outsourced its work to the very artists and industries it wished to control (film was a notable exception, remaining the purview of Home Ministry inspectors).[46] Writers, actors, musicians, and visual artists organized themselves into patriotic associations defined by their respective media, and convened to draw up regulations both to promote the war and to forestall censorable infractions. This self-policing was not unlike the neighborhood associations (tonarigumi) that organized to enforce internal discipline, prepare civil defense measures, determine rations of food and other essentials and identify individual members whose patriotic enthusiasm was inadequate. Members of *tonarigumi* were expected to surveil and rat each other out if their contributions and attitudes were deemed "un-Japanese" (*hikokumin*).

Service in patriotic arts societies was something that their members usually declined to publicize later. When researching how jazz musicians navigated the wartime environment, I found evidence of this self-policing policy in a brief newspaper article, and an attempt to conceal participation in it. Columbia Records' staff composer/arranger Hattori Ryōichi wrote in his memoir that during the war he inserted "Tiger Rag" into a "light music" radio program. When asked if that was not American jazz, he responded, "No, this is a courageous Malayan song about tiger hunting. If you listen you'll realize that there are a lot of sounds that resemble a tiger's roar. I think it's perfect for a time of crisis." Yet the newspaper article from 1943 named Hattori and three other jazz musicians and critics as members of a committee charged with weeding Anglo-American songs, records, and scores from popular music. "Tiger Rag" appeared on a list of some one thousand banned songs that Hattori himself had helped draft.[47] After the war Hattori, like most of his peers, chose to tell stories of sly sedition rather than of cooperation with the wartime state.

This story illustrates one crucial difference between the cultural climates of the Sino- and Russo-Japanese Wars and World War II: there was a sustained effort to purge commercial entertainment and everyday life of all Anglo-Americana. In the implementation it became clear to the less self-delusional how impossible this task would be. Even Prime Minister Tōjō Hideki (1884–1948) was infuriated to learn that "Light of the Fireflies" (with Japanese lyrics set to the melody of the Scot-English folk song "Auld Lang Syne") was on the initial list of banned songs. There were also efforts to purge the language of English loanwords, which resulted in baseball being renamed *yakyū*, along with its terminology: "safe" (*sēfu*) became *anzen*, "foul" (*fauru*) became *kengai* (out of range), *dame* (no good), and the like. Umpires never completely mastered the terms before professional baseball was shut down in 1944. Musical terms and instruments were Japanized in laughably convoluted ways. Trombonists had it particularly bad, since their instrument was rechristened *nukisashi magari kin chō rappa*.

If a cultural cleanse was not daunting enough, there was the far greater challenge of envisioning what popular entertainment would look like when sanitized. Wartime arguably presented an opportunity for cultural innovation, which the relative brevity of the war curtailed. Few, if anyone, advocated a wholesale return to the "purer" indigenous popular culture of the Edo period, which was neither relevant nor wholesome. Modern electronic media were here to stay, but their organization and content required overhauling, per the recurrent slogans "New Order" (*shin taisei*) and "National Spiritual Mobilization" (*kokumin seishin sōdōin*). In 1940 the government ordered movie studios, recording companies, and theatrical troupes to consolidate. This made it easier to oversee cultural production, but it was also a form of punishment: ten drama film studios were merged into three, with a quota of two "national policy" films per month, in part because the film industry had been too laggardly in producing them before. Rare film stock would be withheld for noncompliance.[48]

Patriotic Japanese were conflicted about popular culture, recognizing its importance for lifting flagging spirits yet also condemning its frivolity: "The result was a mélange of inconsistent official prohibitions and desultory popular amusements."[49] Entertainers' troupes (*geinōjin imondan*) visited the front and factories to comfort troops and workers, while the Patriotic Women's Association carried banners in the street exclaiming, "Luxury is the enemy!" (*zeitaku wa teki da!*). One priggish woman hurled that slogan at the wrong person when she accosted glamorous diva Awaya Noriko, who had just returned from a tour of Southeast Asia. "Hey, this is my preparation for battle! Can I go onstage with an unpainted face?" Awaya retorted. "A singer's stage makeup is no more a 'luxury' than a soldier's helmet is!"[50] Thus a technical violation of wartime law—in this case, bans on cosmetics and hair perms—could be cast as supremely patriotic.

Unsurprisingly, the war militarized the content of popular culture. War films such as *The Legend of Tank Commander Nishizumi* (*Nishizumi senshachō den*, 1938) became standard fare, despite the fact that film studios had little to no experience in that genre. If men were heroes on the battlefield, women were heroines on the home front. Women in wartime films were "both realists and fatalists," William Hauser writes, "prepared to enjoy what they have, but anticipating that they may face future suffering. They represent social stability and the maintenance of the family ... They acknowledge the risks, yet refuse to be broken by their fear of the unknown."[51] The masculine ideal in war films was the "young officer or humble conscript who performs his duty without question and is distinguished by an appealing lack of guile." For filmic protagonists of both sexes, purity of character and intention were the defining traits.

John Dower detects in these films the message that war is an "ennobling experience" that "purifies" societies.[52] No less an authority than Mussolini insisted that fascism "repudiates the doctrine of Pacifism ... War alone brings up to their highest tension all human energies and puts the stamp of nobility upon the peoples who have the courage to meet it. All other trials are substitutes, which never really put a man in front of himself in the alternative of life and death.[53]

In the 1930s there was also an increase in period films highlighting samurai heroism and *bushidō* Darrell William Davis retroactively describes these as a "monumental" and "sacramental" form of filmmaking that aspired to no less than a prescriptive definition of "Japaneseness" itself and the fascistic purification of popular culture. "The monumental style, as one of the most stark representations of Japanese nativism in the mass media, is a radical prescription against the 'baleful influences' in manners and morals that engulfed Japanese cities through the 1930s."[54] The primary example is Mizoguchi's two-part, four-and-a-half-hour *Genroku Chūshingura* (1941–2), probably the most artistically well-regarded cinematic retelling of the Akō Vendetta (see Chapter 3). Its austerity and languid pacing are striking; the anticipated action scene, in which the vendetta is carried out, takes place *off-screen*. The focus instead is on the quiet determination and courage of the forty-seven *rōnin* as they conspire. Although the themes of self-sacrifice and redemptive violence are inherent to the subject matter, the efficacy of Mizoguchi's film as "propaganda" is questionable. Period films were safer for screenwriters and directors than were contemporary war films, in that they memorialized the *bushidō* ethos but did not require direct engagement with potentially more controversial, censorable themes about the ongoing war. Still, after defeat several auteur filmmakers openly regretted their wartime careers. "In wartime," Kurosawa Akira (1910–98) admitted, "we were all like deaf-mutes."[55]

In popular music there were efforts in the early 1940s to initiate a "light music revolution" (*kei ongaku kakumei*) that purged the excesses of jazz, but as the war dragged on *gunka* became virtually ubiquitous—and more graphic. "Divine Soldiers of the Sky" ("Sora no shinpei," 1942) describes the bodies of godlike, "babyfaced" paratroopers being "smashed into fleshy gun-powder" (*nikudanbun to kudaku tomo*).[56] A less gory militarism pervaded comedy, which endured the dour, dark wartime climate. In the early years of the war many *rakugo* and *manzai* (comic dialogue) routines centered on the misadventures of dull-witted bumpkin conscripts adjusting to army life, or occasionally even on the excessively imperious officer corps. "[W]artime humor used the background of the military because it was an experience common to its listeners," Barak Kushner observes. Mockery of Chinese and American military prowess was another favored comedic subject. Troupes of comedians also traveled to the front under the name Warawashitai ("we want to make you laugh," a pun on the character *tai* for soldier and the -*tai* verb ending for "want to"). As was also the case with musicians, comedians were occasionally reprimanded by military police (*kenpeitai*), but there is no evidence they were arrested. The main concern of authorities seemed to be sexual innuendo rather than sedition.[57]

The same censorship standards were applied to Japanese colonies, whose populations were mobilized for wartime service via the intense *kōminka* (becoming imperial subjects) policy. *Kōminka* escalated long-standing language policies, which even after decades had made little headway in transforming most Taiwanese and Koreans into fluent Japanese speakers. In the formal colonies musical theater bore the brunt of *kōminka*. In the first decade of the twentieth century, Taiwanese and Koreans had created new genres of musical theater, *gēzǎixì* (performed in colloquial Hokkien) and *ch'anggŭk*, respectively. Although both had roots in older performance genres, they were modern in most other respects and among the most popular forms of entertainment under Japanese rule.

Taiwanese *gēzǎixì* was scorned in Republican China as "not Chinese enough," and by Japanese as "too Chinese." Colonial officials set up a committee to oversee *gēzǎixì*'s reform, which entailed a purge of Chinese music and instruments; the adoption of realistic, spoken theater like *shingeki*; and the performance of "imperial subject" plays in Japanese. A so-called "reform theater" (T: *gáiliônghì*; J: *kairyōgi*) mixed elements of *gēzǎixì* with *shingeki* to appease both Taiwanese audiences and Japanese authorities. Yet whenever Japanese police were absent, actors would switch to orthodox *gēzǎixì*.[58] Korean *ch'anggŭk*, though not banned outright like *gēzǎixì*, became a vehicle for both wartime propaganda and a crash course in Japanese. Spoken portions (*aniri*) of old *p'ansori* tales were delivered, and new operas written and performed, in Japanese (poorly, one theatergoing official sniffed).[59] "The colonizers saw both merit and harm in the verbal artistry of *p'ansori* and *ch'anggŭk*," *p'ansori* scholar/performer Chan E. Park concludes. "It offered effective deliverance of their political messages to the masses, on the one hand, but a dangerous vehicle of rebellion, if 'misapplied,' on the other." An artistic low point for *ch'anggŭk* was a two-part play staged in October 1944 that depicted an Anglo-American imperialist assault on Asia, to which "enlightened" Koreans responded by pledging loyalty to the Japanese emperor and going to war on his behalf.[60]

It is disconcerting to see how extensively children's culture was militarized. By 1944 children spent almost all of their school time doing military drills, sewing and decorating "thousand-stitch belts" (*senninbari*, cloth amulets for departing troops), working in munitions factories, and preparing for air raids. Their imaginative lives centered on war, as indicated by *kamishibai* (paper plays), a pictorial storytelling medium. Typically, *kamishibai* shows were performed on streets by bicycling narrators who carried small wooden boxes to exhibit the story cards and sold candy to children who came to watch. My first major research project involved going to the International Institute for Children's Literature in Ōsaka in 1988 to examine sets of wartime *kamishibai*. They told stories about mothers sending their only sons off to war and about Burmese children assisting Japanese soldiers in their fight against the British. Some sets prepared children for civil defense duties, showing them how to build bomb shelters and put out fires ignited by Allied air raids.[61] In his documentary *Die for Japan*, Jeffrey Dym notes that *kamishibai* maintained their thematic and topical focus on *Japanese* people rather than on the enemy. In this regard, they were quite different from contemporaneous American propaganda: Japanese cartoonists made numerous hideous caricatures of US president Franklin Roosevelt and British prime minister Winston Churchill, but their American counterparts—even the future Dr. Seuss—gave free rein to their racist imaginations.[62]

FIGURE 7.2 *Norakuro's Charging Troops (Norakuro no tosshintai), 1933*
(http://apparejipango.blogspot.com/2011/03/norakuro-kodansha-1933.html).

Cartoons and animated films normalized war for children. The black-and-white stray dog Norakuro, protagonist in a serialized comic strip by Tagawa Suihō (1899–1989), was in the military from his inception in 1931. During his initial ten-year run Norakuro earned promotions in the army and embodied the ideal soldier. Strangely, in 1941 the Home Ministry banned the comic as inappropriate for wartime. Norakuro appeared in three films in the mid-1930s, but the best-known wartime animated film was *Momotarō's Sea Eagles* (*Momotarō no umiwashi*, 1943), which depicted the Peach Boy leading a squad of animals aboard an aircraft carrier in an aerial assault on Pearl Harbor (standing in for Ogre Island from the original folktale). A drunken Bluto/Brutus, Popeye the Sailor's nemesis, represents the American enemy. A longer sequel, *Momotarō's Divine Sea Warriors* (*Momotarō no umi shinpei*), appeared in April 1945. A monkey, pheasant, puppy, and bear cub return from the Imperial Naval Academy on furlough to their home village at the foot of Mount Fuji. As paratroopers, they accompany General Momotarō on an assault on the island of Sulawesi (Celebes) in the Dutch East Indies. The local jungle animals assist Japanese forces in clearing and navigating the forests, merrily learning Japanese from Momotarō's varmint brigade. Clearly, they represent local men and women drafted by the military to build airstrips and perform other hard labor at the Pacific front, most of whom did so under duress rather than voluntarily. Despite the stringencies of wartime, at seventy-four minutes, the Momotarō sequel was "the longest, most accomplished work of Japanese animation up to that point," and would remain so until 1958.[63] Despite wartime's morbid emphasis on "honorable war death," no animals were harmed or killed in the production of these films.

Not all pop cultural propaganda was aimed at domestic audiences: propagandists believed they could demoralize encroaching Allied troops in the Pacific with psychological warfare, using cartoon leaflets and their own decadent music. A favorite tactic was to stoke the enemy's emotional and sexual anxieties about women left behind. Australian troops worried that their American allies on furlough were helping themselves to their womenfolk. The *Australia Screams* leaflet depicts a Digger in New Guinea saying, "What was that scream? Something up?" as a Yank holds a struggling Aussie woman, her dress ripped open. "Sh ... Sh ... Quiet girlie. Calm yourself," the Yank warns. "He'll be on the next casualty list. No worry." Japanese "psychological operations" (PSYOPs) baldly exploited lonesome enemy troops' desires for wives, sweethearts, and sex partners (because, unlike the Japanese forces, they had no organized "comfort women" system to satiate their libidos). One cartoon shows a woman in a red beret pleading, "Please! Please come back! Don't die, it's terrible to be dead! We need each other. It would be awful if you're crippled. I wouldn't know what to do if you were." The message hints that women might reject a maimed serviceman as a partner. Another leaflet, labeled "Ticket to Armistice," features a photograph of a nude white woman, alongside text saying,

> USE THIS TICKET, SAVE YOUR LIFE AND YOU WILL BE KINDLY TREATED.
> Follow these instructions:
> Come towards our lines waving a white flag.
> Strap your gun over your left shoulder muzzle down and pointed behind you.
> Show this ticket to the sentry.
> Any number of you may surrender with this one ticket.[64]

NHK joined the PSYOP campaign, aiming shortwave radio broadcasts at Allied troops. "I wonder who your wives and girl friends are out with tonight," English-speaking female announcers (collectively known as "Tokyo Rose") asked coyly on the *Zero Hour* program. "Maybe with a 4F or a war plant worker making big money while you are out here fighting and knowing you can't succeed." Sidelined after ballrooms closed, Japan's best jazz musicians assembled in NHK studios to perform for these broadcasts, accompanying nisei singers who rewrote popular song lyrics to mock the troops. The state-run radio station was the only place in Japan where one could legally play jazz, albeit "for the country's sake."[65]

Clearly popular culture had a symbiotic relationship with modern Japan's warfare. The Sino- and Russo-Japanese Wars coincided with and

FIGURE 7.3 *Australia Screams, 1942, Enemy Leaflet Collection, Sub-series 2: Japanese leaflets, Folder 2: To Australian and American Troops Album, 1/ 3/2/18, Australian War Memorial (https://www.awm.gov.au/findingaids/ guide-enemy-leaflet-collection).*

contributed to the expansion of printed, musical, photographic, and cinematic mass media. In World War II the state was much more proactive in shaping popular culture through censorship and directive, but often did so in collaboration with entertainers, artists, and media companies themselves. The most important thematic continuity in popular culture across all three wars was the exaltation of the *bushidō* mythos, which applied to all Japanese, purportedly giving them a spiritual advantage that compensated for material deficiencies compared to their more "decadent" antagonists. Conflicts with countries that had had profound cultural impacts on Japan—China, Russia, and the United States—entailed a sometimes traumatic reevaluation of them, yet only in World War II did this result in a systematic effort to purge enemy influence from public culture. In this regard, the cultural cleansing resembled European fascist doctrines and practices. Fascist principles of racial purity and superiority, of spirit and sentiment over material and rationality, of the ennobling effects of war, and of the glorification of service unto death for the nation suffused popular culture.

An interesting change is detectable in the popular culture of each successive war: in the first China war, depictions of the enemy were rife and uniformly disparaging; in the Russia war, opponents were visible yet rarely caricatured, the emphasis being instead on the resemblances between Russians and Westernized Japanese; but in World War II, aside from demonic depictions of leaders such as Roosevelt, Churchill, and Chiang, the enemy was almost invisible. Emphasis was placed instead on Japanese soldiers, sailors, and civilians who provided exemplary service in battle or on the home front. Although depictions of women and men were highly gendered—meaning their respective roles and contributions were distinct, indicating a gender-based division of labor—both sexes were held accountable for wartime service, and both were shown in movies, cartoons, photography, and literature carrying out those duties.

Popular culture probably had no serious impact on the Japanese military's fortunes at the front. Nonetheless, it is likely that soldiers who made suicide charges at the enemy on Iwo Jima, kamikaze pilots who flew their petroleum-laden planes into Allied warships, and divers who steered underwater torpedoes in suicide missions were influenced by popular media that venerated the *bushidō* ideal of "honorable war death." Their willingness to die, taking out as many enemy troops as they could in the process, was a sign of military desperation but gave Japan a momentary psychological advantage. Allied forces struggled to comprehend this mentality. It is not an unfamiliar dilemma today: how does one fight an enemy who does not care to survive the encounter?

CHAPTER EIGHT

Democracy, monstrosity, and pensive prosperity—postwar pop

On August 15, 1945, when Emperor Hirohito announced via radio broadcast that his subjects must "endure the unendurable" and surrender to the Allies, sixty-seven Japanese cities lay in ruins. Air raids under the command of US Air Force Colonel Curtis LeMay (1906–90) had decimated urban Japan with low-altitude, nighttime incendiary attacks intended to break the will of the Japanese people. On August 6 and 9, Hiroshima and Nagasaki, respectively, were practically wiped off the map with the first and only atomic weapons used in combat (so far). In the first few years of the US occupation of Japan (1945–52), Japanese who lived in cities suffered starvation in the bleak shadows of bombed-out buildings that hardly qualified as shelter.

Nine years after the end of the war, on November 3, 1954, Tōhō studios released a science fiction film in which broad swaths of Tokyo were obliterated once again. Onscreen, emergency relief workers and scientists with Geiger counters tended to the bloodied, broken, irradiated bodies of young and old alike. All but the youngest members of the audience had witnessed such scenes in real life; some were old enough to also recall the aftermath of the 1923 earthquake. Some theatergoers wept, re-traumatized by what they watched, but Tokyo, Ōsaka, and other Japanese cities were in for even more onscreen devastation over the next two decades, in a series of movies emphasizing the "profound vulnerability of Japan."[1] That 1954 film was titled *Gojira*; a heavily edited 1956 version for American consumption anglicized its title as *Godzilla*. In a film series that initially continued until 1975, the atomic-powered reptilian behemoth and his friends and foes—Mothra,

Ghidorah, Radon (anglicized Rodan), Gamera, Anguirus, and American guest star King Kong—used urban landscapes as *sumō* rings. Monster movies (*kaijū eiga*) highlighted the fragility and impermanence of modern life and its monuments, while also pitching technology as humanity's salvation. These films were not only popular overseas but also shaped international conceptions of Japanese and their mass entertainment. Anticipating the alternately technophilic and technophobic animated films that enthralled increasingly large subcultures around the world in the 1990s, *kaijū eiga* of the 1960s–70s were stamped with a specifically Japanese brand that chipped away at the stereotype of the "borrower nation" whose culture was entirely derivative. Yet in their amusement at unconvincing special effects (*tokusatsu*) and lips out of sync with dubbed English voices, foreign viewers missed the role of monster films within a broader cultural phenomenon in postwar Japan, which I call "pensive prosperity."

In the first three decades after the war, Japan's economy expanded by leaps and bounds, becoming the world's second largest by the late 1960s and early 1970s. Average standards of living, social mobility, educational levels, urbanization, and consumerism grew exponentially. Neighboring countries such as the "Four Asian Tigers"—South Korea, Taiwan, Hong Kong, and Singapore—sought to replicate Japan's "economic miracle" through its model of "state-guided capitalism" and export-driven development encouraged by US Cold War policies.[2] By the 1980s American policymakers and corporations, amnesic about US contributions to the situation, expressed a mixture of admiration and resentment toward Japan's economic might. Until the bursting of the price asset bubble in 1991, postwar Japan was a success story, and the concomitant hubris found expression in mass entertainment.

But popular culture provided cautionary counternarratives, as well, sometimes through genres such as *kaijū eiga*, which seemed devoid of any deep thematic meaning whatsoever. Mass entertainment articulated, if sometimes obliquely, an intensified "anti-modern ambivalence," nostalgia for native places (*furusato*) and "discourses of the vanishing" Japan, and a pensive, dystopian acknowledgment of the delicacy and impermanence of it all.[3] Some may regard this sentiment as the retention of *mono no aware*, the epiphanic, Buddhist-informed, poignant pleasure that courtiers of the Heian era (794–1185) took in recognizing the transience, impermanence, and perishability of all things in this illusory world. Yet resort to such facile, anachronistic cultural explanations is unsatisfying. The more immediate experiences of disruptive modernization, industrial poisoning of people and ecosystems, government tyranny, natural disaster, and a cataclysmic war informed the postwar malaise and disaffection of Japanese.

To be sure, popular culture expressed optimistic, national triumphalism: the 1964 Tokyo Olympics and the debut of the Shinkansen bullet train are but two examples.[4] National egotism and anxiety cohabited as themes in popular entertainment. *Gojira* itself modeled this: the titular creature's havoc is mitigated somewhat by the scientific genius and *bushido*-like moral heroism of Dr. Serizawa, who creates an "oxygen destroyer" weapon of comparable lethality to atomic weaponry, yet deliberately dies when deploying it to slay the dragon, lest its secrets ever fall into the wrong hands.[5] In contrast to the United States' irresponsible, if indirect, destruction of Tokyo via nuclearsaurus, Japan displayed its moral superiority over its conquerors and occupiers by saving the world from hypothetical destruction. Unintentionally, it echoed Hirohito's benevolent determination to end the war for the "common prosperity and happiness of all nations" and to avoid the "total extinction of human civilization."[6] Japan 1, United States 0.

In the five decades after the war popular culture was so diverse that it is almost impossible to identify a single comprehensive, intellectually responsible theme or characterization. To the aforementioned "pensive prosperity," then, I would add the following: popular culture became notably more technologically focused and driven; more prone to a nationalistic nostalgia; more diverse through the cultivation of niche markets, "micro-masses," and "consumer individualization";[7] and less beholden to a rigid, rigorous censorship regime than ever before. Many of these trends emerged in the crucible of occupation by Japan's former enemy and its later subservient position under the US "nuclear umbrella." Indeed, one of the sources of postwar ambivalence was enjoying the benefits of this Cold War security arrangement, while building a national identity of antinuclear pacifism based on Japan's singular experience of atomic warfare.

Occupation

Whatever its shortcomings, abuses, and failures—and they were legion—the US occupation of Japan was a pleasant surprise for all involved. At least it was a much less horrific experience than either Americans or Japanese anticipated. American troops, well aware that Japanese of all ages had been indoctrinated and trained to fight invaders to the death, instead met hungry children waving the Stars and Stripes, not bamboo spears. Japanese who predicted massacres and unchecked sexual violence (as Japanese and Soviet troops committed routinely) encountered American soldiers with bags full of gum, candy, and nylon hose.

The Supreme Commander of Allied Powers (SCAP)—designating both the occupation administration and its head, General Douglas MacArthur—embarked on a campaign to reinvent Japan as a demilitarized, democratic society. In his magisterial study of the occupation, Dower argues that its successes are attributable both to the sincere idealism of many SCAP officials and to the fact that the occupation gave Japanese rights and liberties for which many thousands had suffered decades of persecution, public humiliation, imprisonment, and execution. SCAP conferred these with the stroke of a pen. SCAP took full advantage of mass media and popular entertainment to disseminate its agenda: divesting the emperor of his sovereignty (retaining him only as a "symbol of the State and of the unity of the People"); promulgating a new, yet-to-be-amended constitution; prosecuting selected high-profile wartime leaders as Class A war criminals; breaking up corporate conglomerates (*zaibatsu*); instituting fundamental land reforms; legalizing labor unions; granting political rights to women; and dismantling Japan's military.

Japanese were well aware of the "inherent contradiction of democracy by fiat" and realized that MacArthur had powers above and beyond anything the monarch had ever enjoyed.[8] He was, in fact, the emperor's patron, not unlike Oda Nobunaga and Toyotomi Hideyoshi had once presented themselves. To the chagrin of many Americans and not a few Japanese, MacArthur decided unilaterally not to prosecute Hirohito as a war criminal. Media culture itself provided proof enough of an "exasperating" paradox. Japanese were now free to say whatever they wanted about the emperor (*and* his mama), to promote socialism (initially, at least), feminism or any other cause or ideology; to lambaste public officials publicly; and to demonstrate, agitate, and cogitate in an environment without "thought crimes." But they could not criticize SCAP personnel and policies or depict occupation troops in public media. A perusal of the Japanese press in the late 1940s and early 1950s yields precious little information about the occupation. It was in plain sight on the streets, but in the mass media it was invisible. Censorship itself was unmentionable. Dower writes,

> The policy of censoring the existence of censorship itself cast a taint of hypocrisy on the Americans and compared poorly with the old system of the militarists and ultranationalists, who until the late 1930s had allowed excised portions of texts to be marked in publications with Xs and Os. At least prewar readers knew that *something* had been excised; they could even count the Xs and Os and try to guess what. It is not surprising, then, that some writers who experienced censorship under both systems were cynical in their appraisals of SCAP's version of free expression ... [A]t least the Japanese censors had served tea.[9]

Popular culture of the occupation era, then, was as profoundly shaped by the limits of permissibility as that of wartime. Oversight was split between two units: SCAP's Civil Censorship Detachment (CCD) was responsible for suppressing "feudal," militaristic content, and its Civil Information and Education section (CIE) for disseminating democratic propaganda. Filmmakers, more than any constituency other than news media, saw the least change in their methods of operation. Theirs was the most tightly regulated of all entertainment industries under both the militarist and the SCAP regimes, told what sorts of films they could not produce, provided with "suggestions" or "recommendations" for subject matter and subjected to pre- and postproduction review. CCD proscribed period films featuring samurai, for instance, because in the previous decade such movies had promoted militarism and *bushidō*. CIE issued directives that movies promote democratic values, individualism, and feminism. Studios obliged, if for no other reason than they were simply relieved not to be prosecuted for their earlier propagandistic productions. "The speed with which the Japanese studio heads changed their policy from promoting war to promoting democracy astounded their employees," Kyoko Hirano writes, and fostered general cynicism about the entertainment industry's unprincipled opportunism.[10]

Many of the films produced under the occupation "lacked conviction" and were criticized as every bit as "crudely propagandistic" as wartime movies, but now Japanese audiences were openly amused by them. The silliest directive was CIE chief David Conde's insistence that Japanese films include kissing scenes, because—alluding to the surprise attack on Pearl Harbor—"Japanese tend to do things sneakily. They should do things openly." Onscreen kisses had been prohibited for decades and were excised from foreign films. Now public displays of affection were considered crucial to the creation of an open, democratic society. The first kissing scene, between Ikuno Michiko (1924–) and Ōsaka Shirō (1920–89) in *Twenty-Year-Old Youth* (*Hatachi no seishun*, 1946), set off a public debate about the "Japaneseness" of kissing, but CIE officials held firm that Japanese should "express publicly actions and feelings that heretofore had been considered strictly private" for a democratic, free society to take root.[11] Incidentally, Ikuno, apparently unsure where Ōsaka's mouth had been, reportedly put gauze in her mouth before kissing him.

Gratuitous onscreen kissing was a relatively wholesome manifestation of the sexualized entertainment of the occupation years generally known as *kasutori bunka* (hooch culture), named for the "drink of choice among those artists and writers who made a cult out of degeneracy and nihilism."[12] Striptease, pornographic print media, and streetwalking *pan-pan* girls made for a more sexualized public culture than had existed since the times of the Edo-period pleasure districts. Moralists who denounced *kasutori* culture paid almost no heed to the plights of women who publicly exposed their nude bodies out of economic desperation caused by war, defeat, inflation, and exploitation by both Japanese miscreants and American troops.

Cinema and radio were the central concerns of CIE, but on semi- and unofficial levels occupation troops promoted Americana among Japanese to facilitate democratization. Herbert Passin (1916–2003), a former CIE official and sociologist of Japan, recalled several "idiosyncratic interpretations of 'democratization'": "I remember meeting young military-government officers in the provinces who were absolutely convinced that square dancing was the magic key to transforming Japan into a democratic society."[13]

Popular music was in fact an important component of living under and remembering occupation: it "involved the working out of new questions about freedom in relation to the exploding market of mass culture."[14] NHK radio featured democratic propaganda with a few morsels of American music through such programs as *New Pacific Hour*, but Japanese could also tune in to WVTR, the US Armed Forces Radio Service, to listen to jazz, "hillbilly," and pop music from the States. American popular music was certainly not completely new to Japanese, but never had they had such steady access to it in all its variety. That variety was a challenge to Japanese musicians hired as day laborers for gigs at rank- and race-segregated servicemen's clubs and cabarets: white officers' clubs preferred Glenn Miller/Guy Lombardo dance orchestras; black enlisted men wanted bebop or R & B; and southern whites demanded country and western.[15]

Many Americans staunchly believed baseball would democratize Japan. American authorities proactively and enthusiastically assisted in the "binational project" of resurrecting professional and semipro industrial leagues as "a new national iconography of peace, democracy and freedom, signifying both a continuity with an idealized yesteryear and a clean break from the rejected past." This campaign was "invested with complex political agendas, social purposes, and cultural symbolism" that bound the United States and Japan together as Cold War allies. Spectatorship increased substantially, making baseball much more prominent in popular culture than it had been before the war. SCAP was predictably diffident toward Japan's other favorite sport, *sumō*, requisitioning its major arena on December 26, 1945.[16]

It was no accident that democratization meant Americanization. Few if any Japanese thought of it otherwise, and Americans were unapologetic about it. Japanese critiques of the occupation as cultural imperialism continue in public discourse today. These are not totally without merit, yet it is also true that what Japanese considered their cultural traditions did not fare so badly during and after the occupation. In fact, several prominent SCAP officials (some of whom earned PhDs on the GI Bill and became the second generation of North American Japan studies professors) were advocates for indigenous arts and amusements. James Brandon offers compelling evidence to debunk the longstanding myth that SCAP suppressed kabuki. It fared far worse under the wartime state, which closed theaters and admonished actors "to take up more useful occupations." SCAP, however, suppressed a mere dozen of the "most blatantly militaristic and feudalistic" plays out of 350 scripts the Shōchiku entertainment company submitted for inspection. "By November 1949, *kabuki* was free of government censorship for the first time in its history." If anyone held the upper hand in negotiations regarding kabuki, it was Shōchiku, which wound up conceding nothing: "Despite paying lip service to a new, democratic Japan, Shōchiku never wavered from its aim of performing the traditional, feudal repertory in all its grotesque glory." And occupation officials fell in love with it.[17] They were no more willing to tamper with a 350-year-old art form than MacArthur was to abolish the oldest surviving monarchical dynasty on Earth. So Japanophilia among SCAP personnel enabled traditional arts and culture to thrive again.

Contemporary opinions about the US occupation vary wildly. People at polar ends of the ideological spectrum criticize it stridently. Political conservatives protest the Tokyo Tribunal's "victor's justice" and Japan's being held solely accountable for the war, SCAP's arrogance and intrusiveness, and the Americanization of popular culture. For rightists all of this overshadows the unprecedented effort of a victorious power to rehabilitate and revive its former enemy and the popularity of MacArthur and occupation reforms among most Japanese at the time.[18] When the occupation ended, they set about undoing as much of its legacy as they possibly could, but despite occasional noise they have (for now) failed to amend the 1947 Constitution, whose singular renunciation of warfare, Article 9, remains both immensely popular and a source of national pride among most Japanese. If for conservatives the occupation went too far, for leftists it did not go far enough. Political liberals are disillusioned by SCAP's failure to deliver on its initial promise, its retention of the emperor, its ultimate failure to bust *zaibatsu* conglomerates and its anticommunist "reverse course" after 1948, which prioritized Cold War strategic interests. For them, MacArthur's unsuccessful effort to *re*militarize Japan for participation in the Korean War tarnishes his reputation considerably.[19]

High times, no nukes

With a major boost from the occupation's economic policies and the Korean War, Japan in the 1950s embarked on an economic recovery that by the 1960s had morphed into campaigns for "high-speed growth" (*kōdo seichō*) and "income doubling" (*shotoku baizō*). From 1955 Japan became essentially a one-party democracy, as the conservative Liberal Democratic Party (LDP) dominated the Diet until 1993. Relieved of major defense outlays while under Cold War America's protection, Japanese government and industry were able to focus on infrastructural development and export of a variety of goods, particularly cars and consumer electronics. It was in the early postwar era that the urban population surpassed the rural one, that white-collar corporate employment as a "salaryman" became the aspiration of many men, and housewifery the ideal for women. Domestic consumption of goods, services, and entertainment were crucial aspects of this recovery.

Whatever its benefits, there were drawbacks to the scale, pace, and priorities of state-guided high-speed growth. The process of economic development was hardly smooth, but fraught with tension, protest, and occasional violence. Edward Abbey's oft-cited, seldom-heeded maxim "Growth for the sake of growth is the ideology of a cancer cell" seemed prescient.[20] Many Japanese came to realize by the 1970s that improvements to quality of life and alignment with the United States in the Cold War were counterbalanced by serious threats to physical and mental health, family life, the natural environment, gender equality, and national security.[21] In the 1950s mercury emissions from the Chissō plant poisoned hundreds in the fishing village of Minamata, and arsenic in Morinaga milk formula sickened infants nationwide. Government and industry responded to these emergencies with sloth-like speed and the compassion of a tree frog. The agonizingly slow response to care for and compensate the thousands of victims, via a convoluted certification process, paralleled the fate of so-called *hibakusha*, radiation-poisoned survivors from Hiroshima and Nagasaki.[22]

Although popular culture served as a distraction from all of this, it also provided powerful critiques of environmental destruction, unresponsive government, social dislocation and injustice, single-minded "growthism," and the psychological stresses that the "credential society" (*gakureki shakai*) put on families, workers, students, and communities. *Hibakusha* were perhaps the injured constituency most active in responding to their plight through cultural production. Fictional and documentary films, autobiographical and semifictional literature, manga and anime, songs, and drawings and paintings documented their struggles with pain and social discrimination.[23] One well-known example is that of Sasaki Sadako (1943–55), a girl who was exposed to radiation at Hiroshima as a toddler and died of leukemia at age twelve. In her last weeks of life in a nursing home, Sasaki started to make a string of 1,000 origami (folded paper) cranes, a good-luck talisman in folk legend. After her death this craft project became a popular, collaborative activity around the world, symbolizing antinuclear pacifism.[24]

Perhaps the most famous antiwar work by a *hibakusha* is the cartoon *Barefoot Gen* (*Hadashi no Gen*) by Hiroshima survivor Nakazawa Keiji (1939–2012). Drawing on his own experiences as a boy caring for his mother and baby sister in the aftermath of the atomic attack, Nakazawa produced a manga serial for *Weekly Shōnen Jump* (1973–85), which was later adapted for anime in 1983 and 1986.[25] Nakazawa pulled no punches: the destruction of bodies by the blast is graphically rendered and is not for the squeamish, and his baby sister perishes. *Gen* mercilessly excoriated the wartime regime, brainwashing education, and even the occupation (at one point he witnesses American soldiers harvesting organs for medical experiments). But the cartoonist also depicted kindness between strangers, quasi-family relationships created between victims, and persistent hope.

Hibakusha art was part of a broader cultural critique of nuclear warfare in mass media, of which *Gojira* was an early example. Based on the real-life irradiation of the crew of the *Lucky Dragon* #5 fishing vessel by US nuclear testing in the Bikini Atoll on March 1, 1954, the story warned about the unforeseen, uncontrollable consequences of atomic weaponry and radiation, emphasizing American culpability and Japanese victimization. Atomic blasts were also responsible for awakening the Thyreophoran Anguirus (1955), the Pteranodon Radon (1956), the Heterocera Mothra (1961), the Chelonian Gamera (1965), and the Gargantuan Frankenstein monsters Sanda and Gaira (1965–66). One of the things that distinguish the 1954 *Gojira* from these later *kaijū* films is the graphic depiction of the creature's ravages. "Death and suffering are depicted matter-of-factly in Godzilla's attacks; radiation is not just something mysterious, antiseptic, or theoretical," William Tsutsui observes, "but is an unrelenting lethal force unleashed against nature and humankind alike. Even Godzilla's skin, thick and furrowed like the keloid scars that afflicted the survivors of Hiroshima and Nagasaki, evoked the agony of irradiation."[26] The seriousness of the original film has been undercut by its numerous kid-friendly sequels, which recast the saurian stomper as a hero who protects Japan from other giant varmints, all of whom became "something akin to household pets."[27] By 1968's *Destroy All Monsters*, characters onscreen are laughably blasé about further rounds of *kaijū* pandemonium.

Unsurprisingly, the 1956 American version of *Godzilla* mutes criticism of US nuclear militarism. Film executives recognized and neutralized its potential to offend American audiences, via an editing process "reflecting metaphorically the reality of contemporary power relations" between Japan and the United States. The *New York Times* critic reassured audiences that, although they "might regard [Godzilla] as a symbol of Japanese hate for the destruction that came out of nowhere and descended upon Hiroshima one pleasant August morn[,] ... the quality of the picture and childishness of the whole idea do not indicate such calculation. Godzilla was simply meant to scare people."[28] "One of the commodities [Tōhō Studios] sold was artistic integrity and pride," Guthrie-Shimizu surmises. The virtual erasure of antinuclear themes in later American *Godzilla* reboots is particularly irksome. In the 1998 version, *French* nuclear testing in the South Pacific (which had indeed transpired in 1996) transforms a Komodo dragon into the giant monster that devastates Panama and New York. In the 2014 movie, *naturally occurring* radiation created Godzilla and his nemeses the "MUTOs" (Massive Unidentified Terrestrial Organisms).The nuclear "tests" of the 1950s had in fact been top-secret efforts to kill the beasts. In other words, humans—Americans, particularly—were off the hook for the creation of *kaijū*. A dream scenario for those who deny the Anthropocene.

Monster films were by no means the only vehicles for criticism of the atomic age. An "atomic bomb literature" (*genbaku bungaku*) emerged, consisting of fictional and nonfictional works by survivors and sympathizers "who have the memory of a likely future in which all human experience concludes." *Genbaku* author Ōe Kenzaburō remarked that such works are not only historical accounts of Hiroshima and Nagasaki but "also highly significant vehicles for thinking about the contemporary world over which hangs the awesome threat of vastly expanded nuclear arsenals ... [and] a means for stirring imaginative powers to consider the fundamental conditions of human existence; they are relevant to the present and to our movement towards all tomorrows."[29] One of the most famous *genbaku* novels, *Black Rain* (*Kuroi ame*, 1965), by Ibuse Masuji (1898–1993), went on to address the stigma attached to *hibakusha*, with a story of a young woman whose custodial uncle is unable to negotiate a marriage for her because she was in Hiroshima when the bomb fell.[30] Kurosawa Akira's 1955 film *Record of a Living Being* (*Ikimono no kiroku*) also stirs the conscience with the story of a retiree, played by the redoubtable Mifune Toshirō (1920–97), who plans to relocate his entire family to Brazil to escape an impending nuclear holocaust. Synopses of the film regularly describe Mifune's Nakajima Kiichi as paranoid and delusional, but Kurosawa implies that his family's complacency might be more deranged (this theme was echoed thirty years later in another Kurosawa production, 1985's *Ran*, in which one character wails, "In a mad world, only the mad are truly sane!").

Identity crisis

A ubiquitous subtext of so much postwar popular culture was anxiety about Japanese identity and its potential atrophy amid the relentless onslaught of Americana. The swift resurrection of *jidaigeki* samurai cinema after SCAP went home was one manifestation of this. Kinugasa Teinosuke's (1896–1982) *Gate of Hell* (*Jigokumon*, 1953), Kurosawa's *Seven Samurai*, and Inagaki Hiroshi's (1905–80) *Samurai Trilogy* (1954–56) are examples, but probably unrepresentative: for every period film later lauded as a masterpiece— usually by foreign critics—there were perhaps a dozen more lucrative ones that have since been forgotten.

Although Kurosawa always insisted that he made his films for Japanese audiences rather than for foreign art house theaters and festivals, his notoriety at home was the result of his ascendant reputation in Europe and North America. Kurosawa became a household name whose films were not (always) flops, but not what ordinary Japanese preferred, either. Andrew Horvat argues that Kurosawa's "moralist" tendencies and implicit critiques of wartime totalitarianism were "perhaps not all that welcome by the majority of his audience at home in the years immediately after Japan's defeat." Japanese critics chafed somewhat at the adulation Americans and Europeans heaped upon the director after *Rashōmon*'s Venice Film Festival victory. They argued that foreign audiences were simply mesmerized by the "exoticism" of Kurosawa's *jidaigeki*, which "define[d] Japanese identity" for them—though that would not explain the acclaim of 1952's *To Live* (*Ikiru*), which was set in modern times.[31] Kurosawa was thus saddled with the reputation of being Japan's most "Western" director, the polar opposite of the more "Japanese" elegiac themes and understated, poetic style of Ozu Yasujirō (1903–63).[32]

Another genre that enjoyed a postwar, postoccupation resurgence was the *yakuza* film, which romanticized gangsters as modern-day samurai, who lived by codes of chivalry (*ninkyō*) and dutiful loyalty (*jingi*). Occasionally they were portrayed as Robin Hood–like champions of the people against The Man (remember him?). *Yakuza* films date back to the silent era, overlapping *jidaigeki* with period settings. In the genre's 1960s "golden age," contemporary gangster heroes encountered the same age-old *ninjō-giri* conflicts that had been a staple of Japanese narratives since the Edo period. Studios could present much the same thematic material—a celebration of "traditional values" purportedly peculiar to Japan—without the added expense of *jidaigeki*.[33] By the 1970s *jidaigeki* and *yakuza* films both declined in production and popularity, but since the 1990s the latter genre has enjoyed a revival, with increasingly graphic violence and a more nihilistic than *bushidō*-like sensibility. The famous maverick actor/director/writer Kitano "Beat" Takeshi has become the Quentin Tarantino of *yakuza* fare, infusing the formulaic genre with superior craftsmanship and thematic depth, while also indulging in over-the-top displays of bloodbathing.

In the late 1950s, cinematic narratives of rebellious, listless teenagers infatuated with American youth culture—that is, acting "un-Japanese"— were produced in sufficient quantities to qualify as a genre: "sun-tribe" (*taiyōzoku*) films. As was also the case in the United States, there was a moral panic about juvenile delinquency, which provided fodder for pulp fiction and movies. Starting in 1956 with *Crazed Fruit* (*Kuruta kajitsu*) and *Season of the Sun* (*Taiyō no kisetsu*), *taiyōzoku* movies evolved from sensationalist and lurid to serious critiques of the corrupt capitalist growthism of adults, as the root of youthful disaffection. The best known and most well regarded of these films was Ōshima Nagisa's (1932–2013) *Cruel Stories of Youth* (*Seishun zankoku monogatari*, 1960), hailed as the progenitor of *la Nouvelle Vague japonaise*. However, viewers were more likely to see the decline of Japanese cultural values in youthful dissipation, indolence, and insolence than in the obsessions of the parental generation guiding economic growth. That is, like 1936's *Ōsaka Elegy*, *taiyōzoku* films could yield opposite readings, depending on the viewer's ideological or political stance.

Probably the most overtly nostalgic cinematic offering was the 48-film series *It's Tough Being a Man* (*Otoko wa tsurai yo*, 1969–95), starring Atsumi Kiyoshi (1928–96) as the wandering sales-tramp Tora-san. A lovable loser who pines both for his hometown and the "Madonna" (leading lady) du jour of each hamlet he visits—with whom he invariably strikes out—Tora-san was the Japanese counterpart of Chaplin's Little Tramp, both "free spirits living on the fringes of society and … instantly recognizable figures who always wear the same clothes." Director Yamada Yōji (1931–) cranked out about two Tora-san films a year until Atsumi's death, building a loyal, aging fan base to whom the bucolic Japan projected onscreen was precious.[34]

Japanese cultural identity was a principal concern (along with liquor and separated lovers) of *enka* songs. Postwar *enka* were based on the sentimental lyrics and "Koga melodies" of interwar songsmith Koga Masao. The *yonanuki* pentatonic melodies and the formulaic lyrical sentimentalism remained, but *enka*'s musical settings were eclectic, featuring different combinations of jazz orchestration, string sections, traditional indigenous instruments (*shamisen*, *shakuhachi*, or *koto*), and occasional Spanish guitar inflections. Yano defines *enka* as a ballad genre that originated in the twentieth century (Nippon Columbia named it in 1973), yet "sounds timelessly old" as a result of "collective forgetting" or "genesis amnesia" similar to that which obscures the invention or renovation of other Japanese traditions. "The erasure of passing time is in fact part of its attraction," she contends: in *enka*, the perplexing transformation of postwar Japanese society "is managed through nostalgia." If *enka* has a single identifiable message, it is "We long for our past Japanese selves."[35]

Enka producers were not merely churning out hit songs but also peddling an exoticized, elegiac vision of "Japan," a place whose essence has not changed, where women love with single-minded, self-destructive devotion, and where men stoically pursue the selfless *otoko no michi* (man's path). *Enka* has performed two important social functions: "it is a technology for creating national and cultural memory and it is an archive of the nation's collective past." As an artistic response to and commentary on the extraordinary changes Japanese witnessed in the twentieth century, the genre critiques the dehumanizing forces of modernity and posits a premodern utopia in which "cultural nationalism is unnecessary" because a purer, more humane and emotionally enriching existence prevailed.[36] The longing for one's pastoral home was a response to urbanization; the oftentimes gendered lyrics expressed nostalgia for more clearly defined markers of femininity and masculinity; the parting of lovers suggested lack of control over one's fate; self-medication with alcohol provided the only viable, if ephemeral, relief.

These functions give *enka* the "cultural weight" that has enabled it to remain a viable cultural commodity in defiance of millennial market forces and music trends. "An affinity for *enka* is said to run in the (Japanese) blood; those who dislike it have allowed themselves to be seduced away from their own innate Japaneseness."[37] In spite of its clearly declining profitability in the last two decades, record companies continue to invest in the production of *enka*, and NHK has tenaciously spotlighted *enka* as the national popular song style on its *Red and White Song Competition* (*Kōhaku uta gassen*) program every New Year's Eve since 1951 (on television since 1953). Today, many consider *enka* outdated and *furu-kusai* (old smelling). But as long as nostalgic nativism retains its potency, Yano asserts, *enka* will have an audience.

Enka produced postwar Japan's most popular star, Misora Hibari (1937–89). Scholars agree that the most comparable figures in Western popular culture would be Elvis Presley, Frank Sinatra, and Edith Piaf, "loved by some and reviled by others." Alan Tansman states that detractors dismiss Misora as "an uneasy reminder of a gloomy past better left behind, [and] the queasy schmaltz of an outdated culture," while devotees see in her "the essence of a much-vaunted Japanese spirit of forbearance—specifically, of postwar forbearance."[38] Her death in 1989 at age fifty-two followed six months after that of Emperor Hirohito, bringing the Shōwa era to a symbolic close. Misora's career began at age eight when she performed at a Yokohama concert hall and made her first recording as a Koga protégé at twelve. She also appeared in some 150 films between 1949 and 1981, recorded 1,200 songs, and sold tens of millions of albums and singles.[39] Deborah Shamoon detects significant shifts in Misora's image over the course of her career, a persona "reflect[ing] the cultural changes in Japan in the postwar years, specifically the reassertion of native cultural values after the U.S. Occupation." At the height of *kasutori* culture and "literature of the flesh" (*nikutai bungaku*), Misora's image was that of a "precocious, scandalously sexualized child. When she made the transition to teen film star, her image changed radically from disruptive and risqué to conservative and chaste." In Shamoon's estimation, "Hibari appears as something of a blank slate onto which the nation projected its hopes and anxieties." Highlighting her potency as a signifier of nostalgic nationalism, Michael Bourdaghs adds that "her singing represented a decolonized, authentically Japanese voice."[40]

New toys

We have seen the impact each new mass media technology—woodblock and press printing, still and moving photography, film projection, recorded sound and radio broadcasting—had on popular culture in Japan. Because it built upon existing electronic media, the dissemination of television was perhaps not quite as epochal, but it was hardly negligible. In 1953, public service broadcaster NHK launched its television channel (for which all viewers with a television are supposed to pay annual subscription fees), followed closely by the *Yomiuri* newspaper's commercial station Nippon Television (NTV). Between 1955 and 1964, four additional commercial news channels went on the air.

Television transformed the private home into a site for entertainment and information, more so even than radio had before. Japan's film studios felt it like a punch to the gut: as television set ownership grew, movie attendance plummeted precipitously. Two major live broadcast events—the 1959 royal wedding of Crown Prince Akihito to his commoner bride, Michiko, and the 1964 Tokyo Olympics—demonstrated the advantages of television over movies, particularly its potential for solidifying national community. Television's challenge helps explain the increased production of movies with overtly sexual themes (so-called "pink" movies and *roman poruno*, "romance pornography") and effects-heavy, science fiction/fantasy *tokusatsu* films in the 1960s, as studios sought desperately to drag viewers out of their homes for wild spectacles. But television stations responded with their own *tokusatsu* programming, such as *Moonlight Mask* (*Gekkō kamen*, 1958–59), *Ultraman* (*Urutoroman*, 1966–67), and *Giant Robot* (*Jaianto robo*, 1967–68), the English-dubbed version of which (entitled *Johnny Sokko and His Flying Robot*) my brother and I watched as boys.

Jayson Chun says that television transformed Japan's "relatively diverse society" into "one large electronic audience partaking in a vast national consumer culture," centered in and on Tokyo. "The Japanese reigned as the heaviest users of television in the world, with people watching more hours of TV every day than people in any other country." The impact on daily routines and habits was rapid and astonishing: "In 1965, twelve years after the introduction of this new device, Japanese spent more time each day watching television than eating, doing hobbies and conversing with other people combined."[41] Chun's "social history" approach to Japanese television highlights "interactions" between viewers and programming, emphasizing not only TV's role in mediating people's sociopolitical awareness, experiences, and memories but also their responses and subsequent actions. This framework serves as a metonym for hegemony: although it is easy to imagine what Ōya Sōichi called "a nation of a hundred million idiots" spending untold hours looking at television, as Chun argues there was both a vigorous public discussion about television's ramifications and grassroots action motivated by televisual exposure to government corruption, terrorism, the Vietnam War, leftist protests, pollution, and other consequences of single-minded economic development.

Furthermore, television intensified and extended electronic media's role in defining the "social landscape" and boundaries of the Japanese nation, a process Yano argues began with recording and radio technologies in the interwar years (see Chapter 5). In other words, postwar Japan had become a truly "mass society" in which television offered shared experiences that transcended geographical and social boundaries. The 1964 Tokyo Olympics was crucial to this process: a televisual spectacle throughout the archipelago and around the world, a monumental national event signifying Japan's ascendancy from the humiliation and despondency of defeat and occupation. World War II had prevented Tokyo from hosting in 1940, so "the connection between the Second World War and the Tokyo Olympics was at the forefront of people's minds" throughout the Games.[42] It was a connection Japanese organizers opted not to obscure, but rather to highlight. As shown in Ichikawa Kon's (1915–2008) documentary film *Tokyo Olympiad* (1965), the person appointed to carry the torch and light the Olympic flame at the opening ceremony was university student Sakai Yoshinori (1945–2014), who was born in Hiroshima within two hours of the atomic blast.[43]

The pressure on Tokyo to look its best and to make foreign competitors and spectators feel comfortable was matched perhaps only by the pressure on Japanese athletes to perform at or beyond their capacities, before an audience of millions. Happily, they were the third most successful team in the medal count. One "gift from the gods" was the women's volleyball team, "The Witches of the Orient," captained by Kasai Masae (1933–2013) and coached by Daimatsu Hirobumi (1921–78), an army veteran who implemented a military-style, "homicidal training" (*satsujin taisō*) regimen that bordered on the sadistic.[44] The domestic and foreign press characterized the Witches as the female embodiments of the timeworn *bushidō* and *gaman* (perseverance and self-denial) ethics that they considered the essence of national character. In the first Olympiad to feature volleyball, Japan thumped its Cold War nemesis the USSR in the gold medal match, doing wonders for Japanese women's athletics in the years to come. Ever since, Japanese women have been more successful in international competition than their male counterparts.

To be sure, hosting the Olympics involved massive disruption in the form of demolition of old buildings, renovation of the cityscape, relocation of residential homes and businesses, and considerable public expense. The Games' cultural impact extended to everyday habits that linger to this day: when diners receive glasses of water at the beginning of a meal in a restaurant, they are the beneficiaries of a hospitable custom for foreign guests that began during the Tokyo Olympics. More to the point here, domestic sales of transistor radios and televisions soared as people tried to stay apprised of NHK's extensive coverage.[45]

Technologies were obviously important to the growth and spread of popular music, an area in which American influence was most conspicuous. Jazz enjoyed two extended moments in the spotlight of youth culture: the early 1950s' "jazz boom" dominated by bombastic drummer George Kawaguchi's (1917–2003) hard-driving Big Four, and the flood of American jazz acts that followed in the wake of Art Blakey and the Jazz Messengers' triumphant 1961 tour of Japan. Jazz coffeehouses (*jazu kissa*), small spaces where customers could listen to imported LPs on hi-fi stereo systems and occasional live performances, became popular hangouts for youth, especially for college student radicals in the late 1960s who protested Japan's supporting role in the Vietnam War.[46] As it did in the United States, rock and roll eventually displaced jazz as the music of youthful rebellion. The clean-cut pop-rock of crooner Sakamoto Kyū (1941–85) and Beatlesque Group Sounds fueled a boom in sales of electric guitars (*ereki būmu*) and amplification equipment.[47] Japan became synonymous with quality high-fidelity audio systems around the world, raising the bar for listeners overseas. Having watched two full-grown men place a ¥100 coin under a heavy speaker just to hear how it affected sound quality, I can vouch for the obsessive audiophilia that often takes priority over the music itself. When Sony introduced the portable cassette player known as the Walkman in 1979, consumer audio technology seemed to have reached perfection. People could now listen to music of their own choice privately anywhere, anytime, shutting out environmental and parental noise. As you cradle your iPod, remember who its technological grandparent is.

Besides recordings, broadcasts, singing contests, and concerts, one of the most important entertainment technologies for the dissemination of popular music was karaoke (inexplicably anglicized as "carry-oh-kee"). Karaoke means "empty orchestra," referring to instrumental tracks over which participants sing into a microphone piped through the same public address system, in taverns, rented rooms ("boxes") or private homes. Karaoke replaced itinerant guitarists and accordionists (*nagashi*) who wandered between taverns entertaining drinkers. Karaoke began in the 1970s as part of all-male, team building among middle-aged corporate employees, who were generally expected to get drunk together after work rather than go home. Hiro Shimatachi asserts that karaoke has become an "electric geisha—a modern invention that plays the socializing role traditionally performed by a hostess, who employs her entertainment skills to draw out guests and establish camaraderie." Karaoke, Bill Kelly adds, is "a technological innovation which provides a new medium for the expression of an established tradition of performing in front of others, as a means of demonstrating—not consciously but implicitly—an individual's membership within a collectivity."[48]

Originating as a quasi-ritualistic activity among the "*enka* generation" of middle-aged salarymen, karaoke repertoire and singing styles were profoundly shaped by *enka* conventions, an immediate turnoff for many younger Japanese.[49] By the mid-1980s, however, karaoke became a pastime in which people of all ages and backgrounds participated, in part because a greater variety of music had been karaoke-ized—having once "sung" James Brown's "Get Up (I Feel Like Being a) Sex Machine" in a Yokohama karaoke box, I can testify to this firsthand. Although neither skill nor competition have been significant aspects of karaoke culture in Japan (karaoke-as-talent-contest is an Americanized variant), in the 1990s it was not uncommon for people to polish their singing at home in preparation for the next visit to the bar or box.

Karaoke illustrates just how extensively postwar popular culture relied on innovations in consumer technologies (frequently modified foreign inventions). Indeed, fuel-efficient automobiles, transistor radios, mechanized toys, home and portable stereo systems, and the Walkman became signature items "made in Japan." Media culture also expressed a widespread faith in technology not only to make everyday life more convenient but also to rescue Japanese from doomsday scenarios. In nearly every *kaijū* movie, for example, the Self-Defense Forces (Jieitai, SDF) deploy high-tech weaponry and are directed from command centers that resemble the bridge of the *Enterprise* from *Star Trek*—indeed, viewers might wonder if Japan ever actually demilitarized after the war. These films also featured genius scientists working with top secret intelligence and special forces to protect the homeland with futuristic devices like those in the more over-the-top James Bond films like 1967's *You Only Live Twice* (which, incidentally, was set in Japan). Admittedly, their weapons rarely discouraged *kaijū* from romping through Tokyo, Nagoya or Ōsaka.

And yet Japanese popular culture also became known for dystopian visions of technology run amok, even integrating with human flesh to create cyborg monstrosities. Calling this material technophobic would be an overstatement, but at best it was ambivalent about the prominence of technology in everyday life, sometimes suggesting that rampant materialism had rendered Japanese spiritually vacuous. Through the so-called "mecha" (*mekka*) genre of manga and live-action and animated films, Japanese filmmakers explored the boundaries of humanness and the threat of technologies to blur, penetrate, and overrun them. To be sure, the artistic self-consciousness with which writers, directors, and actors probed these themes varied wildly, as did audience receptions and readings of them. The most sophisticated material, critiquing blithe technophilia through apocalyptic scenarios, did not appear until the late 1980s and 1990s, when awareness and disaffection with the effects of economic growth and technological development set in.

Cartoon country

Modern manga and animated films date from the Meiji and Taishō periods, but their ascendency as a dominant and prototypical form of Japanese popular culture occurred in the postwar era. Manga monthlies are the size of phonebooks: in the 1980s more paper was used for manga than for toilet tissue, and in the 1990s manga constituted almost half of all published material.[50] There are manga and anime for every social niche and identity, but people read and watch prodigiously outside their "logical" genres. For decades manga have been used for everything from history texts to instructional manuals to earthquake preparedness brochures. In the 2000s anime constituted nearly 40 percent of filmmaking. Annual revenues in the animated film industry hover around ¥200 billion.

Several scholars have speculated about the relatively peculiar popularity of these expressive forms in Japan. Frederik Schodt argues that "Japanese are predisposed to more visual forms of communication owing to their writing system." Schodt and Brigitte Koyama-Richards also describe manga as a "synthesis" between Western cartoon art and a long tradition of humorous, satirical caricature and illustrated printed matter dating back to antiquity, including doodles drawn on planks in the seventh-century Buddhist temple Hōryūji in Nara and the twelfth-century Frolicking Animals (*Chōjūgiga*), Farting Contest (*Hōhi gassen*), and Penis Size Contest (*Yōbutsu kurabe*) picture scrolls.[51] Other scholars are more inclined to think manga and anime are a response to modern social problems. Since the Meiji period manga has served as agitprop and critiques of established power structures. Manga and anime, some say, provide temporary release and wish fulfillment in the high-pressure postwar "credential society."

Postwar cartoon art's most influential figure, universally revered as "God of Comics" (*manga no kamisama*), was a physician, Dr. Tezuka Osamu (1928–89). Once he decided to be a full-time cartoonist, Tezuka was astonishingly prolific—"a one-man dream factory"—producing hundreds of volumes of manga and television anime episodes.[52] His oeuvre was part of a general trend to redefine manga not just as "humorous pictures" but as comic strips and books with serious messages.

Although Tezuka always claimed Walt Disney (1901–66) and Max Fleischer (1883–1972) as heroes, he was also well versed in indigenous visual humor, and is renowned for creating what many describe as a uniquely Japanese cartoon aesthetic, including the expressive large eyes of cartoon characters. He wrote and drew manga adaptations of Western stories as well as a monumental series on the life of Siddhartha Gautama (*Buddha*, 1972–83).[53] Among the thousands of characters he invented, Tezuka's best-known creation is Tetsuwan Atom (Astro Boy). The nuclear-powered boy robot starred in manga (1952–68) and ignited the first anime boom after making the jump to television in 1963. Atom used his super-powers to fight injustice and keep peace. In this respect, he embodied Japan's pacifist nationalism. In one story he traveled back in time to 1969 to rescue innocent Vietnamese peasants from indiscriminate US Air Force bombing, no doubt a compelling fantasy for millions who decried Japan's supporting role in the Indochina war yet felt helpless to stop it.[54]

The sheer variety of narrative themes, moods, and tones in Tezuka's work is impressive. Suzanne Phillipps identifies three narrative patterns over the four decades of his cartooning career: a "classical" period (1947 to mid-1960s), in which he focused on science fiction and adventure stories for children and developed a stable of recurring characters (his "star system") who appeared in virtually any tale he chose; a "horror-gothic" period (1970s) during which Tezuka followed the trend for more realistic drawings and dramatic, adult-themed stories (*gekiga*), in which "right and wrong became blurred, reason and common sense vanished and, often, the figures discovered evil in themselves as something endemic in their character[s] that they could not shake off"; and a "historic-realistic" period (mid-1970s–1989), in which Tezuka told stories of characters living through "times of momentous social upheaval" (for example, *Black Jack*, *Buddha*) and crafted "revisionist" or alternate histories.[55]

By contrast, Philip Brophy sees more continuity in Tezuka's work, arguing that his *gekiga* "are more than mere examples of opportune synchronicity to a clichéd 1960s zeitgeist of social change." Despite their "cute" (*kawaii*) faces, his early manga featured characters who were "consistently innocent yet abused, open-minded yet harshly judged, debilitated yet regenerative ... The faces of Astro Boy and his counterparts embody a peculiar postwar traumatization akin to many depictions of doe-eyed waifs from the era." "Culturally contextualized," Brophy concludes, "Tezuka's paragons of cuteness bear only the slightest resemblance to Walt Disney's beaming cherubs."[56] Tezuka's work thus engaged and responded not only to readers' tastes but to historical moments in which they lived. No less than Misora Hibari and Godzilla, his characters and stories drew their power from the collective trauma of mass destruction and slaughter during the war, defeat, and occupation, and from the more negative consequences of economic development. This sensitivity endears him further to Japanese and makes him an icon of the late Shōwa era. Like Misora, he is memorialized with a museum in his hometown, Takarazuka.[57]

Perhaps Japan's most beloved comic was the four-panel newspaper manga *Sazae-san*, created and drawn by Hasegawa Machiko (1920–92), who used the titular character to champion feminism throughout most of the postwar period. Hailing from Saga prefecture on Kyūshū island, Hasegawa started publishing *Sazae-san* in April 1946, in Fukuoka's *Fukunichi* newspaper, before relocating to Tokyo and taking her cartoon heroine to the liberal *Asahi*, where its run ended in 1974. *Sazae-san* became a radio comedy show in 1955 and a Fuji Television anime program in 1969—it is now the longest-running cartoon show in history.[58] Interestingly, despite its origins as a stridently feminist comic strip in which Mrs. Fuguta (Isono) Sazae resisted the old-fashioned patriarchy of household life and struggled to feed the family with occupation-era rations, the show has become the object of nostalgia for postwar family values. "In contrast to Hasegawa's attempts to be topical and make the comic strip world of the Isonos up to date," William Lee writes, "the producers of the television anime have deliberately suppressed such topicality in order to create an image of family life frozen in some vaguely defined, idyllic past."[59]

In contrast, the earless robot cat Doraemon represented a future technotopia in which androids deploy gadgets to solve human problems. At the bidding of Nobi Sewashi, Doraemon travels back in time from the twenty-second century to befriend and aid the boy Nobita—Sewashi's ancestor—to alter and improve the trajectory of his posterity. With an endless supply of futuristic gadgets in his pocket, Doraemon usually has the fix for Nobita's various challenges. Like *Sazae-san*, *Doraemon* debuted as a manga series (1969–96) but became an animated television program that continues to run.

Manga and anime attracted more diverse and more adult audiences in the 1970s. This was the era in which so-called *shōjo* manga, authored by female cartoonists and aimed at young girls, appeared. It was also the time in which *hentai* (perverted) cartoons began presenting deviant, sadomasochistic sexuality and graphic violence that were impossible to depict or enact in real life. Although *hentai* cartoons are at the forefront of debates about freedom of expression, protection of children from explicit, age-inappropriate material and degrading, misogynistic depictions of women in mass media, such material remains within surprisingly easy reach to any convenience store customer.[60]

Compared to other popular media, by its very nature manga is a medium through which nonprofessionals can deliver alternative messages and express countercultural sensibilities. Since the late 1970s manga readers have doubled as writers and artists, creating their own self-published *dōjinshi* (fan fiction) stories using established characters. Originally written as parodies or tributes to popular manga, *dōjinshi* allow fans to "reenchant commodities" by exploring different aspects of characters' personalities, telling canonical stories from alternate perspectives, or creating entirely new scenarios, settings or "mash-ups" for them. Fans have written sexual fantasies involving characters such as Sailor Moon, either contriving or drawing out eroticism latent in the original sources. For some four decades now, fans have met at big conventions such as Comiket and Big Sight at which they share, trade, and sell *dōjinshi* to fellow writers. Manga thus enables an inclusive, participatory model of cultural production, in which commercialism does not preclude consumer creativity.

In concluding this brief survey of postwar popular culture, it is worth revisiting some themes from earlier in the book, to assess changes, continuities, parallels, and divergences. As had been true since the Edo period, popular culture both spurred and was driven by technological innovations in mass reproduction and marketing. The dissemination of cultural products and leisure activities was of enormous importance in imagining and crafting a national community, as well as normalizing an ideal of the urban middle-class nuclear family. Appropriation and adaptation of foreign words, customs, material culture, fashion, and visual and performance art continued apace, generating intensive angst about the dilution of cultural traditions, though hardly enough to actually prevent the deluge.

In the postwar decades, that influence emanated mostly from the United States, Japan's former adversary, occupier, and Cold War ally and protector. Even after the occupation ended, Americana's presence in the mediascape remained conspicuous. Referring to popular music, Carolyn Stevens remarks that the distinction between "Western music" (*yōgaku*) and "Japanese music" (*hōgaku*) remained salient, but consumers' "purchasing power" transformed them from "conquered" objects of cultural imperialism to "customers" with a range of choices. "*Yōgaku* represented international sophistication and authenticity and imparted social status on the listener; *hōgaku* was culturally immediate and addressed the audience's emotional needs in ways that *yōgaku* could not."[61]

Japanese popular culture had never been so liberated from state censorship as in the postwar decades. Complete constitutional freedom of expression was delayed by the occupation, and informal social pressures were usually enough to keep many mouths shut—but not all of them. Victims of industrial poisoning, atomic warfare, and eviction from ancestral homelands for public works projects, and opponents of the Vietnam War, residual patriarchal attitudes, and structures and lies about national history spoke long and loud, frequently forcing a government response. Activists and dissidents used mass media and cultural expression to promote their respective causes.

Actually, political speech was less prone to censorship than "obscenity" (*waisetsu butsu*), a standard applied in the prohibition of screening Ōshima Nagisa's unedited *roman poruno* film *In the Realm of the Senses* (*Ai no korīda*, 1976) (to be fair, many other countries also banned the uncut version). The true story of Abe Sada (1905–75), who in 1936 erotically asphyxiated her lover, cut off his genitals and carried them around for three days before her arrest, *Realm* required its leads, Matsuda Eiko and Fuji Tatsuya, to engage in a variety of unsimulated sex acts on camera.[62] Cultural producers like Ōshima pushed the limits of postwar obscenity laws that they considered ambiguous, incongruent, and arbitrary. What Anne Allison calls "pubic realism"—graphic depictions of genitalia and pubic hair—was verboten until 1991, but had the dual effects of eroticizing hairless young girls and fetishizing "hair" (*hea*) to the degree that one of the defining cultural trends of the 1990s was an explosion of *hea nūdo* (hair nude) pictorials, featuring women whose pubic hair was exposed.[63]

Yet erotic expression was less important to most Japanese than critiquing, even obliquely, the costs of postwar recovery. Neither the priority given to capitalist industrial growth nor the anticommunist security arrangement went uncontested, as ordinary people utilized mass media to highlight the dangers of nuclear warfare, industrial disease, cultural atrophy, and ecological devastation. Even rubber-suited *kaijū* stomping around on miniaturized cityscapes reminded Japanese about the perilous ephemerality of life in the atomic age. Through popular culture, producers, artists, and audiences worked out the trauma, nostalgia, nuclear nightmares, futuristic visions, sexual politics, and political and economic aspirations of the nation, with fewer state-imposed constraints than ever before.

CHAPTER NINE

Millennial Japan as dream factory

Recall Douglas McGray's 2009 *Foreign Policy* article in the Introduction, in which he argues that "gross national cool" has enabled Japan to "redefine superpower." Japan's GNC is a stellar example, he contends, of political scientist Joseph Nye's concept of "soft power," "the ability to shape the preferences of others" in diplomacy through the use of cultural attractiveness and likability rather than "hard power" (threats of military action or economic sanctions). "Power is the ability to influence the behavior of others to get the outcomes one wants in world politics," Nye asserts, "because other countries—admiring its values, emulating its example, aspiring to its level of prosperity and openness—want to follow it ... This soft power—getting others to want the outcomes that you want—co-opts people rather than coerces them."[1] Although soft power "doesn't quantify easily," McGray speculates that Japan's contributions to the globalization of cultural media will likely have implications beyond the realm of commercial entertainment.

Since World War II, Hollywood movies, popular music, television, fashion, and democratic ideals have made the United States the most prominent beneficiary of soft power. However, Iwabuchi Kōichi believes that Japan's rising profile as a source of popular entertainment "recenters" globalization. His analysis of corporate media discourse reveals that "the appeal of Japanese popular culture [supposedly] lies in its subtle indigenization of American popular culture, making it suitable to 'Asian tastes.'" Thus "Japan has had a special leading role in constructing the sphere of Asian popular culture. The hybrid nature of Japanese popular culture is also seen to present modern, liberal facets of Japanese society to other parts of Asia." The ultimate objective of the entertainment industry's strategy, Iwabuchi states, is "improving Japan's image as an oppressor in Asia," to overcome its record of "imperial aggression in the region."[2]

This chapter necessarily ranges outside of the borders of Japan, because at the millennium Japan's popular culture is irreversibly integrated into the entertainment culture of a globalized society and has been affected and shaped by its popularity overseas. The Internet made Japanese cultural products much more accessible than they were when I began my studies in the late 1980s, and Japan's entertainment industry far more aware of and responsive to a transnational audience than ever before. Many students in my late-1980s cohort studied Japanese language to gain the cultural competence to negotiate trade deals between US and Japanese corporations, but a number of my students now want to become professional translators of manga, write subtitles for imported anime or become consultants to Japanese video game designers (yes, such jobs exist).[3]

Fans' levels of commitment to *japonaiserie* range from occasional interest to the deep involvement (charitably speaking) of so-called "weaboos," parodied in the *Saturday Night Live* skit "J-Pop America Funtime Now!"[4] An autocorrect corruption of "Waponese" (white Japanese wannabe), a "weaboo" refers to someone so obsessed with J-Cult "to the point that the person views Japanese culture as superior to their own (and all other cultures)," who gratuitously—and "incorrectly"—inserts Japanese words when speaking, and whose knowledge of Japan is derived exclusively from cartoons.[5] In some cases, however, interest in Japan broadens and deepens, to include traditional culture, religion, cuisine, and history. People who grew up on Japanese entertainment comprise many of the next generation of Japan scholars. What draws them? Why do cultural products made primarily for Japanese audiences resonate with people abroad? How did Japan become such a prominent "dream factory" for global entertainment? It was not always so.

From imitator to creator

Borrowing from other cultures "is as Japanese as eating rice." That is the theme of a 1991 educational documentary entitled *The Japanese Version*, which provides a snapshot of popular culture immediately preceding Japan's decades-long economic slump, colloquially known as the "Lost Two Decades" (ca. 1991–2010).[6] The video's subject is the massive influence of Americana on modern Japanese culture, emphasizing Japanese adaptations of American cultural practices, imagery, and objects. These adaptations sometimes render their own culture unfamiliar to Americans and also create and perpetuate Japanese stereotypes and caricatures of Americans as free-spirited, cool, unpredictable, and aggressive. The term *akogare* (yearning, admiring) appears throughout the film to describe the attitudes of many Japanese toward US culture.

Despite some unfortunate orientalist stereotyping in the script (for example, "thinking the Japanese way"), the documentary is both informative and humorous, and gives Japanese and American expatriates opportunities to speak about what Americana means to them and how it fits, or not. We meet Ami Shin, who quit his job as a designer of kindergarten classrooms to open a rent-by-the-hour "love hotel." He decorated suites with American flags and a boxing ring bed with *Peanuts* characters on the wall. Asked why a *Muppet Show* poster hangs in a Playboy Club-themed room, he responds, "It's eclectic! That's what makes it interesting." "People are looking for what they don't have at home," he explains. "Japanese have trouble expressing themselves. They work too much. That's why they like these places." We then meet an engaged couple who chose Tamahimeden wedding chapel for their opulent Western-style, Christian wedding. "Wearing a white wedding dress and a veil, walking the virgin road, every Japanese girl has that dream," the bride says. Asked if they are themselves Christians, the couple laugh, "No. Not at all!" We also hear from a couple of teenagers with fuzzy upper lips that Elvis Presley "is a god."

My favorite segment examines a "theme bar" decorated as an Old West saloon. Customers dress as cowboys and adopt nicknames like "Cal" and "Doc Suzuki," watch rodeos on television, and listen to a live band performing Johnny Paycheck's "Take This Job and Shove It." "I think my life is sort of like a cowboy's," one salaryman explains. "You know, I ride a train to work; that's sort of like riding a horse. And my office is kinda like a ranch. I shouldn't say this, but roping in customers is how I make a living." Regarding the symbolism of the cowboy, another says, "You guys [Americans] have it all wrong. It's not about being an individual. It's about working together. Whenever those guys had a problem, they'd gather together and figure out how to solve it. That's why those [television] shows [*Rawhide* and *Laramie*] were so popular in Japan: they used teamwork." This cheeky fellow's revisionist lecture to Americans is amusing, but also indicates the sense of ownership that Japanese feel about culture appropriated from abroad and the authority with which they invest it with their own meanings and self-stereotypes.

In the film, Belgian journalist Ian Buruma explains that, although Americans might find Japanese understandings and uses of imported culture to be "superficial," a more charitable and analytical perspective is that cultural practices and objects have "different associations" for Japanese than for non-Japanese. Even though Japanese may miss the deeper meanings of foreign cultures, he says, they are not always interested in knowing those meanings anyway. At ordinary, casual levels of engagement, cultural activities and products from abroad are uprooted, decontextualized, and made useful to Japanese to meet local interests, functions, and real or perceived needs.

The Japanese Version illustrates what Joseph Tobin calls "domestication," "to indicate a process that is active ... , morally neutral (unlike imitation or parasitism), and demystifying (there is nothing inherently strange, exotic, or uniquely Japanese going on here)." It also "suggests that Western goods, practices and ideas are changed (Japanized) in their encounter with Japan."[7] Social scientists now use the term "glocalization" (supposedly coined by Japanese economists as *dochakuka*) to explain this process by which glo-balized ideas and practices from one part of the world are rendered local by people elsewhere. Glocalization means "the simultaneity—the co-presence—of both universalizing and particularizing tendencies," rather than the out-right erasure of local culture by global forces.[8]

One of the best examples of glocalization in contemporary J-Cult is hip-hop, particularly the strategies that Japanese MCs use to rap in their native language while maintaining hip-hop's characteristic "flow" (rhythmic phrasing). With no rhyming conventions in their native tongue, rappers use word inversions to create rhymes, concocting "ways to exploit the gram-matical and phonological features of their own language while upholding a rap aesthetic," Noriko Manabe observes. "Once Japanese rappers played their own instrument—the Japanese language—for its unique aural qual-ities, they found it was perfectly suitable for rap." Ian Condry likewise lauds the "language creativity" of MCs, to whom "language is as malleable as sculptor's clay, which they mold using 'proper Japanese,' slang, derogatory terms, regional variations, gendered forms and bilingual puns." Condry further argues that although hip-hop conventions such as rapping, break dancing, and deejaying initially traveled via American mass media, their dif-fusion actually transpired at the grassroots level—in the *genba* (actual site) of nightclubs and recording studios—despite corporate reluctance to pro-mote hip-hop in Japan.[9]

For many observers, Japanese or not, glocalization rarely results in any-thing more than a superficial veneer of "internationalization" (*kokusaika*), a buzzword in the 1980s. But there are notable exceptions to this cri-tique, as many Japanese who develop an interest in foreign cultures prize "authenticity" and earnestly study them in context. Certain music genres exemplify this particularly well. Several of the Japanese jazz aficionados and performers whom I met in the early 1990s had developed strong inter-ests in African American history and the civil rights and anticolonial lib-eration movements, to better understand the environments in which jazz developed. Marvin Sterling encountered Japanese who had established reg-gae bands and sound systems, learned patois and dance-hall routines, and even set up rural Rastafarian communes out of an intense enthusiasm for Afro-Jamaican culture. Similarly, as a performer embedded in the Música de Maestros ensemble that toured Japan, Michelle Bigenho met some Japanese who so desired "intimacy" with Andean music that they moved to Bolivia to learn the indigenous and *mestizo* languages, cultures, and lifestyles behind it and became accomplished performers. Bigenho's interlocutors were drawn into "affective economies of desire" and "nostalgia for something perceived as lost in modern life."[10]

In all three of these cases, some Japanese aficionados have imagined tenu-ous bonds of allegiance and ethnohistorical connections, affinities or parallels to justify or explain their fervid identification with foreign musical cultures. A common element to these specific discourses is an anti-imperialist ethos of solidarity among peoples of color (a reversal of the Meiji-era obsession with demonstrating Japan's honorary whiteness). In the 1960s jazz critics and musicians developed an elaborate discourse around the concept of Japanese as "yellow Negroes" with peculiar affinities with black people. Subjugated and humiliated by Euro-Americans, people of both African and Japanese ancestry allegedly had abandoned their respective cultural heritages. But by the 1960s, like black intellectuals and artists who sought to recover linkages to African heritage through jazz, their Japanese counterparts engaged in a parallel effort to reconnect with their ethnonational roots through impro-vised music. Three decades later, Japanese "dreads" expressed a similar, even more elaborate mythistorical concept built on the Rastafarian identifica-tion with the lost tribes of Israel. Sterling's informant Ras Tanki claims that one of those tribes had settled in the Japanese archipelago and founded the Yamato imperial dynasty. To establish an imaginary "racial link," Bigenho reports that some Japanese and Bolivians look even further back in time to a common "prehistoric indigenous ancestor." She attributes this to a desire for intimacy and "ingroup identification between two different nationalist peoples who find connections through a common experience of being under the political domination of the United States."[11]

Specious ethnogenetic theories aside, the reward for Japanese enthusiasts' intensive commitments to these forms of musical expression has been recog-nition and stamps of approval from native practitioners. For instance: jazz artist Akiyoshi Toshiko was named a National Endowment for the Arts Jazz Master in 2007; Kudō "Bashment" Junko was the first non-Jamaican to win the Dancehall Queen contest in Montego Bay in 2002; Shishido Makoto prevailed in a competition to fill the *charango* chair in the Andean folklore band Los Kjarkas; and at the 1999 World Clash between Jamaican-style sound systems, Japan's Mighty Crown took first place with the "agnostic, subculturally deep patois needed to 'big up' their sound system and down their rivals."[12]

The difference between this more impassioned engagement with "authen-tic" foreign cultures and the more casual, "superficial" approach is probably more of degree than kind. At any level of cultural interface the consumed object or practice serves a function or fulfills a desire or perceived need peculiar to individuals and groups, who produce their identities through consumptive activities. John Russell detects this self-fashioning in the "con-sumption of blackness" in millennial Japan. He deems it a "site of resistance against Japanese social and behavioral norms and white cultural hegemony." The fetish among young Japanese women for sexual encounters with black men constitutes a "discourse of complaint" about "traditional gender roles and expectations." For these women ("yellow cabs"), "Consumption of the

black body and its essence liberates one's full potential, one's 'true self.'"
Russell critiques these rituals of resistance as lacking "any clear subversive
direction or intent, since it reifies difference as racial, uncritically accepts
American racial imagery, rejects meaningful dialogue with blacks and con-
firms rather than problematizes Japanese identity." As the ultimate taboo or
transgression, sex with black men becomes an activity bereft of true emotional intimacy or respect and rather a gesture of defiance against Japanese
attitudes about racial purity and control of female sexuality.[13]

It is demonstrably true that "there is nothing inherently strange, exotic,
or uniquely Japanese going on here," yet Japan's reputation as a singularly
voracious poacher and virtuosic adapter of other cultures has endured
nonetheless. Certainly, Japan's long record of observing, appropriating and
adapting ideas, institutions, technologies, and entire epistemological systems
from continental East Asia, Western Europe, and the United States makes it
seem historically credible. However, claiming it is a peculiar national trait
underestimates both how extensive and transformative intra- and transnational cultural influence is elsewhere, and how disruptive and controversial cultural appropriation has been in Japanese society.

In any event, the imitator stereotype is unrecognizable to most millennial
Japanophiles today, to whom Japan is a font of seemingly inexhaustible
creativity, innovation and bold experimentalism, especially in the realms of
consumer electronics, visual design, and storytelling. They have grown up
in an entertainment milieu in which *Dragon Ball Z* and *Naruto* are after-
school staples and American cartoons such as DC Comics' *Teen Titans*
(2003–06) imitate anime conventions. Many fans and scholars posit the
complexity of characterization, unbridled fantasy and dystopian scenarios
of Japanese visual narratives (anime and manga) as the antitheses of vapid
"Disneyfied" American cultural offerings.[14] It is a facile, subjective, and analytically useless distinction. Still, it is undeniable that J-Cult has become
so appealing to international audiences that some will consume any- and
everything Japanese. Their brand loyalty is peerless.

Dream factory

Japan's rise to entertainment superpower took decades and went undetected
initially. Iwabuchi characterizes many of the most successful cultural products exported from Japan as culturally "odorless," in that their Japanese
origins were not odoriferous to everyone.[15] The Japanese settings of monster films of the 1960s and 1970s were unmistakable, but Sony electronics,
arcade games such as Namco's *Pac-Man* (1980) and Nintendō's *Donkey
Kong* (1981) and *Mario Brothers* (1983), Bandai's Transformers toy line
(1984), and children's television shows like *Mighty Morphin Power Rangers*
(1993, originally *Super Sentai*) did not particularly "smell" Japanese. By the

late 1990s, however, the Japanese provenance of entertainment products became both more obvious and a selling point: anything with a Japanese fragrance had almost instant cachet because of its association with other popular items. Even the names of individual entertainment companies— Nintendō, Studio Ghibli, Sony, Sanrio, and Bandai, among others—became household words elsewhere in the world.

From its inception in the 1910s, the animated film industry harbored "dreams of export," which only intensified during the occupation years, when full-length color Disney films were shown in Japan.[16] The 1958 release of *Hakujaden* (screened in the United States as *Panda and the Magic Serpent*), based on a Chinese folktale, realized the longstanding aspiration to create a film of comparable style and scope to Disney's. *Astro Boy* (1963–64), *Kimba the White Lion* (1966–67), and *Speed Racer* (1967–68) were the most popular television anime adapted for overseas broadcast in English, followed by *Battle of the Planets* (1978–79) and *Star Blazers* (*Space Cruiser Yamato*, 1979–80). French, Spanish, Arabic, Québécois, Taiwanese, and Italian adaptations of anime programs were broadcast in the late 1960s and 1970s.[17]

The current international anime boom and the consequent interest in translated manga with a distinctive subcultural following began in the mid-1980s, in part because of the introduction of home video technologies (VHS and laserdiscs). The straight-to-video release of sci-fi cartoon *Dallos* (1983) and other anime made repeated viewing, sharing, and dubbing possible. At the same time, animators and audiences developed an interest in more "mature" animated material: indeed, pornographic anime featuring "violent, eroticized horror" became "the standard bearers for Japanese animation in many foreign territories in the 1990s." So-called *hentai* subject matter is no longer the main point of entry into anime fandom, but in the 1980s and 1990s it was part of the medium's allure to many overseas aficionados, "gaining a higher profile than in its home market."[18]

Most scholars agree that Ōtomo Katsuhiro's *Akira* (1988) is "almost singlehandedly responsible for the early 1990s boom in anime in the English language." Its stunningly detailed, hand-drawn visualization of postapocalyptic catastrophe and the metamorphosis of the human body and its critique of mindless technophilia; "social isolation, political corruption, scientific hubris"; and resistance to unjust social and political institutions have made *Akira* emblematic of anime for many fans. Although sci-fi/fantasy accounts for only a portion of anime production, it is clearly the most conspicuous and popular genre, despite its discomforting visions of the future. Fans of the mecha genre of robot and cyborg fantasies are sometimes compelled to think beyond the coolness of piloting giant humanoid machines and, rather to contemplate their "destructive and dehumanizing potential."[19]

Social scientists have been investigating other aspects of Japanese popular culture's global appeal for over a decade now, while recognizing that no single quality accounts for its magnetism. One word that recurs frequently in such research is "cute" (a flourishing academic field—"cute studies"—is devoted to this aesthetic feature of consumer culture).[20] Many observers regard cuteness (*kawaisa*) as a distinctive and fundamental attribute of J-Cult, facilitating its global appeal. Everything from handwriting to food and from clothing to accessories is assessed for its *kawaisa*; so, too, are human females. In *Hip Hop Japan*, of all places, Condry introduces the term "cutismo" ("a kind of pressure analogous to male machismo") as an aesthetic ideal of childish innocence, inexperience, charm, and vulnerability. Indeed, at least since the 1970s, *kawaii* has become the ultimate word of praise in the Japanese language, particularly for girls and female pop singers.[21]

So-called idol (*aidoru*) singers, "girl groups," and "boy bands" have been fixtures in popular music since the 1970s, adored for their approachability, youthful innocence, and *kawaisa*, and presented as role models in the "public socialization" of youth. Selected by talent agencies at competitions, idols' sweetness (*kawairashisa*) is typically more important than their singing abilities. Like the Puerto Rican boy band Menudo (1977–2009), groups like Morning Musume and AKB48 have rotating memberships, as singers "age out" and are replaced by younger ones. They also have morality clauses in their contracts, intended to maintain their virginal images. In 2013, when AKB48 member Minami Minegishi confessed on YouTube that she had violated her contract by having a one-night stand with a member of a boy band, she shaved her head and was demoted to "trainee" (she was reinstated later that year).[22] Like former Mouseketeers Britney Spears, Christina Aguilera, and Miley Cyrus, idol acts have generated controversy with increasingly sexualized material and performances as they age, in part because infantile *kawaisa* remains important to their appeal.

Kawaisa is also a desirable and bankable attribute of cartoon characters and animals. It is both fascinating and amusing to witness municipalities throughout Japan compete to out-cute one another with their official cartoon mascots, known as *yurui kyarakutā* ("loose" or "gentle" characters, abbreviated *yurukyara*). City governments have tried to attract businesses and tourists by spending millions of yen developing appealingly *kawaii* critters and characters—often based on local folklore, history, wildlife or produce—to promote themselves regionally and nationally. Not all *yurukyara* are created equal: they range from the national favorites, samurai cat Hikonyan (Hikone), rosy-cheeked bear Kumamon (Kumamoto prefecture) and walking pear Funasshi (Funabashi), to the exquisitely lame Okazaemon of Okazaki, Nara's creepy (*kimochi warui*) antlered Buddhist acolyte Sento-kun (an escapee from the Island of Dr. Moreau?) and the menacing Melon Bear (Meronkuma) of the rapidly depopulating coal town of Yubari, Hokkaidō.[23] As the subject of local children's nightmares, Melon Bear is unlikely to encourage them to stay in Yubari. Local cuties can reap millions of yen for cities through merchandising alone, generate tourism revenues and create jobs. A Japan Local Character Association exists to create some semblance of harmony in what is actually a harshly competitive and character-bloated environment. Fretting about "cuteness overload" and the amount of public monies devoted to hitting the *kawaisa* jackpot with the next round-headed, twinkle-eyed star, officials hope to "cull" the cuties.[24] Cutismo—the pressure to be *chō kawaii* (super cute)—thus afflicts entire communities, who place their hopes for economic revitalization on the adorable, plush shoulders of cartoon varmints.

Kawaisa fills cultural and social needs as well as public coffers. It serves as yet another vehicle for the expression of nostalgia that evokes "emotional attachments" to childhood or sometimes to native traditions. Cute characters have instrumentalist value, as well, for they are said to "relieve loneliness and reduce stress."[25] Laura Miller explains zoomorphism—the attribution of human traits to animals—as a "psychological mechanism that allows us to redirect attention and emotions away from areas thought to be indelicate or troublesome" and "renders potentially dangerous or sensitive topics as safe and acceptable." Cute critters are thus deployed to "defuse the preachy quality of authoritative admonishments," focusing attention on their *kawaisa* rather than on the potentially offensive message itself. Because many girls use *kawaii* to mean "groovy, cool, nice, or interesting," Miller adds that its narrow interpretation as "cute" "results in the continuing trivialization of girl culture, while also allowing us to deny that it could possibly contain forms of agency or power."[26] In her formulation, *kawaisa* becomes another area for hegemonic struggle, between entertainment corporations (for example, Sanrio, the cutest company on earth) and girls' assertions of cultural independence.

Informants for Christine Yano's study of Sanrio's global cute crusade indicate that young adult women—who perhaps have outgrown cute consumerism—understand *kawaisa*'s role in gender politics.

> There is some notion of obedience or weakness in the concept of kawaii. We [Japanese] often use the word kawaii for babies and puppies that are smaller, weaker, and thus need to be protected. Kawaii has lots of components of femininity, such as obedience, dependency, and weakness.

> Basically, kawaii is associated with infancy that covers feelings of the need to protect the object. In other words, kawaii is a symbol of dependency. However, girls started to describe so many things as kawaii recently, so my definition of kawaii changed to include the meaning of "trendy."[27]

Bandai's Tamagotchi virtual pet game is one transparent example of *kawaisa* as a vehicle for gender programming: aimed at *shōjo* (teen girls), it pushes the government's desperate pronatal agenda by socializing them to become nurturing mothers.[28]

Perhaps *because* of its utility for reinforcing traditional notions of female delicacy and dependency, and for displacing unpleasant thoughts, the *kawaisa* aesthetic has arguably been Japan's most successful cultural export to East and Southeast Asian countries, which have enthusiastically joined its unannounced campaign to cuten up our ugly world. Dignified machinery such as jet airplanes now feature Sanrio characters romping around the fuselage.[29] When flying Taiwan's Eva Airlines, one can obtain a boarding pass from a kiosk shaped like Hello Kitty's bow-ribboned head, stroll the cabin in Hello Kitty slippers, rest one's head on a Hello Kitty pillow and vomit into Hello Kitty sick bags.

If cute is not their bag, Japanophiles can find pleasure in the mystic, martial machismo of the romanticized Japanese warrior. The mythos of samurai as honorable, superhuman, selfless heroes is almost intolerable to people like myself who have read extensively about the merciless bloodletting and rapacious cruelty of which they were capable. I take notoriously sadistic glee in bursting students' balloons here. For instance, in 2016 I took a group of students to view the Ear Mound (*mimizuka*) in Kyōto, where the ears and noses of nearly forty thousand Koreans slaughtered by honorable samurai were piled. Paid by the kill, *bushi* brought these curios as proof of their productivity on the peninsula during the 1590s' invasions. They had killed so many that they could not possibly ship back all the heads to settle accounts. That little story, plus disclosure of the warriors' penchant for pederasty (see Chapter 2), usually does the trick.

At any rate, fans revere samurai for their quasi-mystical, Force-like combat skills, based on philosophical/spiritual bases not codified until martial arts "traditions" were invented in the late Meiji era.[30] Another myth about warriors is that they were incorruptible defenders of "honor" and high principles. Yet samurai were more like gangbangers today, looking for any provocation or perceived slight as an opportunity to display their machismo. From medieval times into the Edo period, incidents of "self-redress" (*jiriki kyūsai*) for petty "disses" were so endemic that *daimyō* promulgated harsh laws to execute both parties to a fight, regardless of who started it (*kenka ryōseibai*). Still, the appeal of "honor" to contemporary audiences suggests widespread disaffection with a modern world in which everything and everyone is for sale, and where sacrificing oneself for a higher purpose seems foolish.

The romanticized samurai is of Japanese, not Western origin, of course: it extends from the Edo-period stage to the films of Bandō Tsumasaburō and Kurosawa Akira, from the television series about blind swordsman *Zatōichi* (1974–79) to the animated *Samurai Champloo* (2004–05), and foreign films such as *Ghost Dog* and the Tom Cruise vehicle *The Last Samurai*. The latter film is particularly loathsome if one knows anything about Japanese history, or is sensitive to racial not-so-very-subtexts. Set in the context of an uprising against the Meiji government by disaffected *bushi*, Cruise's US Army Captain Nathan Algren (based loosely on the French military adviser Jules Brunet, 1838–1911) sides with the noble Katsumoto (Watanabe Ken, in the Saigō Takamori role) in a quixotic struggle to preserve the *bushidō* lifestyle in the face of modernization. Algren's white privilege serves him well in

Japan: he masters "no-mind" (*mushin*) combat techniques in four months and defeats five Japanese who have studied those techniques all their lives; he attracts the romantic interest of the widow of a warrior he killed himself; he has a personal audience with the emperor, persuading him to keep swords and shun Howitzers; and he gets to be the titular Last Samurai.

Wide(r) world of sport

Besides cuties, warriors, cartoons, toys, sushi, and video games, Japan has produced individual athletes and national sport teams that perform well internationally. Coaches and trainers worldwide study and sometimes imitate Japanese athletic training methods and philosophies emphasizing overall fitness, discipline, and team spirit.[31] Moreover, participation in the international sporting community has aided Japan's efforts to "internationalize" its society and culture since the 1980s.

Thirty-one years after pitcher Murakami Masanori became the first Japanese to break into Major League Baseball (1964–65), Nomo Hideo became a national hero as a star hurler for various US teams (1995–2008). Named Rookie of the Year with the Los Angeles Dodgers in 1995, and pitching a no-hitter in his debut for the Boston Red Sox the following year, Nomo became an MLB fan favorite. Japanese television newscasts kept viewers in the homeland apprised of his every appearance on the mound. Covering Japanese players abroad eventually became too big a job: in the two decades after Nomo's debut, over forty Japanese players were recruited into the Majors. Since his arrival in 2001, outfielder and slugger Suzuki Ichirō has set a number of American League records and become one of MLB's most beloved players. "There's nobody like Ichiro in either league—now or ever," one sportswriter gushed. "He exists strictly within his own world, playing a game 100 percent unfamiliar to everyone else … Ichiro is a stylist in his every move, from his stroke to his sliding catches to his laser-like throws."[32]

Japanese footballers have come a long way since their ignominious loss at the 1936 Olympics, gradually placing players in European leagues—Nakata Hidetoshi (A. S. Roma and Parma), Nakamura Shunsuke (2007 Scottish Footballer of the Year with Celtic), Honda Keisuke (A. C. Milan), and Kagawa Shinji (Borussia Dortland)—and performing well internationally. The Samurai Blue men's national squad has qualified for the FIFA World Cup tournament consistently since 1998 and took the Asian Cup four times between 1992 and 2011. This was partially the result of the professional J-League, which replaced the amateur Japan Soccer League (1965–92), and its youth academies that groom new talent. In its first two years (1993–95) the J-League was wildly popular, leading some to fret that it would surpass baseball as Japan's favorite spectator sport.[33]

The 2011 FIFA World Cup victory of the women's national team— Nadeshiko (Pink) Japan—was Japan's greatest international athletic accomplishment. Nadeshiko also made it to the 2012 Olympics gold medal match and 2015 World Cup final, falling both times to the United States, but nonetheless earning accolades for resolute, disciplined play. With no professional women's league comparable to the J-League, Nadeshiko's achievements are even more remarkable. If the degree of gender equality in a country can be measured by the strength of its women's national football teams, it is significant that despite lingering patriarchal attitudes and structures, Japan's has defeated North American and northern European sides in international play.[34] That said, as is the case in the United States and elsewhere, there are significant disparities in investment and remuneration between female and male footballers.

Kelly argues that the rising prominence of football has inaugurated a new era of "flexible sports citizenship" that undermines the logic of ethnic and state nationalism. Whereas baseball and sumō, which supposedly embody national characteristics such as "samurai spirit" and "dignity" (hinkaku— a strange term to describe overweight men in thongs slamming into each other, no?), have accepted foreign players and wrestlers only grudgingly and with much handwringing, FIFA-affiliated football makes it nearly impossible "to maintain hard and fast sporting ethnic verities." Over four hundred European, South American, and even South Korean footballers have played in the J-League, as have a dozen so-called zainichi (ethnic Koreans born in Japan yet denied citizenship). The flow of players across national boundaries into and out of Japan is "adjudicated by FIFA eligibility rules and not by nation-state citizenship law." Kelly concludes that football is no "panacea for a Japan that is struggling to reimagine the parameters of its national community," but it is "broadening the realm of the possible and extending the horizon of expectations" for players, coaches, and fans.[35] This "broadening" has even had an impact on sumō, although not everyone is delighted by it. Since the 1990s Mongolian, Hawaiian, Bulgarian, Brazilian, Estonian, and Russian wrestlers have entered the top division. In 1993 Hawaiian Akebono Tarō became the first foreign yokozuna (Grand Champion). Mongolian rikishi Hakuhō Shō became the fourth foreign-born yokozuna at the age of twenty-two, and at this writing has set records for number of victories in the top division. Some grumble that foreigners have inborn physical advantages over Japanese, but most spectators have become accustomed to non-Japanese rikishi in the top ranks of the sport and cheer them on.[36]

Tizzies

Popular culture's power to incite moral panic has hardly diminished since the Edo period. No less so than in the United States, where popular culture has been blamed for everything from teen pregnancies and mass shootings to postliteracy and a coarsened public sphere, many in Japanese government and civil society blame mass media (*masukomi*) for a variety of social ills. The hideous slayings of four schoolgirls aged four to seven in 1988–89 by necrophiliac cannibal Miyazaki Tsutomu (1962–2008)—the so-called Otaku Murderer—lent a sinister cast to the increasingly prevalent social isolation of (mostly male) youth who spent practically all their waking hours holed up in their bedrooms consuming *hentai* material.[37] Known as *hikikomori* (social withdrawal) and otaku (literally "your house"), these obsessive, reclusive social maladapts were not only ridiculed for their inability to navigate Japan's pressure-cooker credential society but also demonized as potentially violent perverts who threatened public safety. Interestingly, the foreign appropriation of otaku by non-Japanese, as a term of prideful self-reference for nerds with a particular interest in J-Cult, has somewhat neutralized the implicit ominousness of the word in Japan. Foreign usage is thus transforming the semantics of otaku in Japanese.[38]

What scholars now call "girls' culture" has distressed some contemporary Japanese. One of the most successful genres to emerge from the *dōjinshi* (fan fiction) manga market is *yaoi*, or "boys love," stories of homoerotic relationships between boys (sometimes using established characters), written primarily by females for females. Patrick Galbraith explains that "*yaoi* is an acronym for 'no climax, no punch line, no meaning' (*yama nashi, ochi nashi, imi nashi*)," and refers to a "transgressive" emotional intimacy based on the protagonists' "mutual status as abject and vulnerable." There is an aesthetic ideal for *yaoi* stories, comparable to older terms such as *aware* and *iki* (Chapter 1): *moe*, a "euphoric response" to the intimacy between characters. Self-described "rotten girls" (*fujoshi*) who create, consume, and discuss *yaoi* among themselves "are not particularly political in their play or pursuits of pleasure," but that does not necessarily mean there are no political *implications* to their activities.[39] At the turn of the millennium, women have either delayed or rejected marriage, and Japan's birth rate has plummeted, in part because they reject traditional patriarchal spousal relationships. Even when they "grow out of" their *yaoi* stage, they have been socialized to a standard of emotional intimacy that could make them choosier about potential partners. In a country in which creative solutions to impending demographic disaster, including pronatal government initiatives, are rife, some consider the preoccupation of young women with (perhaps) unrealistic expectations of emotional intimacy to be a national quandary.

Though its prevalence has been greatly exaggerated, the press whipped up concern about another aspect of girls' culture: the *enjo kōsai* (compensated dating) trend, in which schoolgirls voluntarily offered sexual companionship to middle-aged sugar daddies, in exchange for expensive luxury items.[40] These girls took advantage of the "Lolita complex" (*rorikon*) evident in manga and other media. The sexualization of prepubescent and teen females has made a "clothing fetish" of the "sailor suit" school uniform, as alluring to some men as Victoria's Secret lingerie is to others.[41] Despite the expenses incurred, for men *enjo kōsai* was not only a way to indulge *rorikon* fantasies but also a cheaper alternative to bar hostesses, women who—like geisha—are paid to entertain and flirt with male customers. "What the media finds most irritating about [*enjo kōsai*]," Miller observes, "is that the young women involved feel no shame or remorse at all … [They] themselves express disdain, pity, or contempt for the men they see themselves as exploiting, rather than the other way around."[42]

A different sort of parental concern about popular entertainment's impact on young people resulted from the "Pokemon Shock" of December 16, 1997, in which flashing strobe effects on the televised cartoon sent nearly seven hundred children to the hospital with photo-paroxysmal response and, in some cases, epileptic seizures. Some characterize the incident as "mass hysteria," but it certainly helped boost international interest in the anime program and its associated toys and video games.[43] Tajiri Satoshi insists he created Pokemon (Pocket Monsters) "to promote social interaction" among children; however, others detect a more nefarious agenda. Though symbolized by the darling mascot Pikachū, the Pokemon phenomenon has been surprisingly controversial, with allegations that it promotes Satanism, Nazism, animal abuse, and avarice.[44] Certainly, the franchise's crass slogan "Gotta catch 'em all!" leaves little to the imagination about its raison d'être. Collecting and trading Pokemon cards became a standard—and costly—childhood activity in a number of countries at the turn of the millennium.

Critics in Japan and abroad maintain that Japanese popular culture promotes violence, sexual perversion, acquisitiveness, and regressive gender programming. An article in *The Onion*, a US satire website, entitled "Japan Pledges to Halt Production of Weirdo Porn That Makes People Puke" summarizes this reputation better than I ever could, gleefully depicting the "revolting depravity" of the Japanese entertainment industry as an international crisis. Fictional "proposed new measures include a 50 percent reduction in live-eel anal insertions, and a requirement that portrayals of group sex involving seven or more individuals feature at least four human participants. Also under consideration is a zero-tolerance policy covering all 'prurient uses' of colostomy bags." "We honestly had no idea people did not enjoy this stuff," Cultural Affairs Minister Nakai Kazuhiro states in the piece. "We are deeply ashamed for whatever it is about these films that has made people around the world vomit so vigorously."[45]

Like all satire, this is exaggerated and not entirely fair, but is not entirely baseless, either. Part of the problem is that many in the West still regard cartoons as children's entertainment, so their use for violent and pornographic expression seems particularly repugnant. The fact is that cartoons can depict fantasies that are impossible to enact in real life, and many Japanese cartoonists have taken full advantage of that capacity. But not all Japanese find *hentai* material acceptable. One of the great riddles about contemporary Japan is how *hentai* violence, sex, and violent sex can be so widely available in cartoons, with little if any measurable impact on crime rates, which are low compared to the United States. Anti-*hentai* groups are not so sure that is true, in part because sexual crimes are underreported—the statistics are artificially low.

Another criticism of Japanese cartoon media is the lack of ethnic diversity among its characters. Human or cyborg characters are "read" as Japanese (or *mukokuseki*, without nationality), regardless of phenotypical features such as Tezuka-style round eyes or hair color. Indeed, uninitiated foreign observers might think all cartoon characters are Caucasian. The paucity of dark-skinned characters—especially in heroic roles—is conspicuous. There are real-world repercussions for this absence, as racial tensions sometimes plague fan conventions and cosplay events. Many otaku of color encounter prejudice from hard-core weaboos who meticulously judge each other for verisimilitude. "If an African-American was cosplaying Sailor Moon for example," one observer writes, "I would find it strange that there would be more comments about the color of her skin than the craftsmanship of her attire. I found it strange because most of these characters are Japanese in origin, so for a Caucasian cosplayer to comment critically against a cosplayer of color to me seems hypocritical." However, dark-skinned fans object to lighter-skinned players "brownfacing" to represent characters accurately.[46]

Manga and anime are also subject to sharp feminist critiques. Many observers consider *shōjo* manga (girls' comics) as regressive, featuring doe-eyed, sexually inexperienced *kawaii* girls who buy *kawaii* things and prattle on about *kawaii* boys.[47] Yet others point out that Japanese cartoons also regularly feature powerful, decisive, clever, and independent girls and women. Filmmaker and Studio Ghibli founder Miyazaki Hayao has deliberately created heroic protagonists who subvert conventional elements of *shōjo* imagery:

> I felt this country only offered such things as crushes and romance to 10-year-old girls, though, and looking at my young friends, I felt this was not what they held dear in their hearts, not what they wanted ... [For *Spirited Away*] I created a heroine who is an ordinary girl, someone with whom the audience can sympathize ... [I]t's not a story in which the characters grow up, but a story in which they draw on something already inside them, brought out by the particular circumstances.[48]

Whereas *shōjo* and their obligatory *kawaisa* are "commonly associated with consumerism" and passivity, "with the regressive tendency to escape from social realities," Miyazaki's girl heroines retain "the nurturing and caring attributes of femininity," while also making them "active supporters of the oppressed victims of greedy power-mongers, even crusaders for social reform, rather than self-absorbed narcissists."[49]

Another alternative to the stereotypically ditzy *shōjo* is the "beautiful fighting girl" (*sentō bishōjo*). As a symbol of female empowerment, this icon of Japanese cartoon art is not unproblematic. Given the long-standing traditions of helpless damsels in distress in various artistic and storytelling media, it is understandable that many consumers idolize girls or women who use skillful combat to protect themselves and defend others (*if* one accepts the premise that the path to gender equality is best served by women replicating the violent behavior of men). However, emphasis on the physical attractiveness and desirability of "fighting girls," with slender waists, long legs, conventionally pretty faces and hair, skimpy or form-fitting outfits, and ample, gravity-defying breasts, perpetuates unrealistic standards of beauty and promotes rather than undermines sexual objectification of women. In popular culture it is acceptable for women to fight, as long as they are still objects of (male) carnal desire, or at least not "butch."

If the capacity for violence is "masculine," the appeal of the fighting girl is that she has both that capacity *and* the conventionally "feminine" virtues of cuteness or sexiness. In her interpretation of Takeuchi Naoko's manga and television cartoon *Sailor Moon* (1992–97), Anne Allison writes, "This fable of fierce flesh, as I call it—girls who show off their bodies yet are fierce fighters just like male superheroes—defies easy categorization as either (or simply) a feminist or sexist script." Allison's interviews with Japanese and American girls who like *Sailor Moon* indicate that part of its attraction is that one can be both an adept fighter and conventionally "girly" or sexy, interested in both fashion and romance.[50]

It is worth noting here the remarkable impact of Japan's "beautiful fighting girl" on American cinema in the last twenty years.[51] Certainly, there are independent folkloric traditions of warrior women in the United States, Europe, China, and elsewhere, but until recently they have not been prominent onscreen—Wonder Woman, a character created in 1941, did not star in her own film until 2017. Whereas the *Alien* franchise's Ellen Ripley stood virtually alone as a cinematic female action hero for years, Lara Croft, Selene (*Underworld*), Alice Abernathy (*Resident Evil*), Black Widow (Marvel), Rey (*Star Wars*), Mystique (*X-Men*), Buffy the Vampire Slayer, and Xena have made damsels in distress all but obsolete. Even some recent "Bond girls" are cunning assassins or proficient martial artists.

Finally, cartoons and film have been at the center of controversies about national history, particularly collective memories of Japan's imperial and wartime past. In his cartoon epic *Phoenix* (*Hi no tori*, 1954–88) Tezuka Osamu offered an alternate narrative of the Yamato imperial dynasty's origins, countering the imperial (*tennōsei*) mythology with which he and his generation had been relentlessly indoctrinated before World War II. His story of "merciless emperors and shoguns in a repeating cycle of oppression, persecution, and destruction" controverted notions of the imperial family's intrinsic morality and benevolence.[52]

Cartoons "have been influential carriers of war memory for many decades," Hashimoto Akiko contends. *Pitiful Elephants* (*Kawaisōna zō*, 1951), *Barefoot Gen*, *Grave of the Fireflies* (*Hotaru no haku*, 1988), and other cartoons "nurture negative emotions about the Asia-Pacific War and war in general," and "have been equally successful in shaping young children's

antipathy toward lethal violence, exposing them to the sheer meaningless-
ness and horror of mass death."[53] Such cartoons thus socialize young people
for citizenship in a pacifist public sphere. Indeed, as members of the Japan
Teachers Union, their instructors comprise one of Japan's most vocal constituencies critical of the wartime past, right-wing obscurantism and revi-
sionism, and resurgent ultranationalism.[54]

In the 1990s, with renewed public awareness of wartime atrocities—
specifically military sex-slavery (*jūgun ianfu*, "comfort women"), forced
labor systems, and the 1937 Nanjing Massacre—a right-wing backlash
ensued, intent on minimizing the severity of such incidents, denying their
occurrence altogether or claiming the Allies committed comparable crimes.
Seeking to restore national honor, resurrect the "seamless suturing" of a
collectivist society (*kyōdōtai*), and eradicate "masochistic history," highly
organized, well-funded organizations with political support from several
LDP politicians (including two-time prime minister Abe Shinzō) have used
manga, film, and school textbooks to circulate their views. With his 1998
comic *On War* (*Sensōron*) cartoonist Kobayashi Yoshinori hoped to promote a "remasculinized Japanese nationalism" to counter the "consumer-
ist individualism imposed by the United States."[55] Kobayashi's provocative
query on the cover of his manga—"Will you go to war, or will you stop
being Japanese?"—and his focus on the "anonymity and ordinariness" of
suicidal special forces (*tokkō*) seek to elicit from boys the self-sacrificial
ethos of wartime.[56]

Recent films have presented Japan's "holy war" in a more complimen-
tary light. Itō Shun'ya's *Pride* (1998) offered a sympathetic portrayal of
wartime prime minister Tōjō as the victim of "victor's justice." *Merdeka
17805* (2001) attempted to demonstrate the sincerity of Japan's "holy" crusade for Asian independence by depicting a Japanese soldier who stayed in
Indonesia after the surrender, to resist Dutch efforts to reinstate colonial
rule. The kamikaze homage *The Eternal Zero* (*Eien no zero*, 2013), *Men of
the* Yamato (*Otokotachi no* Yamato, 2005), and *The Truth About Nanjing*
(*Nankin no shinjitsu*, 2008) indicate that apologists and deniers can and do
use entertainment media to get their messages out. The lessons and legacies
of Japan's war are among the most controversial topics discussed through
popular media.

Softer than the rest

Many Japanese officials and intellectuals see in J-Cult's global appeal a
solution to almost three decades of economic malaise and ongoing regional
hostilities. They are optimistic that Japan's cultural influence will lead to
a more cohesive (East) Asian "community," wherein "the dense circulation of popular culture" creates a sense of regional identity or "we-ness."
"Popular culture consumption creates a special bond based on a shared

experience" of lifestyles and media diversions that constitute "a shared language for transnational communication." The youth of the consumers themselves, who supposedly will "lead the creation of an East Asian community in various fields, including security, the economy, the environment, education, and culture," gives some observers hope "that the impact of popular culture on an East Asian regional identity will be long-lasting and incremental."[57]

It is not at all clear that Japan's cultural appeal has helped achieve its foreign policy goals. The People's Republic of China (PRC) and the Republic of Korea (ROK), both important markets for Japanese cultural products, are not at all satisfied by Japan's recent efforts to defuse regional tensions related to unresolved historical resentments.[58] Koreans and Chinese are perfectly comfortable playing Nintendō games while angrily protesting Japanese claims to sovereignty over the Liancourt/Tokdo/Takeshima and Diàoyú/Senkaku island chains, respectively.[59] A 2013 poll found that 77 percent of South Koreans and 90 percent of Chinese had an "unfavorable" view of Japan. Given these two countries' proximity, these numbers are arguably of greater importance than Americans' generally positive opinion of Japan.[60] The cosplay generation of Asians on whom the optimists are counting to lay these issues to rest has a daunting task.

China and South Korea also now compete with Japan for the hearts and minds of young Asians. Their respective governments attempt to deploy soft power themselves, using their own comparably cool cultural products to promote tourism, trade, and foreign policy objectives. China's government-sponsored Confucius Institutes at overseas universities support Mandarin language education and Chinese studies.[61] The ROK's Ministry of Culture works with entertainment companies to capitalize on the "K[orean]-Wave" (hallyu) sweeping millennial Asia. Even rapper PSY's immensely popular—if undignified—2012 music video "Gangnam Style" is considered appropriate for such purposes. The Imagine Your Korea campaign aspires to attract twenty million tourists by promoting South Korea as a "leader of popular culture" and a "trendy and innovative" destination.[62]

By contrast, Japan's government has been relatively slow to recognize and exploit the potential benefits of the Cool Japan brand. Competition from Korea's "outsize popular influence" has prompted the Ministry of Education, Trade, and Industry (METI) to create a Cool Japan Fund that gives direction to a soft power assault, heavily reliant on the global popularity of cartoons.[63] Established in 2011, METI's Creative Industries Policy "promotes overseas advancement of an internationally appreciated 'Cool Japan' brand, cultivation of creative industries, promotion of these industries in Japan and abroad and other related initiatives from cross-industry and cross-government standpoints."[64]

All three of these initiatives are plagued with limitations and contradictions. Several academic institutions have terminated their Confucius Institute agreements due to predictable restrictions on political speech and

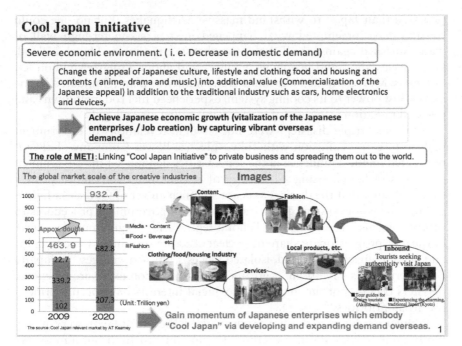

FIGURE 9.1   *Cool Japan Initiative, July 2014, Ministry of Economy, Trade, and Industry, (http://www.meti.go.jp/policy/mono_info_service/mono/creative/file/1406CoolJapanInitiative.pdf).*

academic freedom. Academics allege that "North American universities permit Confucius Institutes to advance a state agenda in the recruitment and control of academic staff, in the choice of curriculum, and in the restriction of debate." The PRC's soft power initiative has backfired: "Other nations promote positive images of themselves for the sake of political profit. China lies and censors, and the world sees through its con."[65] It may draw more tourists to the Korean peninsula, but skeptics doubt that the ROK's own charm offensive will smooth tensions over the Tokdo/Takeshima islets dispute or drive a wedge between China and North Korea.[66] With reference to Japan's relatively tardy Cool Japan campaign, some ask a more philosophical question: "[I]sn't a government-driven attempt to manufacture 'cool,' well, just the opposite?"[67]

Shaken and stirred

On March 11, 2011, a magnitude 9.0 earthquake—the fourth strongest ever recorded—occurred off the coast of Miyagi prefecture, shaking people as far away as central Japan. No country on earth is better built or better prepared than Japan to withstand massive earthquakes. But no one could possibly have preempted what happened next: a six-meter-high wall of water smashed against the Tōhoku (northeast) coastline of Honshū island. Over twenty thousand people were killed, and about a quarter million left homeless. Moreover, the Fukushima Daiichi nuclear plant, inundated by the waves, lost power to its cooling system, experienced fuel rod meltdowns and released radiation into the water and surrounding air and soil.[68]

As if this "triple disaster" were not enough, revelations of government malfeasance and collusion with Tokyo Electric Power Company (TEPCO) decimated public confidence in the state. Critics denounced the government and TEPCO for choosing a "strategy of reassurance over one of protection," insisting that the disaster was not so much an act of God as "a failure of both the whole system of nuclear power and government procedures to protect citizens." The struggling Tōhoku region and its aging populace have borne a disproportionate share of nuclear reactors sustaining big city lights and vending machines in odd, isolated places. "Nuclear villages" in Japan's rural peripheries have been at greater risk of radiation exposure whenever disasters occur—not the first time provincial interests have been sacrificed for urban priorities.[69]

Popular responses to the disaster throughout the rest of Japan were mixed. On the one hand, consumers refused to buy not just food but almost *any* commodity (including lumber and fireworks) from Tōhoku, for fear of contamination, virtually stifling any chance of economic recovery there. On the other hand, despite radiation concerns, thousands of volunteers descended on the region to assist and comfort their fellow citizens. The widespread belief in contemporary Japan's "relationless society" (*muen shakai*) proved to be only partially true.

Analyzing the effects of what is now called 3/11 on Japanese "imaginations," Uno Tsunehiro writes, "Through exposure to considerable violence, people's attention is drawn to the structure of their world. It is not a matter of what the earthquake or accident changed but rather how they emphasized existing connections."[70] The disaster occurred when "precarity" was already recognized as a normal condition of "labor and life." Allison claims "precarious Japan" is the product of the "liquidization in socioeconomic relations" since the late 1980s, with the neoliberal "turn to flexible employment and its transformation of work and the workplace," and a consequent "rhythm of social impermanence." Precarity itself is "differentially distributed," as the people of Tōhoku realized all too well. The degree of precarity "depends on where one lives and where one is situated in the socioeconomic landscape of nation, workplace, and home."[71]

Tokyo's slow, inept response to 3/11 and its perfunctory relief efforts bred an almost unprecedented, widespread cynicism among people that was expressed in various cultural media. Not since the anti–Vietnam War protests had popular culture—*by* and *for* the people (*minshū bunka*)—been so darkly sardonic and bitterly indignant. But it also stirred citizens to confront fundamental cultural and structural problems. Antinuclear activism, which had subsided noticeably since the early postwar era, revived and conjoined with peace movements that opposed the Abe administration's moves to circumvent Article 9 via "reinterpretation" and to install a US-style, surveillance and national security regime. Just as 3/11 has brought despair and suffering—which the domestic and international press minimized by reporting on the inbred stoic forbearance of Japanese people (*gaman*)—it also motivated positive action for fundamental reforms.

Stepping into Meiji street singer Soeda Azenbō's geta (wooden sandal-clogs), musicians used "sound demo[nstration]s" to demand specific reforms of "national energy policies" and "long-term political change." From 2011 to 2013, rap, reggae, punk, techno acts, and even drum corps used "presentational and participatory" performance modes to raise awareness, attract protesters, and agitate against the reactivation of nuclear power plants throughout the archipelago. Although underground subcultural genres such as these tend to attract "people who are different," rather than "the mainstream ... listening to AKB48," sound demos nonetheless proved effective for mobilizing citizen activism in service to "multiple causes."[72]

March 11 has had a wide and deep impact on expressive culture, not just as a form of protest but as a means to healing. The revival of local *matsuri* and "socially engaged art" has been important for "rebuilding struggling communities, helping disadvantaged populations, and connecting people with local history and culture."[73] Unsurprisingly, 3/11 manga appeared, most prominently Shiriagari Kotobuki's *Manga Ever Since: 2011.3.11*, which was awarded the Imperial Medal of Honor for Culture in 2014. Shiriagari "depicts the daily shocks and absurdities following in the wake of 3.11," with a "sloppy" (*zonzai*) sensibility and black humor, "and links them to the working lives, domestic spaces, and collective psyche of his readers."[74] Many films have addressed the tragedy and its aftermath, including *3.11: A Sense of Home* (2011), a collaboration between twenty-one directors, each of whom contributed a short film of three minutes, eleven seconds.[75] Since 2014, a 3/11 film festival has commemorated each anniversary of the disaster in Tokyo's Chiyoda ward.[76] There is also a growing corpus of literature on the disaster, which in some cases draws on the legacy of postwar *hibakusha* literature.[77]

Japanese popular culture remains a central site for hegemonic struggle: personal and collective identities, public memory of Japan's imperial and wartime past, gender values, standards of "decency," and Japan's role in global affairs, rather than being consensually "fixed," are instead up for continuous debate. The state and the entertainment industry have grandiose hopes that the global popularity of J-Cult will redound to the country's other interests. Yet the cultural products with which these interests hope to attract admirers and tourists often project images, raise questions or promote behaviors that do not align well with this agenda. Through the process of glocalization, popular culture gives Japanese and non-Japanese alike means for constructing alternative identities and life-styles, making connections and creating real or virtual communities with others, and reinventing themselves as different from whatever mainstream alienates them. Japan's entertainment industry has made piles of money providing those materials and through the Cool Japan campaign now does so—at least partially—"for the country's sake." In this sense, as in any hegemonic relationship, the corporatists and the customers need each other, occasionally cede ground to one another and continue the uneasy dance to global capitalism's endless tune.

AFTERWORD

Contemplating cool

Cuteness. Apocalypse. Exoticism. Technotopia. "Weirdo Porn That Makes People Puke." What makes Cool Japan cool? Some say it is the result of brilliant marketing and crossover strategies developed, implemented, and improved in tandem with postwar economic growth. These strategies include what has been called "convergence" or "media mix," a "divergent prolif-eration of content across multiple media forms."[1] A franchise's characters might appear in video or card games, toys, comics, animated or live-action movies and television shows, office supplies, and everyday accessories. Soundtracks for video games and anime are released as CDs and audio files and constitute "the main vehicle for delivering J-Pop to a worldwide audi-ence."[2] It is possible for consumers to literally surround themselves with Japanese "character goods" that express who they are or want to be.

Others assert that the aesthetic "quality" of the products themselves explains Japan's coolness (*kakkō yosa*). Timothy Craig highlights J-Cult's craftsmanship, creativity, its tendency to depict "life in all its dimensions," without moralizing or concealing its "unpleasant aspects" and its refreshing lack of cynicism—again, in contrast to American fare—as traits that appeal to global audiences. Allison praises the distinctive "expressive strength" of Japanese artists. Susan Napier describes anime as "uncompromising" and "complex," telling stories with a "dark tone" that resist "the predictabil-ity of Disney (or other Hollywood fare overall, for that matter)." Tsutsui concurs:

> [T]here does seem to be something intrinsic to Japanese mass entertainments—their style, their content, their message—that is distinct-ive and broadly appealing, especially in contrast to the familiar fare of Hollywood blockbusters, prime-time television, and the *Billboard* Top 40 music charts ... [I]t is insistently and unapologetically different from the

familiar and often predictable products of the Magic Kingdom, Marvel Comics, and the top Paris fashion houses.[3]

As poor as my opinion of most American entertainment is, I find it neither intellectually defensible nor analytically useful to position it as the inferior counterpart to Japan's, which can be every bit as formulaic, vapid, and uninspired. Remember, *Zootopia* (2016), one of the most sophisticated movies ever made about prejudice in all its forms, is a Disney movie. That said, for fans this difference in aesthetic quality is very real, no matter how many counterexamples one provides. It is a mind-set impossible for scholars to ignore, though it need not be endorsed.

To some degree, at least, affective attachment to Japanese popular culture is generational. Millennials may connect with J-Cult in part because they have grown up with it; it has shaped their tastes as consumers. But some J-Cult also addresses and depicts some of the unique dilemmas and scenarios they face living on a warming planet, governed by corrupt, dysfunctional political systems and exploited by a "flexible," unpredictable, amoral neoliberal global capitalist economy. And they are expected to fix this mess. Postapocalyptic, dystopian scenarios, human-technology interfaces, youthful rebellion against unjust socioeconomic and political structures, liberation, and self-definition—these recurrent themes in some of the more sophisticated Japanese entertainment have particular resonance for the millennial generation. This generation is also the least racist, sexist, nationalist, homophobic, and environmentally oblivious ever to walk the earth. By "offer[ing] an endless array of possibilities to a world that seems increasingly fettered by the intractable realities of ethnic, religious, and national identifications," Japanese cartoons naturally entice these people.[4] Granted, this would only account for the appeal of specific media (mostly manga and anime) to a particular generation, whereas J-Cult products and fandom are more diverse. Doraemon is not a viable dystopian cipher.

Napier regards the current popularity of J-Cult as the latest in a succession of "Japan booms" that began in the late nineteenth century and rendered Japan a "fantasyscape" in Western imaginations (although foreigners' cherished images are almost invariably products of prodigious Japanese self-stereotyping). Japanophiles escape to an exotic parallel universe to experience the pleasure of "temporary alternative lifestyles" with "different kinds of values that implicitly and sometimes explicitly call into question aspects of Western ideology."[5] Its very alterity may be part of Japanese culture's appeal, but that begs the question of why *other* places outside of Europe and North America do not have the same draw. To invoke Iwabuchi's delightful olfactory metaphor yet again, Japan's *parfum* is apparently more pleasing.

For some, that agreeable aroma emanates from incense-scented Japanese traditions: this line of thinking presents J-Cult as the product of centuries of cultural evolution, a heritage of thematic concerns, sensibilities, historical events and personages, artistic techniques, aesthetic principles, and folklore specific to Japan. Allison refers to an "aesthetic proclivity" and unconscious "animist sensibility" originating in Shintō belief. One of anime's distinctive traits, Zília Papp maintains, is its connection to a "process of visual evolution" of representing folkloric monsters (yōkai): anime is the medium in which "new, changing roles will be assigned to yōkai in alignment with changing realities related to twenty-first century social and environmental changes and traumas related to them." "Japanese comics do not exist in a vacuum," Kinko Itō avers, "they are closely connected to Japanese history and culture … and reflect both the reality of Japanese society and myths, beliefs, and fantasies that Japanese have about themselves, their culture and the world."[6] Some scholars contend that familiarity with vernacular religions, traditional customs, and indigenous performing arts are all but indispensable for understanding contemporary cultural forms.[7]

This is not entirely untrue: it is indisputable that artists and creative industries have mined centuries of history, art, literature, religion, and folklore for content and stylistic inspiration. If nothing else, the fact that J-Cult is communicated in the Japanese language—with its built-in affirmations of status distinctions and webs of obligation—infuses it with a distinctively Japanese fragrance. The trick is to acknowledge this without endorsing ahistorical, reductive, "monocultural" thinking that oversimplifies and stereotypes. "Since Japanese culture is a problematical construct rather than a given reality," Yoshio Sugimoto writes, "it should not be taken to refer to any bounded entity" in which ethnic, class, and regional distinctions are negligible.[8] The Japanese scent is stronger in some cultural products than in others. More often than not, "traditions" are of relatively recent invention and result from centuries of cross-cultural admixture, and cultural products reflect more recent histories, sensibilities, and concerns than older ones.

Besides, there are many artists, entertainers, and consumers who use popular culture to *deliberately subvert* the notion of a timeless, homogeneous, prescriptive Japanese cultural essence. In *Princess Mononoke* (*Mononoke hime*, 1997), Miyazaki Hayao de-centers the dominant patriarchal Yamato imperial polity at the core of Japanese identity by creating an Emishi protagonist, through whom he provides "alternatives to the master narratives" and a "provocative, heterogeneous, and often bleaker view" of national history. The character Eboshi embodies ancient traditions of matriarchal rule. "[T]he [male] emperor, whose usual role was to bring the forces of nature into harmony with his court and subjects, is shown as inimical to nature as he sends forces to fight the forest gods."[9] Refusing to be hemmed in by ethnonational boundaries, self-described "yellow b-boys … suggest the possibilities for a transnational cultural politics of race that improvises on their understandings of hip-hop's core values." Young women who use *kawaii* expansively—and thereby resist Hello Kitty's enchanting tyranny—reject conventional, infantilized notions of *shōjo* femininity.[10] These are but three examples of people refusing to let an immutable notion of Japanese ethnicity, culture or history contain

and constrain their personalities, imaginations, desires, tastes, mannerisms, and identities. It may be attractive to some foreigners (and some
Japanese nationalists) to think of Japanese culture as something easily
packaged in an elegant lacquered box, but to some Japanese, that box is
a prison.

Part of the problem with any overarching theory of Japanese entertainment's global appeal is determining what is representative. Is the dystopian
Akira representative of cartoons more generally, in terms of artistry and
thematic depth? Are internationally read authors Murakami Haruki or
Yoshimoto Banana typical of Japanese fiction writers? Is Chairman Kaga
(Takeshi)'s campy grandiosity as host of *Iron Chef* (*Ryōri no tetsujin*,
1993–99, a Fuji Television cook-off program) paradigmatic of Japanese
television? Is there anything identifiably "Japanese"—aesthetically, the-
matically or historically—that binds these examples together? The reader
probably realizes by now that I will answer "No." Aside from being created (although not necessarily *manufactured*) by people who inhabit
a nation-state called Nippon/Japan, by and for people who speak its
national language, there is nothing tying the saccharine *kawaisa* of Hello
Kitty to the brutal cinematic cyberpunk of *Tetsuo the Iron Man* (1989).
And why must there be?

NOTES

INTRODUCTION

1 Douglas McGray, "Japan's Gross National Cool," *Foreign Policy* 130 (May–June 2002): 44–54.

2 Brian Moeran coined this neologism because it "neatly expresses the fashionable nature of Japanese popular culture, which has to some extent become a cult form among many young people in the Asian region." "Soft Sell, Hard Cash: Marketing J-Cult in Asia," Working Paper 76, Department of Intercultural Communication and Management, Copenhagen Business School, 2004, 2.

3 *The Rush Limbaugh Show*, Premiere Networks, October 28, 1994.

4 Sung-Gun Kim, "The Shinto Shrine Issue in Korean Christianity under Japanese Colonialism," *Journal of Church and State* 39, no. 3 (Summer 1997): 503–21.

5 Wm. Theodore de Bary et al., eds., *Sources of Japanese Tradition*, 2nd ed., vol. 1: *From Earliest Times to 1600* (New York: Columbia University Press, 2001), 100–3 and 107.

6 Quoted in de Bary et al., *Sources*, vol. 1, 6–8.

7 The official imperial genealogy is available from the Imperial Household Agency at http://www.kunaicho.go.jp/e-about/genealogy/img/keizu-e.pdf.

8 Quoted in de Bary et al., *Sources*, vol. 1, 7. See Jennifer Jay, "Imagining Matriarchy: 'Kingdoms of Women' in Tang China," *Journal of the American Oriental Society* 116, no. 2 (April–June 1996): 220–9.

9 Hiroko Sekiguchi, "The Patriarchal Family Paradigm in Eighth-Century Japan," in *Women and Confucian Cultures in Premodern China, Korea, and Japan*, eds. Dorothy Ko, JaHyun Kim Haboush, and Joan Piggott (Berkeley: University of California Press, 2003), 27–46.

10 Hitomi Tonomura, "Women and Inheritance in Japan's Early Warrior Society," *Comparative Studies in Society and History* 32, no. 3 (July 1990): 592–623; de Bary et al., *Sources*, vol. 1, 415–17.

11 See de Bary et al., *Sources*, vol. 1, 47–8 and 50–4.

12 Quoted in Wm. Theodore de Bary et al., eds., *Sources of Japanese Tradition, 1600–2000*, 2nd ed., vol. 2, *Part One: 1600–1868* (New York: Columbia University Press, 2006), 204–5.

13 George Wilson, *Patriots and Redeemers in Japan: Motives in the Meiji Restoration* (Chicago: University of Chicago Press, 1992), 63 and 130.

CHAPTER ONE

1 Norman F. Cantor and Michael S. Werthman, eds., *The History of Popular Culture to 1815* (New York: Macmillan, 1968), xxii.

2 Carol Gluck, "The People in History: Recent Trends in Japanese Historiography," *Journal of Asian Studies* 38, no. 1 (November 1978): 25–50.

3 Matthew Arnold, *Culture and Anarchy: An Essay in Political and Social Criticism* (London: Smith, Elder and Co., 1869), viii and xvi.

4 Arnold, *Culture and Anarchy*, 14, lv and lvi. See also Lawrence Levine, *Highbrow/Lowbrow: The Emergence of Cultural Hierarchy in America* (Cambridge: Harvard University Press, 1988), 223–4; and John Storey, *Inventing Popular Culture: From Folklore to Globalization* (Malden, MA: Blackwell, 2003), 16–21.

5 Paul DiMaggio, "Cultural Entrepreneurship in Nineteenth-Century Boston," *Media, Culture and Society* 4 (1982): 33–50; Levine, *Highbrow*, 86–90, 104, 132, 171, and 219; and Storey, *Inventing*, 34–40.

6 Walter Benjamin, "The Work of Art in the Age of Mechanical Reproduction" (1936), trans. Harry Zohn, Marxists Internet Archive, https://www.marxists.org/reference/subject/philosophy/works/ge/benjamin.htm.

7 Storey, *Inventing*, 92.

8 "Batman and the War on Terror," *New York Times* (hereafter *NYT*), July 21, 2008, http://theboard.blogs.nytimes.com/2008/07/21/batman-and-the-war-on-terror/?_r=0; Ron Briley, "The Dark Knight: An Allegory of America in the Age of Bush?" History News Network, August 25, 2008, http://historynewsnetwork.org/article/53504; reelchanger, "The Hero We Need: An In-Depth Analysis of Batman in Post-9/11 America," Reel Change, July 6, 2012, https://reelchange.net/2012/07/06/the-hero-we-need-an-in-depth-analysis-of-batman-as-post-911-america/.

9 Why do we like what we like? In an NPR commentary, Swiss philosopher Alain de Botton suggests that "we're drawn to call something beautiful whenever we detect that it contains in a concentrated form those qualities in which we personally or our societies, more generally, are deficient." "The Psychology and Taste, and Choice," *All Things Considered*, National Public Radio (hereafter NPR), November 9, 2006, http://www.npr.org/templates/story/story.php?storyId=6463387.

10 Pierre Bourdieu, *Distinction: A Social Critique of the Judgment of Taste* (1979; London: Routledge, 2010), 5, 49, and 238–9.

11 Storey, *Inventing*, 1 and 15–16. On Japanese usages, see Marilyn Ivy, "Formations of Mass Culture," in *Postwar Japan as History*, ed. Andrew Gordon (Berkeley: University of California Press, 1993), 240–2.

12 Peter Burke, *Popular Culture in Early Modern Europe*, 3rd ed. (Farnham: Ashgate, 2009), 7–8, 14, and 71–2.

13 Burke, *Popular*, 23–48; Storey, *Inventing*, 16.

14 Dwight MacDonald, "A Theory of Mass Culture," in *Mass Culture: The Popular Arts in America*, ed. Bernard Rosenberg and David Manning White

(New York: Free Press, 1957), 62; and José Ortega y Gasset, "The Coming of the Masses," in Rosenberg and White, *Mass*, 45.

15 Dominic Strinati, *An Introduction to Theories of Popular Culture* (London: Routledge, 1995), 226. See also Herbert Gans, *Popular Culture and High Culture: An Analysis and Evaluation of Taste*, 2nd ed. (New York: Basic Books, 1999), 8–13.

16 Levine, *Highbrow*, 224.

17 Strinati, *Introduction*, 80.

18 Lawrence Levine, "The Folklore of Industrial Society: Popular Culture and Its Audiences," *American Historical Review* 97, no. 5 (December 1992): 1373 (emphasis in original).

19 William Kelly, ed., *Fanning the Flames: Fans and Consumer Culture in Contemporary Japan* (Albany: SUNY Press, 2004), 6.

20 T. J. Jackson Lears, "Making Fun of Popular Culture," *American Historical Review* 97, no. 5 (December 1992): 1422–3 (emphasis added).

21 Antonio Gramsci, *Selections from the Prison Notebooks* (London: Lawrence and Wishart, 1971), 161; Strinati, *Introduction*, 165–71.

22 Strinati, *Introduction*, 56. Although Gramsci's critique addressed capitalism, hegemony describes socialist/communist societies equally well. China's Cultural Revolution (1966–76) and Democratic Kampuchea (1975–79) both gave young people a sense of power and control over the revolution while carrying out Mao Zedong's and Pol Pot's respective ambitions, without endangering Chinese Communist Party or Khmer Rouge control. Communist parties in Cuba, North Korea, Russia, and elsewhere mobilized the masses to topple ancien régimes, yet subordinated their interests to party ideologies.

23 Benjamin, "Work."

24 Max Gluckman, *Rituals of Rebellion in South-East Africa* (Manchester: Manchester University Press, 1954).

25 Tom Frank, "Alternative to What?" in *Sounding Off! Music as Subversion/Resistance/Revolution*, ed. Ron Sakolsky and Fred Wei-han Ho (Brooklyn, NY: Autonomedia, 1996), 113 and 114.

26 Ariana Hernández-Reguant, "Copyrighting Che: Art and Authorship under Cuban Late Socialism," *Public Culture* 16, no. 1 (Winter 2004): 1–30.

27 John Storey, *Cultural Theory and Popular Culture: An Introduction*, 6th ed. (Harlow: Pearson, 2012), 84.

28 Gerald Groemer, "The Rise of 'Japanese Music,'" *The World of Music* 46, no. 2 (2004): 9–33; Bonnie Wade, *Composing Japanese Musical Modernity* (Chicago: University of Chicago Press, 2014), 1–2.

29 Groemer, "Rise," 11–12. See Scott Cook, "'Yue Ji'—Record of Music: Introduction, Translation, Notes, and Commentary," *Asian Music* 26, no. 2 (Spring–Summer 1995): 1–96; and Walter Kaufmann, *Musical References in the Chinese Classics* (Detroit: Information Coordinators, 1976). Japanese had access to the *Akhak kwebŏm*—a detailed compendium of court music compiled by Sŏng Hyŏn (1439–1504)—because of two invasions of the Korean peninsula in the 1590s, during which they looted the libraries of the Yi royal

house. The oldest surviving manuscript was kept by the Owari Tokugawa house, and is located in the Hōsa Library in Nagoya (http://housa.city.nagoya.jp/index.html).

30 Donald Keene, "Japanese Aesthetics," *Philosophy East and West* 19, no. 3 (July 1969): 293–306.

31 Kuki Shūzō, *Iki no kōzō* (Tokyo: Iwanami Shoten 1930). English translations are available in Kuki Shūzō, *Reflections on Japanese Taste: The Structure of Iki* (Sydney: Power Publications, 2007), and Hiroshi Nara, *The Aesthetics of Detachment: The Aesthetic Vision of Kuki Shūzō* (Honolulu: University of Hawai'i Press, 2004). See also Leslie Pincus, *Authenticating Culture in Imperial Japan: Kuki Shūzō and the Rise of National Aesthetics* (Berkeley: University of California Press, 1996); and Michael Marra, *A History of Modern Japanese Aesthetics* (Honolulu: University of Hawai'i Press, 2001).

32 Nara, *Aesthetics*, 18–22.

33 Nishiyama Matsunosuke, *Edo Culture: Daily Life and Diversions in Urban Japan, 1600–1868*, trans. Gerald Groemer (Honolulu: University of Hawai'i Press, 1997), 56.

34 Nara, *Aesthetics*, 1–2.

35 See for example Burke, *Popular Culture*, 50–6; Anne E. McLaren, *Chinese Popular Culture and Ming Chantefables* (Leiden: Brill, 1998), 8–9; David G. Johnson, Andrew J. Nathan, and Evelyn S. Rawski, eds., *Popular Culture in Late Imperial China* (Berkeley: University of California Press, 1985); Carter Vaughn Findley, *Ottoman Civil Officialdom: A Social History* (Princeton: Princeton University Press, 1989), 52 and 139; Juan R. I. Cole, "Iranian Culture and South Asia, 1500–1900," in *Iran and the Surrounding World: Interactions in Culture and Cultural Politics*, ed. Nikki Keddie and Rudi Matthee (Seattle: University of Washington Press, 2002), 18; Stephen P. Blake, *Shahjahanabad: The Sovereign City in Mughal India 1639–1739* (Cambridge: Cambridge University Press, 1991), 150–60; Farhat Hasan, *State and Locality in Mughal India: Power Relations in Western India, c. 1572–1730* (Cambridge: Cambridge University Press, 2004), 102.

CHAPTER TWO

1 John Dougill, *Kyoto: A Cultural History* (Oxford: Oxford University Press, 2006), 153–4.

2 *Kabukimono* (crooked fellows) described seventeenth-century deviant samurai ruffians who roamed the streets of Edo looking for fights. See Eiko Ikegami, *The Taming of the Samurai: Honorific Individualism and the Making of Modern Japan* (Cambridge: Harvard University Press, 1997), 205–6.

3 Quoted in Donald Shively, "*Bakufu* versus *Kabuki*," *Harvard Journal of Asiatic Studies* 18, no. 3/4 (December 1955): 327.

4 Shively, "*Bakufu*," 326.

5 *Tokusei rei* (virtuous government decrees) were issued by medieval *bakufu* to provide debt relief for peasants who were in arrears with moneylenders. The lenders were compelled to cancel all debts. *Tokusei* were often responses to threatened or actual rural uprisings. Nobunaga's policies thus guaranteed that lenders in his jurisdiction would never face the possibility of losing money by forgiving debts.

6 Quoted in David J. Lu, *Japan: A Documentary History* (Armonk, NY: M. E. Sharpe, 1997), 189.

7 Donald Shively, "Popular Culture," in *The Cambridge History of Japan*, vol. 4, ed. John Whitney Hall (Cambridge: Cambridge University Press, 1991), 733–42.

8 "Tokugawa seiken hyakkajō" (1605), translated and cited in Shively, "*Bakufu*," 337.

9 The term "geisha" (artistic person) originally applied to male "party masters" also known as *takimochi*, who "sang, pranced, and told jokes and stories" like court jesters. Lesley Downer, *Women of the Pleasure Quarters* (New York: Broadway Books, 2001), 96. See also Tanaka Yūko, "Development of the Geisha Tradition," *Japan Echo* 30, no. 6 (December 2003), www.japanecho.co.jp.

10 Quoted in Donald Shively, "The Social Environment of Tokugawa Kabuki," in *Studies in Kabuki: Its Acting, Music, and Historical Context*, ed. James R. Brandon, William Malm, and Donald Shively (Honolulu: University of Hawai'i Press, 1978), 4.

11 Susan Griswold, "The Triumph of Materialism: The Popular Fiction of 18th-Century Japan," *Journal of Popular Culture* 29, no. 1 (Summer 1995): 235–45; Sarah Thompson and H. D. Harootunian, *Undercurrents in the Floating World: Censorship and Japanese Prints* (New York: Asia Society Galleries, 1991), 27.

12 Victor Turner, *The Forest of Symbols: Aspects of Ndembu Ritual* (Ithaca: Cornell University Press, 1967), 99, 106, and 110; cf. Arnold van Gennep, *The Rites of Passage* (1909; London: Routledge, 1960).

13 Howard Hibbett, *The Floating World in Japanese Fiction* (1959; Rutland, VT: Tuttle, 1975), 10. See also Haruo Shirane, ed., *Early Modern Japanese Literature: An Anthology, 1600–1900* (New York: Columbia University Press, 2008), 29–33.

14 See C. Andrew Gerstle, "The Culture of Play: Kabuki and the Production of Texts," *Oral Tradition* 20, no. 2 (2005): 188–216.

15 See Peter Kornicki, *The Book in Japan* (Leiden: Brill, 1998); and Andrew Kamei-Dyche, "The History of Books and Print Culture in Japan: The State of the Discipline," *Book History* 14 (2011): 270–304. See also Simon Eliot and Jonathan Rose, eds., *A Companion to the History of the Book* (Malden, MA: Wiley-Blackwell, 2009).

16 Shively, "Popular," 726.

17 See Richard Lane, *Images from the Floating World: The Japanese Print* (Oxford: Oxford University Press, 1978); Amy Reigle Newland, *Hotei Encyclopedia of Japanese Woodblock Prints* (Amsterdam: Hotei, 2005).

18 Ernest Fenollosa, *The Masters of Ukiyoe: A Complete Historical Description of Japanese Paintings and Color Prints of the Genre School* (New York: W. H. Ketchum, 1896), 1 and 115.

19 Kitao Masayoshi, *Bakemono chakutōchō* (Edo: Senkakudō, 1788). A digitized copy of Kitao's book is available at the Tokyo Archive web site: http://archive.library.metro.tokyo.jp/da/detail?tilcod=0000000005-00000007.

20 Michael Dylan Foster, *Pandemonium and Parade: Japanese Monsters and the Culture of Yōkai* (Berkeley: University of California Press, 2009), 4 and 6. See also Foster, *The Book of Yōkai: Mysterious Creatures of Japanese Folklore* (Berkeley: University of California Press, 2015).

21 Peter Kornicki, Mara Patessio and G. G. Rowley, eds., *The Female as Subject: Reading and Writing in Early Modern Japan* (Ann Arbor: Center for Japanese Studies, 2010), 4 and 5; Peter Kornicki, "Women, Education, and Literacy," in Kornicki et al., *Female*, 23–5. An English translation of *Onna daigaku* is available in Basil Hall Chamberlain, *Women and Wisdom of Japan* (London: John Murray, 1905), 33–46.

22 Itasaka Noriko, "The Woman Reader as Symbol," in Kornicki et al., *Female*, 106–7.

23 See http://www.lib.berkeley.edu/EAL/about/collections.html.

24 Mary Elizabeth Berry, *Japan in Print: Information and Nation in the Early Modern Period* (Berkeley: University of California Press, 2006).

25 Timon Screech, *Sex and the Floating World: Erotic Images in Japan 1700–1820*, 2nd ed. (London: Reaktion Books, 2009), 51.

26 Quoted in Shirane, *Early Modern*, 514.

27 Arthur O'Keefe, "Western Media Cherry-Pick Facts and Phalli to Fit the 'No Vagina' Narrative in Japan," *Japan Times* (hereafter *JT*), July 3, 2016, http://www.japantimes.co.jp/community/2016/07/03/voices/western-media-cherry-pick-facts-phalli-fit-japan-no-vagina-narrative/#.V3qDsVdqpQa; Chris Kitching, "Size Matters: Revellers Carry Gigantic Phalluses through Streets of Japanese City for One of World's Most Unusual Festivals," *Daily Mail*, April 7, 2015, http://www.dailymail.co.uk/travel/travel_news/article-3028751/Revellers-carry-giant-phalluses-streets-Kawasaki-City-Japan-Kanamara-Matsuri-festival.html.

28 T. Fujitani, *Splendid Monarchy: Power and Pageantry in Modern Japan* (Berkeley: University of California Press, 1996), 117, 188, and 190.

29 Gary Leupp, *Male Colors: The Construction of Homosexuality in Tokugawa Japan* (Berkeley: University of California Press, 1995), 28–46.

30 Screech, *Sex*, 56.

31 Screech, *Sex*, 11.

32 Most of these stories have been translated into English: *Five Women Who Loved Love*, trans. Wm. Theodore de Bary (Rutland, VT: Tuttle, 1956); *The Life of an Amorous Man*, trans. Kenji Hamada (Rutland, VT: Tuttle, 1963); *The Life of an Amorous Woman, and Other Writings*, trans. Ivan Morris (Norfolk, CT: New Directions, 1963); and *The Great Mirror of Male Love*, trans. Paul Schalow (Stanford: Stanford University Press, 1991). Excerpts from

Great Mirror were previously published in *Comrade Loves of the Samurai*, trans. Edward Powys Mathers (1928; Rutland, VT: Tuttle, 1972).

33 Saikaku, *Comrade*, 36 and 52.

34 Ihara Saikaku, *The Japanese Family Storehouse, or the Millionaires' Gospel Modernised*, trans. G. W. Sargent (London: Cambridge University Press, 1959), xxvi; Alfred Haft, "Affirming the Life Erotic: Yoshida Hanbei's *Kōshoku kinmō zui*," *Japan Review* 26 (2013): 104.

35 Translated in Leupp, *Male*, 205–18.

36 Stanleigh Jones, *The Bunraku Puppet Theatre of Japan: Honor, Vengeance, and Love in Four Plays of the 18th and 19th Centuries* (Honolulu: University of Hawai'i Press, 2013), 1 and 2; Shively, "Social," 41. Several Chikamatsu plays are available in English translation: Asataro Miyamori, *Masterpieces of Chikamatsu: The Japanese Shakespeare* (London: Kegan Paul, 1926); Donald Keene, *Major Plays of Chikamatsu* (New York: Columbia University Press, 1961, 1990), and an abbreviated version, *Four Major Plays of Chikamatsu* (New York: Columbia University Press, 1998); and C. Andrew Gerstle, *Chikamatsu: 5 Late Plays* (New York: Columbia University Press, 2001).

37 http://www.youkiza.jp/about/rekishi.html. See also B. Kure, *The Historical Development of Marionette Theater in Japan* (New York: Columbia University Printing Office, 1920); *Ito ayatsuri no mangekyō: Yūkiza 350-nen no ningyō shibai* (Tokyo: INAX, 2009); and Mari Boyd, "Surviving and Succeeding: The Yūki-za Marionette Theater Company," in *Rising from the Flames: The Rebirth of Theater in Occupied Japan, 1945–1952*, ed. Samuel Leiter (Lanham, MD: Lexington Books, 2009), 217–30.

38 Shively, "Social," 40; Shively, "*Bakufu*," 355–6.

39 Shively, "Social," 45, 29, and 34–6; Shively, "*Bakufu*," 348–9.

40 Groemer, "Rise," 10 and 12–16.

41 Alison McQueen Tokita, "Music in *Kabuki*: More Than Meets the Eye," in *The Ashgate Research Companion to Japanese Music*, ed. Alison McQueen Tokita and David Hughes (Farnham: Ashgate, 2010), 243.

42 Gerald Groemer, "Popular Music before the Meiji Period," in Tokita and Hughes, *Ashgate*, 261 and 274.

43 J. L. Anderson, "Spoken Silents in the Japanese Cinema; or Talking to Pictures: Essaying the *Katsuben*, Contextualizing the Texts," in *Reframing Japanese Cinema: Authorship, Genre, History*, ed. Arthur Nolletti and David Desser (Bloomington: Indiana University Press, 1992), 261–4.

44 Ronald Toby, "Imagining and Imaging 'Anthropos' in Early-Modern Japan," *Visual Anthropology* 14, no. 1 (1998): 19–44; Berry, *Japan*, 224–6.

45 Georg Schurhammer, *Francis Xavier: His Life and Times*, vol. 4, trans. M. Joseph Costelloe (Rome: Jesuit Historical Institute, 1982), 199–213.

46 Ronald Toby, *State and Diplomacy in Early Modern Japan: Asia in the Development of the Tokugawa Bakufu*, 2nd ed. (Stanford: Stanford University Press, 1991), 64–76.

47 George McCune, "Exchange of Envoys between Korea and Japan during the Tokugawa Period," *Far Eastern Quarterly* 5, no. 3 (May 1946): 308 and 317.

48 Song Chiwŏn, "Chosŏn t'ongsinsa rŭl t'onghaebon Cho-Il munwha kyoryu ŭi myŏnmyŏn," *Ilbon pipyŏng* 5 (2011): 302, http://s-space.snu.ac.kr (HYC); and Doyoung Park, "A New Perspective on the Korean Embassy (Chōsen tsūshinshi): The View from the Intellectuals in Tokugawa Japan," *Studies on Asia* Series IV, 3, no. 1 (March 2013): 10, http://studiesonasia.illinoisstate.edu/seriesIV/documents/Park_Studies_March2013.pdf.

49 Ronald Toby, "Carnival of the Aliens: Korean Embassies in Edo-Period Art and Popular Culture," *Monumenta Nipponica* 41, no. 4 (Winter 1991): 420, 421, 436, and 456.

50 *Kugyŏk haehaeng ch'ongjae*, 12 vols. (Seoul: Minjok Munhwa Ch'ujinhoe, 1974–1981), and Database of Korean Classics, http://db.itkc.or.kr/itkcdb/mainIndexIframe.jsp [HYC].

51 Yi Kyŏngwŏn. "Chosŏn t'ongsinsa suhaeng akdae ŭi ŭmak hwaldong koch'al," *Hanguk ŭmakhak nonjip* 2 (1994): 342 and 615–16 [HYC].

52 Kim Sŏngil, *Haesarok* 4 sŏl, byŏn, ji— "pogwan-i ŭmakŭl chŏhande taehansŏl," 1609 [HYC].

53 Hong Ujae, *Tongsarok* 8th month, 4th day, 1682 [HYC].

54 Shin Yuhan, *Haeyurok*, 9th month, 3rd day, 1719 [HYC].

55 Cho Myŏngch'ae, *Posa ilbon simu kyŏnrok*, 2nd month, 1748 [HYC].

56 Im Sugang, *Tongsa ilki, Mungyŏnrok*, n.d., 1711 [HYC].

57 Shin, *Haeyurok*, 10th month, 9th day, 1719 [HYC].

58 Park, "New," 17–18.

59 Shin, *Haeyurok*, n.d. [HYC]. Saying that Japanese music sounded "Buddhist" was a pointed dig, given the Chosŏn regime's official hostility to the religion.

60 The epithet *tōjin* referred to foreigners in the Edo period. It literally meant "Tang [Chinese] people," referring to the Tang Dynasty (618–935), but was applied generally to Koreans, Ryūkyūans, and Chinese (Westerners were usually called *nanban*, "southern barbarians"). Toby translates *tōjin* as "Chinamen" to convey its pejorative connotation.

61 Toby, "Carnival," 453–4.

62 Tsu no matsuri ni nokoru tōjin gyōretsu, http://www.bunka.pref.mie.lg.jp/rekishi/kenshi/asp/arekore/detail.asp?record=71; and Kawagoi tōjin soroi parēdo, http://tojinsoroi.com.

63 Kate Wildman Nakai, "The Naturalization of Confucianism in Tokugawa Japan: The Problem of Sinocentrism," *Harvard Journal of Asiatic Studies* 40, no. 1 (June 1980): 165 and 181; Tessa Morris-Suzuki, *Reinventing Japan: Time Space Nation* (Armonk, NY: M. E. Sharpe, 1998), chapters 2, 4, and 7; David Howell, *Geographies of Identity in Nineteenth-Century Japan* (Berkeley: University of California Press, 2005), 3–7.

64 Ronald Toby, "'Ketōjin' no tōjō o megutte: kinsei Nihon no taigai ninshiki, tashakan no ichi sokumen," in *Kyōkai no Nihon shi*, ed. Murai Shōsuke, Satō Makoto and Yoshida Nokuyuki (Tokyo: Yamakawa shuppansha, 1997), 264. Justin McCurry, "Japanese Bureaucrats Face Up to the Clean-Cut Look," *The Guardian*, May 20, 2010, https://www.theguardian.com/world/2010/may/20/japan-isesaki-beard-ban.

65 In an official chronicle on Hideyoshi's life (*Taikōki*, 1626), Oze Hoan wrote, "Besides his usual false beard [*tsukurihige*], Lord Hideyoshi also ordered false eyebrows, blackened with iron." See also Okanoya Shigezane, *Shogun and Samurai: Tales of Nobunaga, Hideyoshi, and Ieyasu* (1943), trans. Andrew and Yoshiko Dykstra, 111, http://scholarspace.manoa.hawaii.edu/handle/10125/309.

66 Keene, *Four*, 87, 90, and 112; Toby, " 'Ketōjin,' " 268–73. See Jonathan Spence, *Coxinga and the Fall of the Ming Dynasty* (Stroud: History Press, 2011).

67 Toby, " 'Ketōjin,' " 268; Richard Siddle, "The Ainu: Construction of an Image," in *Diversity in Japanese Culture*, ed. John Maher and Gaynor Macdonald (London: Kegan Paul, 1995), 73–84.

68 Shigemi Inaga, "Reinterpretation of the Western Linear Perspective in Eighteenth- and Nineteenth-Century Japan," in *Dodonæus in Japan: Translation and the Scientific Mind in Tokugawa Japan*, ed. Willy vande Walle and Kazuhiko Kasaya (Leuven: Leuven University Press, 2001), 149–65.

CHAPTER THREE

1 Julie Nelson Davis, *Utamaro and the Spectacle of Beauty* (London: Reaktion Books, 2008), 217–43.

2 Howard Hibbett, *The Chrysanthemum and the Fish: Japanese Humor since the Age of the Shoguns* (Tokyo: Kōdansha, 2002), 89.

3 Hibbett, *Chrysanthemum*, 89.

4 Nishiyama describes an unprecedented "aesthetic of evil" in kabuki of the early- to mid-nineteenth century, with "scenes of gruesome murder" and "stylish" depictions of "villain lovers" and "virtuous bandits." "Evil as seen here was no longer confined to the character traits of solitary villains on the stage. Instead, it had been transformed into something that gave expression to the energy of the commoner populace" (*Edo*, 223–5).

5 Shively, "*Bakufu*," 339, 354, and 356.

6 "If names be not correct, language is not in accordance with the truth of things. If language be not in accordance with the truth of things, affairs cannot be carried on to success ... [A] superior man considers ... that what he speaks may be carried out appropriately. What the superior man requires is just that in his words there may be nothing incorrect." *Analects of Confucius*, bk. 13, 3: 4–7 (trans. James Legge).

7 Irwin Scheiner, "Benevolent Lords and Honorable Peasants: Rebellion and Peasant Consciousness in Tokugawa Japan," in *Japanese Thought in the Tokugawa Period, 1600–1868: Methods and Metaphors*, ed. Tetsuo Najita and Irwin Scheiner (Chicago: University of Chicago Press, 1978), 41 and 52. See also Berry, *Japan*, 232.

8 James Scott, *Domination and the Arts of Resistance: Hidden Transcripts*, rev. ed. (New Haven, CT: Yale University Press, 1992), 3–4.

9 Shirane, *Early Modern*, 12 and 197–9.

10 Cited and translated in Screech, *Sex*, 43.

11 Jones, *Bunraku*, 13, 78, and 81; Nishiyama, *Edo*, 223.

12 See Donald Keene, trans., *Chūshingura—The Treasury of Loyal Retainers* (New York: Columbia University Press, 1971). Henry D. Smith III has written extensively on the Akō Vendetta from a variety of perspectives and has posted his articles to the Internet: http://www.columbia.edu/~hds2/hds2_chushingura.html.

13 Donald Shively, "Chikamatsu's Satire on the Dog Shogun," *Harvard Journal of Asiatic Studies* 18, no. 1/2 (1955): 159–80.

14 C. Andrew Gerstle, "Heroic Honor: Chikamatsu and the Samurai Ideal," *Harvard Journal of Asiatic Studies*, 57, no. 2 (December 1997): 308, 316, and 325.

15 Quoted in de Bary et al., *Sources* vol. 2, pt. 1, 195, 204, and 241–6. This "Confucian populism"—based on Mèngzǐ's (Mencius, ca. 372–289 BCE) interpretations of Confucius—was also emphasized in the commentaries of Wáng Yángmíng (1472–1529) of China, and Chŏng Tojŏn (1342–98), Yu Hyŏngwŏn (1622–73) and Chŏng Yagyong (1762–1836) of Korea. See Mark Setton, "Confucian Populism and Egalitarian Tendencies in Tonghak Thought," *East Asian History* 20 (December 2000): 121–44.

16 Gerstle, "Heroic," 312.

17 Gerstle, "Heroic," 315 and 320.

18 Shively, "Popular," 744.

19 Lu, *Japan*, 212–15.

20 Anne Walthall, "Peripheries: Rural Culture in Tokugawa Japan," *Monumenta Nipponica* 39, no. 4 (1984): 380 and 382; Nishiyama, *Edo*, 95–112.

21 Howell, *Geographies*, 57–8.

22 Yamaga Sokō, *Shidō* (date unknown), quoted in de Bary et al., *Sources*, vol. 2, pt. 1, 192–4.

23 Roger Ames, "Bushido: Mode or Ethic?" *Traditions* 10 (1980): 59–79. Canonical *bushidō* texts in translation include Yamamoto Tsunetomo, *Hagakure: The Book of the Samurai*, trans. William Scott Wilson (Boston: Shambhala, 2012); Thomas Cleary, *Code of the Samurai: A Modern Translation of the Bushidō Shoshinshū of Taira Shigesuke* (Rutland: Tuttle, 1999); Miyamoto Musashi, *The Book of the Five Rings*, trans. William Scott Wilson (Boston: Shambhala, 2012); and Thomas Cleary, *Training the Samurai Mind: A Bushido Sourcebook* (Boston: Shambhala, 2009).

24 Yamamoto, *Hagakure*, 3, 59, and 20.

25 See Lu, *Japan*, 175–82, 206–8; de Bary et al., *Sources*, vol. 1, 420–32; and de Bary et al., *Sources*, vol. 2, pt. 1, 12–14.

26 Ogura Eiichirō, *Ōmi shōnin no rinen—Ōmi shōnin kakin senshū* (Hikone: Sunrise Publishing, 2003), 36–40.

27 de Bary et al., *Sources*, vol. 2, pt. 1, 265–72.

28 Shirane, *Early*, 68; de Bary et al., *Sources*, vol. 2, pt. 1, 272–5.

29 Hibbett, *Floating*, 50, 61, and 114.

30 Shirane, *Early*, 68.

31 See Constantine Vaporis, *Breaking Barriers: Travel and the State in Early Modern Japan* (Cambridge: Harvard University Council on East Asian Studies, 1994); and Laura Nenzi, *Excursions in Identity: Travel and the Intersection of Place, Gender, and Status in Edo Japan* (Honolulu: University of Hawai'i Press, 2008).

32 Satoko Naito, "Beyond *The Tale of Genji*: Murasaki Shikibu as Icon and Exemplum in Seventeenth- and Eighteenth-Century Popular Texts for Women," *Early Modern Women* 9, no. 1 (Fall 2014): 47–78.

33 Nishiyama, *Edo*, 181.

34 Nishiyama, *Edo*, 187–9; Hibbett, *Floating*, 16–17.

35 Nishiyama, *Edo*, 204–8.

36 Naritaya Official Website, http://www.naritaya.jp/english/.

37 Shively, "Social," 8.

38 Shively, "Popular," 745–7. See also Dougill, *Kyoto*, 177–80.

39 Hibbett, *Floating*, 24; Nishiyama, *Edo*, 49–51; Walthall, "Peripheries," 386 and 391; Griswold, "Triumph," 237 and 243–4.

40 See Gregory Smits, *Seismic Japan: The Long History and Continuing Legacy of the Ansei Edo Earthquake* (Honolulu: University of Hawai'i Press, 2014).

CHAPTER FOUR

1 Quoted in Donald Keene, *Emperor of Japan: Meiji and His World, 1852–1912* (New York: Columbia University Press, 2002), 117.

2 In his *Kaika sakuron* (1867), Yoshikawa Tadayasu (1824–84) rephrased Sakuma's concept as "Japanese spirit, Western techniques" (*wakon yōsai*), which became better known. Chinese and Korean reformist intellectuals coined similar phrases: "Chinese learning for fundamental principles, Western learning for practical application" (*Zhōngxué wéi tǐ, xīxué wéi yòng*, abbreviated as *tǐ-yòng*); and "Eastern way, Western tools" (*tongdo sŏgi*), respectively.

3 See Mizusawa Shigeo, *Nakano Takeko to jōshitai* (Aizuwakamatsu: Rekishi Shunjū, 2002); and Stephen Turnbull, *Samurai Women 1184–1877* (Oxford: Osprey, 2010), 62.

4 James Huffman, *Creating a Public: People and Press in Meiji Japan* (Honolulu: University of Hawai'i Press, 1997), 2.

5 Herbert Spencer, "The Social Organism," *Westminster Review* 73 (January–April 1860): 51–67.

6 Hiraku Shimoda, "Tongues-Tied: The Making of a 'National Language' and the Discovery of Dialects in Meiji Japan," *American Historical Review* 115, no. 3 (June 2010): 724.

7 "Tokyo yose torishimari kisoku," February 10, 1877, at http://www.digital.archives.go.jp.

8 Nishiyama, *Edo*, 236, 240, and 250.

9 Andrew Markus, "The Carnival of Edo: *Misemono* Spectacles from Contemporary Accounts," *Harvard Journal of Asiatic Studies* 45 (1985): 499–500 and 519.

10 See Frederick Schodt, *Professor Ridley and the Imperial Japanese Troupe: How an American Acrobat Introduced Circus to Japan—and Japan to the West* (Berkeley: Stone Bridge Press, 2012).

11 Markus, "Carnival," 518, 528–30, and 535–40; Nishiyama, *Edo*, 228–30 and 242–7.

12 M. William Steele, "Edo in 1868: The View from Below," *Monumenta Nipponica* 45, no. 2 (Summer 1990): 133.

13 Fujitani, *Splendid*, 7–9, 139–41, and 172–80.

14 Robert Eskildsen "Of Civilization and Savages: The Mimetic Imperialism of Japan's 1874 Expedition to Taiwan," *American Historical Review* 107, no. 2 (April 2002): 416–17.

15 Fujitani, *Splendid*, Chapter 3.

16 Kim Kisu, *Ildong kiyuje*, vol. 2, *yunŭm, pujusik*, 1876 [HYC].

17 Ury Eppstein, "Musical Instruction in Meiji Education: A Study of Adaptation and Assimilation," *Monumenta Nipponica* 40, no. 1 (1985): 1–3; Christine Yano and Hosokawa Shūhei, "Popular Music in Modern Japan," in Tokita and Hughes, *Ashgate*, 345–6.

18 Quoted in Eppstein, "Musical," 9 and 10.

19 Eppstein, "Musical," 21–31.

20 Eppstein, "Musical," 32 and 37.

21 William Malm, "The Modern Music of Meiji Japan," in *Tradition and Modernization in Japanese Culture*," ed. Donald Shively (Princeton: Princeton University Press, 1971), 269 and 300; E. Taylor Atkins, *Blue Nippon: Authenticating Jazz in Japan* (Durham, NC: Duke University Press, 2001), 51–2; Carolyn Stevens, *Japanese Popular Music: Culture, Authenticity and Power* (London: Routledge, 2006), 13–14.

22 James Millward, "Chordophone Culture in Two Early Modern Societies: A *Pipa-Vihuela* Duet," *Journal of World History* 23, no. 2 (June 2012): 248–50.

23 Wade, *Composing*, 97–108.

24 A facsimile of the program for *Yoshiie*, the play Grant saw, is available at https://archive.org/details/dramaticentertai00slsnrich. Heinrich attended a June 7 performance, and Grant on July 16.

25 Faith Bach, "Breaking the *Kabuki* Actors' Barriers: 1868–1900," in *A Kabuki Reader: History and Performance*, ed. Samuel Leiter (Armonk: M. E. Sharpe, 2002), 153–4.

26 Yuichirō Takahashi, "*Kabuki* Goes Official: The 1878 Opening of the Shintomi-za," in Leiter, *Kabuki*, 126–9; cf. Levine, *Highbrow*.

27 Takahashi, "*Kabuki*," 140–2; A. Horie-Webber, "Modernisation of the Japanese Theatre: The Shingeki Movement," in *Modern Japan: Aspects of*

History, Literature and Society, ed. W. G. Beasley (Berkeley: University of California Press, 1977), 153–4.

28 *Tokyo nichinichi shinbun* July 11, 1888, quoted in Loren Edelson, "The Female Danjūrō: Revisiting the Acting Career of Ichikawa Kumehachi," *Journal of Japanese Studies* 34, no. 1 (Winter 2008): 79–80. See also Jean-Jacques Tschudin, "Danjūrō's *katsureki-geki* (realistic theatre) and the Meiji 'Theatre Reform' Movement," *Japan Forum* 11, no. 1 (1999): 83–94.

29 Ichikawa Kumehachi, "Geidan hyakuwa," *Engei gahō* (April 1907): 85, quoted in Edelson, "Female Danjūrō," 85.

30 Philippe Burty and Jules Claretie coined the term *Japonisme* in publications in 1872–73.

31 Vincent Van Gogh, letter to Theo Van Gogh, July 5, 1888 (#640), http://vangoghletters.org/vg/letters/let640/letter.html; see also Inspiration from Japan, Van Gogh Museum, http://www.vangoghmuseum.nl/en/stories/inspiration-from-japan.

32 Scholarship on *japonaiserie/japonisme* is voluminous; recent studies include: Pamela Genova, *Writing Japonisme: Aesthetic Translation in Nineteenth-Century French Prose* (Evanston: Northwestern University Press, 2016); Gabriel Weisberg and Anna-Maria von Bonsdorff, *Japanomania in the Nordic Countries, 1875–1918* (New Haven, CT: Yale University Press, 2016); Markéta Hánová et al., *Japonisme in Czech Art* (Prague: National Gallery in Prague, 2014); and Ricard Bru i Turull and Amalia Ran, *Erotic Japonisme: The Influence of Japanese Sexual Imagery on Western Art* (Leiden: Hotei Publishing, 2014).

33 See Susan Napier, *From Impressionism to Anime: Japan as Fantasy and Fan Cult in the Mind of the West* (New York: Palgrave Macmillan, 2007).

34 Quoted in Roger Bowen, *Rebellion and Democracy in Meiji Japan* (Berkeley: University of California Press, 1980), 206–8.

35 Irokawa Daikichi, *The Culture of the Meiji Period*, ed. Marius Jansen (Princeton: Princeton University Press, 1988), 44–50 and 208.

36 This is a somewhat misleading term of convenience to describe many different groups (feminists, liberal politicians, socialists, Christian reformers, disinherited samurai, tenant farmers, anarchists, temperance societies and educators) agitating for a variety of causes, with precious little common purpose between them. The main thing holding them together was the fact that they were most active at the same time, the 1870s and early 1880s.

37 Quote in Brett Walker, *Toxic Archipelago: A History of Industrial Disease in Japan* (Seattle: University of Washington Press, 2011), 99.

38 Portrait of the Week #13: Charles Wirgman, Japan Society of the UK, http://www.japansociety.org.uk/29845/portrait-of-the-week-13/. See Jozef Rogala, *The Genius of Mr. Punch—Life in Yokohama's Foreign Settlement—Charles Wirgman and the Japan Punch, 1862–1887* (Yokohama: Yūrindō, 2004).

39 Peter Duus, "Weapons of the Weak, Weapons of the Strong—the Development of the Japanese Political Cartoon," *Journal of Asian Studies* 60, no. 4 (2001): 981 and 989.

40 Duus, "Weapons," 976–7.

41 Duus, "Weapons," 978, and "The *Marumaru Chinbun* and the Origins of
    the Japanese Political Cartoon," *International Journal of Comic Art* 1, no. 1
    (1999): 42–56.

42 See Fukuzawa Yukichi, *The Autobiography of Fukuzawa Yukichi*, trans. Eiikchi
    Kiyooka (New York: Columbia University Press, 2007).

43 Fukuzawa Yukichi, *Bunmeiron no gairyaku* (1875), translated by David
    Dilworth and G. Cameron Hurst III as *An Outline of a Theory of Civilization*
    (New York: Columbia University Press, 2009), 17–24.

44 Duus, "Weapons," 984.

45 Gerald Groemer, "Singing the News: *Yomiuri* in Japan during the Edo and
    Meiji Periods," *Harvard Journal of Asiatic Studies* 54, no. 1 (1994): 245, 248,
    and 260.

46 Michael Lewis, *A Life Adrift: Soeda Azembō, Popular Song, and Modern Mass
    Culture in Japan* (London: Routledge, 2009), xxix–xxxi. This is a translation
    of Azenbō's autobiography *Azenbō ryūseiki* (Tokyo: Nagoya Shobō, 1941).

47 See the story of feminist Fukuda Hideko (1865–1927) in Mikiso Hane,
    ed., *Reflections on the Way to the Gallows: Rebel Women in Prewar Japan*
    (Berkeley: University of California Press, 1988), Chapter 2.

48 Lewis, *Life*, 15–16.

49 Lewis, *Life*, 22–6, 35, 36, 58, and 60.

50 Lewis, *Life*, 91–2.

51 M. Cody Poulton, *A Beggar's Art: Scripting Modernity in Japanese Drama,
    1900–1930* (Honolulu: University of Hawai'i Press, 2010), 20.

52 Lee Soon-jin, "The Genealogy of Shinpa Melodramas in Korean Cinema," 39,
    www.koreanfilm.or.kr; cf. Kang Yŏnghŭi, "Ilche kangchŏmgi sinp'a yangsik e
    Taehan hwa yŏn-gu," MA thesis, Seoul National University, 1989.

53 "Japanese Actors in Chicago," *NYT*, October 15, 1899: 7.

54 "The Japanese Players," *NYT*, April 1, 1900: 18.

55 "Madame Sada Yacco, Japan's Greatest Emotional Actress," *Harper's Bazaar*,
    March 24, 1900: 12 and 33.

56 Kamiyama Akira, "The Dynamics of Melodrama: *Shinpa*," trans. Hisako
    Omori, *SOAS Occasional Translations in Japanese Studies* 6 (2014): 7.

57 Andrew Gordon, *A Modern History of Japan from Tokugawa Times to the
    Present*, 3rd ed. (New York: Oxford University Press, 2014), 75.

CHAPTER FIVE

1 Henrik Ibsen, *A Doll's House and Other Plays*, trans. Peter Watts
    (London: Penguin, 1965), 228.

2 Her other roles included *Hamlet*'s Ophelia (1911), George Bernard Shaw's
    Strange Lady in *Man of Destiny* (1912), the titular roles in *Magda* (1912),
    Oscar Wilde's *Salomé* (1913), *Anna Karenina* (1916), and *Carmen* (1919),
    Katusha in Lev Tolstoi's *Resurrection* (1914), and Anisha in his *Power of*

Darkness (1916). Her song in *Resurrection* became Japan's first hit record, selling about as many discs as there were phonographs in that country.

3 Phyllis Birnbaum, *Modern Girls, Shining Stars, the Skies of Tokyo: 5 Japanese Women* (New York: Columbia University Press, 1999), 15 and 27; "Matsui Sumako," Kindai Nihonjin no shōzō, http://www.ndl.go.jp/portrait/datas/332.html.

4 See Barbara Satō, *The New Japanese Woman: Modernity, Media, and Women in Interwar Japan* (Durham, NC: Duke University Press, 2003), and Dina Lowy, *The Japanese "New Woman": Images of Gender and Modernity* (New Brunswick, NJ: Rutgers University Press, 2007).

5 Theodore F. Cook, "Making 'Soldiers': The Imperial Japanese Army and the Japanese Man in Meiji Society and State," in *Gendering Modern Japanese History*, ed. Barbara Molony and Kathleen Uno (Cambridge: Harvard University Press, 2008), 259–94; Satō, *New*, 64–65.

6 Alys Eve Weinbaum et al., eds., *The Modern Girl around the World: Consumption, Modernity, and Globalization* (Durham, NC: Duke University Press, 2008), 1–2.

7 Mitsuyo Wada-Marciano, *Nippon Modern: Japanese Cinema of the 1920s and 1930s* (Honolulu: University of Hawai'i Press, 2008), 77; Birnbaum, *Modern*, 181.

8 The English translation is titled *Naomi*, trans. Anthony Chambers (Rutland, VT: Tuttle, 1985).

9 Donna Guy, "Editor's Note," *Journal of Women's History* 16, no. 3 (Fall 2004): 6.

10 Miriam Silverberg, *Erotic Grotesque Nonsense: The Mass Culture of Japanese Modern Times* (Berkeley: University of California Press, 2006), 71; Wada-Marciano, *Nippon*, 13–14.

11 Kawabata Yasunari, *The Scarlet Gang of Asakusa*, trans. Alisa Freedman (Berkeley: University of California Press, 2005), 5–6 and 31. See also Silverberg, *Erotic*, 188–95.

12 Miriam Silverberg, "Constructing the Japanese Ethnography of Modernity," *Journal of Asian Studies* 51, no. 1 (February 1992): 30–54.

13 Ōbayashi Sōshi, *Minshū goraku no jissai kenkyū: Ōsaka-shi no minshū goraku chōsa* (Osaka: Ōhara Shakai Kenkyūjo, 1922), 75–7; Jeffrey Hanes, "Media Culture in Taishō Osaka," in *Japan's Competing Modernities: Issues in Culture and Democracy, 1900–1930*, ed. Sharon Minichiello (Honolulu: University of Hawai'i Press, 1998), 268 and 283–4.

14 Harry Harootunian, *Overcome by Modernity: History, Culture, and Community in Interwar Japan* (Princeton: Princeton University Press, 2000), 149–52 and 178–86.

15 Ōya Sōichi, "Modan sō to modan sō," *Chūō kōron*, February 1929, 181.

16 Tessa Morris-Suzuki, "The Invention and Reinvention of 'Japanese Culture,'" *Journal of Asian Studies* 54, no. 3 (August 1995): 763; see also Harootunian, *Overcome*, 15–16, 57–8.

17 Jordan Sand, *House and Home in Modern Japan: Architecture, Domestic Space, and Bourgeois Culture, 1880–1930* (Cambridge: Harvard University

Asia Center, 2006), 194–8, 203–4, 228, and 410n1; and Harootunian, *Overcome*, 58–9.

18 Roy Starrs, "Japanese Modernism Reconsidered," in *Rethinking Japanese Modernism*, ed. Roy Starrs (Leiden: Global Oriental 2012), 3; Miriam Bratu Hansen, "The Mass Production of the Senses: Classical Cinema as Vernacular Modernism," *Modernism/Modernity* 6, no. 2 (1999): 71. See Elise Tipton and John Clark, eds., *Being Modern in Japan: Culture and Society from the 1910s to the 1930s* (Honolulu: University of Hawai'i Press, 2000), 7; Wada-Marciano, *Nippon*, 7; and Harootunian, *Overcome*, xvi–xvii.

19 Silverberg, *Erotic*, 13–14 and 32–3.

20 Gennifer Weisenfeld, *MAVO: Japanese Artists and the Avant-Garde, 1905–1931* (Berkeley: University of California Press, 2001).

21 Soeda, *Life*, 231.

22 Quoted in Wm. Theodore de Bary et al., comps., *Sources of Japanese Tradition, 1600–2000*, 2nd ed., vol. 2, pt. 2: *1868–2000* (New York: Columbia University Press, 2006), 163.

23 Andrew Gordon, *Labor and Imperial Democracy in Prewar Japan* (Berkeley: University of California Press, 1991), 13, 14–15, and 25; Minichiello, *Japan's*, 3.

24 Gordon, *Modern*, 170.

25 Jan Bardsley, *The Bluestockings of Japan: New Women Essays and Fiction from Seitō, 1911–16* (Ann Arbor: University of Michigan Center for Japanese Studies, 2007).

26 See Heather Bowen-Struyk, "Proletarian Arts in East Asia," special issue of *positions: east asia cultures critique* (Fall 2006); introduction excerpted in *Asia-Pacific Journal* (hereafter *APJ*) 5.5.0 (April 2, 2007), http://apjjf.org/-Heather-Bowen-Struyk/2409/article.html.

27 There was a movement for female suffrage, leaders of which had an audience with Prime Minister Hamaguchi Osachi (1870–1931) in 1929, but gains in women's political participation were limited to a 1922 reform measure that lifted a decades-old ban on women's participation in political events.

28 Komatsu Hiroshi, "Some Characteristics of Japanese Cinema before World War I," in Noletti and Desser, *Reframing*, 231.

29 Anderson, "Spoken," 262–4; Donald Richie, *A Hundred Years of Japanese Film* (Tokyo: Kōdansha, 2001), 22 and 23.

30 Aaron Gerow, *Visions of Modernity: Articulations of Cinema, Nation, and Spectatorship, 1895–1925* (Berkeley: University of California Press, 2010), 44–9.

31 Kyoko Hirano, *Mr. Smith Goes to Tokyo: Japanese Cinema under the American Occupation, 1945–1952* (Washington, DC: Smithsonian Books, 1994), 42.

32 Komatsu, "Characteristics," 241, Gerow, *Visions*, 49.

33 Anderson, "Spoken," 284–9; Daisuke Miyao, "Before *Anime*: Animation and the Pure Film Movement in Pre-war Japan," *Japan Forum* 14, no. 2 (2002): 199.

34 The characters for *benzi* would normally be pronounced *piānsū* in Taiwanese and *biànshì* in Mandarin, so *benzi* is probably a corruption of the Japanese word. Thanks to Jui-ching Wang for her assistance on this matter.

35 Hiroshi Komatsu, "The Foundation of Modernism: Japanese Cinema in the Year 1927," *Film History* 17 (2005): 368.

36 Hideaki Fujiki, "*Benshi* as Stars: The Irony of the Popularity and Respectability of Voice Performers in Japanese Cinema, *Cinema Journal* 45, no. 2 (2006): 68–70, 73–4, and 78–9; Anderson, "Spoken," 292.

37 Joseph Anderson and Donald Richie, *The Japanese Film: Art and Industry* (expanded ed.) (Princeton: Princeton University Press, 1982), 29; Richie, *Hundred*, 20.

38 Fujiki, "*Benshi*," 77 and 79.

39 See Joanne Bernardi, *Writing in Light: The Silent Scenario and the Japanese Pure Film Movement* (Detroit: Wayne State University Press, 2001).

40 Gerow, *Visions*, 1–3, 10, and 11.

41 Quoted in Anderson and Richie, *Japanese*, 41.

42 Miyao, "Before *Anime*," 196; Fujiki, "*Benshi*," 69–70.

43 Miyao, "Before *Anime*," 198–201. Examples of some of these "folkloric" animated films are available in Zakka Films' *The Roots of Anime* DVD, http://www.zakkafilms.com/film/the-roots-of-japanese-anime—until-the-end-of-ww-ii/. A new website called Japanese Animated Film Classics has put several interwar and wartime films in the public domain online for free viewing. http://animation.filmarchives.jp/index.html.

44 Atkins, *Blue Nippon*, 68; Anderson and Richie, *Japanese*, 73.

45 Richie, *Hundred*, 44.

46 Wada-Marciano, *Nippon*, 1–2.

47 Atkins, *Blue Nippon*, 65–7. The public broadcasting network initially consisted of stations in Tokyo (JOAK), Ōsaka (JOBK), Nagoya (JOCK) and Keijō/Kyŏngsŏng/Seoul (JODK).

48 Christine Yano, "Defining the Modern Nation in Popular Song, 1914–1932," in Minichiello, *Japan's*, 248 and 251.

49 Soeda, *Life*, 174–5 and 192–5.

50 Tōru Mitsui, "Introduction: Embracing the West and Creating a Blend," in *Made in Japan: Studies in Popular Music*, ed. Tōru Mitsui (New York: Routledge, 2014), 7; Stevens, *Japanese*, 14.

51 Atkins, *Blue Nippon*, 70, 78, 81–2, and 98–9.

52 Atkins, *Blue Nippon*, 129 and 132–9; Yano and Hosokawa, "Popular Music," 347–8.

53 E. Taylor Atkins, "The Dual Career of 'Arirang': The Korean Resistance Anthem That Became a Japanese Pop Hit," *Journal of Asian Studies* 66, no. 3 (August 2007): 658.

54 Andrew Jones, *Yellow Music: Media Culture and Colonial Modernity in the Chinese Jazz Age* (Durham, NC: Duke University Press, 2001), 54.

55 See Hugh de Ferranti and Alison Tokita, eds., *Music, Modernity and Locality in Prewar Japan: Osaka and Beyond* (Farnham: Ashgate, 2013).

56 Kawabata, *Scarlet*, 32.

57 Alison Tokita, "Takarazuka and the Musical *Modan* in the Hanshin Region, 1914–1942," in Starrs, *Rethinking*, 410.

58 Tanizaki, *Naomi*, 123.

59 Silverberg, *Erotic* 76.

60 Atkins, *Blue Nippon*, 57–9, 64, 72, and 73.

61 Yano, "Defining," 260–1; Atkins, *Blue Nippon*, 96–113.

62 Cricket was played almost exclusively by expatriates until the 1980s. The first match (June 25, 1863, in Yokohama) occurred when the British Legation anticipated an attack by angry *sonnō jōi* terrorists, so that armed guards would be present. Michael Galbraith, "Death Threats Sparked Japan's First Cricket Game," *JT*, June 16, 2013, http://www.japantimes.co.jp/news/2013/06/16/national/history/death-threats-sparked-japans-first-cricket-game/#.WCDDJneZNSx. See also Justin McCurry, "After 150 Years, Japan Is Finally Falling in Love with Cricket," *The Guardian*, July 29, 2016, https://www.theguardian.com/world/2016/jul/29/after-150-years-japan-is-finally-falling-in-love-with-cricket. Enthusiasts founded the Japan Cricket Association in 1984.

63 Quoted in Ivan Hall, *Mori Arinori* (Cambridge: Harvard University Press, 1973), 361; Robin Kietlinski, *Japanese Women and Sport: Beyond Baseball and Sumo* (London: Bloomsbury, 2011), 20–1; Masako Gavin, "Abe Isoo and Baseball: New Social Relations Beyond the Family-State Institution," in Starrs, *Rethinking*, 455–6.

64 Elise Edwards, "Theorizing the Cultural Importance of Play: Anthropological Approaches to Sports and Recreation in Japan," in *A Companion to the Anthropology of Japan*, ed. Jennifer Robertson (Malden, MA: Blackwell, 2005), 281 and 283.

65 Kietlinski, *Japanese*, 131.

66 Included on *The Roots of Anime* DVD.

67 Quoted in Kietlinski, *Japanese*, 58–65; Dennis Frost, *Seeing Stars: Sports Celebrity, Identity, and Body Culture in Modern Japan* (Cambridge, MA: Harvard University Press, 2010), 130–48.

68 Gavin, "Abe," 460–4; Miho Koishihara, "Sports Culture," in *The Cambridge Companion to Modern Japanese Culture*, ed. Yoshio Sugimoto (Port Melbourne: Cambridge University Press, 2009), 327–9.

69 Sayuri Guthrie-Shimizu, *Transpacific Field of Dreams: How Baseball Linked the United States and Japan in Peace and War* (Chapel Hill: University of North Carolina Press, 2012).

70 See Robert Fitts, *Banzai Babe Ruth: Baseball, Espionage, and Assassination during the 1934 Tour of Japan* (Lincoln: University of Nebraska Press, 2012); and 1934 Japan Tour Footage, http://baseballhall.org/discover/1934-japan-tour-footage-uncovered.

71 John Horne and Derek Bleakley, "The Development of Football in Japan," in *Japan, Korea and the 2002 World Cup*, ed. John Horne and Wolfram Manzenreiter (London: Routledge, 2002), 90–2; Wolfram Manzenreiter, *Sport and Body Politics in Japan* (New York: Routledge, 2014), 196–7.

72 Harold Bolitho, "*Sumō* and Popular Culture: The Tokugawa Period," in *The Japanese Trajectory: Modernization and Beyond*, ed. Gavan McCormack and Yoshio Sugimoto (New York: Cambridge University Press, 1988), 22.

73 The Tokyo and Osaka associations merged in 1927 to complete the process. http://www.sumō.or.jp/kyokai/history.

74 Allen Guttmann and Lee Thompson, *Japanese Sports: A History* (Honolulu: University of Hawai'i Press, 2001), 108–5; Frost, *Seeing*, 67.

75 R. Kenji Tierney, "From Popular Performance to National Sport: The 'Nationalization' of *Sumo*," in *This Sporting Life: Sports and Body Culture in Modern Japan*, ed. William Kelly and Atsuo Sugimoto (New Haven, CT: Council on East Asian Studies, Yale University, 2007), 67.

76 Inoue Shun, "The Invention of the Martial Arts: Kanō Jigorō and Kōdōkan Judo," in *Mirror of Modernity: Invented Traditions of Modern Japan*, ed. Stephen Vlastos (Berkeley: University of California Press, 1998), 163–4 and 172.

77 William Kelly, "Introduction: Sports and Sport Studies in Japan," in Kelly and Sugimoto, *Sporting Life*, 9. On *bushidō* in baseball, see Robert Whiting, *The Chrysanthemum and the Bat: Baseball Samurai Style* (New York: Dodd Mead and Co., 1977), and *You Gotta Have Wa: When Two Cultures Collide on the Baseball Diamond* (New York: Macmillan, 1989).

78 Kiku Kōichi, "Bushidō and the Modernization of Sports in Japan," in Kelly and Sugimoto, *Sporting Life*, 43 and 45.

79 Frost, *Seeing*, 10–11, 106–8, and 172–4.

80 Edward Seidensticker, *Tokyo from Edo to Showa 1867–1989: The Emergence of the World's Greatest City* (Rutland, VT: Tuttle Classics, 2010), chapter 3.

81 See Minamoto Ryōen, "The Symposium on 'Overcoming Modernity,' " in *Rude Awakenings: Zen, the Kyoto School, & the Question of Nationalism*, ed. James Heisig and John Maraldo (Honolulu: University of Hawai'i Press, 1994), 197–229; Harootunian, *Overcome*, 29–30 and 34–93; and Richard Calichman, ed., *Overcoming Modernity: Cultural Identity in Wartime Japan* (New York: Columbia University Press, 2008).

CHAPTER SIX

1 Jürgen Osterhammel, *Colonialism: A Theoretical Overview* (Princeton: Markus Weiner, 2005), 16–17.

2 Jordan Sand, "Imperial Tokyo as a Contact Zone: The Metropolitan Tours of Taiwanese Aborigines, 1897–1941," *APJ* 12.10.4 (March 10, 2014), http://www.japanfocus.org/-Jordan-Sand/4089/article.html.

3 Robert Tierney, *Tropics of Savagery: The Culture of Japanese Empire in Comparative Frame* (Berkeley: University of California Press, 2010), 2 and 21.

4 Edward Said, *Orientalism* (New York: Vintage, 1978), 204 and 273.

5 V. I. Lenin, *Imperialism, the Highest Stage of Capitalism: A Popular Outline* (1916), accessed at Lenin Internet Archive, http://www.marxists.org/archive/lenin/works/1916/imp-hsc/index.htm.

6 Marius Jansen, "Japanese Imperialism: Late Meiji Perspectives," in *The Japanese Colonial Empire, 1895–1945*, ed. Ramon Myers and Mark Peattie (Princeton: Princeton University Press, 1984), 76.

7 Andre Schmid, "Colonialism and the 'Korea Problem' in the Historiography of Modern Japan: A Review Article," *Journal of Asian Studies* 59, no. 4 (2000): 951–76.

8 Louise Young, *Japan's Total Empire: Manchuria and the Culture of Wartime Imperialism* (Berkeley: University of California Press, 1997), 354.

9 See Michael Auslin, *Negotiating with Imperialism: The Unequal Treaties and the Culture of Japanese Diplomacy* (Cambridge, MA: Harvard University Press, 2006).

10 Michael Robinson, "Mass Media and Popular Culture in 1930s Korea: Cultural Control, Identity and Colonial Hegemony," in *Korean Studies: New Pacific Currents*, ed. Dae-Sook Suh (Honolulu: Center for Korean Studies, University of Hawai'i Press, 1994), 59.

11 *Moga* = T: *o-niau* (lit., "black cat"); K: *modŏngŏl*; Ch: *módēng xiǎojiě/nǚláng/ nǚzǐ. Mobo* = T: *o-káu* (lit., "black dog"); K: *modŏnboi*; Ch: *módēng nánzǐ*.

12 Park Chan Seung, "Colonial Modernity and the Making of Mokpo as a Dual City," *Korea Journal* 48, no. 3 (2008): 105. See Tani Barlow, "Introduction: On 'Colonial Modernity,'" in *Formations of Colonial Modernity in East Asia*, ed. Tani Barlow (Durham, NC: Duke University Press, 1997), 1–20, and "Debates over Colonial Modernity and Another Alternative," *Cultural Studies* 26, no. 5 (2012): 617–44; Gi-Wook Shin and Michael Robinson, eds., *Colonial Modernity in Korea* (Cambridge: Harvard University Press, 1999); Komagome Takeshi, "Colonial Modernity for an Elite Taiwanese, Lim Bo-Seng," in *Taiwan under Japanese Colonial Rule, 1895– 1945: History, Culture, Memory*, ed. Ping-hui Liao and David Der-Wei Wang (New York: Columbia University Press, 2010); Younghan Cho, "Colonial Modernity Matters? Debates on Colonial Past in South Korea," *Cultural Studies* 26, no. 5 (2012): 645–69; Yamauchi Fumitaka, "(Dis)Connecting the Empire: Colonial Modernity, Recording Culture, and Japan-Korea Musical Relations," *The World of Music* (new series) 1, no. 1 (2012): 143–206; and E. Taylor Atkins, "Colonial Modernity," *Routledge Handbook of Modern Korean History*, ed. Michael Seth (London: Routledge, 2016), 124–40.

13 Michael Baskett, *The Attractive Empire: Transnational Film Culture in Imperial Japan* (Honolulu: University of Hawai'i Press, 2008), 21–2; Kim Ryŏsil "*Ariran* to wa nani deatta ka? Kankoku kōnichi minzoku eiga no keisei," *Eizōgaku/Iconics* 72 (2004): 18, 20, and 21–2; Roald Maliangkay, "Classifying Performances: The Art of Korean Film Narrators," *Image & Narrative* 10 (2005), http://www.imageandnarrative.be.

14 Guo-Juin Hong, *Taiwan Cinema: A Contested Nation on Screen* (New York: Palgrave Macmillan, 2011), 22–3. See also Ru-Shou Robert Chen, "Taiwan Cinema," in *Encyclopedia of Chinese Film*, ed. Yingjin Zhang and Zhiwei Xiao (London: Routledge, 1998), 48–9; and Flannery Wilson, *New Taiwanese Cinema in Focus: Moving within and beyond the Frame* (Edinburgh: Edinburgh University Press, 2014), 16–17. *Tákáu* was a homophone for Takao, the Japanese name for the southern Taiwanese city Kaohsiung.

15 See Hui-Hsuan Chao, "Musical Taiwan under Japanese Colonial Rule: A Historical and Ethnomusicological Interpretation" (PhD diss., Department of Music, University of Michigan, 2009), 43–4,

16 Categories of popular music in colonial Korea were generally vernacular equivalents of those in Japan: *kayo* = *kayōkyoku*; *yuhaengga* = *ryūkōka*; *sin minyo* = *shin min'yō*; *ch'angga* = *shōka*; *jazu songu* = *chaejŭ song*.

17 Miyeon Hwang, "Chŏlla-pukdo kwŏnbŏn ŭi unyŏng-kwa kisaeng hwangdong ŭl tonghan sikminji kŭntaesung yŏnku" (PhD diss., Chonbuk National University, 2010), 162–3 [HYC].

18 "Hyŏng-hyŏng saek-saek ŭi kinyŏm sosik, ŭmak, yŏnju, radio," *Tong-a ilbo*, May 3, 1927 [HYC].

19 Michael Robinson, "Broadcasting, Cultural Hegemony, and Colonial Modernity in Korea, 1924–1945," in Shin and Robinson, *Colonial*, 65.

20 Ho Woisaeng, "Rekkodŭ ŭi yŏlgwang sidae," *Pyolgŏn'gon* 67, November 1, 1933: 30–1; "'Kŏri ŭi kkwe kkori' ın yŏl tae kasu rŭl naebonaen—chaggok chaksasa ŭi koshimgi," *Samchŏlli* November 1, 1935: 150–1 [HYC].

21 Eu-jeong Zhang, "What It Means to Be a 'Star' in Korea: The Birth and Return of Popular Singers," *Korea Focus*, September 2010, http://www.koreafocus. or.kr/design2/layout/content_print.asp?group_id=103227 [HYC].

22 "Chŏnju kwŏnbŏn honggun chungang esŏ yŏngjuhŏe," *Maeil sinbo*, May 17, 1936; and "Chŏnju sŏn hyangt'o yŏne taehŏe ch'ongram koak kamu taep'yŏ chent'ŭ," *Chosŏn ilbo* April 24, 1938 [HYC].

23 Robinson, "Broadcasting," 65–8; Yano, "Defining," 260–1; "Ŏhak kangjwa nŭn chŏngmal silkko Chosŏn ŭmak i choso," *Tong-a ilbo*, March 2, 1939 [HYC]; Min-Jung Son, "Young Musical Love of the 1930s," *The Korean Popular Culture Reader*, ed. Kyung Hyun Kim and Youngmin Choe (Durham, NC: Duke University Press, 2014), 255 and 271.

24 Chien-Yu Lin and Ping-Chao Lee, "Sport as a Medium of National Resistance: Politics and Baseball in Taiwan during Japanese Colonialism, 1895–1945," *International Journal of the History of Sport* 24, no. 3 (March 2007): 320, 325–6, 328, and 331. Documentary footage of the 1931 Taiwan team can be seen at https://www.youtube.com/watch?v=U0XbOf0fPA0.

25 The offending picture appears in *Tong-a ilbo*, August 13, 1936: 2. Son's victory and the medal ceremony were filmed and included in Leni Riefenstahl's documentary film *Olympia* ("Part 1: Festival of the Nations," 1:40:19-1:52:41). See also Jung Hwan Cheon, "Bend It Like a Man of Chosun: Sports Nationalism and Colonial Modernity of 1936," in Kim and Choe, *Korean*, 199–227.

26 Government-General of Chōsen, *Annual Report on Administration of Chosen*
    [*sic*] (Keijō: Government-General of Chōsen, 1936–37), 177. See also Gwang
    Ok, "The Political Significance of Sport: An Asian Case Study—Sport, Japanese
    Colonial Policy and Korean National Resistance, 1910–1945," *International
    Journal of the History of Sport* 22, no. 4 (2005): 649–70.

27 Orientalist Nude Photographs by Jean Geiser, http://mobile.wikilove.com/
    Tag:Orientalist_nude_photographs_by_Jean_Geiser; The Dutch East Indies
    in Photographs, 1860–1940, http://www.geheugenvannederland.nl/?/en/
    collecties/nederlands-indie_in_fotos,_1860-1940; Inge Oosterhoff, "Greetings
    from the Colonies: Postcards of a Shameful Past," http://www.messynessychic.
    com/2015/06/11/greetings-from-the-colonies-postcards-of-a-shameful-past/
    ; Without Sanctuary—Photographs and Postcards of Lynching in America,
    http://withoutsanctuary.org; Aboriginal Headhunters, http://www.taipics.com/
    abo_headhunters.php.

28 Nayoung Aimee Kwon, "Conflicting Nostalgia: Performing *The Tale of
    Ch'unhyang* in the Japanese Empire," *Journal of Asian Studies* 73, no. 1
    (February 2014): 113–41; E. Taylor Atkins, Primitive Selves: Koreana in
    the Japanese Colonial Gaze, 1910–1945 (Berkeley: University of California
    Press, 2010), 134–5; and Jennifer Robertson, *Takarazuka: Sexual Politics and
    Popular Culture in Modern Japan* (Berkeley: University of California Press,
    1998), 22, chapter 3.

29 Robertson, *Takarazuka*, 96.

30 Annika Culver, *Glorify the Empire: Japanese Avant-Garde Propaganda in
    Manchukuo* (Vancouver: University of British Columbia Press, 2013), 6.

31 See *The 1904 World's Fair: Looking Back at Looking Forward*, Missouri
    Historical Museum, http://www.mohistory.org/exhibits/Fair/WF/HTML/
    About/. See also Michael Hawkins, *Making Moros: Imperial Historicism and
    American Military Rule in the Philippines' Muslim South* (DeKalb: Northern
    Illinois University Press, 2012), 48–9; Pamela Newkirk, *Spectacle: The
    Astonishing Life of Ota Benga* (New York: Amistad, 2015); and Greg Allen,
    "'Living Exhibits' at 1904 World's Fair Revisited—Igorot Natives Recall
    Controversial Display of Their Ancestors," *Morning Edition*, NPR, May 31,
    2004, http://www.npr.org/templates/story/story.php?storyId=1909651.

32 Nathalie Curtin, "The Music of Many Lands: Songs and Their Singers as
    Represented in St. Louis Fair Exhibits," *NYT*, September 25, 1904: 30. See also
    Frederick Starr, *The Ainu Group at the Saint Louis Exposition* (Chicago: Open
    Court, 1904); James Vanstone, "The Ainu Group at the Louisiana Purchase
    Exposition, 1904," *Arctic Anthropology* 30, no. 2 (1993): 77–91; and James
    Rodgers, "Hidden Collections—Stories from the Archive," American Museum
    of Natural History, http://images.library.amnh.org/hiddencollections/tag/1904-
    st-louis-worlds-fair/.

33 Lisa Hiwasaki, "Ethnic Tourism in Hokkaido and the Shaping of Ainu
    Identity," *Pacific Affairs* 73, no. 3 (Autumn, 2000): 393–412; Kenneth Ruoff,
    *Imperial Japan at Its Zenith: The Wartime Celebration of the Empire's 2600th
    Anniversary* (Ithaca, NY: Cornell University Press, 2010), 7–8, 82, and 105.

34 Paul Barclay, "Peddling Postcards and Selling Empire: Image-Making in Taiwan under Japanese Colonial Rule," *Japanese Studies* 30, no. 1 (May 2010): 82. See also Sidney C. H. Cheung, "Men, Women and 'Japanese' as Outsiders: A Case Study of Postcards with Ainu Images, *Visual Anthropology* 13, no. 3 (2000): 227–55; and Digital Scholarship Services' East Asia Collection, http://digital.lafayette.edu/collections/eastasia.

35 Barclay, "Peddling," 86–7.

36 See Eskildsen, "Civilization," 396 and 402; Sand, "Imperial"; and Leo Ching, *Becoming "Japanese": Colonial Taiwan and the Politics of Identity Formation* (Berkeley: University of California Press, 2001), 137–48.

37 Atkins, *Primitive Selves*, 182–4.

38 Prasenjit Duara, *Sovereignty and Authenticity: Manchukuo and the East Asian Modern* (Lanham: Rowman & Littlefield, 2004), 16–20 and 78.

39 Young, *Total*, 68–78.

40 Young, *Total*, 350–1; Culver *Glorify*, 5.

41 Kari Shepherdson-Scott, "Conflicting Politics and Contesting Borders: Exhibiting (Japanese) Manchuria at the Chicago World's Fair, 1933–34," *Journal of Asian Studies* 74, no. 3 (August 2015): 539–64.

42 Although northern China was indeed infested with predatory mounted robber bands, Japanese used the term "bandits" to designate local militias and resistance fighters—anyone who resisted them.

43 "Buyō ni seishin suru Chōsen umare no bishōjo," *Yomiuri shinbun* August 13, 1928: 3; Ch'oe Sŭng-hŭi [Sai Shōki], "Watakushi no jijoden: doryoku to namida no itsuwaranu kako," *Fujin kōron* June 1935.

44 Sang Mi Park, "The Making of a Cultural Icon for the Japanese Empire: Choe Seung-hui's US Dance Tours and 'New Asian Culture' in the 1930s and 1940s," *positions: east asia cultures critique* 14, no. 3 (2006): 606 and 610.

45 Baskett, *Attractive*, 77–8.

46 Peter High, *The Imperial Screen: Japanese Film Culture in the Fifteen Years' War* (Madison: University of Wisconsin Press, 2003), 572; Baskett, *Attractive*, 81–2.

47 Edgar Pope, "Songs of the Empire: Continental Asia in Japanese Wartime Popular Music" (PhD diss., University of Washington, 2003), 3 and 321–2.

48 Atkins, *Blue Nippon*, 134–9. Sugii's recordings are obtainable now in a four-volume series: *Japanese Jazz and Salon Music, 1936–1941*, https://itunes.apple.com/us/album/japanese-jazz-salon-music/id415125229.

49 Robertson, *Takarazuka*, 96.

50 Young, *Total*, 373.

51 Kimberly Kono, "Imperializing Motherhood: The Education of a 'Manchu Girl' in Colonial Manchuria," in *Reading Colonial Japan: Text, Context, Critique*, ed. Michele Mason and Helen Lee (Stanford: Stanford University Press, 2012), 238.

52 *The Manual of Home Cuisine* (*Katei shokuji tokuhon*, 1941), trans. Helen Lee, in Mason and Lee, *Reading*, 143.

53 Tierney, *Tropics*, 114–33.

54 Shimada quoted in Faye Yuan Kleeman, *Under an Imperial Sun: Japanese Colonial Literature of Taiwan and the South* (Honolulu: University of Hawai'i Press, 2003), 17–18; Tierney, *Tropics*, 145–6. See also Naito Sudo, *Nanyo-Orientalism: Japanese Representations of the Pacific* (Amherst, NY: Cambria Press, 2010). Dankichi was based on Mori Koben (1869–1945), a pioneering businessman in what became Japan's South Seas Mandate. The comics are collected in Shimada Keizō, *Bōken Dankichi*, vols. 1–4 (Tokyo: Kōdansha, 1976).

55 Hyungjun Han, "Adventure Stories and Geographical Imagination in Japanese and Korean Children's Magazines, 1925–1945," *Japan Forum* 28, no. 1 (2016): 102–5.

56 Kim Brandt, *Kingdom of Beauty: Mingei and the Politics of Folk Art in Imperial Japan* (Durham, NC: Duke University Press, 2007), 34–5 and 222; Tierney, *Tropics*, 10, 57, 61, 88, 115, and 180–1; Atkins, *Primitive Selves*, 78–93.

57 Atkins, *Primitive Selves*, 165–7.

CHAPTER SEVEN

1 Nitobe Inazō, *Bushido: The Soul of Japan* (1899; Tokyo: Kōdansha USA, 2012).

2 Oleg Benesch, *Inventing the Way of the Samurai: Nationalism, Internationalism, and Bushido in Modern Japan* (Oxford: Oxford University Press, 2014), 8, chapters 3 and 4. See also Karl Friday, "Bushidō or Bull? A Medieval Historian's Perspective on the Imperial Army and the Japanese Warrior Tradition," *History Teacher* 27, no. 3 (May 1994): 339–49; and Stewart Lone, "Between Bushido and Black Humour," *History Today* 55, no. 9 (September 2005): 20–7.

3 "War News," *Japan Weekly Mail* November 3, 1894: 509.

4 Charles Cabry Dix, *The World's Navies in the Boxer Rebellion (China 1900)* (London: Digby, Long & Co., 1905), 295–6 and 298; italics in original.

5 "Russian and Japanese Troops," *NYT* January 13, 1904: 8; "When the War Is Over," *NYT* June 12, 1904: 8.

6 Stewart Lone, *Japan's First Modern War: Army and Society in the Conflict with China, 1894–95* (Houndsmills: Macmillan, 1994).

7 Yŏng-ho Ch'oe, "The Kapsin Coup of 1884: A Reassessment," *Korean Studies* 6 (1982): 105–24.

8 S. C. M. Paine, *The Sino-Japanese War of 1894–1895: Perceptions, Power, and Primacy* (Cambridge: Cambridge University Press, 2002), 4, 9, and 295–332.

9 "Protests against Japan: Russia, France, and Germany Object to Cession of Territory," *NYT* April 25, 1895: 5; "Japan Yields to Russia," *NYT* May 7, 1895: 1. See also Lone, *Japan's*, 175–7, and Paine, *Sino-Japanese*, 288–90.

10 Lone, *Japan's First*, 54–6 and 98.

11 See Donald Keene, "The Sino-Japanese War and Japanese Culture,"
    in *Landscapes and Portraits: Appreciations of Japanese Culture*
    (Tokyo: Kōdansha International, 1971), 268–70; and Kiyochika's War section
    in John Dower, "Throwing Off Asia III—Woodblock Prints of the Sino-
    Japanese War," MIT Visualizing Cultures, http://ocw.mit.edu/ans7870/21f/
    21f.027/throwing_off_asia_02/toa_essay02.html.

12 See Jung-Sun Han, "Empire of Comic Visions: Japanese Cartoon Journalism
    and Its Pictorial Statements on Korea, 1876–1910," *Japanese Studies* 26, no. 3
    (December 2006): 283–302.

13 Keene, "Sino-Japanese," 274.

14 Soeda, *Life*, 47–52. Soeda's wartime song "Chakurai bushi," performed
    by Tsuchitori Toshiyuki, can be heard at https://www.youtube.com/
    watch?v=jJV3Ehy4VpI.

15 Keene, "Sino-Japanese," 272–3 and 282–5.

16 Kamei's photographs are collected in the book *Nisshin sensō jūgun shashinjō*
    (Tokyo: Kashiwa Shobō, 1992). He was also the subject of a History Channel
    (Japan) documentary (https://www.historychannel.co.jp/detail.php?p_
    id=00195).

17 The occurrence and scale of the event was disputed in the Western press,
    which generally praised imperial forces for their conduct toward civilians. See
    Frederic Villiers, "The Truth about Port Arthur," *North American Review* 160,
    no. 460 (March 1895): 325–30; and Daniel Kane, "Each of Us in His Own
    Way: Factors Behind Conflicting Accounts of the Massacre at Port Arthur,"
    Journalism History 31, no. 1 (2005): 23–33.

18 Lone, *Japan's*, 100.

19 M. K. Gandhi, *Indian Opinion* March 25, 1905: 185–6, http://gandhimuseum.
    org/MGM/INDIAN%20OPINION.htm. See Mustafa Kamil Pasha, *al-Shams
    al-mushriqa* (*The Rising Sun*; Cairo: Matba'a al-Liwa,' 1904); Michael
    Laffan, "Mustafa and the *Mikado*: A Francophile Egyptian's Turn to Meiji
    Japan," *Japanese Studies* 19, no. 3 (December 1999): 269–86; Steven Marks,
    "'Bravo Brave Tiger of the East!' The Russo-Japanese War and the Rise of
    Nationalism in British Egypt and India," in *The Russo Japanese War in Global
    Perspective: World War Zero*, ed. John W. Steinberg et al. (Leiden: Brill, 2005),
    609–27; Paul Rodell, "Inspiration for Nationalist Aspirations? Southeast
    Asia and the 1905 Japanese Victory," in Steinberg, *Russo-Japanese*, 627–54;
    Gerhard Krebs, "World War Zero? Re-assessing the Global Impact of the
    Russo-Japanese War 1904–05," *APJ* 10.21.2 (May 2012), http://apjjf.org/2012/
    10/21/Gerhard-Krebs/3755/article.html; and Orhan Kologlu, "Turkish and
    Islamic Perspective of Japanese Modernisation: The Role of Japanese Victory
    over Russia (1904–05) Instigating Mid-Easters to Explore the Far-East,"
    Turkish Review Of Middle East Studies 11 (January 2000): 9–42.

20 John Steinberg, "Was the Russo-Japanese War World War Zero?" *Russian
    Review* 67 (January 2008): 1–7.

21 Naoko Shimazu, "Patriotic and Despondent: Japanese Society at War, 1904–
    5," *Russian Review* 67 (January 2008): 48. See Shumpei Okamoto, "The

Emperor and the Crowd: The Historical Significance of the Hibiya Riot," in *Conflict in Modern Japanese History: The Neglected Tradition*, ed. Tetsuo Najita and J. Victor Koschmann (Princeton: Princeton University Press, 1982), 258–75.

22 Kobayashi Kiyochika and Koppi Dōjin, *Ghosts from the Crushing Defeat* (*Mecha make no bōrei*), print #83, from *Long Live Japan: A Hundred Victories, a Hundred Laughs* (*Nihon banzai—hyakusen, hyakushō*), 3rd series, 1904, https://cdn.loc.gov/service/pnp/jpd/00900/00929v.jpg. See also the Lavenberg Collection of Japanese Prints, http://www.myjapanesehanga.com/home/artists/kiyochika-kobayashi-1847-1915-/long-live-japan-one-hundred-victories-one-hundred-laughs-. The character compound for *banzai* (literally 10,000 lives, but used as a cheer meaning "Long live the emperor!") seems intended as a pun. It can also be read *manzai*, which means "comic dialogue." So the title could just as easily be translated as "Comic Japan."

23 See *nishiki-e* at "Throwing Off Asia III—Woodblock Prints of the Russo-Japanese War (1904–05)," MIT Visualizing Cultures, http://ocw.mit.edu/ans7870/21f/21f.027/throwing_off_asia_03/toa_vis_04.html.

24 Shimazu, "Patriotic," 38.

25 Daibō Masaki, "Nichiro sensō kiroku eigagun no katarogingu—Josefu Rōsentāru satsuei *Ryojun no kōfuku* no fukusū bājon," http://www.momat.go.jp/ge/wp-content/uploads/sites/2/2015/01/19_pp.42–65.pdf; James Chapman, *A New History of British Documentary* (Houndmills: Palgrave Macmillan, 2015), 21; Richie, *Hundred*, 20.

26 *Kōbe shinbun*, December 9, 1904, cited in High, *Imperial*, 5; italics in original.

27 Stewart Lone, "Remapping Japanese Militarism: Provincial Society at War 1904–1905," *Japanese Studies* 25, no. 1 (May 2005): 60; High, *Imperial*, 5–6. One film (from the Huntley Film Archives) mixing real and faux footage is viewable at https://www.youtube.com/watch?v=lD1kyodeu9Q.

28 See Iida Sueharu, *Nichiro sensō taishō gunka—kaisen no maki* (Tokyo: Kinkōdō, 1904), http://school.nijl.ac.jp/kindai/CKMR/CKMR-00209.html#22, and Chintō Sanjin and Hashimoto Hideyoshi, *Nichiro sensō gunka* (Tokyo: Shunkōdō, 1904).

29 Several versions of the song are available on the Internet. This translation (slightly amended) is from https://www.youtube.com/watch?v=9gazaHoS5Ig.

30 Junko Oba, "To Fight the Losing War, to Remember the Lost War: The Changing Role of *Gunka*, Japanese War Songs," in *Global Goes Local: Popular Culture in Asia*, ed. Timothy Craig and Richard King (Vancouver: University of British Columbia Press, 2002), 225–45.

31 Naoko Shimazu, "The Myth of the 'Patriotic Soldier': Japanese Attitudes Towards Death in the Russo-Japanese War," *War & Society* 19, no. 2 (October 2001): 81 and 84–5.

32 Soeda, *Life*, 110.

33 David Wells and Sandra Wilson, eds., *The Russo-Japanese War in Cultural Perspective* (Houndmills: Palgrave Macmillan, 1999), 2; and "A View from the

East? Slavic Studies in Japan," Association for Slavic, East European, and Eurasian Studies, March 26, 2014, http://www.aseees.org/news-events/aseees-blog-feed/view-east-slavic-studies-japan. Russians reciprocated with interest in Japan: see Rosamund Bartlett, "Japonisme and Japanophobia: The Russo-Japanese War in Russian Cultural Consciousness," *Russian Review* 67 (January 2008): 8–33.

34   Shimazu, "Patriotic," 35 and 41–4; Lone, "Remapping," 63.

35   Yosano Akiko, "Kimi shi ni tamau koto nakare," *Myōjō*, September 1904: 51–2. Translation by Janine Beichman, in *The Columbia Anthology of Modern Japanese Literature*, ed. J. Thomas Rimer and Van Gessel, vol. 1, *From Restoration to Occupation, 1868–1945* (New York: Columbia University Press, 2005), 302–3.

36   Shimazu, "Patriotic," 29.

37   Sandra Wilson, "The Past in the Present: War in Narratives of Modernity in the 1920s and 1930s," in Tipton and Clark, *Being*, 179–80 and 182.

38   Young, *Japan's*, 96–7; Akira Iriye, *Pearl Harbor and the Coming of the Pacific War: A Brief History with Documents and Essays* (Boston: Bedford/St. Martin's, 1999), 57 and 90–1.

39   Article 11 simply reads, "The Emperor has the supreme command of the Army and Navy" (*Tennō wa rikukaigun o tōsui su*). Dai Nippon teikoku kenpō, 6, http://www.digital.archives.go.jp/.

40   Alan Tansman, *The Aesthetics of Japanese Fascism* (Berkeley: University of California Press, 2009), 1–3.

41   Robert Paxton, *The Anatomy of Fascism* (New York: Vintage, 2005), 219–20.

42   Tansman, *Aesthetics*, 1–3, and Alan Tansman, ed., *The Culture of Japanese Fascism* (Durham, NC: Duke University Press, 2009), 1–18.

43   Reto Hofmann, *The Fascist Effect: Japan and Italy, 1915–1952* (Ithaca, NY: Cornell University Press, 2015), 2, 6–7, and 88. Culver contends that "Manchukuo was more thoroughly fascistic than Japan itself" (*Glorify*, 140).

44   Yoshimi Yoshiaki, *Grassroots Fascism: The War Experience of the Japanese People*, trans. Ethan Mark (New York: Columbia University Press, 2015).

45   Ruoff, *Imperial*, 24–5.

46   Gregory Kasza, *The State and the Mass Media in Japan, 1918–1945* (Berkeley: University of California Press, 1988), 57–8. Makino Mamoru, *Nihon eiga ken'etsu shi* (Tokyo: Gendai Shokan, 2003) provides a thorough account of the history of film censorship, including original documents.

47   Atkins, *Blue Nippon*, 143 and 157.

48   Richie, *Hundred*, 96–7, Kasza, *State*, 242–8.

49   Thomas Havens, *Valley of Darkness: The Japanese People and World War Two* (Lanham, MD: University Press of America, 1986), 148.

50   Atkins, *Blue Nippon*, 127.

51   William Hauser, "Women and War: The Japanese Film Image," in *Recreating Japanese Women, 1600–1945*, ed. Gail Bernstein (Berkeley: University of California Press, 1991), 300.

52 John Dower, *Japan in War & Peace: Selected Essays* (New York: New Press, 1993), 35–6.

53 Benito Mussolini, "The Social and Political Doctrine of Fascism" (*Enciclopedia Italiana*, 1932), The History Guide: Lectures on Twentieth Century Europe, http://historyguide.org/europe/duce.html.

54 Darrell William Davis, *Picturing Japaneseness: Monumental Style, National Identity, Japanese Film* (New York: Columbia University Press, 1996), 45 and 49.

55 Akira Kurosawa, *Something Like an Autobiography*, trans. Audie Bock (New York: Knopf, 1982), 146.

56 "Sora no shinpei" (Umeki Saburō, lyrics; Takagi Tōroku, music), from *Senji kayō*, CD (King KICX 8428, 1997).

57 Barak Kushner, *The Thought War: Japanese Imperial Propaganda* (Honolulu: University of Hawai'i Press, 2006), 90, 95, and 98.

58 Hsieh Hsiao-mei, "Music from a Dying Nation: Taiwanese Opera in China and Taiwan during World War II," *Asian Theatre Journal* 27, no. 2 (Fall 2010): 279–81.

59 Teramoto Kiichi, Counselor of the Chōsen National Mobilization League, griped that Koreans had made much better progress in Japanizing their clothing and residences than their speech. "Bunka no naisen ittai (ifuku, jūtaku, kokugo)," *Chōsen* 344 (January 1944): 65–8.

60 Chan E. Park, *Voices from the Straw Mat: Toward an Ethnography of Korean Story Singing* (Honolulu: University of Hawai'i Press, 2003), 103; Andrew Killick, *In Search of Traditional Korean Opera: Discourses of Ch'anggŭk* (Honolulu: University of Hawai'i Press, 2010), 97–101. See also Yi T'aehwa, *Ilje kangjŏmgi ŭi p'ansori munhwa yŏngu* (Seoul: Pagijŏng, 2013).

61 Nihon Kyōiku Kamishibai Kyōkai, *Bōkū shidō gageki 1: shōidan* (Tokyo: Dai Nihon Gageki Kabushiki Kaisha, 1941); Dai Nihon Bōkū Kyōkai, *Bōkūgo* (Dai Nihon Gageki Kabushiki Kaisha, n.d.); Kitajima Eisaku and Koyano Hanji, *Amakudaru shinpei* (Tokyo: Nihon Kyōiku Gageki Kabushiki Kaisha, 1944); Yanai Takao, Takei Shōhei, and Koyano Hanji, *Aiki minami e tobu* (Tokyo: Nihon Kyōiku Gageki Kabushiki Kaisha, 1944); and Nihon Kyōiku Kamishibai Kyōkai, *Biruma shōnen to sensha* (Tokyo: Dai Nihon Gageki Kabushiki Kaisha, 1944).

62 Jeffrey Dym, *Die for Japan: Wartime Propaganda Kamishibai (paper plays; kokusaku kamishibai)*, https://www.youtube.com/watch?v=lFavUjEYc7Y. See Shimizu Isao, *Taiheiyō sensōki no manga* (Tokyo: Bijutsu Dōjinsha, 1971); John Dower, *War without Mercy: Race and Power in the Pacific War* (New York: Pantheon, 1986); Richard Minnear, *Dr. Seuss Goes to War: The World War II Editorial Cartoons of Theodor Seuss Geisel* (New York: New Press, 2001); and Kinko Itō, "Manga in Japanese History," in *Japanese Visual Culture: Explorations in the World of Manga and Anime*, ed. Mark MacWilliams (Armonk: M. E. Sharpe, 2008), 33–5.

63 Jonathan Clements, *Anime: A History* (London: Palgrave Macmillan, 2013), 74. *Sea Eagles* appears on the *Roots of Anime* DVD; *Divine Sea Warriors* is viewable (sans subtitles) at https://www.youtube.com/watch?v=9Ne-0e6P4jo.

64 Enemy Leaflet Collection, Australian War Memorial, https://www.awm.gov.au/findingaids/guide-enemy-leaflet-collection/#S1; Propaganda Leaflets Aimed at Undermining Morale, Australians at War, http://www.australiansatwar.gov.au/stories/stories_war=W2_id=135.html; Japanese PSYOP During WWII, http://www.psywarrior.com/JapanPSYOPWW2b.html;

65 Atkins, *Blue Nippon*, 157–8.

CHAPTER EIGHT

1 William Tsutsui, *Godzilla on My Mind: Fifty Years of the King of the Monsters* (New York: Palgrave Macmillan, 2004), 16–18.

2 *The Economist*, September 1–8, 1962. See Ezra Vogel, *Japan as Number One: Lessons for America* (New York: Harper & Row, 1979); Chalmers Johnson, *MITI and the Japanese Miracle: The Growth of Industrial Policy, 1925–1975* (Stanford: Stanford University Press, 1982); and Takahiro Fukada, "Looking Back at 'Japan as No. 1': A Rising Star No Longer, Nation Has Suffered Numerous Setbacks Since 1979,'" *JT*, November 11, 2010, http://www.japantimes.co.jp/news/2010/11/11/national/looking-back-at-japan-as-no-1/#.V5zLv1c8KrU.

3 Marilyn Ivy, *Discourses of the Vanishing: Modernity, Phantasm, Japan* (Chicago: University of Chicago Press, 1995).

4 Asahi Shinbun Company, *Media, Propaganda and Politics in 20th-Century Japan*, trans. Barak Kushner (New York: Bloomsbury, 2015), 187–93.

5 Susan Napier, "Panic Sites: The Japanese Imagination of Disaster from *Godzilla* to *Akira*," *Journal of Japanese Studies* 19, no. 2 (Summer 1993): 331–2.

6 "Imperial Rescript on Surrender," in de Bary et al., *Sources*, vol. 2, pt. 2, 317–19.

7 Ivy, "Formations," 253–4.

8 John Dower, *Embracing Defeat: Japan in the Wake of World War II* (New York, W.W. Norton, 1999), 70.

9 Donald Keene, *Dawn to the West: A History of Japanese Literature*, vol. 3 (New York: Henry Holt, 1984), 967; Dower, *Embracing*, 410. See page 411 for a list of taboo subjects under SCAP censorship.

10 Hirano, *Mr. Smith*, 148, 152–3. See also Richie, *Hundred*, 107–15.

11 Hirano, *Mr. Smith*, 154–70; Mark McLelland, "'Kissing Is a Symbol of Democracy!' Dating, Democracy, and Romance in Occupied Japan, 1945–1952," *Journal of the History of Sexuality* 19, no. 3 (September 2010), 516–24.

12 Dower, *Embracing*, 148–54. *Kasutori* referred to the lees or dregs of rice, sweet potato or other distilled alcoholic drinks.

13 Herbert Passin, "The Occupation—Some Reflections," in *Showa: The Japan of Hirohito*, ed. Carol Gluck and Stephen Graubard (New York: Norton, 1992), 119.

14 Michael Bourdaghs, *Sayonara Amerika, Sayonara Nippon: A Geopolitical Prehistory of J-Pop* (New York: Columbia University Press, 2012), 15.

15 Atkins, *Blue Nippon*, 171–2 and 175–9; Stevens, *Japanese*, 62–3.

16 Sayuri-Guthrie, *Transpacific*, chapter 7; Seidensticker, *Tokyo*, 468–9.

17 James Brandon, "Myth and Reality: The Story of *Kabuki* during American Censorship, 1945–1949," *Asian Theatre Journal* 23, no. 1 (Spring 2006): 2–3, 5, 79, and 83.

18 Sodei Rinjirō, *Dear General MacArthur: Letters from the Japanese during the American Occupation*, trans. Shizue Matsuda (Lanham: Rowman & Littlefield, 2006).

19 See Mari Yamamoto, *Grassroots Pacifism in Post-War Japan: The Rebirth of a Nation* (Abington: RoutledgeCurzon, 2005).

20 Edward Abbey, *The Journey Home* (1977; New York: Plume, 1991), 183.

21 See Laura Hein, "Growth versus Success: Japan's Economic Policy in Historical Perspective," in Gordon, *Postwar*, Chapter 7.

22 See W. Eugene Smith and Aileen Mioko Smith, *Minamata: Life—Sacred and Profane* (Tokyo: Sōjusha, 1973); Timothy George, *Minamata: Pollution and the Struggle for Democracy in Postwar Japan* (Cambridge: Harvard Asia Center, 2001); Esther Inglis-Arkell, "The Effects of Japan's 1955 Poison-Milk Coverup Persist to This Day," February 10, 2015, http://io9.gizmodo.com/the-effects-of-japans-1955-poison-milk-coverup-persist-1684903422; Joe Moore, *The Other Japan: Conflict, Compromise, and Resistance since 1945*, new ed. (Armonk: M. E. Sharpe, 1997); and W. Sasaki Uemura, *Organizing the Spontaneous: Citizen Protest in Postwar Japan* (Honolulu: University of Hawai'i Press, 2014).

23 See Mick Broderick, ed., *Hibakusha Cinema: Hiroshima, Nagasaki and the Nuclear Image in Japanese Film* (1996; London: Routledge, 2009); Jerome Shapiro, "Atomic Bomb Cinema: Illness, Suffering, and the Apocalyptic Narrative," *Literature and Medicine* 17, no. 1 (1998): 126–48; Matthew Edwards, *The Atomic Bomb in Japanese Cinema: Critical Essays* (Jefferson, NC: McFarland, 2015); Hibakusha Stories, http://www.hibakushastories.org.

24 The Sadako Story, Hiroshima International School, http://www.hiroshima-is.ac.jp/index.php?page=sadako-story.

25 Nakazawa Keiji, *Barefoot Gen*, vols. 1–10 (San Francisco: Last Gasp, 2004–10), originally serialized in *Shōnen Jump*, 1973–85.

26 Tsutsui, *Godzilla*, 33.

27 Sayuri Guthrie-Shimizu, "Lost in Translation and Morphed in Transit: Godzilla in Cold War America," in *In Godzilla's Footsteps*, ed. William Tsutsui and Michiko Itō (Gordonsville: Palgrave Macmillan, 2006), 59.

28 Guthrie-Shimizu, "Lost," 55; Bosley Crowther, "Monsters Again: Old Creatures in New But Familiar Films," *NYT*, May 6, 1956: 129.

29 Quoted in John Whittier Treat, *Writing Ground Zero: Japanese Literature and the Atomic Bomb* (Chicago: University of Chicago Press, 1995), 2 and 20.

30 Masuji Ibuse, *Black Rain*, trans. John Bester (Tokyo: Kōdansha, 2012). Imamura Shōhei's 1989 film adaptation is equally powerful.

31 Andrew Horvat, "Kurosawa Akira's Contested Legacy—Contrasts in Japanese and American Perceptions of *Rashomon*," *IHJ Bulletin* 28, no. 1 (2008), 23, 27, and 29.

32 See David Bordwell, *Ozu and the Poetics of Cinema* (Princeton: Princeton University Press, 1988).

33 Mark Schilling, *The Yakuza Movie Book: A Guide to Japanese Gangster Films* (Berkeley: Stone Bridge Press, 2003), 23–5.

34 Mark Schilling, *The Encyclopedia of Japanese Pop Culture* (New York: Weatherhill, 1997), 271.

35 Christine Yano, *Tears of Longing: Nostalgia and the Nation in Japanese Popular Song* (Cambridge: Harvard University Asia Center, 2002), 3, 44, 178, and 183.

36 Yano, *Tears*, 4, 8, 17–19, 60, 89, and 178.

37 Yano, *Tears*, 184.

38 Alan Tansman, "Mournful Tears and Sake: The Postwar Myth of Misora Hibari," in *Contemporary Japan and Popular Culture*, ed. John Whittier Treat (Honolulu: University of Hawai'i Press, 1996), 105. See also Bourdaghs, *Sayonara*, Chapter 2.

39 "Hibari Misora, Japanese Singer, 52," *NYT*, June 25, 1989, http://www. nytimes.com/1989/06/25/obituaries/hibari-misora-japanese-singer-52.html; Misora Hibari Official Website, http://www.misorahibari.com; Shōwa jidai o daihyō suru dai sutā! Misora Hibari, http://www.misorahibariza.jp.

40 Deborah Shamoon, "Misora Hibari and the Girl Star in Postwar Japanese Cinema," *Signs* 35, no. 1 (Autumn 2009): 133 and 153; Bourdaghs, *Sayonara*, 69.

41 Jayson Makoto Chun, *"A Nation of a Hundred Million Idiots"? A Social History of Japanese Television, 1953–1973* (New York: Routledge, 2007), 4–6 and 9.

42 Kietlinski, *Japanese*, 87–94. See William Tsutsui and Michael Baskett, ed., *The East Asian Olympiads 1934–2008: Building Bodies and Nations in Japan, Korea, and China* (Leiden: Global Oriental, 2011).

43 *Tokyo Olympiad* is available at the Olympics YouTube channel, https://www. youtube.com/watch?v=WHt0eAdCCns.

44 Iwona Merklejn, "The Taming of the Witch: Daimatsu Hirobumi and Coaching Discourses of Women's Volleyball in Japan," *Asia Pacific Journal of Sport and Social Science* 3, no. 2 (2014): 115–29; Guttmann and Thompson, *Japanese*, 198–9; Robert Whiting, "'Witches of the Orient' Symbolized Japan's Fortitude," *JT*, October 21, 2014, http://www.japantimes.co.jp/sports/ 2014/10/21/olympics/witches-of-the-orient-symbolized-japans-fortitude/ #.Vmbn8IRqpQY;

45 Guttmann and Thompson, *Japanese*, 199–200.

46 Atkins, *Blue Nippon*, 210–11 and 233–4; Hiraoka Masaaki, *Shōwa jazu kissa no densetsu* (Tokyo: Heibonsha, 2005); Michael Molasky, *Jazu kissaron: sengo no Nihon no bunka o aruku* (Tokyo: Chikuma Shobō, 2010).

47 Bourdaghs, *Sayonara*, 87 and 123–4. Sakamoto's song "I Look Up as I Walk" (1961) became a US hit as "Sukiyaki."

48 Junko Kitagawa, "Music Culture," in Sugimoto, *Cambridge*, 271; Hiro Shimatachi, "A Karaoke Perspective on International Relations," in *Japan Pop!*

Inside the World of Japanese Popular Culture, ed. Timothy Craig (Armonk: M. E. Sharpe, 2000), 101; and Bill Kelly, "Japan's Empty Orchestras: Echoes of Japanese Culture in the Performance of Karaoke," in *The Worlds of Japanese Popular Culture: Gender, Shifting Boundaries and Global Cultures*, ed. D. P. Martinez (Cambridge: Cambridge University Press, 1998), 84.

49 Kelly, "Empty," 80.

50 Frederik Schodt, *Manga! Manga! Manga! The World of Japanese Comics* (New York: Kōdansha, 1983), 12 and 28–9, and *Dreamland Japan: Writings on Modern Manga* (Berkeley: Stone Bridge Press, 1996), 21–2.

51 Schodt, *Manga!*, 25; Brigitte Koyama-Richards, *One Thousand Years of Manga* (Paris: Flammarion, 2014); Natsu Onoda Power, *God of Comics: Tezuka Osamu and the Creation of Post-World War II Manga* (Jackson: University Press of Mississippi, 2009), 19–20, 22, and 24.

52 Frederik Schodt, *The Astro Boy Essays: Osamu Tezuka, Mighty Atom, and the Manga/Anime Revolution* (Berkeley: Stone Bridge Press, 2007), x.

53 *Buddha* (New York: HarperCollins, 2014) is an eight-volume box set of the series in English translation. See also Mark MacWilliams, "Japanese Comic Books and Religion: Osamu Tezuka's Story of the Buddha," in Craig, *Japan Pop!*, 109–37.

54 "The Angel of Vietnam," serialized in *Sankei shinbun*, 1967–69; available in English in *Astro Boy*, vol. 7 (Milwaukie, OR: Dark Horse, 2002). See Schodt, *Astro*, 131–6.

55 Suzanne Phillipps, "Characters, Themes, and Narrative Patterns in the Manga of Osamu Tezuka," in MacWilliams, *Japanese*, 68–90.

56 Philip Brophy, "Osamu Tezuka's *Gekiga*: Behind the Mask of *Manga*," in *Manga: An Anthology of Global and Cultural Perspectives*, ed. Toni Johnson-Woods (New York: Continuum International, 2010), 129–30.

57 http://tezukaosamu.net/en/museum/.

58 "Sazae-san Enters Guinness World Records as Longest-Running Animated TV Series," *Japan Today*, September 7, 2013, http://www.japantoday.com/category/entertainment/view/sazae-san-enters-guinness-world-records-as-longest-running-animated-tv-series.

59 William Lee, "From *Sazae-san* to *Crayon Shin-chan*: Family *Anime*, Social Change, and Nostalgia in Japan," in Craig, *Japan Pop!*, 193.

60 Schodt, *Dreamland*, 49–59.

61 Stevens, *Japanese*, 63.

62 See David Desser, *Eros Plus Massacre: An Introduction to the Japanese New Wave Cinema* (Bloomington: Indiana University Press, 1988), 97–8; Maureen Turim, *The Films of Oshima Nagisa: Images of a Japanese Iconoclast* (Berkeley: University of California Press, 1998); Christine Marran, "So Bad, She's Good: The Masochist's Heroine in Postwar Japan, Abe Sada," in *Bad Girls of Japan*, ed. Laura Miller and Jan Bardsley (New York: Palgrave Macmillan, 2005), 81–96, and *Poison Woman: Figuring Female Transgression in Modern Japanese Culture* (Minneapolis: University of Minnesota Press,

2007); and William Johnston, *Geisha, Harlot, Strangler, Star: A Woman, Sex, and Morality in Modern Japan* (New York: Columbia University Press, 2012).

63 Anne Allison, *Permitted and Prohibited Desires: Mothers, Comics, and Censorship in Japan* (Durham, NC: Duke University Press, 1996), Chapter 7.

CHAPTER NINE

1 Joseph Nye, *Soft Power: The Means to Success in World Politics* (New York: Public Affairs, 2004), 2 and 5.

2 Iwabuchi Kōichi, *Recentering Globalization: Popular Culture and Japanese Transnationalism* (Durham, NC: Duke University Press, 2002), 19.

3 Video Games Jobs in Japan—Join the Japanese Games Industry, http://www.gamesjobsjapan.com.

4 https://vimeo.com/30767628. Few of my students find this amusing.

5 Chris Kincaid, "Am I a Weeaboo? What Is a Weeaboo Anyway?" Japan Powered, Aug. 30, 2015, http://www.japanpowered.com/otaku-culture/am-i-a-weeaboo-what-does-weeaboo-mean-anyway.

6 *The Japanese Version*, DVD, dir. Louis Alvarez and Andy Kolker, Center for New American Media, 1991. See Center for New American Media, http://www.cnam.com/flash/index.html and Internet Movie Database, http://www.imdb.com/title/tt0361766/.

7 Joseph Tobin, ed., *Re-made in Japan: Everyday Life and Consumer Taste in a Changing Society* (New Haven, CT: Yale University Press, 1992), 4.

8 Roland Robertson, "Comments on the 'Global Triad' and 'Glocalization,' " in *Proceedings: Globalization and Indigenous Culture*, Institute for Japanese Culture and Classics, Kogakuin University, 1997, http://www2.kokugakuin.ac.jp/ijcc/wp/global/15robertson.html.

9 Noriko Manabe, "Globalization and Japanese Creativity: Adaptations of Japanese Language to Rap," *Ethnomusicology* 50, no. 1 (Winter 2006): 1–2, 27 and 30; Ian Condry, *Hip-Hop Japan: Rap and the Paths of Cultural Globalization* (Durham, NC: Duke University Press, 2006), 5, 61–2, 137, and 151.

10 Marvin Sterling, *Babylon East: Performing Dancehall, Roots Reggae, and Rastafari in Japan* (Durham, NC: Duke University Press, 2010), 49, 151, 199, and 228; and Michelle Bigenho, *Intimate Distance: Andean Music in Japan* (Durham, NC: Duke University Press, 2012), 8, 34, and 171–2.

11 Atkins, *Blue Nippon*, 248–55; Sterling, *Babylon*, 49, 101–3, 151, and 199; and Bigenho, *Intimate*, 173.

12 Atkins, *Blue Nippon*, 248–55, and https://www.arts.gov/honors/jazz/toshiko-akiyoshi; Sterling, *Babylon*, 8–9, chapters 2 and 3, and Mighty Crown—The Far East Rulaz, http://www.mightycrown.com/ (there are several YouTube videos of Kudō's salacious dances); Bigenho, *Intimate*, 13 and 116–17, and Minato Kobori, "Makoto Shishido," *Cocha Banner* January 2009, http://www.cocha-banner.org/issues/2009/january/makoto-shishido/.

13 John Russell, "Consuming Passions: Spectacle, Self-Transformation, and the Commodification of Blackness in Japan," *positions* 6, no. 1 (1998): 119 and 135; cf. Karen Kelsky, *Women on the Verge: Japanese Women, Western Dreams* (Durham, NC: Duke University Press, 2001), 4.

14 Susan Napier, "Confronting Master Narratives: History As Vision in Miyazaki Hayao's Cinema of De-assurance," *positions* 9, no. 2 (Fall 2001): 469 and 471; William Tsutsui, *Japanese Popular Culture and Globalization* (Ann Arbor, MI: Association for Asian Studies, 2010), 16 and 37.

15 Iwabuchi, *Recentering*, 24–7.

16 Clements, *Anime*, 93; cf. Gerow, *Visions*, 113.

17 Clements, *Anime*, 106–8; Jonathan Clements and Helen McCarthy, *The Anime Encyclopedia: A Century of Japanese Animation*, 3rd ed. (Berkeley: Stone Bridge Press, 2015), 612–13.

18 Clements, *Anime*, 157–60, 165, and 171; Clements and McCarthy, *Anime*, 614.

19 Clements and McCarthy, *Anime*, 17; Steven Brown, *Tokyo Cyberpunk: Posthumanism in Japanese Visual Culture* (New York: Palgrave Macmillan, 2010), 3; Susan Napier, *Anime: From Akira to Howl's Moving Castle* (New York: Palgrave Macmillan, 2005), 36, 40, and 86.

20 See for example *East Asian Journal of Popular Culture* 2, no. 1 (April 2016), special "cute studies" issue edited by Kate Taylor-Jones, Ann Heylen, and John Berra, http://www.intellectbooks.co.uk/journals/view-issue,id=3066/.

21 Condry, *Hip-Hop*, 22 and 165; Sharon Kinsella, "Cuties in Japan," in *Women, Media and Consumption in Japan*, ed. Lise Skov and Brian Moeran (Honolulu: University of Hawai'i Press, 1995), 220–54.

22 Hiroshi Aoyagi, *Islands of Eight Million Smiles: Idol Performance and Symbolic Production in Contemporary Japan* (Cambridge: Harvard Asia Center, 2005); Stevens, *Japanese*, 59–60; Ian Martin, "AKB48 Member's 'Penance' Shows Flaws in Idol Culture," *JT*, February 1, 2013, http://www.japantimes.co.jp/culture/2013/02/01/music/akb48-members-penance-shows-flaws-in-idol-culture/#.V3AX7ldqpQY.

23 See Hikonyan Official, http://hikone-hikonyan.jp; Kumamon Official, http://kumamon-official.jp; Yuka Miller, "Japan: Love and Hate Story of the Mascot Character, 'Sento-kun,' Global Voices, April 22, 2008, https://globalvoices.org/2008/04/22/japan-love-and-hate-story-of-the-mascot-character-sento-kun/; Richard Hendy, "Yubari, Japan: A City Learns How to Die," *The Guardian*, August 15, 2014, https://www.theguardian.com/cities/2014/aug/15/yubari-japan-city-learns-die-lost-population-detroit; "Melon Bear Mascot Terrifies Children in Japan," https://www.youtube.com/watch?v=6koOKPvy0-Y.

24 Nihon gotōchi kyrakutā kyōkkai, http://kigurumisummit.org; "Japanese Mascots," *Last Week Tonight with John Oliver*, May 15, 2015, https://www.youtube.com/watch?v=1iXOaUJyFB4&feature=share; Euan McKirdy, "Japanese Cuteness Overload Could Result in Mascot Cull," CNN, May 12, 2014, http://edition.cnn.com/2014/05/12/world/asia/osaka-mascot-cull/.

25 Anne Allison, "Cuteness as Japan's Millennial Product," in *Pikachu's Global Adventure: The Rise and Fall of Pokémon*, ed. Joseph Tobin (Durham, NC: Duke University Press, 2004), 34–5 and 46.

26 Laura Miller, "Japan's Zoomorphic Urge," *ASIANetwork Exchange* 17, no. 2 (Spring 2010): 69–70, and "Cute Masquerade and the Pimping of Japan," *International Journal of Japanese Sociology* 20 (2011): 24 and 26.

27 Quoted in Christine Yano, *Pink Globalization: Hello Kitty's Trek Across the Pacific* (Durham, NC: Duke University Press, 2013), 43.

28 "Finding Companionship in a Digital Age," *Next Generation*, October 1997: 60.

29 Hello Kitty Jet Travels with You!, http://evakitty.evaair.com/en/.

30 I have co-taught a class on Knights and Samurai with my medieval history colleague, Valerie Garver. Students often ask us whether a knight or a samurai would prevail in mortal combat. Neither of us cares. But students typically vote 2-to-1 that a samurai would thump a knight.

31 James Surowiecki, "Better All the Time: How the 'Performance Revolution' Came to Athletics—and Beyond," *New Yorker*, November 10, 2014, http://www.newyorker.com/magazine/2014/11/10/better-time; Jon Anderson, "Kaatsu Training Is Blowing Fitness Researchers' Minds," *Military Times*, February 6, 2015, http://www.militarytimes.com/story/life/diet-fitness/2015/02/06/get-stronger-go-longer-kaatsu-is-blowing-researchers-minds-bode-miller-comeback/22878671/.

32 Bruce Jenkins, "Closing the Deal—Ichiro, Byrnes Like No One Else in Game Today," *San Francisco Chronicle*, July 28, 2004, http://www.sfgate.com/sports/jenkins/article/Closing-the-deal-Ichiro-Byrnes-like-no-one-3325193.php.

33 James Sterngold, "Tokyo Journal; Japan Falls for Soccer, Leaving Baseball in Lurch," *NYT*, June 6, 1994, http://www.nytimes.com/1994/06/06/world/tokyo-journal-japan-falls-for-soccer-leaving-baseball-in-lurch.html.

34 Kuang Keng Kuek Ser, "The Strong Connection between Gender Equality and a Kickass National Women's Soccer Team," Public Radio International, June 30, 2015, http://www.pri.org/stories/2015-06-30/strong-connection-between-gender-equality-and-kickass-national-womens-soccer.

35 William Kelly, "Japan's Embrace of Soccer: Mutable Ethnic Players and Flexible Soccer Citizenship in the New East Asian Sports Order," *International Journal of the History of Sport* 30, no. 11 (2013): 1241–3. For a contrasting view, see Cesare Polenghi, "Opinion: J. League Must Embrace Global Football Culture," Football Channel Asia, June 30, 2015, http://footballchannel.asia/2015/06/30/post5070/.

36 Daniel Krieger, "In Japan, Sumo Is Dominated by Foreigners," *NYT*, January 24, 2013, http://www.nytimes.com/2013/01/25/sports/25iht-sumo25.html.

37 Schodt, *Dreamland*, 43–59.

38 The Japan National Tourist Organization (JNTO) includes on its website an "Invitation to an 'Otaku' Tour: Immersing Yourself in Japanese Anime and Comics," which states, "Just as 'wabi' and 'sabi' became key words for understanding Japanese culture, the term 'moe', which refers to the

enthusiasm of the 'Otaku', has become a major key word for describing unique Japanese sentiment and taste." http://www.jnto.go.jp/eng/indepth/exotic/animation/. See Mizuko Ito, Daisuke Okabe, and Izumi Tsuji, eds., *Fandom Unbound: Otaku Culture in a Connected World* (New Haven, CT: Yale University Press, 2012).

39 Matthew Thorn, "Girls and Women Getting Out of Hand: The Pleasure and Politics of Japan's Amateur Comics Community," in Kelly, *Fanning*, 169–87; Patrick Galbraith, "*Fujoshi*: Fantasy Play and Transgressive Intimacy among 'Rotten Girls' in Contemporary Japan," *Signs* 37, no. 1 (September 2011): 219–40.

40 "U.N. Official's Claim that 13% of Japanese Girls Engage in 'Compensated Dating' Angers Government," *JT*, November 10, 2015, http://www.japantimes.co.jp/news/2015/11/10/national/u-n-officials-remarks-girls-compensated-dating-japan-angers-tokyo/#.V1MBFFdqpQY.

41 Tamaki Saitō, *Beautiful Fighting Girl*, trans. J. Keith Vincent and Dawn Lawson (Minneapolis: University of Minnesota Press, 2011), 57.

42 Laura Miller, "Those Naughty Teenage Girls: Japanese Kogals, Slang, and Media Assessments," *Journal of Linguistic Anthropology* 14, no. 2 (December 2004): 239. On bar hostesses, see Anne Allison, *Nightwork: Sexuality, Pleasure, and Corporate Masculinity in a Tokyo Hostess Club* (Chicago: University of Chicago Press, 1994).

43 Jonathan Clements, *Anime: A History* (London: Palgrave Macmillan, 2013), 177; Benjamin Radford, "The Pokémon Panic of 1997," *Skeptical Inquirer* 25, no. 3 (May/June 2001), http://www.csicop.org/si/show/pokemon_panic_of_1997.

44 Allison, "Cuteness," 42; Damien McFerran, "Pokémon's Controversial History," *Nintento Life*, October 19, 2012, http://www.nintendolife.com/news/2012/10/feature_pokemons_controversial_history; "Demonic Child Entertainment," http://www.demonbuster.com/demonicc.html.

45 *The Onion* 45, no. 7 (February 10, 2009), http://www.theonion.com/article/japan-pledges-to-halt-production-of-weirdo-porn-th-2657.

46 Max Eddy, "Cosplayers Speak Out on Racism in the Fandom," *PC Magazine*, October 13, 2013, http://www.pcmag.com/article2/0,2817,2425583,00.asp; E. Ortiz, "The Face of Cosplay: Racism & Cosplayers of Color," Nerd Caliber, http://www.nerdcaliber.com/the-face-of-cosplay-racism-cosplayers-of-color/; Lauren Rae Orsini, "Torn Between Cosplay and Reality—Racial Barriers Spur Controversy," *Daily Dot*, August 29, 2012, http://www.dailydot.com/society/cosplay-brownface-whitewashing-racial-controversy/; Emily Jan, "A 'Con' For Everyone," *The Atlantic*, February 19, 2016, http://www.theatlantic.com/entertainment/archive/2016/02/sailor-moon-drake-and-pikachu-walk-into-a-room/463110/.

47 See Mizuki Takahashi, "Opening the Closed World of *Shōjo* Manga," in MacWilliams, *Japanese*, 114–36; and Masami Toku, *International Perspectives on Shojo and Shojo Manga: The Influence of Girl Culture* (New York: Routledge, 2015).

48　"Interview: Miyazaki on *Sen to Chihiro no kamikakushi*," *Animage*, May 2001, trans. Ryoko Toyama at GhibliWiki, http://www.nausicaa.net/miyazaki/interviews/sen.html.

49　Freda Freiberg, "Miyazaki's Heroines," *Senses of Cinema*, July 2006, http://sensesofcinema.com/2006/feature-articles/miyazaki-heroines/.

50　Saitō, *Beautiful*, 41–2, 47, and 57; Anne Allison, "Sailor Moon: Japanese Superheroes for Global Girls," in Craig, *Japan Pop!*, 259 and 269, and *Millennial Monsters: Japanese Toys and the Global Imagination* (Berkeley: University of California Press, 2006), 137, 155. See also Kanako Shiokawa, "Cute But Deadly: Women and Violence in Japanese Comics," in *Themes and Issues in Asian Cartooning: Cute, Cheap, Mad and Sexy*, ed. John A. Lent (Bowling Green, KY: Bowling Green State University Popular Press, 1999), 93–125. The star and director of *Wonder Woman* (2017) also praise their hero for being "strong and kind and wonderful and badass, but beautiful." See Nurith Aizenman, "Is Wonder Woman Suited to Be a U.N. Ambassador?" *All Things Considered*, NPR, October 20, 2016, http://www.npr.org/sections/goatsandsoda/2016/10/20/498569053/is-wonder-woman-suited-to-be-a-u-n-ambassador.

51　Saitō, *Beautiful*, 127–33.

52　Rachael Hutchinson, "Sabotaging the Rising Sun: Representing History in Tezuka Osamu's *Phoenix*," in *Manga and the Representation of Japanese History*, ed. Roman Rosenbaum (London: Routledge, 2013), 18 and 36. See Tezuka Osamu, *Phoenix*, trans. Jared Cook and Frederik Schodt, 11 vols. (San Francisco: Viz Media, 2003–7).

53　Akiko Hashimoto, "'Something Dreadful Happened in the Past': War Stories for Children in Japanese Popular Culture," *APJ* 13.30.1 (July 27, 2015), http://apjjf.org/2015/13/30/Akiko-Hashimoto/4349.html. See also Hashimoto, *The Long Defeat: Cultural Trauma, Memory, and Identity in Japan* (New York: Oxford University Press, 2015), chapter 4.

54　Birth of JTU, http://www.jtu-net.or.jp/english/birth.html.

55　Mark Driscoll, "Kobayashi Yoshinori Is Dead: Imperial War/Sick Liberal Peace/Neoliberal Class War," *Mechademia* 4 (2009): 291–2. See Kobayashi Yoshinori, *Sensōron* (Tokyo: Gentōsha, 1999).

56　Rumi Sakamoto, "'Will You Go to War? Or Will You Stop Being Japanese?' Nationalism and History in Kobayashi Yoshinori's Sensoron," *APJ* 6.1.0 (January 1, 2008), http://apjjf.org/-Rumi-SAKAMOTO/2632/article.html.

57　Nissim Kadosh Otmazgin, "A New Cultural Geography of East Asia: Imagining a 'Region' through Popular Culture," *APJ* 14.7.5 (April 2016), http://apjjf.org/2016/07/Otmazgin.html; Hiro Katsumata, "Japanese Popular Culture in East Asia: A New Insight into Regional Community Building," *International Relations of the Asia-Pacific* 12 (2012): 159–60.

58　Martin Jacques, "China and Japan: Two Nations Locked in Mutual Loathing," *The Telegraph*, August 20, 2012, http://www.telegraph.co.uk/news/worldnews/asia/japan/9487658/China-and-Japan-two-nations-locked-in-mutual-loathing.html; Elise Hu, "The Past Haunts the Present for Japan's Shinzo Abe," *Morning Edition*, NPR, April 28, 2015,

http://www.npr.org/sections/parallels/2015/04/28/402480866/the-past-
haunts-the-present-for-japans-shinzo-abe, and "Best Frenemies: Japan, Korea
Mark 50th Anniversary Despite Rivalry," *All Things Considered*, NPR, June
29, 2015, http://www.npr.org/sections/parallels/2015/06/23/416661086/
best-frenemies-japan-korea-mark-50th-anniversary-despite-rivalry.

59 Mark Selden, "Small Islets, Enduring Conflict: Dokdo, Korea-Japan Colonial
Legacy and the United States," *APJ* 9.17.2 (April 25, 2011), http://japanfocus.
org/-Mark-Selden/3520/article.html.

60 Pew Research Center, "Japanese Public's Mood Rebounding, Abe Highly
Popular," July 11, 2013, http://www.pewglobal.org/2013/07/11/japanese-
publics-mood-rebounding-abe-strongly-popular/; Bruce Stokes, "What
Japanese and Americans Think about Each Other," Pew Research Center,
March 20, 2013, http://www.pewglobal.org/2013/03/20/what-japanese-and-
americans-think-about-each-other/.

61 Confucius Institute Headquarters (Hanban), http://english.hanban.org/node_
10971.htm; John Sudworth, "Confucius Institute: The Hard Side of China's
Soft Power," BBC News, December 22, 2014, http://www.bbc.com/news/
world-asia-china-30567743.

62 PSY, "Gangnam Style," YouTube, https://www.youtube.com/
watch?v=9bZkp7q19f0; Imagine Your Korea—Brand Identity, http://www.
imagineyourkorea.com/brand-storywwww. The popularity of *hallyu* in Japan
elicited a nasty backlash in the form of Yamano Sharin's four-volume manga
entitled *Manga kenkanryū* (Hating the Korea Wave) (Tokyo: Shin'yūsha,
2005–9). See Rumi Sakamoto and Matthew Allen, "'Hating the "Korean Wave'
Comic Books: A Sign of New Nationalism in Japan?" *APJ* 5.10.0 (October 1,
2007), http://apjjf.org/-Rumi-SAKAMOTO/2535/article.html.

63 "Japan's Soft Power—Squaring the Cool," *The Economist*, June 16, 2014,
http://www.economist.com/blogs/banyan/2014/06/japans-soft-power.

64 METI Cool Japan / Creative Industries Policy, http://www.meti.go.jp/english/
policy/mono_info_service/creative_industries/creative_industries.html.

65 "Another Confucius Institute to Close," *Inside Higher Ed*, October 1, 2014,
https://www.insidehighered.com/quicktakes/2014/10/01/another-confucius-
institute-close; David Volodzko, "China's Confucius Institutes and the Soft
War," *The Diplomat*, July 8, 2015, http://thediplomat.com/2015/07/chinas-
confucius-institutes-and-the-soft-war/.

66 Dana, "The Korean Wave and the Question of Soft Power," *Seoulbeats*,
September 21, 2012, http://seoulbeats.com/2012/09/the-korean-wave-and-the-
question-of-soft-power/.

67 "Japan's Soft Power."

68 See Richard Samuels, *3.11: Disaster and Change in Japan* (Ithaca: Cornell
University Press, 2013).

69 Aileen Mioko Smith and Mark Selden, "Bringing the Plight of Fukushima
Children to the UN, Washington and the World," *APJ* 9.41.4 (October 10,
2011); Jeff Kingston, "Mismanaging Risk and the Fukushima Nuclear Crisis,"
APJ 10.12.4 (March 12, 2012), http://www.japanfocus.org/-Jeff-Kingston/3724;

and Hiroshi Onitsuka, "Hooked on Nuclear Power: Japanese State-Local Relations and the Vicious Cycle of Nuclear Dependence," *APJ* 10.3.1 (January 15, 2012), http://apjjf.org/2012/10/3/Hiroshi-Onitsuka/3677/article.html.

70 Uno Tsunehiro, "Imagination After the Earthquake: Japan's *Otaku* Culture in the 2010s," trans. Jeffrey Guarneri, *Verge: Studies in Global Asias* 1, no. 1 (Spring 2015): 126.

71 Anne Allison, *Precarious Japan* (Durham, NC: Duke University Press, 2013), 7–10.

72 Noriko Manabe, *The Revolution Will Not Be Televised: Protest Music after Fukushima* (New York: Oxford University Press, 2015). For more on Japan's thriving underground music scenes, see Condry, *Hip-Hop*; Jennifer Milioto Matsue, *Making Music in Japan's Underground: The Tokyo Hardcore Scene* (London: Routledge, 2011); and David Novak, *Japanoise: Music at the Edge of Circulation* (Durham, NC: Duke University Press, 2013).

73 Tony McNicol, "The Power of Tohoku's Festivals," NHK World, http://www.nhk.or.jp/japan311/tmrw2-fest.html; The Tohoku Region's Summer Festivals, http://www.tohokumatsuri.jp/english/index.html; Socially Engaged Art in Japan Symposium, University of Washington Walter Chapin Simpson Center for the Humanities, November 12–14, 2015, https://simpsoncenter.org/projects/socially-engaged-art-japan. See also Hiroko Furukawa and Rayna Denison, "Disaster and Relief: The 3.11 Tohoku and Fukushima Disasters and Japan's Media Industries," *International Journal of Cultural Studies* 18, no. 2 (March 2015): 225–41.

74 Shiriagari Kotobuki, *Ano hi kara no manga: 2011.3.11* (Tokyo: Entā Burein, 2011); Mary Knighton, "The Sloppy Realities of 3.11 in Shiriagari Kotobuki's Manga," *APJ* 11.26.1 (June 30, 2014), http://apjjf.org/2014/11/26/Mary-Knighton/4140/article.html; "Depicting Fukushima in Manga," NHK World, http://www.nhk.or.jp/japan311/kuro-manga.html.

75 *3.11: A Sense of Home* trailer, https://www.youtube.com/watch?v=Gpalik11eas.

76 3.11 Film Festival, http://www.3331.jp/schedule/en/002332.html. See also Tim Graf and Jakob Montrasio's *Salvage and Salvation*, https://vimeo.com/141396760, and *Souls of Zen—Buddhism, Ancestors, and the 2011 Tsunami in Japan*, http://soulsofzen.com.

77 See for example Rachel Dinitto, "Narrating the Cultural Trauma of 3/11: The Debris of Post-Fukushima Literature and Film," *Japan Forum* 26, no. 3 (2014): 240–60.

AFTERWORD

1 Allison, *Millennial*, 9–10; Marc Steinberg, *Anime's Media Mix: Franchising Toys and Characters in Japan* (Minneapolis: University of Minnesota Press, 2012), vii.

2 Stevens, *Popular*, 30 and 34.

3 Craig, *Japan Pop!*, 6–14; Allison, *Millennial*, 224–5; Napier, *Anime*, 9; Tsutsui, *Japanese*, 35–6.

4 Napier, *From Impressionism*, 210.

5 Napier, *From Impressionism*, 3 and 10–12.

6 Allison, *Millennial*, 12–13; Zília Papp, *Traditional Monster Imagery in Manga, Anime and Japanese Cinema* (Folkestone: Global Oriental, 2011), 210; Itō, "Manga," 26.

7 Jolyon Baraka Thomas, *Drawing on Tradition: Manga, Anime, and Religion in Contemporary Japan* (Honolulu: University of Hawai'i Press, 2012), 18–19; and Stevie Suan, *The Anime Paradox: Patterns and Practices through the Lens of Traditional Japanese Theater* (Leiden: Global Oriental, 2013), 8.

8 Yoshio Sugimoto, "'Japanese Culture': An Overview," in Sugimoto, *Cambridge*, 1–9.

9 Napier, "Cinema," 478–9.

10 Condry, *Hip-Hop*, 20; Miller, "Cute," 26.

INDEX